EQUIVALENT SUBSTITUTIONS

1 cup corn syrup	1 cup sugar plus ¼ cup liquid when used to replace one-half of the sugar
1 cup honey	1 to 1¼ cups sugar plus ¼ cup liquid
1 ounce chocolate	3 tablespoons cocoa plus 1 teaspoon fat
1 cup butter	1 cup margarine ⅞ to 1 cup hydrogenated fat ⅞ cup lard ⅞ cup rendered fat
1 cup coffee cream (20%)	3 tablespoons butter plus about ⅞ cup milk
1 cup heavy cream (40%)	⅓ cup butter plus about ¾ cup milk
1 cup fresh sweet milk	½ cup evaporated milk plus ½ cup water 4 tablespoons dried whole milk plus 1 cup water 3 tablespoons dried skim milk plus 1 cup water 1 cup sour milk or buttermilk plus ½ teaspoon baking soda 1 cup skim milk plus 2 teaspoons fat
1 teaspoon double-acting baking powder	1½ teaspoons phosphate baking powder 2 teaspoons tartrate baking powder ½ teaspoon soda plus 1 cup sour milk or buttermilk ½ teaspoon soda plus 1 tablespoon vinegar or lemon juice added to 1 cup sweet milk ½ teaspoon soda plus ½ to 1 cup molasses
1 cup all-purpose flour	1 cup plus 2 tablespoons cake or pastry flour ½ cup whole wheat flour plus ½ cup flour ½ cup bran plus ½ cup flour ½ or 1 cup rye plus ½ cup or no flour ⅓ or ½ cup cornmeal plus ⅔ or ½ cup flour ½ or 1 cup rice flour plus ½ cup or no flour ¼ or ⅓ cup soybean plus ¾ or ⅔ cup flour

AMERICA'S
COOK BOOK

Revised Edition

Marguerite Dodd

AMERICA'S COOK BOOK

Revised Edition

CHARLES SCRIBNER'S SONS

New York

This book published simultaneously in the
United States of America and in Canada—
Copyright under the Berne Convention

1 3 5 7 9 11 13 15 17 19 C/MD 20 18 16 14 12 10 8 6 4 2

Printed in the United States of America
Library of Congress Catalog Card Number 73-19551
ISBN 0-684-10126-2

Books by Marguerite Dodd

America's Homemaking Book
America's Cook Book

CONTENTS

CONTENTS

AMERICA'S
COOK BOOK

Revised Edition

INTRODUCTION

This book is designed for both the novice and the experienced cook. It will introduce the new homemaker to the art of cooking in an easy step-by-step fashion, will serve as a refresher course to the cook who has long since been whipping up her delicious three-a-day meals by rule of thumb, and for both will provide a handy reference to hundreds of basic recipes and their many variations.

New Style Recipes

In leafing through the book you will see that the recipes are presented in a new and easy-to-follow method. There are no long paragraphs of complicated text to slow you up when you are trying to cope with a new dish. Instead, each recipe is presented in a two-column form, which the eye can easily separate and follow. At the left, in heavy type, you will see at a glance all the ingredients needed. This will serve as your shopping list, or as a counter list when you begin to work.

The ingredients are listed in the order in which you will use them, and when several are used together, or one following the other, they appear in a continuous group. When there are several steps to the recipe, the ingredients used in one step are separated by a space from the next group.

Following each ingredient, the quantity to be used is specified in lighter type, and the form in which it is used; that is, beaten, chopped, minced, et cetera.

Set off to the right, the procedure for using each ingredient in turn is described as briefly and simply as possible. If you have ever been discouraged in trying to follow a new recipe that confuses ingredients, quantities, and methods all in one long paragraph, I think you will like the simplicity of this system.

We have tried to identify the recipes with names that are well known or easily recognizable. When we have borrowed from foreign cookery we have usually called it by a name that will identify the ingredients and tried to improve the method of preparation in line with modern practice. Sometimes, when a foreign name is well known, we have included it.

Menus

In the Pantry Shelf Section, and in the sections on main course dishes such as meat, poultry and fish, you will find listed on many of the right-hand pages suggested menus which include the recipes given on that page and the one opposite. These will help the cook provide variety in her meal planning and will suggest food combinations that are compatible.

In planning menus we are concerned with several things. We think of the need for a "well-balanced" diet, which means that every meal should have an assortment of the various foods that provide what the body requires to replace its worn-out tissues. The problem is to provide these building materials in forms that the family enjoys. Also, menus should be varied to avoid monotonous repetition, and the individual items should avoid sameness, if possible; that is, they should be varied in appearance, color and texture, to help awaken interest and appetite. Variety from day to day is important, but variety doesn't mean strange and often ridiculous ways of combining foods, but rather to know the good basic recipes and then vary them from time to time with other seasonings, accents, sauces.

In planning menus, try to feature the fruits and vegetables that are in season, or plentiful: asparagus in the spring, corn and tomatoes at their midsummer height, berries in their season. Fruit can add infinite variety to the menu: serve it as an accompaniment to the meat course, as a dessert, or as a substitute for a vegetable. This latter can be helpful to the cook whose family is not fond of vegetables. However, we hope that the many interesting ways of preparing them, listed in the vegetable section, will help the cook who has this problem.

Using the Index

Make good use of the index—almost every recipe is listed in several ways: once by its special name, usually under its chief ingredient, and, often, under the special type of dish. We have tried to make it easy for you to find any recipe you want without strenuous searching. Under its special section you will find a recipe for every item mentioned in the menus.

Making Your Cooking Time Count

Why not reduce your cooking hours by quantity cooking? Since you must spend a certain amount of time in the kitchen preparing one meal, why wouldn't it be smart to prepare two—one for today's dinner and one for the freezer? By cooking twice the amount, you can repeat your menu next week or the week after, and the work is already done. When you have a freezer, a second casserole or half a roast can be easily put aside, but even without this great convenience, a certain amount can be stored in the freezing compartment of the refrigerator. Consult the chapter "Frozen Foods" for advice on freezing prepared dishes.

The chapter on Leftovers will suggest many delicious dishes that can be planned in advance when you are buying a roast. In other words, we don't just "use up" leftovers these days—we plan for them and make sure we have them on hand.

Using the Cook Book

Read the recipe carefully; assemble all ingredients listed in heavy type in the left-hand column. Set the oven, if needed, at the indicated temperature.

Measure carefully, using standard measuring cups and spoons—all measurements are level. Invest in a nested set of 4 cups holding ¼, ⅓, ½ and 1 cup. Level cups and spoons with a spatula. Level ingredients in a glass cup by holding it up to eye level.

Larger quantities. Most of the recipes in this book will make 4 average servings, with the exception, of course, of cakes or pies, or other items which are standard in size. We felt that 4 servings was a useful amount for many families, and the arithmetic is easy when dividing to serve just 2, or when increasing the amount to serve more than 4.

Follow the directions on temperature. If a recipe calls for low heat, it means just that. If a recipe says to turn heat from high to low, this is difficult to do with an electric burner because the coils will remain hot for some time. Therefore have another burner turned on at its lowest heat, and switch the pan from one to the other.

Consult the back of the book. In addition to a complete Index, you will find:

INFORMATION ABOUT FROZEN FOODS
HOW TO MANAGE ALL TYPES OF STOVES
A LIST OF NECESSARY POTS, PANS, AND TOOLS
A LIST OF SMALL ELECTRICAL APPLIANCES
STORING FOODS
HOW TO USE WINES AND HERBS
A DICTIONARY OF COOKERY TERMS
A CALORIE CHART
RULES FOR KITCHEN SAFETY AND FIRST AID
SETTING THE TABLE

In most recipes that call for sautéing we have specified butter in the list of ingredients because we like the flavor it imparts to food. Other cooking fats or oils may be used according to your preference. At this writing the cholesterol question is still up in the air, but the cook who is interested in her family's nutrition will want to watch for further developments on this question. The final evidence may indicate that we should substitute vegetable oils for animal fats where possible in our diet, to avoid the fatty deposits in our blood vessels that cause heart trouble in later life.

To the New Cook

You will find that the book begins with easy recipes that are made chiefly from ready-prepared foods. We call these "Pantry Shelf Meals," and we believe that this is the easiest way for the brand-new cook to become acquainted with cooking. Instead of tackling a complicated recipe from scratch, with no previous experience, you will get your hand in by going through the motions of combining ready-to-use foods into interesting and practically fool-proof meals. Once you acquire confidence, learn how to handle your stove and equipment, and how to combine foods into an acceptable menu, you will have no hesitancy in trying out new recipes.

To the Experienced Cook

For you, "Pantry Shelf Meals" can serve as a catalog of meals that practically prepare themselves and can be ready in short order. With a well-stocked shelf of canned and packaged foods you will never be at a loss in entertaining unexpected visitors, or on those busy days when there is little time for meal planning. With the help of these recipes you can add to simple dishes a touch of individuality that will turn them into little meals of distinction.

TYRO IN THE KITCHEN

If your entire experience with cooking has been to make a cup of hot cocoa before bedtime, it may seem a bit baffling to assemble several dishes into a menu and have them all ready at one time. The thing to do is to take it in easy stages, starting with simple recipes, and with simple menus that may require the preparation of only one dish at mealtime, with all preliminary work done beforehand. For dinners you might start off with those pantry-shelf meals we talk about in the first chapter. These will help you get used to the whole cooking procedure.

Breakfast

Let's start with first things first, and breakfast is certainly the day's starter. The trouble is too many people think that breakfast can be scamped, or overlooked entirely, and this can become a very bad habit. People going to a day's work, and certainly children going to school, need a nourishing breakfast in order to do efficient work and to maintain health. It is even important for a woman at home who is watching calories, for a satisfying breakfast will make her less likely to crave little snacks during the day. So do a little planning about breakfast menus, and then work out a routine that will spare you that early morning frenzy.

Try to make the menu varied—including fruit, cereal, an egg and meat dish, probably, and some sort of bread, but not always the same cereal, the same egg dish, and the same white toast! Serve fruits in season, sometimes a hot cooked cereal, sometimes the crisp ready-to-eat kind, vary the bacon with ham, sausage, or even an occasional chop, and use the many muffins and buns that are available as well as a variety of toasted breads.

Start off with your first breakfast and all subsequent ones by doing as much as possible the night before. Set the breakfast table with a pretty cloth or mats and cheerful dishes. Set up the toaster with a plate and napkin ready for the hot toast. Put coffee pot, coffee, measuring spoon and cup near the sink, ready to go. Have the fruit washed and ready to prepare, the oranges with the squeezer and glasses on a tray, berries in dishes in the refrigerator, or peaches ready to slice. Set out cereal and cereal dishes, and extras such as jam or marmalade. Trays are very helpful to hold each group of necessary items, particularly if you are eating in the dining room, they will save you endless steps back and forth to the kitchen.

So now when you step into the kitchen in the morning everything is ready to go. First start the coffee (if you are like some of us you may want that first cup before anything else)! Let's say you have planned the following simple menu:

Corn Flakes with Sliced Fresh Peaches
Scrambled Eggs with Crisp Bacon
Buttered Toast · Marmalade
Coffee

Start the bacon, which requires rather long cooking, in the skillet over medium heat so that it can cook while you are doing other things. Just remember to turn it occasionally. When crisp, drain it on paper towels and put it in the oven until needed.

Meanwhile place the corn flakes in the cereal dishes and top with the peaches, peeled and sliced. Sprinkle a little sugar over the peaches and serve them to be eaten while the eggs are cooking. Place bread slices in the toaster.

Follow recipe for scrambled eggs in the egg section and cook them gently. Start the toaster and warm the plates. Stir the eggs as needed and butter the toast as it pops, wrapping it loosely in the napkin to keep warm. Dish out the eggs on individual plates and add strips of bacon. (Assembling the plates on a tray is a step-saver, don't forget.) Remove the cereal dishes and serve the eggs.

After a little practice you will do all this easily in twenty to twenty-five minutes.

Lunch

Lunch can be a meal prepared at your own convenience. Sandwiches may be made ahead of time with materials especially provided, canned soups heated at the last minute, or more elaborate fare started early, perhaps at the same time you are doing the breakfast dishes. Serve a nourishing lunch even though you are home alone to eat it: it will restore your energy for afternoon activities.

For suggestions in packing lunches or preparing the home lunch see the chapter on sandwiches, with its many suggestions, and also the interesting combinations of canned soups in the soup section.

Your First Dinner

For your first dinner you might choose one of the easy pantry-shelf menus in the opening section, or, perhaps, start off with the cook's standby—hamburger. Suppose, for example, you choose the latter and plan the following menu:

Chilled Tomato Juice
Pan-broiled Hamburger with Assorted Relishes
French Fried Potatoes (frozen)
Buttered Green Beans (frozen)
Tossed Green Salad with French Dressing
Hot Crisp Rolls · Butter
Ice Cold Melon
Coffee

This is a menu that can be prepared mostly in advance with about 15 minutes of cooking just before serving time.

MARKETING: The main items will include tomato juice, good quality hamburger, relishes in jars, frozen French fried potatoes and beans, greens for the salad, and whatever melon is in season, honeydew, honeyball, cantaloup, or perhaps one of the rarer (and more expensive) Cranshaw, Persian, or Christmas melons. Be sure you get a ripe one.

Consult the recipes for the items you are serving to see what incidental seasonings and items you will need for sauces, flavorings, and the like. For example, you will need either a bottle of ready-made French dressing or the ingredients to make it according to the recipe.

When you arrive home from marketing put the tomato juice and melon right into the refrigerator. Wash and dry the salad greens, removing any leaves in poor condition, and put them in the refrigerator, either in a hydrator or wrapped loosely in a towel.

PREPARATION: An hour or more before dinner, set the table. Then

· prepare the French dressing
· arrange relishes in relish dish or individual dishes and place in refrigerator
· open tomato juice and pour into glasses, using it as is or flavoring it with Worcestershire sauce or a little onion powder; return to refrigerator until ready to serve. Slice wedges of lemon to serve with it, if desired.
· break salad greens into salad bowl and return to refrigerator
· cut melon and remove seeds; cut in serving size pieces and return to refrigerator
· read directions on frozen food packages

COOKING AND SERVING: 25 minutes before dinner time, start heating oven for potatoes;

· follow directions on package for heating potatoes
· have boiling water ready for beans when needed
· turn to recipe on page 28 for hamburger; allow sufficient time to have them rare or well-done as you like them
· while food cooks, bring out salad, pour dressing over it and toss gently to coat leaves; set tomato juice on plates with lemon slices and carry to table; set out butter, relishes, and fill water glasses if needed
· put rolls in oven to crisp, following directions on package
· check potatoes to make sure they do not get too brown; check beans for doneness
· put plates in warming oven
· melt butter in metal cup or small pan for dressing beans
· when beans are done drain and reserve water for future soups or stews, and pour melted butter over them
· wrap crisp rolls loosely in napkins for serving
· when hamburgers are done, turn out on individual plates with a helping of beans and potatoes on each and serve at once; or, if preferred, the food may be placed on platter and vegetable dishes and served at the table.

PANTRY
SHELF MEALS

The following section is devoted to meals prepared from ingredients that come ready-cooked from the pantry shelf and need only heating, or combining, and seasoning, to shape them into tasty, quickly-prepared menus.

This is an excellent way for the beginner cook to become acquainted with cooking procedures. In fact we have a friend who taught her teen-age daughter to cook by this method. After a period of carefully following the printed directions on canned and frozen foods, and packaged mixes, she acquired enough confidence and dexterity to tackle recipes from scratch.

This seems to us a more interesting way to begin, than with basic Whitesauce Nos. I, II, and III, which is the way we were taught in cooking school, and which seemed like dull work indeed. Today's beginner skips white sauces and replaces them with canned creamed soups. And she comes up with a delicious meal the first time she tries.

EASY CHICKEN FRICASSEE

Precooked Rice, 5-ounce package
Chicken Fricassee, 2 cans
Milk, ½ cup
Salt and **Pepper,** to taste
Curry, ½ teaspoon

To serve 4

Prepare rice according to directions on package. Add chicken and milk. Heat thoroughly and season with salt, pepper and curry.

SALMON QUICKIE

Salmon, 16-ounce can
Cream of Chicken Soup, 1 can
Milk, ½ soup can
Worcestershire, ½ teasp.

In saucepan add salmon to other ingredients and cook over low heat until heated thoroughly.

Precooked Rice, 5-ounce package
Parsley Flakes, 1 teasp.
Pimiento, 1, chopped

To serve 4

Prepare rice according to directions on package, adding parsley and pimiento. Form into ring on hot platter. Pour salmon mixture in center of ring.

5-MINUTE CHILI CON CARNE

Meat Balls, 2 16-oz. cans
Onion, 1 large, chopped
Garlic, 1 clove, minced
Red Kidney Beans, 2 16-ounce cans
Chili Powder, 1 teaspoon
Water, ½ cup

To serve 4

In saucepan combine meat balls, broken apart with fork, with other ingredients. Bring to boil and simmer 20 minutes. Add more chili powder if a hotter chili is desired.

BEANS AND VIENNA SAUSAGE CASSEROLE

Boston Beans, 2 16-ounce cans
Onion Flakes, 1 tablesp.
Worcestershire, 1 tablespoon

Mix first three ingredients in saucepan, heat thoroughly and pour into casserole.

Vienna Sausage, 2 cans
Prepared Mustard

Score sausages, spread with mustard. Arrange on beans and place under broiler until well browned.

To serve 4

HAMBURGER-RAVIOLI CASSEROLE

Ravioli with Beef, 2 16-ounce cans
Meat Balls, 16-oz. can
Red Wine, ¼ cup
Parmesan Cheese, ¼ cup, grated

Separate ravioli, and arrange in shallow casserole. Cut meat balls in half, arrange on top of casserole. Add wine and sprinkle with cheese.

Oven, moderate, 350°

Bake 30 minutes or until thoroughly heated.

To serve 4

TOMATO TUNA

Tuna, 7-ounce can
Celery Flakes, 2 teasps.
Onion Flakes, 2 teasps.
Mushrooms, 3-oz. can, sliced
Tomatoes, 16-ounce can
Flour, 1 tablespoon

Drain oil from tuna into skillet; sauté celery and onion until soft. Drain mushrooms and add to mixture. Add tomatoes, reserving liquid. Mix flour with tomato liquid and add to other ingredients. Bring to boil, simmer few minutes until thickened.

To serve 4

CREAMED CHICKEN AND MUSHROOMS

Cream of Mushroom Soup, 1 can
Mushrooms, Sliced, 3-ounce can
Milk, ½ soup can
Worcestershire, 1 teasp.
Parsley Flakes, 1 tablesp.
Chicken, 2 6-ounce cans

Combine soup, milk and mushrooms with their liquid, in saucepan over low heat. Add Worcestershire, parsley and chicken in small pieces. Heat thoroughly and serve on toast.

To serve 4

CRAB MEAT SKILLET

Mushroom Soup, 1 can
Milk, ½ cup
Crab Meat, 6½-oz. can
Peas, 8-oz. can, drained
Sherry, 2 tablespoons
Paprika
Precooked Rice, 5-ounce package

Combine soup and milk in skillet; bring to boiling point, stirring frequently. Add crab meat and peas; simmer 5 minutes. Add sherry and heat over low heat few minutes more. Garnish with paprika. Serve with bowl of hot rice, prepared according to directions on package.

To serve 4

TUNA SKILLET: Substitute tuna for crab in the above recipe.

LOBSTER SKILLET: Substitute lobster for crab in the above recipe.

CREAMED MEAT AND VEGETABLES

Celery Soup, 1 can
Cream, ½ cup
Chopped Ham, 12-ounce can, cubed
Potatoes, 8-oz. can, diced
Peas, 8-ounce can
Carrots, 8-oz. can, diced
Worcestershire, 1 tablespoon

Mix soup with cream and ham in saucepan and heat. Add drained vegetables and Worcestershire; simmer 5 minutes. Add a little of the vegetable liquid if needed. Save balance for soups or gravies. Serve on toast.

To serve 4

CHICKEN-ASPARAGUS PARMESAN

Cream of Chicken Soup, 1 can
Button Mushrooms, 4-ounce can
Chicken, 6-ounce can

In saucepan combine soup, mushrooms in their liquid, and chicken, broken in pieces. Heat thoroughly.

Asparagus Spears, 1 can
Parmesan Cheese, grated, ½ cup

Place individual portions of chicken mixture on toast; arrange a few asparagus spears on top of each; sprinkle with Parmesan cheese and put under hot broiler until cheese is melted. Serve at once.

To serve 4

MENUS

To extend these menus with a first course consult the chapter "Appetizers"(page 244), and the section on canned-soup combinations in "Soups" (page 108).

EASY CHICKEN FRICASSEE

Canned Cranberry Sauce
Buttered Canned Carrots
Apples and Cheese · Crackers

SALMON QUICKIE

Canned Stewed Tomatoes
Ready-to-Bake Rolls · Whipped Butter
Mixed Canned Pineapple and Grapefruit · Cookies

5-MINUTE CHILI CON CARNE

Corn Mix Muffins · Bought Preserves
Icy Canned Pears in Gingerale

BEANS AND VIENNA SAUSAGE CASSEROLE

Bought Cole Slaw · Vienna Bread · Butter
Chilled Apricots with Kirsch

HAMBURGER-RAVIOLI CASSEROLE

Parmesan Cheese
Packaged Mixed Salad · Bought Salad Dressing
Queen Anne Cherries and Store Cake

TOMATO TUNA

Packaged Mashed Potatoes
Carrot and Celery Sticks
Whole Wheat Bread · Butter · Ice Cream (mix)

CREAMED CHICKEN AND MUSHROOMS

Baked Potato · Buttered Canned Peas
Olives and Celery Sticks
Bought Angel Food Cake · Canned Blueberries

CRAB MEAT SKILLET

Hot Cooked Rice · Buttered Green Beans (canned)
Avocado Halves with Curried Mayonnaise
Butterscotch Pudding (mix)

CREAMED MEAT AND VEGETABLES

Hot Buttered Noodles · Pickled Canned Beets
Apple Mallow

CHICKEN-ASPARAGUS PARMESAN

Toast · Packaged Scalloped Potatoes
Applesauce · Doughnuts

These packaged short cuts can be a boon to the busy homemaker whenever her day is too crowded to allow for more elaborate meal preparation. The working wife, especially, can profit from always having a supply of these foods on hand to serve her in an emergency.

SKILLET BEAN AND BURGER BARBECUE

Meat Balls, 2 16-oz. cans
Dried Lima Beans,
  16-ounce can
Red Kidney Beans,
  16-ounce can
Onion Flakes, 1 package
Brown Sugar, ¼ cup
Catsup, ½ cup
Onions, small, 8-oz. can
Red Wine, ½ cup
Salt and **Pepper,** to taste

Combine all ingredients in skillet; simmer on top of stove or in electric skillet for 30 minutes. Add water if necessary.

To serve 4

10-MINUTE CHICKEN AND RICE

Chicken, 2 6-ounce cans
Onion Flakes, 1 tablesp.
Salt, ½ teaspoon
Pepper, ⅛ teaspoon
Chicken Bouillon,
  1⅓ cups

Combine all ingredients in saucepan and bring to boil.

Precooked Rice, 5-ounce
  package
Parsley, 1 tablespoon,
  minced

Stir rice lightly into chicken mixture; cover, and remove from heat. Let stand 5 minutes. Check seasonings and add more if needed. Serve with a sprinkling of parsley.

To serve 4

TUNA PATTIES

Mashed Potato Mix,
  1 envelope or package
Instant Onion, 1 tablesp.
Tuna, 7-oz. can
Salt, 1 teaspoon
Pepper, ⅛ teaspoon
Fat or **Oil** for browning,
  3 tablespoons

Prepare mashed potato mix according to directions on package, keeping the mixture stiff. Add onions. Pour oil from tuna into other fat, flake tuna and add to potato mix, with salt and pepper. Form into patties and brown in skillet.

To serve 4

SPAGHETTI WITH CLAM SAUCE

Olive or **Salad Oil,**
  2 tablespoons
Salt, 1 teaspoon
Instant Garlic, ¼ teasp.
Oregano, ¼ teaspoon
Celery Flakes, 1 teasp.
Pepper, ⅛ teaspoon
Minced Clams,
  2 7-ounce cans
Spaghetti, 8-ozs., cooked
Parmesan Cheese, grated

In saucepan heat olive oil and add seasonings. Add clams and liquid. Simmer 5 minutes. Serve on portions of cooked spaghetti with grated Parmesan cheese.

To serve 4

TUNA POTATO CRISP

Cream of Mushroom
  Soup, 1 can
Thin Cream, 1 soup can
Sherry, 2 tablespoons
Tuna Fish, 2 7-oz. cans
Potato Chips

Combine soup, cream and sherry. Pour over tuna fish arranged in baking dish. Top with finely crumbled potato chips.

Oven, moderate, 350°

Bake 30 minutes, or until lightly browned.

To serve 4

QUICK SHRIMP AND RICE

Bacon, 4 slices
Precooked Rice,
  5-ounce package
Tomatoes, 16-ounce can
Basil, ½ teaspoon
Green Pepper Flakes,
  1 teaspoon
Black Olives, ¼ cup,
  chopped
Shrimp, 5-oz. can
Salt and **Pepper,** to taste

Sauté bacon in skillet until crisp; drain in paper and pour off all but 1 tablespoon of bacon fat. Add rice and brown lightly. Add tomatoes and simmer 5 minutes. Add basil, green pepper, black olives; devein shrimp and add. Season to taste. Serve with crumbled bacon on top.

To serve 4

CREAMED MUSHROOMS, HAM AND EGGS

Mushroom Soup, 1 can
Milk, 1 soup can
Chopped Ham, 12-ounce
  can

Combine soup and milk in saucepan, heat, stirring until smooth. Cube ham and add to soup.

Mushroom Buttons,
  4-ounce can
Butter, 1 tablespoon
Hard-cooked Eggs, 4
Sherry, 2 tablespoons

Drain mushrooms and brown lightly in butter. Add to soup. Simmer 5 minutes. Quarter eggs and add to soup with sherry just before serving. Stir gently so as not to break eggs.

To serve 4

MENUS

SKILLET BEAN AND BURGER BARBECUE

Cucumber and Carrot Sticks
Rye Bread · Butter
Apple Snow

10-MINUTE CHICKEN AND RICE

Canned Asparagus
Bread and Butter Pickles
Corn Bread (mix) · Butter
Pears and Cheese

SPAGHETTI WITH CLAM SAUCE

Parmesan Cheese
Black Olives · Carrot Sticks
Italian Bread · Butter
Home-Style Canned Peaches

TUNA POTATO CRISP

Hot Buttered Canned Beets
Heat and Serve Rolls · Butter
Canned Prunes in Port Wine

QUICK SHRIMP AND RICE

Green Salad · Bottled French Dressing
Melba Toast · Butter
Pineapple Jamaican

CREAMED MUSHROOMS, HAM AND EGGS

Toasted English Muffins · Jam
Banana-Grape Cup

To vary your meal starters you might plan to serve a creamed soup before non-creamy main courses, or clear soups with heartier meals.

Most of these recipes add something special in the way of sauce or seasoning to the ready-prepared foods. The trick is to taste as you go—make sure the seasoning is the way you like it, adding more than is called for if your palate so dictates.

TONGUE IN RED WINE

Butter, 2 tablespoons
Onion Flakes, 2 tablesps.
Parsley Flakes, 2 tablesps.
Celery Flakes, 2 tablesps.
Tongue, 2 12-oz. cans
Dry Red Wine, ¼ cup
Salt and Pepper, to taste

Melt butter in skillet, add onion, parsley and celery flakes. Stir over low heat until soft. Slice tongue and add to skillet. Heat 5 minutes. Add wine, bring to boil. Remove from heat. Season to taste.

To serve 4

HAM AND SWEET POTATO GRILL

Canned Ham, 1½ lbs.
Sweet Potatoes,
    16-ounce can
Nutmeg, ¼ teaspoon
Brown Sugar, 2 tablesps.

Slice ham; spread with mustard and arrange on broiler pan; broil 5 minutes. Turn over. Arrange potatoes around ham, sprinkle potatoes with nutmeg and brown sugar. Broil 8 minutes or until lightly browned.

To serve 4

BAKED SALMON AND POTATOES PARMESAN

Salmon, 16-ounce can
Potatoes, 16-ounce can
Celery Soup, 1 can
Milk, ½ cup
Worcestershire,
    1 tablespoon
Basil, ½ teaspoon
Parmesan Cheese, ½ cup

In baking dish arrange salmon and sliced potatoes in layers. Mix soup, milk and Worcestershire; heat to boiling point and pour over other ingredients.

Sprinkle cheese over top.

Oven, moderate, 350°

Bake 30 minutes.

To serve 4

CRAB CASSEROLE

Onion Flakes, 2 teasps.
Green Pepper Flakes,
    2 teaspoons
Garlic Powder, ⅛ teasp.
Butter, 2 tablespoons
Tomatoes, 16-oz. can
Worcestershire, 1 teasp.
Rosemary, ½ teaspoon
Rice, 1 cup, cooked
Crab Meat, 2 6-oz. cans
Cheese, ½ cup, grated
    Parmesan

Add onion and pepper flakes and garlic powder to melted butter in skillet and heat briefly. Add tomatoes and seasonings, and bring to boil; simmer 10 minutes over low heat.

Add rice and crab to the tomato mixture, combine well and pour into shallow baking dish. Sprinkle with cheese.

Oven, 375°.

Bake 30 minutes.

To serve 4

CREAMED DRIED BEEF DE LUXE

Dried Beef, 4-oz. pkg.

Mushroom Soup, 1 can
Milk, 1 cup
Sherry, 2 tablespoons
Biscuit-mix Biscuits

Rinse dried beef in cold water to remove excess salt; drain.

Mix soup and milk in saucepan; heat. Add shredded dried beef. Bring to boiling point but do not boil. Add sherry. Serve on hot buttered biscuit-mix biscuits.

To serve 4

SALMON AND ASPARAGUS

Red Salmon, 16-oz. can
Cream of Asparagus
    Soup, 1 can
Milk, 1 cup

Flake drained salmon; combine soup and milk over low heat; add salmon to hot soup and continue heating, stirring constantly, but do not boil.

Asparagus Spears, 1 can
Toast

Heat asparagus spears in separate pan. Arrange salmon mixture on toast and top each serving with several asparagus spears.

To serve 4

CHICKEN FLORENTINE

Chopped Spinach, frozen,
    1 package
Salt and Pepper
Chicken à la King, 2 cans
Parmesan Cheese, grated

Arrange partly thawed spinach in bottom of greased casserole. Sprinkle with a little salt and pepper. Arrange chicken à la king over it. Cover top with grated cheese.

Oven, moderate, 375°

Bake 20 minutes, or until lightly browned.

To serve 4

EVE'S CORNED BEEF HASH WITH RIPE OLIVES

Butter, 3 tablespoons
Corned Beef Hash,
    2 16-ounce cans
Worcestershire, 1 tablesp.
Ripe Olives, ½ cup,
    chopped
Chili Sauce

Melt butter in large skillet. Chop up corned beef, mix with Worcestershire and olives; brown gently, scraping up from bottom from time to time. Serve with chili sauce.

To serve 4

A variety of seasonings will improve packaged foods

MENUS

TONGUE IN RED WINE

Packaged Au Gratin Potatoes
Whole Kernel Canned Corn
Banana Cordiale

HAM AND SWEET POTATO GRILL

Bottled Mustard Sauce
Hot Buttered Spinach (canned)
Lemon-Applesauce Sherbet

BAKED SALMON AND POTATOES PARMESAN

Mixed Canned Green Beans and Corn
Sesame Wafers · Butter
Easy Prune Whip

CRAB CASSEROLE

Glazed Canned Carrots
Pickle Relish
Strawberry Shortcake (frozen berries and mix)

CREAMED DRIED BEEF DE LUXE

on Hot Biscuits (mix)
Garlic-Seasoned Canned Green Beans
Sweet and Sour Beet Shreds
Italian Rum Cake

SALMON AND ASPARAGUS ON TOAST

Canned Peas
Stuffed Olives
Spiced Pears · Date Bars (mix)

CHICKEN FLORENTINE

Parsley Potatoes (canned)
Lettuce Wedges with Russian Dressing
Grapes Sauterne with Sour Cream

EVE'S CORNED BEEF HASH WITH RIPE OLIVES

Quick Creamed Onions
Celery Hearts
Popovers (mix) · Butter
Quick Holiday Dessert

Dried fruits and vegetables are staples in every kitchen

SALMON AND SHRIMP CASSEROLE

Salmon, 16-ounce can
Shrimp, 4½ oz. can
Mushrooms, sliced,
    4-ounce can

Mix salmon, shrimp and drained mushrooms in casserole.

Butter, 2 tablespoons
Flour, 2 tablespoons
Cream, 1½ cups
Dry White Wine, ⅓ cup
Salt, ½ teaspoon
Pepper, ⅛ teaspoon

In saucepan, melt butter, blend in flour, add cream, wine, salt, and pepper. Cook over low heat, stirring constantly until thickened. Pour into casserole.

Instant Mashed Potatoes,
    1 pkg., prepared

Drop spoonfuls of potatoes around edge of casserole to form border.

Oven, moderate, 350°

Bake 30 minutes or until thoroughly heated and potatoes are lightly browned.

To serve 4

HAM HAWAIIAN

Pineapple Chunks,
    16-ounce can
Cornstarch, 1 tablespoon
Sugar, 1 tablespoon
Vinegar, 1½ tablesps.
Mustard, 1 teaspoon, dry
Green Pepper Flakes,
    1 tablespoon
Water, ¾ cup
Chopped Ham, 12-oz. can

Drain pineapple and mix liquid with cornstarch. Add sugar, vinegar, water, mustard, and pepper flakes, and cook until thickened, stirring constantly. Chop ham into bite-size pieces and add with pineapple; heat thoroughly.

Precooked Rice, 5-ounce
    package

Prepare rice according to directions on package and serve with ham.

To serve 4

SALMON LOAF

Salmon, 16-ounce can
Soft Bread Crumbs,
    2 cups
Eggs, 2, slightly beaten
Milk, ½ cup
Onion Flakes, 1 tablesp.
Salt, 1 teaspoon
Pepper, ⅛ teaspoon

Combine ingredients; mix lightly with a fork and put in greased loaf pan.

Oven, moderate, 350°

Bake 30 minutes.

To serve 4

PANNED CORNED BEEF HASH

Fat, 1 tablespoon
Corned Beef Hash, 2 cans
Onion Flakes, 3 tablesps.
Catsup

Melt fat in skillet, add onion flakes and heat until softened. Add hash broken up with fork. Cook slowly letting bottom brown and turning it up as it cooks. Serve with catsup.

To serve 4

BEEF PIE WITH CHEESE CRUST

Beef Stew, 24-oz. can
Packaged Biscuit Mix
Sharp Cheddar Cheese,
    grated, ¼ cup

Empty stew into casserole. Mix biscuit dough as directed on package, adding grated cheese. Pat out into thin layer and cover stew.

Oven, hot, 425°

Bake until stew is heated through and topping is lightly brown, about 20 to 30 minutes.

To serve 4

MENUS

SALMON AND SHRIMP CASSEROLE

Green Salad
Biscuits (ready-to-bake) · Whipped Butter
Figs in Wine · Cookies

HAM HAWAIIAN

Hot Cooked Rice · Green Beans (canned)
Refrigerator Cookies (ready-to-bake)

SALMON LOAF

Quick Creamed Onions and Potatoes
Ripe Olives
Canned Pineapple and Cookies

PANNED CORNED BEEF HASH

Poached Eggs
Celery and Carrot Sticks
Buttered Heated Rye Wafers
Canned Apricots and Cottage Cheese

BEEF PIE WITH CHEESE CRUST

Quick Cole Slaw
Hard Rolls · Butter
Dark Sweet Cherries (canned)

Remember sometimes to use fresh fruit for a first course if it doesn't appear elsewhere in the meal.

Pantry shelf meals with an assist from the freezer.

BAKED TUNA AND ASPARAGUS

Frozen Asparagus Spears, 2 packages **Tuna,** 2 7-ounce cans	Cook asparagus and arrange in bottom of baking dish. Spread tuna over top.
Butter, ¼ cup **Almonds,** ½ cup, sliced **Flour,** 4 tablespoons **Salt,** ¼ teaspoon **Pepper,** ⅛ teaspoon **Milk,** 2 cups **Sherry,** 2 tablespoons	In skillet lightly brown blanched, sliced almonds in butter. Blend in flour, salt and pepper. Add milk and cook slowly until thickened, stirring constantly. Add sherry; pour into baking dish.
Oven, moderate, 350°	Bake 20 minutes.

To serve 4

GUMBO MACARONI WITH SAUSAGES

Macaroni, 8-ounce pkg.	Cook macaroni in boiling water until tender. Drain.
Brown and **Serve Sausages,** 1 package **Butter,** 1 tablespoon	Meanwhile, cook sausages in skillet with butter until lightly browned. Remove sausages from skillet and keep hot.
Chicken-Gumbo Soup, 1 can **Water,** ½ soup can	In skillet heat soup with water. When hot add macaroni. Mix lightly and put in serving dish with sausages on top.

To serve 4

QUICK SHRIMP NEWBURG

Frozen Cream of Shrimp Soup, 1 can **Light Cream,** 1 can **Frozen Shrimp,** 1 pkg,. shelled, raw **Egg Yolks,** 2, beaten **Sherry,** 2 tablespoons	Add cream to frozen soup and thaw slowly over low heat. Bring to boiling point. Add frozen shrimp; cook several minutes until they turn pink. Add a little of the hot mixture to the eggs, stir and add back to mixture. Add sherry. Heat slowly and stir a few minutes. Serve on toast.

To serve 4 or 5

SHRIMP CURRY: Follow the above recipe for Quick Shrimp Newburg, but add two teaspoons curry powder and 2 drops of Tabasco.

STEAMED LOBSTER TAILS

Lobster Tails, frozen, 4–8 (about 2 pounds) **Horse-radish Sauce** (see page 90)	Follow directions on package for cooking. Split tails but leave meat in shell. Serve with Horse-radish sauce.

To serve 4

EASY CORNED-BEEF DINNER

Corned Beef, 16-oz. can **Brussels Sprouts,** frozen, 1 box **Whole Potatoes,** 16-ounce can **Whole Onions,** 16-oz. can **Horse-radish**	Place corned beef in center of skillet; separate Brussels sprouts in skillet with a little boiling water; add potatoes and onions, drained of their liquids. Cover and cook 10 to 12 minutes, or until sprouts are tender. Serve with horse-radish.

To serve 4

TUNA POT PIE

Frozen Peas and **Carrots,** 1 package **Canned Potatoes,** 1 cup, diced **Instant Onion,** 1 tablesp. **Tuna,** 2 7-oz. cans **Celery Soup,** 1 can	Cook frozen vegetables in small amount of boiling water until just tender. Add potatoes and onion. Drain and reserve liquid. Arrange vegetables in casserole, in layers alternating with tuna fish. Combine ⅓ cup of water from vegetables with celery soup. Heat and pour over mixture in casserole.
Biscuit Mix	Make dough for top according to directions on package. Put on top.
Oven, hot, 400°	Bake 20 minutes or until crust is golden brown.

To serve 4

SEAFOOD TRIO

Shrimp Soup, Frozen, 1 can **Cream,** 1 soup can **Crab Meat,** Frozen, 1 package **Lobster,** 1 can **Salt** and **Pepper,** to taste **Sherry,** 2 tablespoons **Chow Mein Noodles,** 1 can	Heat soup and cream together stirring until smooth. Add crab meat and lobster. Bring to boiling point. Add salt and pepper and sherry, heat few more minutes. Serve on chow mein noodles.

To serve 4

BROILED FISH FILLETS

Frozen Fillets, 2 pkgs. **Soya Sauce** **Butter** **Lemon Wedges**	Separate thawed fillets into serving pieces, brush each one with soya sauce and let them remain out of the refrigerator for 10 or 15 minutes. Then brush with butter and cook under broiler until top is lightly browned. Turn fish over, brush with butter and broil until done. Serve with lemon wedges.

To serve 4

TROUT AMANDINE

Frozen Trout, 4
Flour
Salt and **Pepper**
Cooking Oil, 4 tablesps.

Cook trout without thawing. Dredge with flour and season with salt and pepper. Brown in oil in skillet over medium heat, cooking until fork tender and browned evenly on both sides.

Almonds, ¼ cup
Butter, 4 tablespoons
Parsley

To serve 4

Meanwhile blanch almonds and cut into slivers. Sauté lightly in butter until golden brown. Remove trout to hot platter and pour almonds and butter over it. Garnish with sprigs of parsley.

MINUTE STEAKS

Cook steaks without thawing. Melt 2 tablespoons of butter in skillet and sauté steaks over moderate heat, ½ minute on each side. Do not overcook or they will be dry. Allow 2 steaks per person. Serve with bottled steak sauce.

BROWN AND SERVE SAUSAGES

Cook sausages, without thawing, in lightly greased skillet until brown on all sides. Allow 2 or 3 sausages per person.

TUNA PASTRY

Pie Crust Mix, 1 pkg.

Make pastry according to directions on package; chill. Roll out round ⅜" thick and place on floured baking sheet when other ingredients are ready.

Precooked Rice, 5-oz. pkg.
Sliced Mushrooms, 1 can
Butter, 1 tablespoon
Lemon Juice, 1 tablespoon
Tuna, 2 7-oz. cans
Eggs, 2, hard-cooked
Parsley, 1 tablespoon
Salt and **Pepper** to taste
Lemon Butter, see page 91

Oven, hot, 450°

To serve 4

Prepare rice according to directions on package.

Drain mushrooms and heat in butter. Add lemon juice.

Break up tuna with fork. On half of pastry round place a layer of rice; cover it with tuna, mushrooms and egg slices. Sprinkle with parsley, salt and pepper, and cover with remaining rice. Fold pastry over, crimp edges together and gash top in several places.

Bake 15 minutes, or until golden brown. Serve hot with Lemon Butter.

MENUS

BAKED TUNA AND ASPARAGUS

French Fried Potatoes (frozen)
Carrot and Celery Sticks
Frozen Cherry Tarts

GUMBO MACARONI WITH SAUSAGES

New Cabbage Wedges with Sour Cream Sauce
Peach Pie (frozen)

QUICK SHRIMP NEWBURG ON TOAST

Parsley Potatoes · Asparagus (frozen)
Tossed Green Salad
Italian Cream Cheese Custard

STEAMED LOBSTER TAILS

Scalloped Potatoes (package) · Green Peas
Carrot Sticks · Black Olives
Blueberry Pie (frozen)

EASY CORNED-BEEF DINNER

Horse-radish
Brown and Serve Rolls · Butter
Chocolate Walnut Sundae (bought topping)

TUNA POT PIE

Sliced Tomatoes on Lettuce
Whole Wheat Bread · Butter
Peach Parfait

SEAFOOD TRIO

Chow Mein Noodles · Limas and Leeks
Escarole with French Dressing
Hawaiian Ladyfingers

BROILED FISH FILLETS

Lemon Wedges
Spanish Rice (package) · Frozen Broccoli
Frozen Cheese Cake

TUNA PASTRY

Water cress and Tomato Salad
Sharp Cheese and Crisp Crackers

Canned, packaged and frozen foods bring you new freedom—and the ability to entertain at a moment's notice.

CORNED-BEEF PATTIES AND POACHED EGGS WITH CHEESE SAUCE

Corned Beef Hash, 2 cans — Brown slices of corned beef hash in small amount of bacon fat or other fat.

Eggs, 8 or as needed — Poach eggs until just set (see page 112).

Cheese Sauce, 1 jar — Arrange corned beef slices on platter with egg on each one, top with cheese sauce. (Use the ready-prepared kind that just needs to be melted or see Cheese Sauce, page 90.)

To serve 4

SPICY SPAGHETTI

Bacon, 2 slices
Onion, 1 medium
Celery Flakes, 2 teasps.
Green Pepper Flakes, 2 teaspoons
Tomatoes, 24-ounce can
Salt, 1 teaspoon
Pepper, 1/8 teaspoon
Basil, 1/2 teaspoon
Cloves, 1/4 teaspoon
Bay Leaf, 1

In large skillet fry bacon until crisp, and remove. Chop onion and add with celery and green pepper flakes to fat in skillet; cook slowly a few minutes, stirring frequently. Add tomatoes and seasonings, bring to boil and simmer 10 minutes.

Spaghetti, 8-ounce pkg. — Meanwhile cook spaghetti according to directions on package. Drain and add to tomato mixture. Cook 5 minutes, stirring once or twice. Top with crumbled bacon.

To serve 4

SALMON NEWBURG

Butter, 3 tablespoons
Flour, 3 tablespoons
Salt, 1/4 teaspoon
Pepper, 1/8 teaspoon
Milk, 1 1/2 cups

Melt butter in skillet over low heat and blend in flour and seasonings. Add milk slowly, stirring constantly. Cook until thickened.

Egg Yolks, 2, beaten
Sharp Cheese, grated, 2 tablespoons
Salmon, 16-ounce can
Sherry, 2 tablespoons

Add a little of the hot mixture to the beaten eggs, stir and add back to the first mixture. Add cheese and salmon; stir and cook about 2 minutes. Add sherry; cook another minute and serve on toast.

To serve 4

FRANKFURTERS AND KRAUT

Onion, 1 large
Garlic, 1 clove
Caraway Seeds, 2 tablespoons
Pepper, 1/8 teaspoon
Sauerkraut, 16-ounce can
Frankfurters, 1 pound

Chop onion and garlic. Combine with sauerkraut and seasonings in large casserole. Arrange frankfurters on top. Cover.

Oven, moderate, 350° — Bake 40 minutes.

To serve 4

BACON-TUNA-RICE CURRY

Bacon, 1/2 pound — Fry bacon slices slowly until brown and crisp. Drain on paper towels, cool and crumble.

Tuna, 2 7-ounce cans
Rice, cooked, 2 cups
Curry Powder, 2 teasps.
Clove, 1/8 teaspoon
Ginger, 1/4 teaspoon
Celery Salt, 1/2 teaspoon
Minced Onion, 2 teasps.
Tomato Juice, 1/2 cup

Drain tuna and flake with fork. Add rice, bacon, seasonings; stir in tomato juice and combine all together lightly. Turn into buttered casserole.

Oven, moderate, 350° — Bake 30 minutes.

To serve 4

EASY JAMBALAYA

Onion, 2 medium, sliced
Garlic, 1 clove, minced
Green Pepper, 1 large, sliced
Tomatoes, 16-ounce can
Chopped Ham, 12-ounce can, cubed
Thyme, 1/4 teaspoon
Basil, 1/2 teaspoon
Paprika, 1/2 teaspoon
Salt, 1 teaspoon
White Wine, 1/2 cup
Rice, 1 cup, raw
Shrimp, 2 7-ounce cans

Sauté onion, garlic and green pepper in butter until soft. Add tomatoes, ham, seasonings and wine. Bring mixture to a boil, add rice slowly, stirring constantly. Cover, simmer over low heat for 25 minutes, or until rice is tender, adding water if necessary. Add shrimp, heat thoroughly and serve immediately.

To serve 4

CURRIED DRIED BEEF AND SPAGHETTI

Spaghetti. 8-oz. package

Cook spaghetti in boiling salted water until tender. Drain.

Cream of Mushroom Soup, 1 can
Milk, 1 can
Curry Powder, 1 teasp.
Dried Beef, 4-oz. pkg.
Bread Crumbs, 1 cup
Butter, 2 tablespoons

Combine soup with milk in saucepan, add curry powder. Heat, stirring constantly. Break up dried beef in pieces and add to sauce. (If beef seems very salty, rinse in cold water before using.) Bring to boil; add spaghetti. Turn at once into casserole. Top with bread crumbs mixed with melted butter. Put under broiler until crumbs are lightly browned.

To serve 4

CORNED BEEF HASH-STUFFED PEPPERS

Corned Beef Hash, 16-ounce can
Chili Sauce, 2 tablesps.
Green Peppers, 2 large
Tomato Sauce, 1 can

Break up corned beef hash with fork and mix with chili sauce. Cut peppers in half lengthwise, remove seeds, parboil 5 minutes, heap with corned beef hash mixture.

Oven, hot, 400°

Bake 20 minutes or until peppers are tender.

To serve 4

Serve with canned tomato sauce.

QUICK CORNED BEEF AND CABBAGE

Cabbage, small head
Water, ½ cup
Salt, 1 teaspoon
Pepper, ⅛ teaspoon
Dry Mustard, ½ teasp.
Corned Beef, 1 can

Shred cabbage and place in skillet with water and seasonings; cover tightly and cook 10 minutes over low heat. Slice corned beef and arrange slices over cabbage. Cook 5 minutes more, or until meat is heated and cabbage tender.

To serve 4

BEANS AND FRANKFURTERS WITH A DIFFERENCE

Beans with Pork, 2 1-lb. 7-oz. cans
Onion, 1 small, grated
Worcestershire, 1 tablespoon
Prepared Mustard
Frankfurters, 1 lb.

Mix beans, onion and Worcestershire in skillet. Score frankfurters and spread with prepared mustard and place on top of beans. Cover and simmer 15 minutes.

To serve 4

MENUS

Meals ready to serve without advance notice.

CORNED-BEEF PATTIES AND POACHED EGG WITH CHEESE SAUCE

Carrots and Green Pepper Salad
Buttered Toast
Chocolate Ice Cream Roll (bought)

SPICY SPAGHETTI

Egg and Anchovy Salad
Italian Bread · Butter
Brandied Grapes

SALMON NEWBURG

Fresh Peas and New Potatoes
Raspberry Apple Sauce · Brownies (mix)

FRANKFURTERS AND KRAUT

Kidney Bean Salad
Rye Bread · Butter
Melon Compote

CURRIED DRIED BEEF AND SPAGHETTI

Fried Tomatoes · Chutney
Banana Cream Cake

CORNED BEEF HASH-STUFFED PEPPERS

Canned Tomato Sauce
Au Gratin Potatoes (package) · Watercress
Frozen Melon Balls and Strawberries

QUICK CORNED BEEF AND CABBAGE

Mexican Corn
Watermelon Pickles
Rye Bread · Butter
Jelly Cake

BEANS AND FRANKFURTERS WITH A DIFFERENCE

Raw Sauerkraut
Rye Bread · Butter
Danish Dessert (mix)

MENUS

These hot weather menus, to keep the cook cool on days when the temperature soars, need no cooking, or only a little that can be done early in the day. You will find recipes for the main dishes in the sections on Salads and Sandwiches; consult the Index.

SLICED CORNED BEEF (CANNED)

Potato Salad with Savory Mayonnaise
Quartered Tomatoes · Cucumber Strips · Olives
Ice-cold Honeydew Melon

AVOCADO FILLED WITH LOBSTER SALAD

Tomato Aspic
Cream Cheese and Caviar Sandwiches
Raspberry Cooler

ITALIAN STYLE SANDWICH

Tossed Green Salad
Strawberry Mousse

COLD BORSCH

Jellied Salmon Salad
Cottage Cheese
Sesame Crackers · Butter
Blueberry Cobbler

CHILLED ROCK LOBSTER TAILS

Mayonnaise
Green Bean and Potato Salad
Assorted Cheeses with Crackers

SANDWICHES OF ASSORTED LUNCH MEATS

Kidney Bean Salad
Deviled Eggs
Young Radishes · Tiny Carrots · Scallions
Melon Compote

SHRIMP SALAD

Celery Stuffed with Pimiento Cheese
Mixed Pickles
Sponge Layers with Sliced Peaches and Whipped Cream

CHILLED CLAM BROTH (CANNED)

Picnic Salad
Hard Rolls · Butter
Cherry Pie

SEAFOOD BLUEPLATE SANDWICH

Potato Chips
Cucumbers with Yogurt
Chocolate Refrigerator Cake

CANNED HAM WITH CRANBERRY GLAZE

Potato Salad with Sour Cream
Jellied Lobster Ring
Sliced Pineapple and Banana

TOMATOES STUFFED WITH TUNA FISH SALAD

Cucumbers and Onions in Vinegar
Whole Wheat Bread · Butter
Blackberry Duff

TROPICAL CHEF'S SALAD

Biscuits · Whipped Butter
Spice Cup Cakes and Vanilla Ice Cream

3 colorful and delicious fruit plates with meat and cheese accompaniments—to arrange for individual servings.

1. Rolled slices of boiled ham
   Slice of cantaloupe
   Half of banana, cut lengthwise
   2 tomato slices
   Cubes of Cheddar cheese
   Serve with French Dressing for tomato

2. Sliced cold turkey
   Wedge of watermelon
   Sliced peach
   Pineapple cubes
   Few green grapes
   Sprigs of watercress
   Cube of blue cheese

3. Honeydew melon wedge
   Oval slices of banana
   2 slices of orange
   2 green pepper rings
   2 slices of Swiss cheese
   2 slices of broiled bacon as top garnish

Serve these with crisp, crunchy bread or rolls and whipped butter.

Or make an open sandwich, starting with a large slice of dark bread spread with butter and topping it with quarter-inch thick slices of liverwurst overlapping alternate slices of ripe tomato. Garnish the whole with sardine fillets in oil and slices of Spanish onion.

To add interest to menus take advantage of the many delicious ready-to-buy relishes and pickles.

MEAT

Every piece of meat, whether an expensive, tender cut, or a cheaper, tougher portion of an animal, can be delicious if properly cooked. The important thing is to know before purchasing just how you plan to use it. Don't buy meat that is intended for the pot, if you want a fast broil or a rare roast; for the tougher cuts require long, slow cooking in moist heat to make them tasty, and these we make into potroasts and stews, or braise.

Always buy graded meat, and, if possible, government graded meat. It carries the stamp of the United States Department of Agriculture; and the grades in order of quality are USDA Prime, Choice, Good, Commercial and Utility. However, many packers have substituted their own brand names as grades, and these are usually reliable. Always look for the US Inspected and Passed stamp on all meat, which is your guarantee that it was a healthy animal, processed in a sanitary plant.

Regardless of brand, the experienced cook buys meat by eye. Good meat looks good. It has plenty of fat around it, and the fat should be very white—hard and thick on beef, crisp on lamb, waxy and hard on pork, and what little fat there is on veal should be clear white. Beware of meat with thin yellow fat.

Next in importance is color—beef should be dark red, and the bone pink and soft, not gray. Lamb should be rosy in color, not as red as beef, and not dull or gray looking. (Lamb should be small too; to be what is called "spring lamb," the leg will weigh no more than six pounds; a little older lamb, seven. Beyond this size and age, lamb has a stronger flavor and is almost mutton.) Good veal is pale rosy beige in color. Older veal is very pink. Good pork is grayish pink, fine grained.

Knowing a good piece of meat when you see it can mean you will always have good meat on your table. When you shop, be flexible, and buy what looks good.

Though you had your heart set on a rib roast of beef, today, you may find the beef supply low, but there in the case is a tiny leg of lamb, covered in crisp, white fat, that you know will make superb eating. Keep your eyes open for the best, even though you can't use it immediately. You can hold it in your refrigerator a few days, or wrap it for your freezer. (See page 272.)

STORING MEAT

Do not leave meat tightly wrapped. Remove paper, place it in a shallow container and cover loosely with wax paper, or other wrapping, leaving the ends open. Store all meat in the coldest part of the refrigerator and take it out half an hour before cooking.

ROASTING MEAT

Roast meat at a low oven temperature. It will be tenderer and more flavorful, will require less fuel, there will be less shrinkage and your oven will not become spattered and require cleaning. High temperatures can cause as much as 15 to 20% loss in shrinkage.

It is difficult to give exact cooking times, since meat varies greatly in size, shape and the proportion of fat to lean. Therefore, to be sure it reaches just the degree of doneness that you like, always use a meat thermometer. For approximate cooking times required, consult the timetable in the section with each type of meat. This will help you plan the time to put your meat in the oven.

WHAT TO DO WITH THE LEFTOVER ROAST

Part of the reason for having a roast is the number of delicious dishes that can be made from the leftover meat. See the section called "Leftovers" to help you plan the interesting meals ahead.

STORAGE TIMETABLE FOR MEATS

Kind of Meat	Fresh-Storage Limit at 40° or Below	Frozen-Storage Limit at 0° or Below
Beef	Large Cuts, 8 Days	1 Year
	Ground Beef, 2 Days	
Pork and Veal	5 Days	6 Months
Lamb	4–5 Days	9 Months

BEEF   In buying beef look for the United States Department of Agriculture grade stamp. (See Buying Meat, page 21.) USDA Prime is usually sold to fine hotels and restaurants, but a great deal of USDA Choice beef is available in consumer stores. It has a firm white fat covering and the flesh is marbled with fat which makes it tender and flavorsome. Some USDA Good is of good quality, but has less fat and marbling. The lower grades, Commercial and Utility, are useful for braising and pot roasting, but do not make tender oven roasts.

RIB ROAST OF BEEF

A rib roast is probably the most flavorful and succulent cut of beef. Its appearance on the table makes a meal a great occasion. There are 7 ribs, but the first and second ribs are the choicest. All rib roasts are not *prime* rib—see meat grades above.

Standing Rib Roast. A roast with the ribs left in; sometimes sold in the full 10-inch length, sometimes with 3 inches cut off and sold separately as short ribs. The 7-inch cut costs more per pound than the 10-inch. Buy at least 2 ribs.

Rolled Rib Roast. The ribs are removed and the meat rolled and tied. This has the advantage of being easier to carve, but the flavor that the bones impart to the roasting meat will be lost. Buy at least 4 pounds, if already rolled.

HOW TO ROAST BEEF

Plan your roasting time ahead. Try to have the roast finished 10 minutes before serving time. It will slice more easily if it stands a while. Have oven preheated to 325°, or if starting in a cold oven, add 15 minutes to the roasting time.

Do not wash roast. If necessary, wipe it with damp paper towel. Place it in a shallow pan; for a rolled roast, use a rack in the pan. Never use a cover and do not wrap in foil. Both would hold in the steam so that you would then have a steam-cooked roast, or potroast, not a true roasted flavor. Roasting means cooking with *dry* heat.

Do not flour the roast, or put salt on it at the beginning of its cooking. If you wish to season it, wait until the meat is thoroughly seared on the outside.

Insert meat thermometer in the center of the muscle, not near the bone. Make sure the point goes only half-way through and does not come out the other side to rest on the pan. The meat

will be done when the thermometer registers the proper interior temperature. If you have no thermometer, gauge your cooking time by the approximate time per pound in the following chart.

Do not baste or turn during cooking. The melting fat in the meat is self-basting, and to open the oven door unnecessarily only cools the oven. When roast is finished, remove to hot platter and set in warm place. Make gravy with the drippings in the pan, according to the directions below.

ROAST FILLET OF BEEF (Tenderloin)

The fillet or tenderloin is the choicest and most tender part of the beef. It is also the most expensive, but there is no waste. It weighs between 4 and 6 pounds; sometimes it is possible to buy half a tenderloin.

Start roast in hot oven, 450°, on a rack in a shallow pan. Reduce heat to 375°. Use a meat thermometer if you have one. Cook 45 to 50 minutes, or until thermometer registers 140°. Serve on heated platter and cut into inch-thick slices as to resemble small steaks.

ROAST BEEF GRAVY

Pour off most of the clear fat in the roasting pan, leaving about 3 tablespoonsful. Place pan over low heat and add 3 tablespoons of flour, stirring with a wooden spoon until well blended. Have ready 2 cups of hot liquid, preferably from cooked vegetable, or plain water. Pour a little at a time into the pan, blending it with the flour mixture and scraping up the browned fat and juices from the roast. Cook and stir until gravy thickens and takes on a rich color from the browned bits in the pan. If there is not enough browned fat to

TIMETABLE FOR ROASTING BEEF

Roast at 325°	Doneness	Thermometer Reading	Approximate Minutes per pound
Standing Rib	Rare	140°	18–20
	Medium	160°	22–25
	Well Done	170°	30
Rolled Rib	Rare	140°	30
	Medium	160°	35
	Well Done	170°	40–45

color it properly add a few drops of one of the bottled gravy colorings. If the gravy becomes too thick, add more water cautiously.

If there is too much fat in the gravy, so that it rises to the top when poured into a bowl, blot it up with torn pieces of paper toweling. Place one piece at a time on top of the gravy; as it absorbs the grease, discard and replace with a new piece.

A traditional English accompaniment to roast beef:

YORKSHIRE PUDDING

Flour, sifted, 1 cup **Salt,** ½ teaspoon **Milk,** 1 cup **Eggs,** 2	Mix sifted flour and salt; add milk gradually, and beat until smooth. Add eggs, 1 at a time, beat in each until smooth and creamy. Cover bowl and chill thoroughly.
Beef Drippings, ¼ cup	Heat beef drippings in sizzling shallow pan. Pour batter into pan and pop into hot oven.
Oven, hot, 425°	Bake 25 to 30 minutes. Cut in squares and serve with roast.

To serve 4

ITALIAN PICKLED BEEF SLICES

Cooked Beef, 8 slices **Onions,** 2 med., sliced **Olive Oil,** 3 tablesps. **Red Wine** or **Wine Vinegar,** ½ cup **Sugar,** 1 teaspoon **Garlic,** 1 clove, minced **Bay Leaf,** 1 **Parsley,** 1 tablespoon, chopped **Rosemary,** ¼ teaspoon **Consommé,** 1 can	Place cold beef in a shallow dish. In skillet, brown onions in olive oil and add remaining ingredients. Simmer 10 minutes and pour over the sliced beef. Cover and chill about 12 hours.

To serve 4

STEAKS

The finest quality steaks come from US Prime or Choice beef. (See page 21.) A steak can be cooked under the broiler or "pan broiled" but do not "fry" it in fat. Do not overcook a steak until it is dry and tasteless. If your habit is to cook it well done, try it just a little less so, and see if the flavor and tenderness isn't improved.

BUYING A STEAK FOR BROILING

For tender juicy broiled steak you will want one of the following cuts. However, the names of cuts vary regionally, and so do the cuts themselves.

Porterhouse Steak. From the loin, has T-bone and large section of tenderloin. A 1-inch steak weighs about 2 pounds, will serve 2 or 3.

T-Bone Steak. From center of the loin, smaller than porterhouse, tenderloin portion is smaller. A 1-inch steak weighs about 1½ pounds, will serve 2.

Club Steak. From rib-end of loin, no tenderloin, usually boneless. A 1-inch steak weights about ¾ pound.

Strip Steak. A steak cut from the loin without any bone in it. Expensive, but no waste. Weighs ½ to ¾ pound.

Rib Steak (sometimes called Club). Cut from the loin end of the rib. Weighs about ¾ pound.

Sirloin. Good family-size steak.

MENUS

Roast Ribs of Beef or Broiled Steak—simple dinners, yet grand enough for any occasion, and Sauerbraten for hearty eaters, with two delicious ways to use the leftover beef.

ROAST RIBS OF BEEF

Duchess Potatoes · Asparagus
Tossed Green Salad
Hard Rolls · Butter
Lemon Sherbet

PICKLED ITALIAN BEEF SLICES

Corn-Zucchini Casserole · Tomatoes Florentine
French Bread · Whipped Butter
Rum Custard

SLICED BEEF IN SPENDTHRIFT MUSHROOM-SHERRY SAUCE (page 97)

Top-of-the-Stove Corn Pudding
Haitian Sliced Tomatoes
Banana Royale

SAUERBRATEN WITH DUMPLINGS (page 31)

Mashed Turnips · Green Onions and Peas
Creamy Coleslaw
Pumpernickel · Butter
Lemon Snow with Cherry Sauce

BROILED STEAK

French Fried Potatoes · Glazed Onions
Assorted Pickles · Steak Sauce
Hot Rolls · Butter
Chiffon Cake with Seafoam Sauce

ABOVE: *standing rib roast*
RIGHT: *rolled rib roast*

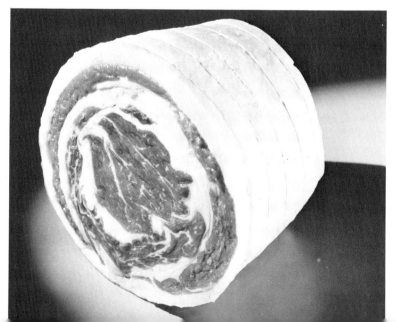

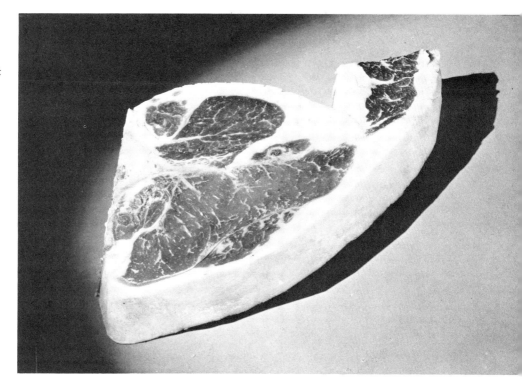

Porterhouse steak

HOW TO BROIL A STEAK

Remove steak from the refrigerator ½ hour before cooking time. If it has an excessive amount of fat, trim some away. With sharp knife cut through outer edge of fat rim at intervals to prevent steak from curling during cooking.

Preheat broiler a few minutes before cooking steak. Place steak on rack over broiler pan. Place broiler pan under heat with steak, if 1-inch thick, 3 inches from heat; if thicker, 4 inches from heat. Time it according to the table below. Transfer to hot platter, season with salt and pepper and serve at once.

STEAK SEASONERS

BOTTLED SAUCES: Worcestershire, steak sauce, horse-radish, relishes.
MUSHROOMS: Sliced mushrooms sautéed in butter.
ONIONS: Sliced onions sautéed in butter.
CHOPPED CHIVES OR SCALLIONS: Added to melted butter.

TIMETABLE FOR STEAKS

Thickness	Doneness	Approx. Minutes per Side
1-inch	Rare	5
	Medium	6–7
2-inch	Rare	10–12
	Medium	13–15

The above cooking times may vary depending on the individual broiler. If you are not familiar with the stove you are using, make a little cut near the steak bone to determine its doneness.

Planked porterhouse steak, with tomatoes and mushrooms

PLANKED STEAK

Prepare Duchess Potatoes (page 149). Broil or panbroil a steak until half-cooked, meanwhile heating a seasoned plank in the oven. Place steak on heated plank, arrange a border of potatoes around the edge of the plank, and place in 350° oven until steak is finished and potatoes lightly browned. Arrange cooked vegetables on the plank around the steak. Season and serve on a platter or special holder.

FILLET MIGNON

Fillets are cut from the tenderloin and are usually an inch or more thick. Broil, or panbroil, as described above, to the desired doneness. Spread with butter, season with salt and pepper. Add 2 tablespoons of water to the pan juices, bring to boil and pour over steak.

BEEF STROGANOFF

Fillet of beef, 1½ pounds **Flour** **Butter,** 3 tablespoons **Onions,** 2 medium, chopped **Mushrooms,** ½ lb., sliced **Salt,** 1½ teaspoons **Pepper,** ⅛ teaspoon **Sherry,** ½ cup **Water,** 1 cup **Sour Cream,** 1 cup *To serve 4*	Cut meat in thin strips; dredge with flour and brown in butter quickly in skillet. Remove meat. Cook onions and mushrooms in skillet until golden; add back meat, salt and pepper. Add sherry and water, bring to boiling point. Remove from heat. Stir in sour cream; heat but do not boil, and serve immediately.

PANBROILED STEAK

Remove steak from refrigerator ½ hour before cooking time. Trim away any excessive fat, and with sharp knife score outer rim of fat at intervals to prevent steak from curling.

Heat large skillet very hot and, without grease, brown steak quickly, first on one side and then on the other. Cook 5 minutes on the second side. Turn steak back to first side, lower heat and cook 5 minutes or more, depending on thickness and desired doneness. Pour off fat during cooking. Remove steak to warm platter and season to taste.

SUKIYAKI

Fillet of Beef, 1½ lbs. **Cooking Oil,** 2 tablespoons **Scallions,** 4 **Celery,** 2 stalks **Mushrooms,** 4 fresh **Spinach,** ½ lb. **Bamboo Shoots,** 2 **Bean Curd,** 2 pieces **Soy Sauce,** ⅓ cup **Beef Stock** or **Consommé,** 1½ cups *To serve 4*	Slice beef into thin cross-sections. Slice vegetables into thin pieces and have each ingredient arranged separately on a large platter. Heat oil in skillet. Add scallions; when they are wilted add beef and brown slightly. Mix soy sauce with beef stock and add ½ to skillet and cook few minutes. Add bean curd, bamboo shoots, spinach and remaining sauce. Cook several more minutes, but do not overcook. Serve with hot boiled rice.

Other vegetables may be added or substituted such as watercress or asparagus. Sliced water chestnuts may be added. Rice wine would be added in Japan—sherry may be used instead and ¼ cup added at end of cooking.

Steaks cut from the less tender portions of beef can be delicious too, if handled properly. Pounding, scoring and the use of tenderizers help break down the tougher fibers.

BROILED FLANK STEAK
(London Broil)

Flank steak is a long, thin boneless steak from the flank. It must be from top quality beef to be good. It will weigh between 1 and 2 pounds.

Place steak on rack of broiling pan and broil 3 inches below heat for 5 minutes on each side. Season with salt and pepper and brush with butter. Cut in very thin slices diagonally across the grain.

CUBE STEAKS

Cube steaks are thin steaks from the round or chuck that have been scored to cut the fibers, thus making them more tender. Panbroil cube steaks (see page 26), cooking them just a few minutes on each side to the desired doneness.

Remove from pan to hot platter and season. To salvage the juices in the skillet, add a few tablespoons of water; stir and scrape over low heat, then pour over steaks.

CHUCK STEAK, MARINATED

Chuck Steak, 3/4″ thick
Tenderizer

French Dressing, 1 cup

Sprinkle steak with tenderizer following directions on bottle.

Add French dressing and let stand overnight in refrigerator. Drain and broil or panbroil.

CHINESE PEPPER STEAK

Flank Steak, 1 pound
Cornstarch, 2 tablesps.
Cooking Oil, 3 tablesps.
Green Peppers, 4 medium sliced
Garlic, 1 clove, minced
Soy Sauce, 2 tablesps.
Consommé, 1 can.
Rice, 1 cup, boiled

To serve 4

Slice meat paper thin across the grain. Put into paper bag with cornstarch and shake it to coat it thoroughly. Heat oil in skillet, add beef and sauté quickly, stirring constantly. Add peppers and garlic; cook until soft, turning them constantly with the meat. Stir in soy sauce. Add consommé; bring to boil. Cook a few minutes or until juice thickens. Serve at once with rice.

SWISS STEAK

Round Steak, 1½ lbs.
Flour, 2 tablespoons
Fat, 2 tablespoons

Shake flour over both sides of steak, brown on both sides in hot fat.

Tomato pureé, 10-oz. can
Water, 1 cup
Garlic, 1 clove, chopped
Onion, 1 medium, chopped
Worcestershire, 1 teasp.
Salt, ½ teaspoon
Pepper, 1/8 teaspoon

To serve 4

Add remaining ingredients and simmer 1 hour or until meat is tender.

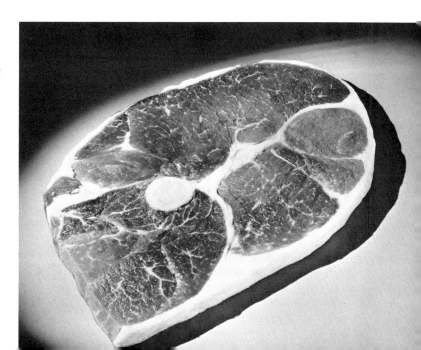

Round steak

HAMBURGER

Buy regular hamburger, if your meat dealer is reliable, or else buy boned chuck and have it ground to order. Hamburger should contain some fat and chuck is fatter and juicier than round. If you prefer to buy round, ask the butcher to add a little suet to it. For patties it should be ground once, twice for meat loaf.

2 pounds of hamburger without additional ingredients will make 4 good servings. For recipes that stretch the meat with rice, breadcrumbs, or the like, you may use less.

With fork gently loosen hamburger and shape into loose patties, handling gently and as little as possible. Do not pack hamburger tight or flatten it while cooking. A little minced onion may be added to the mixture if desired.

BROILED HAMBURGERS

PANBROILED: Place hamburger patties in very hot ungreased skillet. Brown on each side, turning once. Allow 4 to 8 minutes cooking time altogether, depending on how rare or well done you want them. Season and serve.

OVEN-BROILED: Preheat broiler while arranging thick patties on broiler rack. Broil patties 3 inches from heat, turning once. Allow 3 to 6 minutes each side, depending on how rare or well done you want them. Season and serve.

After broiling hamburger on one side, turn over and add one of these toppers; then finish broiling.

A slice of sharp cheddar cheese
Bottled mustard sauce
Prepared mustard
Soft butter or margarine mixed with ¼ teaspoon garlic powder

Or serve cooked hamburgers on hot platter with one of these on the side, or as a topper.

Sautéed Onions
Sautéed Mushrooms
Horse-radish
Mustard
Barbecue Sauce
Pickle Relish
Chili Sauce

HAMBURGER SEASONERS

You can have endless variety by mixing flavorful extras with your hamburgers or adding them as toppers.

Try mixing in one of these to each pound before cooking:

1 tablespoon minced onion
½ teaspoon marjoram
2 tablespoons crumbled blue cheese
1 tablespoon chopped parsley
2 tablespoons catsup
2 teaspoons Worcestershire
½ teaspoon Chili powder

GRILLED ITALIAN HAMBURGER

Hamburger, 1¼ pounds
Parmesan Cheese, ½ cup, grated
Onion, 1 medium, minced
Garlic, 1 clove, minced
Tomato Paste, 2 tablesp.
Water, 2 tablespoons
Egg, 1 beaten
To serve 4

Mix hamburger lightly with cheese, onion and garlic. Combine tomato paste and water and add to meat. Add beaten egg. Mold gently into steak and cook under broiler 10 minutes on each side.

SALISBURY STEAK

Hamburger, 1½ pounds
Salt, 1 teaspoon
Pepper, ¼ teaspoon
Worcestershire, 1 teasp.
Onion, minced, 1 tablesp.
Flour, 2 tablespoons
Mushrooms, 4-ounce can, sliced
Bouillon, 1 cup

To serve 4

Mix hamburger with seasonings and onion and shape into patties. Brown in small amount of fat in skillet and cook to desired doneness. Remove to hot platter. Pour off all but 2 tablespoons of fat, blend in flour. Add undrained mushrooms and bouillon. Cook, stirring constantly until thickened. Season to taste and pour over meat.

HAMBURGER WITH MILK GRAVY

Cook hamburger as in the recipe for Salisbury Steak. Remove to hot platter. Make gravy using milk instead of bouillon. Mushrooms may be omitted if desired, and replaced with ½ cup of additional milk.

CREAMED HAMBURGER

Hamburger, 1 lb.
Onion, 1 medium, minced
Flour, 2 tablespoons
Milk, 2 cups
Worcestershire, 1 teasp.
Salt and Pepper, to taste

To serve 4

Stir hamburger in hot skillet, breaking it up with fork until it loses its red color. Add onion as you stir. Shake flour over meat and blend in. Add milk and cook over low heat until thickened, stirring constantly. Add seasonings.

EDNA'S SALMAGUNDI

Butter, 2 tablespoons
Onions, 2 medium
Green Peppers, 2 medium
Ground Beef, 1½ lbs.
Tomatoes, 16-ounce can
Salt and Pepper, to taste
Basil, 1 teaspoon

Chop onions and peppers and sauté in butter in heavy skillet until soft. Add ground beef and crumble it with a fork. Stir over low heat until beef is seared and is of a uniform light color. Add tomatoes and seasonings, bring to boil, and simmer over low heat for 30 minutes.

Spaghetti, 8-oz. pkg.

To serve 4

Meanwhile, break spaghetti into boiling salted water and cook until tender. Drain and add to meat mixture; stir over heat for a few minutes to blend.

*Pan-broiled hamburgers
with gravy*

HAMBURGER LOAF

Hamburger, 2 pounds	Combine all ingredients lightly
Onion, 1 large, chopped	with a fork. Press gently into
Bread, 3 slices, crumbled	loaf pan.
Salt, 1 teaspoon	
Pepper, ¼ teaspoon	
Marjoram, ½ teaspoon	
Egg, 1, beaten	
Oven, moderate, 350°	Bake 1 hour, or until nicely
	browned on top.

To serve 4 or 5, with leftovers

HAMBURGER POT ROAST

Follow the above recipe for mixing Hamburger Loaf; shape
into loaf with hands; brown it on all sides in fat in a heavy
kettle; put a rack under it. Add ½ cup beef broth or bouillon.
Cover and simmer 40 minutes.

CHILI CON CARNE

Cooking Oil, 1 tablesp.	Sauté onion in oil until golden
Onion, 1, chopped	brown. Add meat and break it
Hamburger, 1 pound	up with a fork, stirring it until
Kidney Beans, 1 can	it loses its red color. Add beans,
Chili Powder, 1 teasp.	seasonings and tomatoes. Cover
Salt and **Pepper,** to taste	and simmer 20 minutes. More
Tomatoes, 16-ounce can	chili powder can be added,
	depending on whether you like
	it very hot. Serve with Tortillas,
To serve 4	(page 188).

HAMBURGER AND RICE

Raw Rice, ½ cup	Melt butter in large frying pan
Butter, 2 tablespoons	and stir rice in it until golden
Onion, 1 medium,	brown. Add onion and cook
chopped	gently until soft; add meat and
Ground Beef, 1 pound	cook until it loses its color,
Bouillon, 1 can	stirring occasionally. Add
Water, 1 can	bouillon and water, bring to
Salt and **Pepper,** to taste	boil, cover and simmer 30
	minutes or until liquid is
	absorbed. Stir occasionally and
	add water if needed. Season to
	taste.

To serve 4

HAMBURGER ORIENTALE

Hamburger, 1 pound	In hot skillet stir hamburger
Corn Starch, 1 tablesp.	around with a fork, separating it
Onion, 1, minced	into small pieces; sprinkle
Mushrooms, 4 ounce can	cornstarch over it and stir as it
Pimiento, 1, chopped	browns. Add onion as it cooks.
Bean Sprouts, 16-oz. can	Add undrained mushrooms,
Soy Sauce, 2 tablesps.	pimiento, drained bean sprouts,
Water, ½ cup	soy sauce and water. Cover and
Hot Boiled Rice	simmer 10 minutes. Add more
	water if it seems dry. Serve with
	hot boiled rice.

To serve 4

MEAT BALLS

Chuck, ground, 1 pound
Dry Bread Crumbs,
  ½ cup
Garlic, 1 clove, minced
Parsley, 2 tablespoons,
  minced
Egg, 1
Salt, ½ teaspoon
Pepper, ⅛ teaspoon

Combine all ingredients; shape into small balls. Brown well in a little fat in skillet. Add sauce ingredients and follow directions for cooking sauce. (See recipes for Spaghetti Sauces, page 125.)

POT ROASTS

Cuts of beef that are not tender enough for oven roasting make delicious pot roasts. They must be cooked very slowly with moist heat to break down the fibers. There should be some fat to add juiciness and flavor.

Since tough meat is the cook's challenge the world around, you will find pot roasts in every language, as some of the titles on these pages will indicate.

In choosing a piece of meat for pot roasting the cooking time and fuel consumed should be weighed against a more expensive cut that cooks more quickly.

See Veal and Lamb sections for other pot roasts.

For a pot roast you might choose:

Boned Rump. A cut from the hip, 4–5 pounds.

Sirloin-Tip. A cut from the side of the round; have it boned and rolled.

Chuck. A fine-flavored cut from the shoulder, very juicy. Can be cooked with the bone in for added flavor, or boned and rolled.

Cross Cut. Cut across the ribs, with sections of ribs in. Good flavor.

Short Ribs. The rib ends of the rib roast.

HOW TO COOK A POT ROAST

Dredge meat with flour; in heavy kettle, brown meat slowly on all sides, in a little fat; sprinkle with salt and pepper and add ½ cup of water. Cover tightly and simmer 2 to 3 hours, or until fork tender.

If all the water dries up, add a little, although the meat itself will create moisture as it cooks. Sliced onion may be added to the pot for flavoring.

For water you may substitute ½ can of onion soup or ½ cup of red wine.

When meat is done remove to platter and keep hot, while making gravy. Cool liquid in kettle and skim excess fat from top. For each cup of liquid in kettle add 1 tablespoon of flour mixed with a little cold water. Heat and stir until it thickens. Add salt and pepper to taste.

A rolled pot roast

BRAISED SHORT RIBS

Beef Short Ribs, 3 lbs.
Onion, 1 medium, chopped
Salt, 2 teaspoons
Pepper, 1/8 teaspoon
Worcestershire, 1 tablespoon

To serve 4

Brown short ribs in their own fat in a heavy kettle. Add seasonings and water; simmer about 2 hours, or until tender. Turn meat several times during cooking.

SAUERBRATEN WITH KARTOFFELKLOESSE
(Potato Dumplings)

Chuck, Boneless, 4 lbs.
Salt, 2 teaspoons
Cider Vinegar, 1 cup
Water, 1 cup
Pickling Spices, 3 tablespoons
Red Wine, 1 cup
Ginger, 1 teaspoon
Sugar, 2 tablespoons
Onions, 3, sliced
Celery, 1/2 cup, sliced

Fat, 3 tablespoons
Flour, 3 tablespoons
Dumplings (page 152)

To serve 4

Sprinkle chuck with salt and place in deep bowl. Combine other ingredients in saucepan, boil, and pour over meat. Place in refrigerator to marinate for 3 or 4 days, turning meat over every day. When ready to cook, remove meat, dry with paper towel; reserve marinade.

Follow directions in "How to Cook a Pot Roast," using marinade for cooking liquid and making gravy. Return meat to kettle with gravy and keep hot until dumplings are cooked.

BEEF POT ROAST BURGUNDY

Proceed as for Sauerbraten, but substitute 3 cups red burgundy for red wine, cider vinegar and water. Omit dumplings.

BEEF À LA MODE

Beef for Pot Roast, 4 lbs.
Red Wine, 2 cups
Salt, 2 teaspoons
Pepper, 1/8 teaspoon

But beef in bowl, sprinkle with salt and pepper and marinate with wine. Let stand in refrigerator several hours, turning meat occasionally. Remove meat and wipe dry. Reserve marinade.

Suet, or other fat, 3 tablespoons
Garlic, 1 clove, sliced
Parsley, 2 tablespoons, minced
Marjoram, 1/4 teaspoon
Bay Leaf, 1
Tomatoes, 1 16-ounce can
Carrots, 8 young, whole
Onions, 12 small white
Celery, 2 stalks, cut up

Flour, 2 tablespoons

To serve 4, with leftovers

Render suet in heavy kettle. Dredge meat with flour and brown on all sides. Add 1 cup of marinade and seasonings; simmer 2 hours. Add vegetables and simmer 45 minutes longer, or until meat and vegetables are tender. Add rest of marinade if needed.

Remove meat and vegetables to heated platter and thicken gravy with flour mixed in a little cold water.

YANKEE POT ROAST

Suet, or other fat, 2 tablespoons
Chuck, 4 pounds
Flour
Salt, 2 teaspoons
Pepper, 1/4 teaspoon
Water, 1/2 cup
Carrots, 1/2 cup, diced
Celery, 1/2 cup, diced
Parsley, 2 tablespoons, chopped
Onion, 1 medium, chopped

To serve 4, with leftovers

Melt fat in heavy kettle. Dredge meat with flour and brown on all sides. Sprinkle with salt and pepper and add water. Cover tightly and simmer 2 hours. Add vegetables and simmer 1 hour longer, or until meat is fork tender. Remove meat to platter and keep hot. Follow directions in "How to Cook a Pot Roast" for making gravy.

POT ROAST WITH DRIED FRUIT

Proceed as for Pot Roast. When meat is half-cooked, add 1/2 pound of dried prunes and 1/2 pound of dried apricots to the kettle, with 1 cup of water, and 1/2 teaspoon of whole cloves. Continue cooking slowly until meat and fruit are tender. Serve pot roast on hot platter surrounded by fruit.

BARBECUED SHORT RIBS

Proceed as for Braised Short Ribs. Add to beef before simmering, 1 can tomato paste, 1 teaspoon chili powder and 1 tablespoon prepared mustard.

BAKED SHORT RIBS WITH VEGETABLES

Short Ribs, 3 pounds, cut in 3-inch pieces
Flour, 2 tablespoons
Salt and **Pepper,** to taste
Stock or **Water,** 1 cup

Oven, slow, 300°

Carrots, 4 young
Onions, 4 small
Frozen Green Beans, 1 pkg., cooked

To serve 4

Dredge meat with flour, season and brown on all sides in heavy kettle or casserole. Add stock, cover.

Bake 2–3 hours or until tender.

Add carrots and onions during last hour. Arrange meat and vegetables on platter, adding cooked beans.

POT ROAST IN SPAGHETTI SAUCE

Beef for Pot Roast, 4 lbs.
Olive Oil, 3 tablespoons
Onion, 1 medium, chopped
Garlic, 1 clove, minced
Oregano, 1 teaspoon
Salt, 2 teaspoons
Pepper, 1/4 teaspoon
Tomato Paste, 2 cans
Water, 2 cans

Thin Spaghetti, 1 pound
Parmesan Cheese, grated

To serve 4, with leftovers

In heavy kettle brown meat on all sides in oil. Add onion and seasonings to kettle and cook a few minutes until onion is soft. Add tomato paste and water; cover tightly and simmer 2 to 3 hours, or until meat is tender. Add more water if necessary. Remove meat to hot platter and slice.

Cook spaghetti and serve on individual plates topped with sauce. Serve grated cheese on the side.

ROLLED FLANK STEAK

Flank Steak, 2 pounds
Onion, 1, finely chopped
Celery, 1 stalk, finely
chopped
Parsley, few sprigs,
chopped
Bread Crumbs, 1 cup
Marjoram, ¼ teasp.
Salt, 1 teaspoon
Pepper, ⅛ teaspoon
Fat, 2 tablespoons
Tomato Juice, 1 cup

Pound flank steak on both sides with knife to tenderize. Cover one side with onion, celery, parsley, crumbs and seasoning. Roll up and tie in center and around each end with string. Brown in hot fat on all sides in heavy kettle, cover with tomato juice, bring to boil and simmer 2 hours.

New Potatoes, 8 tiny
Carrots, 8 young
Salt, 1 teaspoon

Add vegetables and salt, continue simmering until vegetables are tender. Remove to platter and make gravy as described in "How to Cook a Pot Roast."

To serve 4

BOILED BEEF WITH HORSE-RADISH SAUCE

Fresh Beef Brisket,
3 to 4 pounds
Onion, 1 medium, thinly
sliced
Carrot, 1, thinly sliced
Celery, 1 stalk, chopped
Salt, 2 teaspoons
Pepper, ¼ teaspoon

Put meat and vegetables in deep kettle; add enough water to cover. Add seasonings. Bring to boil, simmer, covered, 3 or more hours, until tender. Slice and serve with Horse-radish Sauce.

Horse-radish Sauce
(page 90)

To serve 4, with leftovers

STEWS

Stews, too, are international, and are related to pot roasts in that they are a means of coping with the less tender cuts of meat. In this case, the meat is cut in cubes for faster cooking.

Pressure cookers are wonderful time savers when making stews—2 hours simmering time can be cut to 15 to 30 minutes. Follow directions for using your own cooker. Be sure to brown meat first, for flavor, if recipe calls for it.

See other meat sections for veal, lamb and pork stews.

It is often a good idea to make double the recipe, for stews are sometimes even better when reheated for the second day. Or you might freeze a portion to use later.

BROWN BEEF STEW

Beef Chuck, 2 pounds,
boneless
Flour, 2 tablespoons
Salt, 1 teaspoon
Pepper, ¼ teaspoon
Fat, 2 tablespoons
Onion, 2 med., chopped
Water, 2 cups

Cut beef in 2-inch cubes. Shake in bag with flour, salt, and pepper; brown in fat in heavy kettle. Remove from kettle and sauté onions until golden. Return meat to kettle, add water, bring to boil and simmer covered, 1½ hours or until meat is tender. Add water during cooking if necessary.

Onions, 8 small white
Carrots, 4 to 8, cut in
chunks
Potatoes, 4 medium,
quartered
Parsley, ¼ cup, chopped

Add vegetables, bring to boil and simmer 30 minutes. Add more salt and pepper if necessary.

Flour, 1 tablespoon

Mix flour with a little cold water. Add to gravy to thicken.

To serve 4

BEEF PIE

Use recipe for Brown Beef Stew. Turn stew into casserole, cover with pastry and bake in 450° oven, 20 or 25 minutes.

This is a good way to use left-over stew.

ENGLISH BEEF STEW

Follow the recipe for Brown Beef Stew, but do not brown meat first. Simply put ingredients in kettle with water and simmer until tender.

BOEUF BOURGUIGNON

Beef Chuck, 2 lbs., cut in
2-inch cubes
Onions, 3 med., sliced
Garlic, 1 clove, minced
Pepper, ¼ teaspoon
Bay Leaf, 1
Thyme, ½ teaspoon
Parsley, few sprigs
Marjoram, ½ teaspoon
Burgundy, 1 cup

Combine meat with onions, seasonings and wine in a bowl and let marinate for 2 hours. Drain and reserve marinade.

Flour
Salt Pork, ½ lb., cut in
½-inch cubes

Pat meat dry and dredge with flour. Brown salt pork in heavy kettle, add beef cubes and brown on all sides. Pour marinade over beef, bring to boil, cover tightly and simmer over low heat 1 to 2 hours, or until tender. If more liquid is needed add wine or water.

Mushrooms, ½ lb., sliced
Butter, 1 tablespoon

Just before serving time, sauté mushrooms in butter and add to stew. Thicken gravy with a tablespoon of flour mixed in a little cold water.

To serve 4

HUNGARIAN GOULASH WITH NOODLES

Chuck or Round, 2 lbs.,
  cut in cubes
Fat, 2 tablespoons
Onions, 6 medium,
  sliced fine
Salt, 2 teaspoons
Paprika, 1 tablespoon
Caraway Seeds, 2 teasps.
Pepper, 1/4 teaspoon
Parsley, 2 tablespoons,
  chopped
Bay Leaf, 2, crumbled
Water, 1/2 cup
Broad Noodles, 1 pkg.

To serve 4

Dredge beef cubes in flour;
brown in fat in heavy kettle.
Add onions and seasonings, and
blend together. Add liquids;
bring to boil; cover tightly and
simmer 2 hours or until tender.
Serve with boiled noodles.

OXTAIL STEW

Oxtail Joints, 2 to 3 lbs.
Flour
Fat, 2 tablespoons
Tomatoes, 1 #2 1/2 can
Salt, 2 teaspoons
Pepper, 1/4 teaspoon
Bay Leaf, 1, crumbled
Garlic, 1 clove, minced

Dredge joints with flour and
brown in fat in heavy kettle.
Add tomatoes and seasonings;
bring to boil. Cover and simmer
about 3 hours, or until tender.

Carrots, 4 med., sliced
Onion, 2 med., sliced
Butter, 2 tablespoons
Sherry, 1/4 cup
Water, 1/4 cup

To serve 4

Sauté vegetables in butter, add
to kettle. Add sherry and water;
continue to simmer 20 minutes
longer, or until meat and
vegetables are tender.

STEAK AND KIDNEY PIE

Round Steak, 1 1/4 lbs.
Beef Kidney, 1
Fat, 2 tablespoons
Salt, 1 teaspoon
Pepper, 1/4 teaspoon
Water, 2 cups
Carrots, 6 young, whole
Onions, 12 small white
Flour, 2 tablespoons

Cut steak in 1-inch cubes and
slice kidney, remove membrane;
brown in skillet with fat. Add
seasonings and water, bring to
boil and simmer over low heat
for 1 1/2 hours. Add carrots and
onions and simmer 30 minutes
longer, or until vegetables are
tender. Mix flour smooth with a
little cold water; add to stew
and cook few minutes until
gravy is thickened. If water has
cooked away too much, add a
little.

Pastry (see page 180)
Oven, hot, 425°

To serve 4

Pour stew into casserole, cover
with pastry. Bake 30 minutes,
or until pastry is lightly
browned.

FLEMISH CARBONADE OF BEEF

Beef Chuck, 2 lbs., cut in
  2-inch cubes
Flour
Butter, 2 tablespoons
Salt, 1 teaspoon
Pepper, 1/4 teaspoon
Thyme, 1/2 teaspoon
Bay Leaf, 1, crumbled
Onions, 2 med., sliced
Beer, 1 bottle or can

To serve 4

Dredge beef in flour; brown on
all sides in butter in heavy
kettle. Add salt, pepper, thyme,
bay leaf, and onions. Cook until
onions are golden. Add beer,
bring to boil, cover, and simmer
over low heat 1 to 2 hours, or
until tender.

BEEF AND OKRA STEW

Beef Chuck, 2 pounds,
  cut in cubes
Flour, 2 tablespoons
Fat, 2 tablespoons
Onions, 2 med., chopped
Salt and Pepper, to taste
Water, 2 cups
Green Pepper, 1, chopped
Carrots, 2, diced
Okra, 2 cups, sliced
Tomatoes, 16-ounce can

To serve 4

Follow procedure in Brown
Beef Stew above. Simmer 1 1/2
hours, or until meat is tender.
Add green pepper, carrots and
okra and tomatoes. Simmer
15 minutes.

Note: Frozen or canned okra
may be used.

CURRIED BEEF STEW

Follow recipe for Beef and Okra Stew, omitting carrots,
okra and tomatoes. Thicken gravy with flour mixed with
a little cold water. Flavor with 1-2 teaspoons curry powder
and 1 cup sour cream; heat but do not boil. Serve on rice.

GINGERED BEEF STEW

Round Steak, 1 1/2 lbs. in
  1-inch cubes
Onions, 2 med., sliced
Fat, 2 tablespoons
Boiling Water, 3 cups
Bay Leaf, 1
Salt, 1 1/2 teaspoons
Pepper, 1/4 teaspoon
Caraway Seed, 1 teasp.
Vinegar, 1/4 cup
Green Cabbage, 1 head
Gingersnap Crumbs,
  1/4 cup
Warm Water, 1/4 cup

To serve 4 to 6

Brown beef and onions in fat in
heavy skillet. Add water,
seasonings and vinegar. Bring
to boil, cover and simmer
1 1/2 hours, or until meat is
tender. Add cabbage, cut in
wedges, and simmer 30 minutes
longer, or until tender. Remove
cabbage and arrange around
edge of platter. Remove meat
and place in center. Soften
gingersnap crumbs in warm
water and stir into gravy.
Simmer until thickened and
pour over meat.

CORNED BEEF

Buy 2½ or 3 pounds of corned brisket. Cover with cold water and bring to boil. Simmer 10 minutes, then drain. Cover again with cold water; and cook at simmering temperature 3 hours, or until meat is tender. Let it cool in stock, then remove to platter. Serve with Horse-radish Sauce (page 90). *To serve 4.*

If you have a pressure cooker, the cooking time can be cut to about 1 hour. Simmer corned beef for 10 minutes, drain, then process in pressure cooker according to manufacturer's directions.

CORNED BEEF AND CABBAGE: About 20 minutes before beef is done, add a cabbage cut in wedges, and cook until just tender. Serve meat on hot platter, arrange cabbage around it. Serve with mustard.

CORNED BEEF HASH

Corned Beef, cooked,
  chopped, 2 cups
Potatoes, 4 medium,
  cooked, chopped
Onions, 2 medium,
  chopped
Bouillon or **Milk,** ¼
  cup
Butter, 2 tablespoons
Salt and **Pepper** to taste
Worcestershire Sauce,
  1 teaspoon

To serve 4

Mix corned beef, potatoes, onions, bouillon and seasonings. Melt butter in frying pan, spread hash over bottom of pan and flatten with pancake turner. Cook gently until browned on bottom. Fold over in half and serve on hot platter.

CORNED BEEF HASH AND POACHED EGG: See page 18.

NEW ENGLAND BOILED DINNER

Corned Brisket of Beef,
  2½ to 3 pounds
Potatoes, 4 medium
Carrots, 4 medium
Turnips, 2 medium
Cabbage, 1 head

To serve 4

Cook corned beef according to directions above. Pare and quarter potatoes, carrots and turnips, and wash and quarter cabbage. About ½ hour before corned beef is finished, add vegetables and cook until meat and vegetables are tender. Serve beef on large platter surrounded by vegetables.

BOILED BEEF TONGUE

Fresh Beef Tongue
Onion, 1 medium,
  quartered
Garlic, 1 clove
Pickling Spice,
  2 tablespoons
Salt, 2 teaspoons

Wash tongue, cover with cold water in deep pot, bring to boil. Add seasonings, reduce heat, cover and simmer until tender. Cool enough to handle and skin. Serve hot or wrap in waxed paper and chill in refrigerator.

Serve Boiled Tongue hot with Horse-radish Sauce (page 90) or Raisin Sauce (page 91).

SMOKED TONGUE: Follow the above recipe for Boiled Tongue, but omit salt.

CREAMED DRIED BEEF

Thin White Sauce, 2 cups
  (page 90)
Dried Beef, ¼ pound,
  thinly sliced
Egg, 1, beaten
Sherry, 1 tablespoon

To serve 4

Make white sauce omitting salt. Scald beef if overly salty. Shred and add to white sauce. Cook together over low heat about 5 minutes. Stir a little of the mixture into the beaten egg, then add back to beef. Add sherry just before serving.

VEAL

Young veal is pale rosy beige in color; as the animal grows older the color deepens to rosy red. What little exterior fat it has is firm and clear white. Buy it by USDA Grades (see page 21) if possible, and look for the US Inspected and Passed stamp for wholesomeness. Veal cuts resemble beef in shape, but are, of course, only ⅓ to ½ the size. Veal is usually preferred cooked well done. Slices of veal that are to be skillet-cooked should be tenderized by pounding.

ROAST VEAL

Loin or Rib. These are the sections usually reserved for chops but they make excellent roasts.

Leg. This corresponds with the fresh ham in pork, and is usually sold as cutlets. Whole, it makes a meaty roast for a goodly number of people; or it may be cut into smaller roasts of 4 to 6 pounds.

Rump Roast. An economical family roast, used with the bone in or boned and rolled.

Shoulder. This should be boned and rolled to make carving easier.

HOW TO ROAST VEAL

Plan roasting time by consulting chart and set oven for 325°. Rub surface of meat with cut clove of garlic, or insert several little slivers of garlic in small gashes in the meat. Or flavor with crushed herbs such as thyme, marjoram, or rosemary. Brush surface of meat with melted butter or other fat, or cover it with thin slices of salt pork or bacon.

Place roast on rack in open pan. Do not cover. Insert thermometer in center of roast. Don't let it touch the bone. Roast veal to 180°.

When veal is cooked, remove to hot platter and keep warm while making gravy in roasting pan, following directions for Roast Beef Gravy, page 22.

POT-ROASTED BREAST OF VEAL

Veal Breast, 3 pounds
Fat, 2 tablespoons
Onions, 2, sliced
Garlic, 1 clove, minced
Salt, 1 teaspoon
Pepper, ⅛ teaspoon
Worcestershire, 2 teasps.
Tomatoes, 16-oz. can

Brown veal on all sides in heavy kettle. Combine remaining ingredients, pour over meat, bring to boil. Cover, and simmer 1½ hours, or until tender; turn meat over once or twice, while cooking. Serve with pan juices.

To serve 4 or 5

HERBED VEAL SHOULDER

Veal Shoulder, 3 to 4 lbs., boned and rolled
Flour, 1 tablespoon
Salt, 1 teaspoon
Pepper, ¼ teaspoon
Fat, 2 tablespoons
Garlic, 1 clove, minced
Rosemary, 1 teaspoon
Thyme, 1 teaspoon
Parsley, 1 tablespoon, minced
Water, ½ cup

Dredge veal with seasoned flour. Brown on all sides in heavy kettle in fat. Put meat on rack in kettle; add garlic, herbs and water. Cover tightly and simmer 2 hours, or until tender.

Substitute white wine for the water, if desired.

To serve 4, with leftovers

RUMP OF VEAL AUX FINES HERBES

Fat or Oil, 2 tablesps.
Veal Rump Roast, 4–5 pounds
Salt, 1 teaspoon
Pepper, ⅛ teaspoon
Parsley, 2 tablespoons, chopped
Chives, 2 tablespoons, minced
Basil, 1 teaspoon
Thyme, ¼ teaspoon
Vermouth, ⅓ cup
Water, ⅓ cup

Heat fat in heavy kettle; add meat and seasonings, and brown meat on all sides. Add vermouth and water; cover and simmer 2 hours or until fork tender. Add more water if needed. Make gravy from pan juices. (Page 22.)

To serve 4, with leftovers

VEAL STEW

Follow the recipe for Irish Stew (lamb) substituting neck or breast of veal. The stew may be served with Dumplings (page 67) or on hot Baking Powder Biscuits. If the gravy requires thickening, add 2 tablespoons of flour mixed in a little cold water.

TIMETABLE FOR ROASTING VEAL

Roast at 325°	Thermometer Reading	Approx. Minutes per Pound
Loin or Rib	180°	35 to 40
Leg	180°	30
Rump	180°	35
Shoulder, rolled	180°	35 to 40

VEAL CHOPS SUPREME

**Veal Chops with the
  Kidney Attached,** 4
Flour
Butter, 2 tablespoons
Salt, 1 teaspoon
Pepper, 1/4 teaspoon
Basil, 1/4 teaspoon
Dry Sherry, 1/2 cup

Dredge chops with flour, brown gently in butter in large skillet. Add salt and pepper, basil and dry sherry. Cover tightly and simmer over low heat for 30 minutes or until tender. Add a little water if liquid dries up. When done, remove chops to hot platter.

Mushrooms, sliced,
  4-ounce can
Sour Cream, 1/2 cup

Add mushrooms and liquid to juice in skillet and cook slowly, stirring up brown drippings in pan. Bring to boil, add sour cream, stir and remove from heat. Pour over chops.

To serve 4

VEAL PARMESAN

Veal Cutlet, 1 pound
Parmesan Cheese, grated
Salt, 1 teaspoon
Pepper, 1/8 teaspoon
Oregano, 1/2 teaspoon
Instant Garlic, 1/8 teasp.
Bouillon, 1/2 cup

Cut veal into 4 serving portions and pound thin. Dip the veal slices in the grated cheese to coat them, in the way you would use crumbs. In a large skillet heat the butter and brown the cutlets, over low heat, on both sides. Add seasonings and bouillon; cover, and simmer 30 minutes or until tender. Remove cutlets to warm platter, add a little water to juices in pan, stir over heat and pour over cutlets.

To serve 4

BREADED VEAL CUTLET

Veal Cutlet, 1 1/2 pounds
Flour
Egg, 1
Water, 1 tablespoon
Fine Dry Bread Crumbs
Salt and **White Pepper**

Divide cutlet into serving-size pieces. Sprinkle with salt and pepper. Dredge pieces lightly with flour. Dip in egg, beaten lightly with water added, and then in the breadcrumbs. Chill for 1 hour to make crumbs adhere.

Fat, 4 tablespoons

Heat fat in skillet and brown veal lightly on both sides. Arrange pieces in shallow baking dish.

Oven, moderate, 325°

Bake 40 minutes, or until fork tender.

To serve 4

BREADED VEAL CHOPS: Follow above recipe also for veal chops.

ITALIAN VEAL AND PEPPERS

Veal, 1 1/2 lbs., boneless
Salad Oil, 3 tablespoons
Green Peppers, 2
Mushrooms, 3-ounce can,
  sliced
Tomatoes, 16-ounce can
Basil, 1 teaspoon
Salt, 1 teaspoon
Pepper, 1/8 teaspoon

Cut veal in pieces and brown in hot oil, over low heat. Add chopped peppers and cook, stirring, until soft. Add remaining ingredients, cover, and simmer 30 minutes, or until meat is tender. Serve on hot rice or spaghetti.

To serve 4

Veal chops

MENUS

An antipasto would make an excellent first course for these veal menus.

VEAL CHOPS SUPREME

Green Peas and New Potatoes
Dilled Cucumbers and Tomatoes
Lemon Tort

VEAL PARMESAN

Broccoli · Stewed Tomatoes
Bread Sticks
Peach Upside Down Cake

BREADED VEAL CUTLET

Scalloped Potatoes with Cucumbers
Panned Spinach
Fruit Salad
Ice Cream · Cookies

ITALIAN VEAL AND PEPPERS

Buttered Spaghetti
Hearts of Lettuce with Anchovy Dressing
Mandarin Oranges in Red Wine

Rump roast of veal

Veal cooked in a skillet, Italian style

*Veal cut for stewing, as in
Veal Paprika*

VEAL CHOPS COUNTRY STYLE

Salt Pork, ¼ pound
Veal Chops, 4
Instant Garlic, ¼ teasp.
Parsley, chopped,
  1 tablespoon
Salt, 1 teaspoon
Pepper, ⅛ teaspoon
Onions, 12 small white,
  peeled
Potatoes, 8 small, peeled

To serve 4

Dice salt pork and cook in
skillet until crisp. Remove pork
and reserve. Brown chops on
both sides in fat over low heat.
Add remaining ingredients;
cover and simmer 30 minutes, or
until meat and vegetables are
tender. Return pork to mixture,
heat, and serve.

VEAL IN TUNA SAUCE
(Vitello Tonnato)

Olive or Salad Oil,
  2 tablespoons
Veal Leg, 3 lbs., boneless
Anchovies, 1 can
Sour Pickle, ½
Tuna, 1 7-ounce can
Carrot, 1, sliced
Celery, 2 stalks, sliced
Parsley, few sprigs,
  chopped
Basil, 1 teaspoon
Garlic, 1 clove, minced
White Wine, 1 cup
Egg Yolks, 2
Olive Oil, few drops
Salt and Pepper, to taste

To serve 4, with leftovers

In a heavy kettle brown the
meat on all sides in oil. Add
anchovies, sour pickle, tuna,
vegetables, seasonings and wine.
Simmer 2½ hours, or until meat
is tender. Cool, then chill;
remove meat to platter and slice
thin. Purée remaining mixture in
a blender or food mill. Add
the well-beaten egg yolks and
a few drops of olive oil. Add
salt and pepper to taste. Serve
as sauce for the veal.

VEAL PAPRIKA

Boneless Stewing Veal,
  2 pounds, cut in cubes
Fat, 3 tablespoons
Mushrooms, ½ lb., sliced
Onions, 2, chopped
Beef Bouillon Cube, 1
Water, 1 cup
Salt, 1 teaspoon
Paprika, 1 tablespoon
Sour Cream, 1 cup

To serve 4

Brown veal lightly in fat in
skillet. Add mushrooms and
onions. Cook for 10 minutes,
stirring often. Dissolve bouillon
cube in water and add with
seasonings to veal. Simmer
1½ to 2 hours or until tender.
Add sour cream, stir in and
heat, but do not boil.

WIENER SCHNITZEL

Follow recipe for Breaded Veal Cutlet, but pound veal with
mallet to flatten it before coating with egg and bread crumbs.

After veal is cooked, add 2 tablespoons water, cover tightly
and steam over low heat, 30 minutes or until tender. Add a
little more water, a tablespoon at a time if needed. Turn meat
once or twice. Serve with wedges of lemon.

CASSEROLE OF VEAL AND POTATOES

Boneless Veal Shoulder,
  2 pounds
Mushroom Soup, 1 can
Consommé, 1 can

Oven, moderate, 325°
Instant Mashed Potatoes,
  for 4
Egg, 1, beaten

To serve 4

Cut veal in small cubes and put
in casserole. Add soup and
mix well. Cover casserole.

Bake 2 hours or until meat is
tender. Prepare potatoes, add
beaten egg and form crust on
top of casserole. Return to oven
for 10 minutes or until potatoes
are golden brown.

Veal paprika, with mushrooms and sour cream

VEAL AND HAM PIE

Veal, 2 cups, cooked, diced
Ham, 1 cup, cooked, diced
Cream of Celery Soup, 1 can
Milk, ½ can
Mushrooms, 3-ounce can, sliced, drained
Pimiento, ½, chopped
Pastry (see page 181)

Combine all ingredients in casserole. Cover with pastry.

Oven, hot, 400°

To serve 4

Bake 25 minutes, or until heated through and pastry lightly browned.

VEAL BIRDS

Veal Cutlet, 1½ pounds
Soft Bread Crumbs, 1 cup
Butter, 1 tablespoon, melted
Egg Yolk, 1
Salt and **Pepper,** dash
Parsley, 1 tablespoon

Divide cutlet into 4 portions and pound until thin. Add bread crumbs to melted butter, mixing well. Add beaten egg yolk, salt and pepper and parsley. Place some of the bread mixture on each piece of veal and roll; fasten securely with toothpicks. Dredge with flour.

Butter, 1 tablespoon
Bouillon, ½ cup
Cream, ½ cup

To serve 4

Sauté "birds" in butter, turning until all sides are browned evenly. Add bouillon and simmer, covered, until tender, about 30 minutes. Remove birds to platter, add cream to pan and heat, stirring to mix with pan juices. Pour over "birds."

MENUS

VEAL CHOPS COUNTRY STYLE

Broiled Tomatoes
Cucumbers and Carrot Sticks
Sherry Trifle

VEAL PAPRIKA

Buttered Brown Rice · Glazed Carrots
Black Olives and Celery
Lemony Pears

WIENER SCHNITZEL

Baked Potato · Scalloped Tomatoes
Green Salad with Roquefort Dressing
Coffee-Pecan Molds with Rum
Cream

VEAL AND HAM PIE

Spinach Timbales
Carrot and Green Pepper Salad
Corn Muffins · Butter
Spumoni

CASSEROLE OF VEAL AND POTATOES

Green Salad with Vinaigrette Dressing
French Bread · Butter
Chocolate Bavarian

VEAL BIRDS

Baked Parsnips · Zucchini and Onions
Water cress Salad with French Dressing
Rum Cake

LAMB

The age of lamb can be told by its weight; the leg of young spring lamb weighs between 5 and 6 pounds; the legs of older lamb weigh 7 or 8 pounds. The meat should carry the US Inspected and Passed Stamp, and may have the same Department of Agriculture Grade marks as beef. (See page 21.) The meat should be rosy in color with crisp white fat.

LAMB ROASTS

Leg of Lamb. An economical roast for a family; can be used as one roast, or cut in two. Or chops can be taken off the upper end to be served as a separate meal. The leg can be roasted with the bone in, or boned and rolled.

Shoulder Roast. The shoulder is tender and juicy; it can be prepared with a pocket for stuffing, or it can be boned and rolled for easier slicing.

HOW TO ROAST LAMB

Plan your roasting time and set oven for 325°. Wipe meat with damp paper towel, if necessary, but do not wash. Do not remove the "fell", the thin paper-like covering, as this will help retain the juices.

Make several little slits in fatty portions of the lamb and insert slivers of garlic. (Garlic is practically an essential flavor in cooking lamb, and gives it a pleasant odor while roasting.) Other herbs may also be used for flavoring—rosemary, thyme, marjoram, or mint. Crumble the leaves and rub them on the meat. Sprinkle meat with salt and pepper.

Place meat fat side up on rack in shallow pan; do not cover. Insert meat thermometer in center of roast, not against bone. Roast meat without turning or basting, according to the timetable below.

When cooked, remove lamb to hot platter and make gravy in roasting pan, following directions given for Roast Beef Gravy, page 22.

CROWN ROAST OF LAMB

A crown roast is made of one section of ribs curved into a crown shape, with the ends skewered together; or it may be made of two rib sections, if a larger roast is desired. The meat is trimmed back a little from the ends of the ribs, and before roasting the ends should be wrapped with pieces of foil to keep them from burning. The butcher should loosen the ribs from the backbone, for easy carving.

Follow the procedure for roast lamb. Do not fill the center of the crown with stuffing, as this will increase roasting time. For serving, the crown may be filled with potatoes or whatever vegetable is served with the meal. If desired, the ends of the bones may be decorated with paper frills.

ROAST LEG OF LAMB JARDINIÈRE

Follow directions above for roasting lamb. Surround lamb in roasting pan with several chopped onions, carrots and celery stalks. When lamb is done, remove to platter, pour off fat and mix canned consommé with vegetables to the desired consistency for gravy. The vegetables can be mashed or put through a sieve if a purée is desired.

BROILED LAMB CHOPS

Select loin or rib chops for broiling. They can be double thick, if desired. Arrange chops on broiler rack, sprinkle with garlic salt, and place about 3 inches from heat. Broil on one side, then turn chops and broil other side. A 1-inch thick chop will be medium done in about 6 minutes to each side. A 2-inch chop will take 10 to 12 minutes to a side.

TIMETABLE FOR ROASTING LAMB

Roast at 325°	Desired Doneness	Thermometer Reading	Approx. Minutes per Pound
Leg or Shoulder	Medium	175°	30
	Well Done	182°	35
Rolled Shoulder	Medium	175°	40
	Well Done	182°	45
Crown Roast	Medium	175°	35
	Well Done	182°	40

LAMB CHOPS WITH FRESH FRUIT

Pineapple, 4 peeled slices
Butter, 2 tablespoons
Salt, 1 teaspoon
Pepper, ⅛ teaspoon
Ginger, ¼ teaspoon
Loin Lamb Chops, 4
Bananas, 2 under-ripe,
  peeled and halved
Yams, 4, cooked, peeled
  and halved

Drain juice from pineapple, putting it in small pan with butter and seasonings; heat. Brush chops with mixture and arrange on broiler rack. Broil 4 to 5 minutes. Turn over, brush with sauce; arrange fruit and yams on broiler rack, brush with sauce and broil 4 or 5 minutes.

To serve 4

Canned pineapple slices may be used if preferred.

PANBROILED LAMB CHOPS

Remove extra fat from each chop; brown slowly on both sides in heavy skillet. Pour off fat as it accumulates, so as not to fry meat. Cook to desired degree of doneness, sprinkle with salt and pepper and serve on heated platter.

LAMB POT ROAST

Lamb Shoulder, 3 lbs.,
  boned and rolled
Fat, 3 tablespoons
Garlic, 1 clove, minced
Onions, 2, minced
Cardamon, ¼ teaspoon
  seeds
White Wine, ½ cup

Brown lamb on all sides in hot fat in heavy kettle. Add remaining ingredients; cover tightly, and simmer 2 hours, or until tender. Make gravy with pan drippings. (See page 22.)

To serve 4 to 6

Thyme, basil or poultry seasoning may be substituted for cardamon, if desired.

MENUS

ROAST LEG OF LAMB JARDINIÈRE

Golden Brown New Potatoes · Buttered Zucchini
Green Salad with Avocado Slices
Hot Biscuits · Butter
Strawberries Cointreau

CROWN ROAST OF LAMB

Pan Roasted Potatoes · Glazed Onions
Spring Salad
Hard Rolls · Butter
Strawberry Mousse

BROILED LAMB CHOPS

Creamed Potatoes · Peas with Mint
Carrot Salad
Garlic Bread
Gingerbread with Applesauce

LAMB CHOPS WITH FRESH FRUIT

Green Salad
Oatmeal Bread (mix)
Chocolate Ice Cream

LAMB POT ROAST

Mashed Potatoes · Rainbow Salad
Hard Rolls · Butter
Spanish Cream

*Loin
lamb chops*

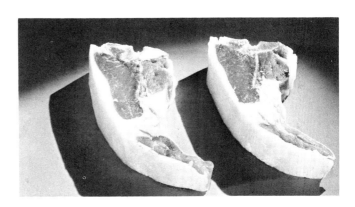

Roast leg of lamb

Rolled shoulder of lamb

Lamb stew with carrots, potatoes, onions and celery

BRAISED LAMB IN SOUR CREAM

Boneless Lamb for Stewing, 2 lbs., cubed
Flour
Butter, 2 tablespoons
Instant Garlic, ¼ teasp.
Basil, 1 teaspoon
Onions, 2, med., chopped
Water, 1 cup
Sour Cream, 1 cup

To serve 4

Dredge lamb with flour, brown in butter in heavy skillet. Add seasonings and onion. Cook over low heat until onion is soft. Add water and simmer 1½ hours, or until tender. Add additional water if needed. When done, add sour cream, stir until hot but do not boil.

IRISH STEW WITH DUMPLINGS

Lamb, Shoulder, Boneless, 1½ pounds
Onion, 1 medium
Carrots, 1 cup, diced
Potatoes, 4 medium
Parsley, few sprigs
Salt and **Pepper,** to taste
Dumplings (see page 64)

To serve 4

Cut lamb in pieces, cover with boiling water and simmer covered, 2 hours. Add vegetables and seasonings, simmer until meat and vegetables are tender. Add dumplings the last 15 minutes of cooking.

MENUS

BRAISED LAMB IN SOUR CREAM

Baked Parsnips · Baby Lima Beans
Endive with Piquante Dressing
Blueberry Charlotte

IRISH STEW WITH VEGETABLES AND DUMPLINGS

Tomato Salad
Chocolate Mousse

LAMB HOT POT

Boneless Lamb for Stewing, 2 pounds
Lamb Kidneys, 3
Potatoes, 4 med., sliced
Onions, 2 med., sliced
Ham, 1 cup, chopped
Mushrooms, ½ lb., sliced
Salt and **Pepper**
Flour
Stock or **Consommé,** 1 cup
Parsley, 2 tablespoons

Oven, Slow, 300°

To serve 4

Cut lamb into cubes, peel and slice kidneys. Arrange a layer of lamb and kidneys on the bottom of a casserole; place a layer of potatoes, onions, ham and mushrooms over it. Repeat until all ingredients are used up. Sprinkle each layer with salt and pepper and a little flour. Add stock and parsley. Cover.

Bake 1½ hours, or until tender.

NAVARIN OF LAMB
(Lamb Stew)

Lamb Shoulder, Boneless, 1½ pounds, cubed
Butter, 2 tablespoons
Parsley, 2 tablespoons
Thyme, ½ teaspoon
Bay Leaf, 1, crumbled
Water, 1 cup
Onions, 8 small
Carrots, 3, quartered
Turnips, 3, quartered
New Potatoes, 8, skinned
Tomatoes, 16-ounce can

To serve 4

Brown lamb on all sides in butter in heavy kettle. Add herbs and water, bring to boil and simmer 30 minutes. Add onions and tomatoes and simmer 30 minutes longer. Add remaining vegetables and continue simmering until tender.

DILLED LAMB

Breast of Lamb, 3 lbs.
Water, 1 cup
Salt, 1 teaspoon
Pepper, ⅛ teaspoon
Dill Seed, 1 teaspoon
Vinegar, 1 tablespoon

Butter, 2 tablespoons
Flour, 2 tablespoons
Egg, 1, beaten
Salt and **Pepper,** to taste

To serve 4

Put lamb into kettle with water, vinegar and seasonings. Cover tightly; bring to boil and simmer 1½ hours, or until tender. Remove lamb to hot platter.

Melt butter in skillet, blend in flour, add liquid in kettle. (You need about 1½ cups; add consommé if needed.) Stir constantly over low heat until thickened. Add a little of the mixture to the egg; add egg to remainder of sauce and mix well. Season to taste.

LAMB PILAF

Lamb Shoulder, 3 lbs., cut in cubes
Onion, 1, chopped
Green Pepper, 1, chopped
Tomatoes, 16-ounce can
Salt, 2 teaspoons
Pepper, ¼ teaspoon
Instant Garlic, ⅛ teasp.
Water, 1 cup
Rice, 1 cup, raw

To serve 4 to 6

Brown lamb in kettle and pour off rendered fat. Add onion, green pepper, tomatoes, water and seasonings. Cover and simmer 1½ hours, or until tender. Add rice; simmer ½ hour more, or until rice is tender and liquid absorbed.

BARBECUED LAMB SHANKS

Lamb Shanks, 4
Vegetable Oil, 2 tablesps.
Onions, 2, sliced
Ketchup, ¼ cup
Water, 1½ cups
Salt, 2 teaspoons
Worcestershire, 1 tablesp.
Vinegar, ½ cup
Brown Sugar, ¼ cup
Dry Mustard, 1 teasp.
Cayenne, dash

To serve 4

Brown shanks on all sides in skillet in hot oil. Pour off oil. Add remaining ingredients. Cover and simmer 2 hours or until tender. Make gravy with pan juices. (See page 22.)

MENUS

Lamb Hot Pot, Navarin of Lamb and Lamb Pilaf are one-dish meals that require only good crusty bread and a light dessert to be complete. Vegetables may be cooked also with the Dilled Lamb and Barbecued Lamb Shanks to turn these into one-pot stove-to-table gourmet affairs, or served separately if preferred. And you can always add a tossed green salad if another course is needed.

PORK

Pork does not carry a government grade stamp, but it should have the US Inspected and Passed Stamp. The meat should be grayish pink and fine grained; the fat, white and hard. *Pork should always be served well done—the cooked meat should be almost white, never pink.* In fact, roast pork is most delicious when it is ready to fall apart.

PORK ROASTS

Loin Roast. This is a long strip extending from the shoulder to the hip of the animal. It can weigh up to 14 pounds and can be roasted in its entirety if desired. However, it is usually cut into three parts:

Center Cut Roast. Choicest and most expensive section from which the center chops are taken. *Rib End*, bony and difficult to carve. *Loin End*, also bony and difficult. When buying the loin, have the butcher free the ribs from the backbone for easier carving.

Fresh Ham. The hind leg, economical with little waste.

Shoulder. Good flavor with more fat than the ham. Can be used with bone in or boned and rolled.

Picnic. Lower part of shoulder. Used either boned and rolled or with bone in. Good flavor.

HOW TO ROAST PORK

Plan your roasting time and try to have the roast finished 10 or 15 minutes ahead of serving time, for easier slicing. Set oven for 325°. Do not wash roast; wipe with a damp paper towel if necessary. Place roast on rack in shallow pan with fat side up. Season with salt and pepper. Do not cover (see page 21). Do not add water.

Insert your meat thermometer in the centre of the roast, not against the bone. Roast meat to 185° on the thermometer without turning or basting. *Pork must be well done to be safe.*

ROAST LOIN OF PORK WITH VEGETABLES

Buy center cut loin roast and follow above directions for roasting. About 1 hour before roast is done, add 8 small peeled potatoes and 8 peeled onions to roasting pan. Season with salt and pepper and turn occasionally as they cook to brown evenly on all sides. Carrots, parsnips and turnips may also be added if desired.

When thoroughly done, remove pork to hot platter and make gravy in roasting pan, following directions given for Roast Beef Gravy, page 22.

BARBECUED PORK

Loin of Pork, 4 pounds	Roast pork according to directions above. Baste from time to time with barbecue sauce made as follows:
Brown Sugar, 3 tablesps.	Mix all ingredients in saucepan;
Salt, 1 teaspoon	boil 1 minute. Spoon over pork.
Pepper, ¼ teaspoon	
Worcestershire, 1 tablesp.	
Instant Garlic, ⅛ teasp.	
Vinegar, ½ cup	
Water, ½ cup	
To serve 4, with leftovers	

SPARERIBS HAWAIIAN

Spareribs, 4 pounds	Brown spareribs in heavy kettle
Onions, 2 med., chopped	or casserole. Pour off fat. Mix
Garlic, 1 clove, minced	onions, garlic, pineapple juice,
Pineapple Juice, 1½ cups	vinegar, seasonings, and corn-
Vinegar, ¼ cup	starch and pour over meat.
Soy Sauce, 1 tablespoon	
Paprika, 1 teaspoon	
Cornstarch, 1½ tablesps.	
Oven, moderate, 350°	Bake 2 hours, or until tender.
To serve 4	

TIMETABLE FOR ROASTING PORK

Roast at 325°	Thermometer Reading	Approx. Minutes per Pound
Loin	185°	45 to 60
Fresh Ham	,,	60 to 65
Shoulder	,,	50 to 60
Picnic	,,	45 to 55

SAVORY FRESH HAM

Fresh Ham Half
Salt, 1 teaspoon
Thyme, 1 teaspoon
Marjoram, 1 teaspoon
Bay Leaf, 1
Onion, 1 med., chopped
Sherry, ½ cup

Brown meat on all sides in heavy kettle; pour off fat. Add remaining ingredients; cover tightly and simmer 3 to 4 hours, or until meat is tender. Liquid in kettle may be used for gravy (page 22), if desired.

PORK GOULASH

Rib End of Loin, 3 lbs.

Remove meat from bone; put bones in kettle, cover with water and simmer 30 minutes.

Flour
Fat, 1 tablespoon
Onions, 3 large, sliced
Salt, 1 teaspoon
Paprika, ½ teaspoon
Parsley, 2 tablespoons, chopped
Marjoram, 1 teaspoon
Sherry, ¼ cup

Cut meat into small pieces, dredge with flour, brown in fat in heavy kettle. Add onion, salt, paprika, parsley, and marjoram. Cook a few minutes until onion is soft. Add sherry and stock from bones (about 1½ cups). Cover tightly and simmer 1 hour, or until pork is tender. Add more stock if necessary.

To serve 4

SKILLET PORK AND RICE

Pork Shoulder, 1 pound, boneless
Fat, 1 tablespoon
Rice, ½ cup, raw
Onion, 1 med., chopped
Salt, 1 teaspoon
Pepper, ⅛ teaspoon
Worcestershire, 1 teasp.
Tomatoes, 16-ounce can
Bouillon, 1 cup

To serve 4

Cut pork in cubes, brown in fat on all sides in skillet. Add rice and stir until lightly browned. Add remaining ingredients, cover, and cook over low heat for 1 hour, or until pork is tender.

PORK AND RICE CASSEROLE

Follow recipe for Skillet Pork and Rice above, putting all ingredients in casserole with browned pork on top. Cover with lid or foil and bake about 1 hour, or until rice and pork are tender. Oven, moderate, 350°.

SWEET AND SOUR PORK

Pork Tenderloin, 1 pound
Cooking Oil, 1 tablesp.
Cornstarch, 1 tablesp.
Pineapple Chunks, 8-ounce can
Vinegar, ¼ cup
Brown Sugar, ¼ cup
Soy Sauce, 1 tablespoon
Frozen Whole Green Beans, 1 pkg.

To serve 4

Cut pork into very thin slices and brown in oil lightly in large skillet. Remove pork from skillet. Mix cornstarch with juice from pineapple chunks, and add to skillet with vinegar, sugar and soy sauce. Cook over low heat, stirring constantly, until clear and thickened. Add pineapple chunks, pork and beans, which have been thawed. Bring to boil and simmer 5 minutes, adding a little water if additional liquid is needed.

CHINESE PORK WITH MUSHROOMS

Boneless Pork Shoulder, 1 pound
Fat, 2 tablespoons
Onion, 1 medium, sliced thin
Celery, 2 stalks, sliced thin
Fresh Mushrooms, ½ pound, sliced
Soy Sauce, 1 tablespoon
Ginger, ¼ teaspoon
Water, ¼ cup
Boiled Rice

To serve 4

Cut pork into thin strips. Brown in fat over low heat; add onion, celery, mushrooms, and seasonings. Cook gently until all are lightly browned. Add water, cover tightly and simmer 10 minutes. Serve with fluffy boiled rice.

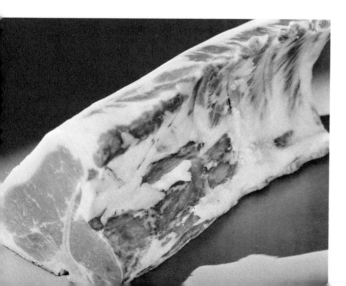

Center cut pork loin roast

Roast pork with apple rings

MENUS

SAVORY FRESH HAM

Corn Pudding · Green Beans
Deep Dish Apple Pie

PORK GOULASH

Noodles · Spinach
Preserved Apple Rings (bought)
Lemon Snow with Custard Sauce

SKILLET PORK AND RICE

Corn on the Cob · Waldorf Salad
Hard Rolls · Whipped Butter
Raspberry Ice

PORK AND RICE CASSEROLE

Broccoli
Sliced Tomato Salad
Apples and Cheese

SWEET AND SOUR PORK

French Fried Cauliflower · Asparagus
Spring Salad
Assorted Rolls · Butter
Cheese Cake

CHINESE PORK WITH MUSHROOMS

Hot Boiled Rice · Buttered Green Beans
Rosy Skillet Apples

Panned pork chops

PORK HOCKS AND SAUERKRAUT

Fresh Pork Hocks, 4
Sauerkraut, 2 pounds, raw
Salt, 1 teaspoon
Pepper, ⅛ teaspoon

To serve 4

Scrub hocks thoroughly and rinse. Cover with water in kettle, add salt and pepper and simmer 1 hour. Remove the hocks and put the sauerkraut in the kettle with the cooking water. Arrange the pork hocks over the top, cover, and simmer 2 hours, or until pork and sauerkraut are tender. Drain and serve on hot platter.

If desired, the sauerkraut may be flavored with bay leaves, or a few sprigs of parsley and green celery tops. Or a tablespoon of caraway seeds may be added during the last hour of cooking.

PORK RIB WITH SAUERKRAUT

The rib end of the loin may be used for the above recipe in place of the pork hocks.

PANNED PORK CHOPS

Pork chops are more certain to be tender and juicy if cooked slowly in a skillet. Cooking them under the broiler the long time required has a tendency to make them dry.

Grease skillet with a little of the fat from the chop. Brown chops quickly on both sides; turn heat low, season, pour off fat, cover, and cook slowly until tender, turning occasionally. Make gravy of pan drippings, if desired. (See page 22.)

SHERRIED PORK CHOPS AND CABBAGE CASSEROLE

Cabbage, 1 head, young
Salt, 1 teaspoon
Pepper, ⅛ teaspoon
Cream, 1 cup

Wash and shred cabbage; put in saucepan with salt and pepper and cream. Simmer 20 minutes.

Pork Chops, 4
Marjoram, ½ teaspoon
Sherry, ½ cup
Parmesan Cheese, grated

Fry chops in skillet until golden brown. Pour off fat. Cover and cook over low heat until tender. Remove chops. Add marjoram and wine. Simmer few minutes and stir, scraping up browned juices in pan.

Put layer of cabbage in shallow casserole. Arrange pork chops on cabbage, with another layer of cabbage on top. Pour pan juices over all. Sprinkle cheese over top.

Oven, moderate, 350°

To serve 4

Bake 45 minutes.

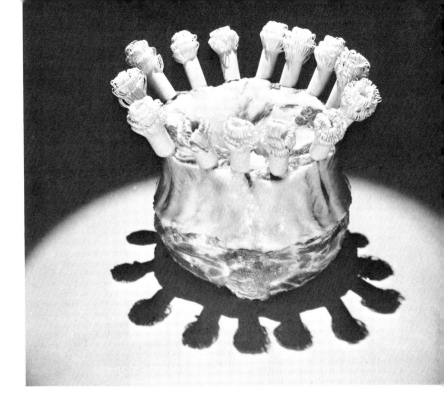

Pork crown roast

BRAISED PORK CHOPS WITH VERMOUTH

Pork Chops, 4, thick
Salt and **Pepper**
Flour
Dry Vermouth, ¼ cup
Water, ¼ cup

To serve 4

Cut off part of outer rim of fat on chops. Render a little in skillet and discard pieces. Dredge chops with flour and brown on both sides in skillet. Pour off fat. Add seasoning, vermouth and water; simmer 1 hour, or until chops are tender. Remove to hot platter. Stir up drippings in pan with a little hot water and pour over chops.

Vermouth may be omitted and water substituted, or sherry used in its place.

BREADED PORK CHOPS

Follow recipe for Breaded Veal Cutlet on page 36.

CROWN ROAST OF PORK

See Crown roast of lamb, page 40, and follow procedure for roast pork, page 45.

MENUS

PORK HOCKS AND SAUERKRAUT

Mashed Potatoes · Fried Apples
Indian Pudding

PANNED PORK CHOPS

Spanish Rice · Succotash
Tossed Green Salad
Apple Betty

SHERRIED PORK CHOPS AND CABBAGE CASSEROLE

Twice Baked Sweet Potatoes
Celery and Carrot Sticks
Apple Sauce · Cookies

BRAISED PORK CHOPS WITH VERMOUTH

Glazed Carrots · Cauliflower
Applesauce
Lemon Chiffon Pie

49

HAM

The pig serves us in two ways; not only with succulent roasts and chops, but with flavorful smoked hams and bacon.

A whole or half ham is one of the most economical buys in the meat department because of the many good things that can follow the original serving: starting with the most popular of sandwiches and ending up with the bone lending its delicious flavor to bean soup. But don't weary the family palate by serving too many ham dishes on successive days—space them out with other meals in between.

TYPES OF HAM

COUNTRY HAM (VIRGINIA, SMITHFIELD, KENTUCKY, ETC.): Requires long slow boiling, 25 to 30 minutes per pound. (See Boiled Smoked Country Ham.)

TENDERIZED HAM: Must be cooked; can be baked without boiling first. Sold bone in or boned and rolled. (See "Baked Smoked Ham".)

READY-TO-EAT HAM: Is tenderized and cooked by processor; sold bone in, or boned and rolled, or canned. Can be eaten without cooking, but to be palatable should be heated. Heating requires over half as long as to cook a tenderized ham. (See "Baked Smoked Ham".)

BOILED SMOKED COUNTRY HAM

Boiling is not necessary for the modern-processed ham: it is ready for baking; but the old-fashioned country smoked ham will still require it. Scrub and rinse ham and place it, rind up, in large kettle. Soak over night. Cover with fresh water and bring to boil; simmer until tender—25 to 30 minutes per pound. After first hour, pour off water; cover with fresh boiling water and continue simmering until tender. If you use a meat thermometer, it will register 170° when done.

Let ham stand in stock until ready to serve. Peel off rind and serve hot or cold with one of the Ham Sauces on pages 90-91.

If desired, score ham and cover it with one of the glazes listed in right column and place in a hot oven, 400°, for 15 minutes. Let it stand for 10 minutes after removing from oven.

TO SCORE AND GLAZE A HAM

Old-fashioned smoked ham with the rind still on should have the rind removed shortly before the ham is done. Remove it from the oven and with a sharp paring knife carefully cut the rind loose. Don't tear it off or break the fat underneath. With a sharp knife make a diagonal cut ⅛-inch deep from one end of the ham to the other, with succeeding cuts one inch apart and parallel to the first all the way across the ham. Now place the second set of lines to form a diamond pattern on the ham. If desired, a clove may be placed in the center of each diamond. Dribble one of the following glazes over the ham and return it to a hot oven for 15 or 20 minutes more, until a glossy brown.

BAKED SMOKED HAM

Place Tenderized or Ready-to-eat Ham on rack in roasting pan. Score ham diagonally in 1-inch squares. Stick a clove into each square. Bake uncovered in slow oven (325°) until thermometer registers 155° for Tenderized (about 25 minutes per pound) or 135° for Ready-to-eat (about 12 to 15 minutes per pound).

If desired, a glaze may be applied half an hour before ham is done. See Glazes, below.

GLAZES FOR BAKED HAM

1. HONEY GLAZE: Dribble ¼ cup of honey over ham, then sift brown sugar over it.

2. CRANBERRY GLAZE: Mash ¾ cup cranberry jelly.

3. PINEAPPLE GLAZE. Mix ½ cup crushed pineapple with ½ cup brown sugar.

4. MUSTARD GLAZE. Mix 1 teaspoon dry mustard with ½ cup molasses.

5. ORANGE GLAZE: ¾ cup orange marmalade.

HAM AND PORK LOAF

Ham, raw, 1 lb., ground **Pork,** fresh, 1½ pounds, ground **Eggs,** 2, beaten **Soft Bread Crumbs,** 1 cup **Milk,** 1 cup **Onion,** 1 small, minced **Mustard,** 1 teaspoon, dry **Parsley,** chopped, 1 tablespoon	Mix all ingredients together and turn into 1 large loaf pan, or into individual loaf or muffin pans.
Oven, moderate, 350° **Sweet** and **Pungent Sauce** (page 91)	Bake 1 hour for individual loaves, 1¾ hours for large loaf. Serve with Sweet and Pungent Sauce.

To serve 4, with leftovers

HAM AND VEAL LOAF. Substitute veal for pork in the above recipe.

*Broiled
ham slices
filled with
hashed brown
potatoes*

BROILED HAM WITH PINEAPPLE

Broil ham on one side as above, and turn slice. Arrange slices of fresh or canned pineapple on ham, brush lightly with butter and broil until light brown.

Fresh or canned pears, apricots or peaches may be substituted for pineapple.

BROILED HAM SLICE

Ham Slice, ¾″ thick
Prepared Mustard,
1 teaspoon

Place ham on broiler rack, spread with mustard, broil 10 minutes, or until thoroughly hot and lightly browned. Turn and repeat on other side.

HAM MOUSSE

Unflavored Gelatin, 1 envelope **Meat** or **Chicken Stock,** 1¾ cups	Soften gelatin in cold stock, dissolve it over low heat. Chill until nearly set.
Ham, cooked, ground, 2 cups **Onion,** grated, 1 tablesp. **Salt** and **Pepper,** to taste **Heavy Cream,** ¾ cup	Add ham and onion to chilled stock. Add seasoning to taste and mix well. Whip cream until stiff and fold into ham mixture. Pour into mold and chill until firm. To serve, unmold on chilled platter.
To serve 4 to 6	

HAM SLICE BAKED IN MILK

Ham Slice, ¾″ thick **Prepared Mustard,** 1 teaspoon **Milk,** 1 cup	Put ham in shallow baking dish, spread with mustard, cover with milk.
Oven, moderate, 350° *To serve 4*	Bake 30 minutes or until fork tender.

HAM WITH GREEN BEANS

Green Beans, 1 pound **Onion,** 1 med., sliced **Celery,** 2 stalks, sliced **Prepared Mustard,** 1 tablespoon **French Dressing,** ½ cup **Ham,** cooked, 8 slices	Cut beans in small pieces and cook in a little boiling salted water until tender. Drain and combine with onion, celery, mustard and French Dressing. Chill. Serve on platter with ham.
To serve 4	

BAKED BONELESS BUTT

Smoked Shoulder Butt, 1½ to 2 pounds **Water**	Cover butt with water, simmer until tender, about 40 minutes per pound.
Oranges, 4 thick slices **Pineapple,** 4 slices **Cranberry Jelly,** ¾ cup	Place butt in shallow baking dish, arrange orange and pineapple slices around it. Mash cranberry jelly and spread over butt and fruit slices.
Oven, hot, 400°	Bake 20 minutes. Let stand 10 minutes before slicing.

BROCCOLI HAM ROLLS

Broccoli Spears, 1 package, frozen **Boiled Ham,** 8 slices **Quick Hollandaise Sauce** (page 91)	Cook broccoli and put 1 stalk on each slice of ham. Roll up and place side by side in shallow baking dish.
Oven, hot, 425° *To serve 4*	Bake 15 minutes. Serve with Quick Hollandaise Sauce.

ASPARAGUS HAM ROLLS: Fresh or frozen asparagus may be substituted for the broccoli.

MENUS

BAKED HAM WITH CRANBERRY GLAZE

Creamed Potatoes · Asparagus
Corn Muffins · Butter
Spumoni

HAM AND PORK LOAF

Succotash · Scalloped Tomatoes
Lemon Snow with Cherry Sauce

BROILED HAM SLICE WITH BROILED PINEAPPLE SLICES

Baked Yams
Tossed Salad with Sour Cream Dressing
Cup Custards

HAM WITH GREEN BEANS

Cucumber and Cottage Cheese Ring
Hot Biscuits · Butter
Applesauce Cake · Lemon Sauce

BAKED BONELESS BUTT

Frozen Lima Beans · Cabbage Casserole
Rye Bread · Butter
Pumpkin Pie

BROCCOLI HAM ROLLS

Hot Mustard Potato Salad
Tomato Aspic
Peach Shortcake

HAM MOUSSE

Green Goddess Salad
Hard Rolls · Butter
Strawberry Glacé

VARIETY MEATS

Do not overlook the many delicious dishes that can be made with these low-priced meats.

BREADED CALF BRAINS

Calf Brains, 2 sets
Egg, 1, beaten
Water, 2 tablespoons
Fine Bread Crumbs
Fat
Salt and **Pepper,** to taste

To serve 4

Remove membranes and slice brains. Dip in egg mixed with water, then in crumbs. Set aside for ½ hour. Fry in deep fat at 370°, or sauté in butter in skillet, cooking each side until lightly browned and thoroughly cooked. Season to taste and serve at once.

PIGS' FEET

Scrub and rinse 4 pigs' feet; cover with cold water, bring to boiling point and simmer 3 hours. Add a tablespoonful of pickling spice and a teaspoonful of salt and continue to simmer another hour, or until tender. Let cool, strain stock and use for making gravy (page 22). Remove skin and bones and add meat to gravy. To serve 4.

JELLIED PIGS' FEET

Cook according to above recipe. Strain stock and add meat to it. Pour into mold and chill until firm.

SAUTÉED LAMB OR PORK KIDNEYS

Allow 2 or 3 lamb, or **1 pork kidney per person**
Garlic, 1 clove, minced
Onion, 1, minced
Butter, 2 tablespoons
Sauterne, ½ cup

Slice kidneys lengthwise, remove white membrane with scissors. Melt butter in skillet until it bubbles, then add kidneys, garlic and onion. Cook kidneys about 2 minutes on each side, or until no longer red. Dredge with a little flour, stir in, then add wine. Continue cooking for about 2 more minutes. Turn into hot serving dish and serve at once.

Kidneys should not be overcooked or they become tough.

KIDNEYS WITH MUSHROOMS

Follow above recipe for Sautéed Lamb or Pork Kidneys. Slice a few fresh mushrooms and cook along with the kidneys. When done, add 1 cup of cream, heat 1 minute, and serve.

CALF BRAIN FRITTERS

Follow the recipe for Fritters on page 140. Simmer brains in a little salted water, covered, for 15 minutes. Pull into pieces and add to fritter batter.

BRAINS À LA KING

See recipe for à la King on page 92.

STUFFED HEART

Heart, 1 beef or 2 calf

Onions, 2, chopped
Celery, ½ cup, chopped
Parsley, 2 tablespoons, chopped
Thyme, ½ teaspoon
Bay Leaf, 1
Fat, 2 tablespoons
Salt, 1 teaspoon
Pepper, ⅛ teaspoon

To serve 4

Wash heart well, remove any remaining blood, arteries and veins, and excess fat.

Stuff heart with as much onion and celery mixed with seasonings as it will hold. Sew edges closed. Brown in fat on all sides in heavy kettle. Arrange any remaining vegetables around heart, cover tightly and simmer until very tender, 2 hours or more. Make gravy with drippings in pan. (See page 22.)

SAUTÉED VEAL KIDNEYS

Have the butcher leave a little of the fat around the kidneys: it is very sweet and delicate in flavor when fried crisp. Slice kidneys into half-inch slices. Use a little of the kidney fat to grease the skillet. Brown kidney slices a few minutes on each side. Season with salt and pepper.

If there is no fat on the kidneys, sauté in a little butter.

One veal kidney will serve one person. Or kidneys can be served along with veal chops. Sometimes the kidney is cut as part of the loin chop, and is cooked with it.

CURRIED TRIPE WITH RICE

Tripe, 1 pound, fresh or pickled

Wash tripe, cut in 2-inch pieces, cover with cold water and bring to boil; drain. Cover with boiling water, cover and simmer 1½ to 2 hours, until tender. Add 1 teaspoon salt to fresh tripe while cooking. Drain and reserve stock.

Fat, 3 tablespoons
Flour, 3 tablespoons
Tripe Stock, 2 cups
Curry Powder, 2 teasps.
Paprika, 1 teaspoon
Rice, 1 cup, boiled

To serve 4

Melt fat in skillet, blend in flour and gradually stir in stock. Cook until thickened. Add meat and seasonings. Serve with hot rice.

BEEF KIDNEY STEW

Beef Kidneys, 2
Butter, 2 tablespoons
Onion, 2 tablespoons, minced
Salt, ½ teaspoon
Pepper, ⅛ teaspoon
Marjoram, ½ teasp.
Water, 2 cups
Noodles, 1 8-ounce package, cooked

To serve 4

Wash kidneys, split in half lengthwise, remove tubes and fat, and outer membrane. Cut into pieces. Sauté in butter lightly, turning so that all sides are cooked. Add onion, and stir 2 minutes. Add seasonings and water; cover, simmer 1 to 1½ hours, or until tender. Serve with boiled noodles.

BROILED LIVER

Brush liver slices with butter, season with salt and pepper and place under broiler; cook 4 to 5 minutes on each side, or until gently browned. One pound will serve 4.

Slices of tomato and Spanish onions may be broiled at the same time and served with the liver.

SAUTÉED LIVER

Calf liver is the tenderest and also most expensive, but liver from young, good quality beef is almost as good. Lamb and pork liver can also be used. Buy liver sliced in half-inch thick slices; remove skin on edges. One pound will serve four.

Melt 3 tablespoons of butter in skillet, dredge liver with flour and brown 3 minutes on each side. Do not overcook, or liver will be dry. Season with salt and pepper and serve at once.

Liver is often served with bacon or with fried onions. Fry bacon crisp and set in warm place while liver is being cooked. Onions may be fried ahead of time and kept hot while liver is being cooked. Or serve with lemon wedges.

SMOTHERED LIVER AND ONIONS

Pork or **Beef Liver,** 1½ pounds, sliced
Flour
Fat, 3 tablespoons
Onion Soup, 1 can

To serve 4

Dredge liver with flour, brown in hot fat in skillet. Add onion soup, bring to boil and simmer over low heat for 20 minutes, or until liver is tender. Remove liver to hot platter; if mixture in pan requires more thickening, add a little flour mixed with cold water. Cook until thickened, stirring constantly.

SAUTÉED SWEETBREADS

Precook 2 pairs of sweetbread in salted water, covered; simmer 15 minutes. Cool, remove membrane and tubes.

Split sweetbreads in halves, sprinkle with salt and pepper and sauté in butter until delicately brown. Serve with lemon butter (page 91). To serve 4.

SWEETBREADS NEWBURG

See recipe for Lobster Newburg (page 79). Substitute 2 pairs sweetbreads, precooked and diced, for lobster.

CREAMED SWEETBREADS

Sweetbreads, 2 pairs
Medium White Sauce, 2 cups
Egg, 1

To serve 4

Precook sweetbreads, as in Sautéed Sweetbreads, and break up into small pieces. Add to White Sauce and heat. Add beaten egg just before serving. Serve on hot toast or croustades, if desired.

SWEETBREADS IN VELOUTÉ SAUCE: Velouté Sauce (page 91) may be substituted for White Sauce in the above recipe.

DEEP-FAT FRIED SWEETBREADS AND BACON

Pre-cook sweetbreads as described in "Sautéed Sweetbreads." Cool. Cut sweetbreads into 1-inch squares and dredge with flour. Wrap each piece in ½ slice of bacon and hold in place with small skewer. Fry in deep hot fat (380°) 5 or 6 minutes, or until browned. Drain on paper towel. Allow one sweetbread per person.

FRIED PHILADELPHIA SCRAPPLE

Slice pan of scrapple into ½-inch thick slices, dredge each slice on both sides lightly with flour and fry in oil or bacon drippings until brown. Serve with vegetables as a lunch dish, or with scrambled eggs for breakfast.

SPICED LAMBS' TONGUES

Simmer 2 pounds fresh lambs' tongues in enough salted water to cover, adding a bay leaf, a few whole cloves, a 1-inch piece of stick cinnamon, and a slice of lemon peel. Serve hot as a main dish, or cold, as part of a cold meat platter. To serve 4.

SAUSAGE

Fresh sausage comes in links or in bulk, by the pound. If using bulk sausage, shape it into flat cakes. Panbroil it until well done, pouring off the fat as it accumulates, and turning to brown both sides evenly.

Or bake sausage links or patties uncovered in moderate oven, 350°, about 30 minutes, or until well done. There should be no pink meat showing when cut.

FRANKFURTERS

Simmer frankfurters in boiling water over low heat for 5 to 10 minutes to plump them; or split and sauté them in a little fat in a skillet until brown on both sides. Or they may be cooked under the broiler until browned on both sides. Serve with mustard or pickle relish.

POULTRY

Poultry is the cook's standby. Chicken is plentiful, economical, and nearly everyone likes it. Turkey is no longer a special treat on holidays, but is available all year round; and in small sizes to accommodate the small family. Ducks are available most of the year and Cornish Hens, the most recent arrival on the poultry market, are growing in popularity.

Poultry can be bought "dressed" or "ready-to-cook." "Dressed" means with the feathers off, but weighed and priced with head, feet and viscera. "Ready-to-cook" birds are eviscerated and the head and feet removed. More than 90% of the poultry sold today is ready-to-cook.

Like meat, poultry can be bought government inspected and government graded, but this practice is not widespread.

Much poultry is sold frozen and a long time is required to thaw a large bird. You will find it impossible to remove the wrapped giblets from the inside of the bird until it is nearly thawed. It is best thawed in the refrigerator, so when buying a hard-frozen turkey, for example, purchase it at least 24 hours before the time you wish to cook it, if it is a small bird, or 2 to 3 days, if a 20-pound bird.

HOW TO ROAST POULTRY

If you are not buying ready-to-cook poultry, have the butcher prepare the bird for roasting. If, however, you are killing your own bird, follow the directions for drawing on this page.

If the bird is frozen, let it thaw (see above).

Inspect the bird to make sure all pinfeathers are removed— if not, pull them with tweezers or by holding them against the blunt edge of a kitchen knife. Any hairs or down can be singed off with a lighted match or soda straw.

To prepare poultry for stuffing, let cold water run into the inside cavity, then dry it thoroughly, removing any small pieces of viscera that might remain. Do not soak the bird in water. Wipe the outside with a damp cloth, or rub it with a cut lemon. Sprinkle body cavities with salt.

Stuff the body and crop cavities with your favorite stuffing (page 73), filling them only about three-quarters full so there will be room for expansion. Close the openings with skewers or with needle and string. Truss the bird by tying the legs close to the body with a string from the end of one drumstick to the other, and tuck the wing tips under the back.

Roast poultry in a slow oven, 325°, for the approximate time given in the timetable. For finest results, use a meat thermometer.

HOW TO SELECT A CHICKEN

Chickens are chosen by age for the way in which they are to be used.

Very young chickens, 2½ pounds (ready-to-eat weight) or under, are called broilers.

Slightly older ones, 2½ to 3½ pounds, are called fryers. They are also used for roasting, costing less per pound than a roasting chicken.

Fully developed chickens, but still young and tender, are for roasting.

Old chickens, called "fowls", are used for fricassees, stews or soups; they require long simmering to become tender.

Capons are unsexed male birds weighing up to 7 pounds. They are larger and plumper than hens, of delicious flavor, and are used for roasting.

In recipes calling for "stewing chickens" younger chickens can always be used, thereby shortening the cooking time.

Ready-to-eat chicken may be bought either whole, split in half, quartered or cut up. It is also sold in pieces that permit you to select the parts your family likes best.

HOW TO DRAW A CHICKEN

With a sharp knife make an incision lengthwise, below the breast, large enough to put your hand through. Work hand in between organs and breastbone. Grasp gizzard, which is round and hard, and pull. It will come out bringing the rest of the entrails. Pull out the kidneys near the back bone and the spongy red lungs lying against the ribs.

Separate heart, stomach and liver from entrails, being careful not to disturb green gall sac attached to liver. Allow a half-inch of liver in removing it.

Cut off head. Loosen neck skin and pull down, exposing neck; cut neck close to body, leaving the skin attached to body. Make cut at base of neck and pull out crop and windpipe. Cut out oil sac at base of tail.

Either cut off the feet or learn the butcher's trick of cutting the skin and breaking the foot at the knee joint, then pulling it so that the tendons are pulled out with it. This is helpful with an older bird that is apt to have tough tendons.

To clean the gizzard, cut a slit on the edge, making sure not to cut the inner sac. Loosen and pull out the inner sac with your fingers; discard it.

HOW TO CUT UP A CHICKEN

If you wish to cut up a drawn chicken into parts for frying, proceed as follows: lift up wing and feel for the joint; with a sharp knife cut through the skin around the joint, then through the flesh and joint itself. Cut off the second wing in the same way. Next cut through the skin between the leg and body and follow with the knife around the outline of the thigh; pull the leg outward until the joint cracks, then cut through the flesh to sever the leg. Repeat on the second leg. Remove the back by cutting toward the back on each side from the opening made to eviscerate the chicken. Press the back and breast in opposite directions until they crack apart. Cut off the neck where it joins the breast. The breast may be left whole or split into 2 parts. The legs may be left whole, or separated at the joint, by bending and cutting through at the joint.

ROAST CHICKEN

Prepare a plump, young roasting chicken according to the directions for roasting poultry. Stuff it with one of the dressings on page 73, and truss it.

Place chicken breast up on a rack in a shallow roasting pan. Cover the breast with a square of foil to prevent it from browning too soon. Roast in slow oven (325°) until tender. (See timetable below.) A meat thermometer inserted in the thigh near the body will register 185° when it is well done. It is done when the drumstick can be moved up and down easily. Uncover the breast for the last 20 minutes so that it may brown.

Serve with Chicken Gravy, see below, or with Giblet Gravy, page 68.

CHICKEN GRAVY

Make gravy in roasting pan, using drippings. Pour off all but 3 tablespoons fat and blend in 3 tablespoons flour, stirring constantly over low heat. Gradually add 2 cups chicken stock or chicken bouillon and cook, stirring until thickened. Milk or light cream may be substituted for part of the stock if desired.

POLYNESIAN CHICKEN

Broiler, 1, quartered
Butter, 3 tablespoons
Pepper, ⅛ teaspoon
Ginger, ¼ teaspoon
Soy Sauce, 1 tablespoon
Dry Mustard, ½ teasp.

Place chicken in shallow baking dish, skin side up. Melt butter and add seasonings; brush chicken with it.

Oven, moderate, 350°

Bake 45 minutes.

Pineapple Chunks,
   8-ounce can
Green Pepper, 1, chopped
Mandarin Oranges,
   1 can, drained
Cornstarch, 2 tablesps.
Vinegar, ¼ cup
Brown Sugar, 2 tablesps.

Combine pineapple and juice, green pepper and oranges in saucepan with cornstarch, brown sugar and vinegar. Heat to boiling point, stirring constantly, and simmer a few minutes. Pour over chicken, cover casserole and bake 15 minutes longer, or until chicken is fork tender.

To serve 4

BAKED CURRIED CHICKEN BREASTS

Onion, 1, medium
Celery, ½ cup, chopped
Green Pepper, ¼ cup, chopped
Butter, 2 tablespoons
Salt, 2 teaspoons
Pepper, ¼ teaspoon
Curry Powder, 2 teasps.
Cornstarch, 1 tablespoon
Chicken Bouillon, 1 cup
Sauterne, 1 cup

Sauté vegetables in butter in skillet over low heat until soft. Add seasonings, cornstarch and bouillon; simmer 5 minutes. Add wine, stir and remove from heat.

Chicken Breasts, 4 split

Put chicken in one layer in wide shallow casserole. Pour sauce over chicken. Cover casserole.

Oven, moderate, 325°

Bake 1 hour.

To serve 4

BROILED CHICKEN

Have broiling chickens cut in halves or quarters depending on size portion desired. Place on broiling rack, skin side down. Brush with melted butter, sprinkle with salt and pepper. Broil about 10 minutes; turn and brush other side with butter, broil 15 minutes. Turn again, brush with butter, and continue broiling until chicken is fork tender. Adjust broiler height so that chicken does not become too brown before it is cooked through.

Mix light cream with pan drippings to make gravy.

Variation. Mix 1 tablespoon melted butter with ¾ cup dry white wine, and 1 tablespoon basil, simmer 5 minutes. Baste chicken during broiling.

BARBECUED CHICKEN

Broiling Chickens, 2,
   split in half
Molasses, 1 tablespoon
Mustard, dry, 1 teasp.
Worcestershire, 2 teasps.
Salt, 1 teaspoon
Pepper, ¼ teaspoon
Vinegar, 2 tablespoons
Butter, ⅓ cup, melted

Put chickens on broiler rack, skin side down. Combine molasses, seasonings, vinegar and butter to make sauce and brush chicken with it. Broil 30 minutes, 4 inches from heat, basting with more sauce. Turn chicken, baste with sauce and broil 5 minutes, baste with remaining sauce and broil 5 more minutes, or until done.

To serve 4

TIMETABLE FOR ROASTING STUFFED CHICKEN

Ready-to-cook Weight Before Stuffing	Approximate Time in 325° Oven
2½–3½ pounds	2–3 hours
3½–4¾ pounds	3–3½ hours
4¾–6 pounds	3½–4 hours

If chicken is not stuffed it will require a little less cooking time.

BARBECUED CHICKEN CHINESE STYLE

Soy Sauce, 4 tablesps.
Salad Oil, 4 tablesps.
Dry Mustard, 1 teaspoon
Ginger, ½ teaspoon
Pepper, ¼ teaspoon
Garlic, 1 clove, minced

To serve 4

Follow the above procedure for Barbecued Chicken, but make the basting sauce of the ingredients listed.

HERB-BROILED CHICKEN

Lemon, 3 tablespoons
Butter, 3 tablespoons
Basil, ¼ teaspoon
Thyme, ¼ teaspoon
Salt and **Pepper**
Broiling Chickens, 2, halved

To serve 4

Combine lemon, butter, herbs, salt and pepper in saucepan and heat to the boiling point. Brush chicken halves arranged on broiler rack. Broil as in Barbecued Chicken.

FRIED CHICKEN

Select a young, tender chicken for frying and have it cut in halves, quarters, or smaller pieces if preferred. Put pieces in paper bag with ¼ cup of flour, 1 teaspoon salt, and a little pepper, and shake the bag until pieces are coated. Heat enough fat in a heavy skillet to cover the bottom (butter, oil or lard as preferred, or a combination). Brown the chicken parts evenly on all sides. Cover skillet, reduce heat and let cook slowly 20 to 30 minutes, or until fork tender.

If a crisp crust is desired, leave the skillet uncovered for the last 10 minutes of cooking.

Serve with gravy, if desired. Pour off all but 2 tablespoons fat and blend 2 tablespoons of flour with it in the skillet; gradually add 2 cups of milk or light cream. Cook slowly, stirring constantly until thickened. Add salt and pepper to taste.

MENUS

Menus for chicken dinners all the year round.

BROILED CHICKEN

Broiled Tomato Halves · Creamed Celery
Whole Cranberry Sauce
Orange Sponge Cake

BARBECUED CHICKEN

Corn on the Cob
Hot Garlic Bread
Fresh Fruit and Camembert Cheese

BARBECUED CHICKEN CHINESE STYLE

Panned Greens
Carrot and Green Pepper Salad
Fresh Pineapple · Almond Cookies

FRIED CHICKEN

Scalloped Potatoes with Cucumbers
Chilled Herb Tomatoes
Corn Bread · Butter
Rhubarb Pie

Broiled chicken

BREADED FRIED CHICKEN

Frying Chickens, 2
quartered
Egg, 1, beaten
Salt, 1 teaspoon
Pepper, ¼ teaspoon
Dry Bread Crumbs

Dip chicken pieces in mixture of egg and seasonings, then dip in breadcrumbs. Let set 15 minutes.

Cooking Oil, ¼ cup

Heat oil in heavy skillet, lightly brown pieces of chicken. Lower heat and cover pan. Cook ½ hour, shaking pan occasionally so chicken will not scorch.

To serve 4

SMOTHERED FRIED CHICKEN

Frying Chickens, 2, cut in
quarters
Salt, 1 teaspoon
Pepper, ¼ teaspoon
Flour, 3 tablespoons
Fat, 3 tablespoons
Dry White Wine, ½ cup
Water, ½ cup

Shake chicken in paper bag with flour, salt and pepper. Brown on all sides in hot fat in large skillet. Add wine and water. Cover and simmer 30 minutes, or until chicken is tender.

To serve 4

POULTRY GLAZE

Chicken Bouillon, 1 cup
Cornstarch, 2 tablesps.

Mix cold bouillon and cornstarch together. Boil, stirring until clear and thickened. Cool off a little and spoon over bird.

To serve 4

BATTER FRIED CHICKEN

Flour, 1 cup
Baking Powder, 2 teasps.
Salt, 1 teaspoon
Egg, 1
Milk, ¾ cup
Frying Chickens, 2 cut up

Sift dry ingredients together, add egg and milk, and stir to blend. Dip each piece of chicken in batter. Fry a few pieces at a time in deep hot fat (375° on your frying thermometer), and fry until golden brown. Keep finished pieces in warm oven while you do the rest.

To serve 4

CHICKEN LIVERS IN WINE

Chicken Livers, 1 pound
Flour
Butter, 3 tablespoons
Sauterne, ½ cup
Water, ½ cup
Parsley

Dredge livers with flour; cook in butter over low heat until lightly browned and done. Season with salt and pepper. Add wine and water, and simmer until thickened, stirring constantly. Put in serving dish and sprinkle with finely chopped parsley.

To serve 4

CHICKEN KIEV

Chicken breasts, 4
Butter, 1 stick

Cut breasts in half, remove bones. Pound flat into thin cutlets. Butter should be chilled hard. Cut in 8 pieces. Put one piece in center of each piece of chicken. Roll chicken around butter and skewer or tie firmly so butter cannot escape in cooking.

Eggs, 2
Cold Water, 2 tablesps.
Fine Dry Bread Crumbs
Fat for Deep Fat Frying

Dip chicken in egg, beaten with cold water, then in crumbs. Fry few pieces at a time in deep fat 3 to 5 minutes. Drain and put on paper towel. Keep finished chicken warm in oven while cooking remaining pieces.

To serve 4

GLAZED BREAST OF CHICKEN

Chicken Breasts, 4, split
in half
Butter, 4 tablespoons
Salt, 1 teaspoon
Pepper, ¼ teaspoon
Poultry Glaze (see
opposite column)

Oven, hot, 400°

Prepare chicken early in day. Sauté pieces in butter until brown on all sides; season. Place pieces in wide baking dish, pour glaze over them and chill until dinner time. Then cover dish with foil or lid for baking.

Bake 30 minutes or until thoroughly heated.

To serve 4

MENUS

BATTER FRIED CHICKEN

Creole Eggplant
Ripe Olives and Carrot Sticks
Raspberry Bavarian

CHICKEN LIVERS IN WINE

Fried Eggplant · Baby Lima Beans
Crisp Radishes and Celery
Hot Biscuits · Whipped Butter
Strawberry Glacé

GLAZED BREAST OF CHICKEN

Baked Tomatoes Stuffed with Rice
Bowl of Watercress · Cranberry and Orange Relish
Coffee Sherbet

CHICKEN KIEV

Baked Potato on Half Shell
Caesar Salad
Chocolate Rum Parfait

Fried chicken with corn

Chicken gumbo, a one-dish meal (see page 66)

CHICKEN IN THE POT

Chicken can be very successfully "roasted" on top of the stove. This is a favorite method used by French cooks, called poulet en cocotte. Following is a basic recipe for this method with five interesting variations.

CHICKEN IN THE POT
(Poulet en Cocotte)

Frying or **Small Roasting Chickens**, 2
Butter, 3 tablespoons
Salt, 1 teaspoon
Pepper, ⅛ teaspoon

To serve 4

Truss chicken; sprinkle with salt and pepper. Melt butter in heavy kettle on top of stove and cook chicken in it, turning from time to time until it is a light golden color all over. Cover pot and continue cooking slowly on top of stove until tender, 40 minutes or longer, depending on size of bird.

CHICKEN COUNTRY STYLE

Roasting Chicken
Butter, 3 tablespoons
Salt, 1 teaspoon
Pepper, ⅛ teaspoon

Salt Pork, or **Bacon**, 4-oz.
Onions, 8–12 small
Carrots, 4
New Potatoes, 16–20 small
Parsley
Salt and **Pepper**

To serve 4

Cook chicken in heavy kettle, as described in Chicken in the Pot, for 30 minutes.

Meanwhile, cut pork into cubes and render in frying pan. Add onions, carrots, potatoes, salt and pepper, and parsley, and cook until lightly browned. Add to chicken; continue cooking until all are tender.

CHICKEN SUPREME

Roasting Chicken
Butter, 3 tablespoons
Chicken Livers, ½ lb.
Pepper, ⅛ teaspoon
Brandy, 1 jigger

Egg Noodles, 8-ounce, medium
Cream, 3 tablespoons

To serve 4

Cook chicken as in Chicken in the Pot. When chicken is half finished add chicken livers. Sprinkle pepper on livers and add the brandy. Cover and cook slowly until livers are just done —about 6 minutes. Remove livers from pot.

Cook noodles according to directions on package. Break up livers with fork; mix with cream in hot noodles. Arrange in bottom of serving dish. Carve chicken and arrange pieces on top of noodles. Pour juices over all and serve immediately.

APPLEJACK CHICKEN

Broiler, cut in serving pieces
Butter, 3 tablespoons
Salt, 1 teaspoon

Applejack, ¼ cup
Apples, 1 pound, peeled, cored and sliced
Pepper, ¼ teaspoon

To serve 4

In heavy kettle on top of stove, cook chicken pieces, turning them until lightly browned all over.

Pour applejack over chicken and add apples; sprinkle with pepper. Cook slowly over low heat for 30 minutes, or until chicken and apples are tender.

CHICKEN IN CREAM

Roasting Chicken
Butter, 3 tablespoons
Salt, 1 teaspoon
Pepper, ⅛ teaspoon
Mushrooms, ¼ pound, sliced
Madeira Wine, ½ cup

Brandy, 1 jigger
Cream, Heavy, 1 cup

To serve 4 to 6

Cook chicken as in Chicken in the Pot, with peeled, sliced mushrooms. Add wine. When tender, remove chicken to platter and carve.

Add brandy to kettle and stir and scrape over low heat. Add cream, stirring constantly until very hot but not boiling. Pour hot sauce over chicken and serve at once.

RIVIERA CHICKEN

Chickens, 2, 2½ pounds
Butter, 3 tablespoons
Salt, 1 teaspoon
Pepper, ⅛ teaspoon

New Potatoes, 16–24, small
Butter, 3 tablespoons
Tomato Paste, 2 tablesps.
Black Olives, 25–35, pitted

Madeira or **Brown Sherry**, 1 wine-glass

To serve 4

Cook chickens whole or in halves on top of stove as described in Chicken in the Pot, for 40 minutes

Toss scraped potatoes in frying pan with melted butter until light golden brown. Add to chicken with tomato paste and olives; cover and cook 30 minutes longer, or until potatoes and chicken are done. Place chicken on hot dish with potatoes around them.

Add Madeira to sauce in pan and pour over chicken.

ITALIAN CHICKEN AND EGGPLANT

Frying Chicken, 1, cut up
Salt, 1 teaspoon
Pepper, ⅛ teaspoon
Butter, 2 tablespoons

Brown chicken in butter in heavy skillet; season. Cover and cook 30 minutes, or until tender. Remove chicken to baking dish.

Eggplant, 1, medium
Salt, 1 teaspoon
Flour

Meanwhile, cut eggplant into 1-inch cubes. Dredge with flour and salt and cook.in skillet until lightly browned and tender, adding more butter if necessary. Remove from skillet.

Onion, 1 medium, sliced
Garlic, 1 clove, minced
Flour, 2 tablespoons
Chicken Bouillon, 1 cup
Dry Red Wine, ½ cup
Olives, Stuffed, ¼ cup, sliced

Add onion and garlic to fat in skillet and cook 5 minutes, or until golden. Blend in flour, add chicken bouillon and wine. Bring to boil and cook until thickened, stirring constantly. Pour over chicken. Add eggplant and olives to chicken.

Oven, hot, 400°

Bake 20 minutes or until heated through.

To serve 4

RED HOT CHICKEN

Roasting Chicken, large, quartered
Butter, 3 tablespoons
Salt and **Pepper**
Fresh Mushrooms, ¼-lb.
Green Pepper, 1 large
Tomatoes, 3–4
Onion, 1 medium
Parsley, 3 tablespoons, chopped
Vinegar, ½ teaspoon
Cream, 2 tablespoons
Pepper, red, enough to be biting

Brown chicken in butter in heavy kettle over low heat. Add vegetables, chopped fine, and seasonings. Cook slowly, so nothing will stick to pan, uncovered, for 5 minutes, stirring from time to time. Cover and cook for 1 hour, stirring from time to time or until chicken is tender and vegetables have disintegrated. Remove chicken, add cream, stirring until mixture is smooth, then add red pepper. Pour over chicken.

To serve 4

CHICKEN CREOLE

Frying Chickens, 2 cup up
Flour in Shaker
Salad Oil, ¼ cup
Garlic, 1 clove, chopped
Bay Leaf, 1
Green Pepper, ½, chopped
Tomatoes, 16-ounce can
Thyme, ½ teaspoon
Salt and **Pepper**
White Wine, ½ cup

Dredge chicken with flour and brown in oil in heavy skillet. Add remaining ingredients; cover; simmer 1 hour or until tender. Add a little water if sauce cooks too dry.

To serve 4

MENUS

CHICKEN IN THE POT

French Fried Eggplant Sticks
Creamed Spinach
Blackberry Cobbler

CHICKEN COUNTRY STYLE

Pennsylvania Pepper Cabbage
Strawberry Shortcake

APPLEJACK CHICKEN

Boiled New Potatoes in Jackets
Panned Brussels Sprouts
Celery Hearts
Angelfood Cake with Chocolate Sauce

CHICKEN SUPREME

Carrot and Green Pepper Salad
Hard Rolls · Butter
Lemon Meringue Pie

CHICKEN IN CREAM

Golden Brown New Potatoes
Cucumber Salad
Rolls with Herb Butter
Currant-Blackberry Flummery

RIVIERA CHICKEN

Spring Salad
French Bread · Butter
Sliced Peaches with Cream

ITALIAN CHICKEN AND EGGPLANT

Hot Buttered Spaghetti with Parmesan Cheese
Bread Sticks
Stewed Green Gage Plums

RED HOT CHICKEN

Baked Potatoes · Tossed Green Salad
Corn Bread · Butter
Coconut Orange Cream

CHICKEN CREOLE

Boiled Rice · Corn on Cob
Crusty French Bread
Chess Pies

HAITIAN CHICKEN

Roasting Chicken, 4 lbs.
Butter, 2 tablespoons
Salt, 1 teaspoon
Pepper, ¼ teaspoon
Chicken Broth, 1½ cups
Celery, ½ cup, sliced
Green Peppers, ½ cup, sliced
Onion, 1 med., chopped
Garlic, 1 clove, chopped
Vinegar, 1 tablespoon
Allspice, ¼ teaspoon

Brown chicken in heavy kettle, as in Chicken in the Pot. Add remaining ingredients to chicken and simmer 1 hour or until tender.

Green Olives, ½ cup, sliced
Flour, 2 tablespoons

Add olives and simmer 10 minutes longer. Remove chicken and add flour blended in a little cold water to sauce. Cook until slightly thickened, stirring all the while. Serve with chicken.

To serve 4

POT-ROASTED STUFFED CHICKEN

Roasting Chicken, 4 to 5 pounds

Stuff chicken with your favorite stuffing, see page 73.

Butter, ¼ cup
Water, 1 cup
Potatoes, 6 medium, peeled
Carrots, 6 young
Onions, small white, 6 peeled
Salt, 2 teaspoons
Pepper, ⅛ teaspoon

Melt butter in Dutch oven and brown chicken on all sides. Add water, cover and simmer on top of stove for 35 minutes. Add vegetables to pot and sprinkle vegetables and chicken with salt and pepper. Cover and continue cooking 30 minutes or until all are tender. Make gravy with pot juices. (See page 56.)

To serve 4 to 6

A stewing chicken could be used, if cooking time allows (about 2 hours) or if you have a pressure cooker. With a pressure cooker, process chicken according to the directions that came with cooker, then add vegetables and process again.

BRAISED SOUTHERN CHICKEN

Frying Chicken, 1, cut up
Salt, 1 teaspoon
Pepper, ⅛ teaspoon
Butter, 3 tablespoons
Marjoram, ¼ teaspoon

Brown chicken on all sides in skillet, add seasonings, lower heat, cover and cook slowly 45 minutes or until chicken is tender.

Potatoes, New, 12 small
Pecans, ¾ cup, shelled

Meanwhile, cook potatoes in jackets and skin them, if preferred. Add potatoes and pecans to chicken. Heat thoroughly, but do not boil.

To serve 4

BRAISED CHICKEN AND MUSHROOMS

Frying Chicken, 1 or 2 quartered
Butter, 3 tablespoons
Salt and Pepper
Onion, 1, sliced
Mushrooms, ¼ lb., sliced
Dry White Wine, ½ cup
Light Cream, 1 cup
Parsley, few sprigs, chopped

Brown chicken lightly in butter. Add onion and mushrooms and seasoning. Cook until onions are golden. Add wine, cover and simmer 40 minutes, or until tender. Add cream, heat but do not boil. Garnish with parsley.

To serve 4

ARROZ CON POLLO

Frying Chicken, 1 or 2 quartered
Olive Oil, 3 tablespoons
Salt
Garlic, 1 clove, minced
Onion, 1 large, sliced
Green Pepper, 1 medium, chopped
Tomatoes, 16-ounce can
Pepper, ¼ teaspoon
Saffron, 1 pinch
Cloves, ¼ teaspoon
Bay Leaf, 1
Sherry, ½ cup
Water, 1 cup
Rice, 1 cup, raw

Brown chicken on all sides in oil; add salt and garlic, onion and pepper; continue cooking few minutes until they are golden in color. Add tomatoes, seasonings, sherry and water to chicken and simmer 10 minutes. Add rice to chicken, cover and simmer 30 minutes or until chicken and rice are tender. Add a little water if necessary to complete cooking. Rice should be dry when served.

Peas, 1 cup, cooked
Pimiento, few slices

Add peas to finished dish. Garnish with pimiento.

To serve 4

BRAISED CHICKEN IN SHERRY

Scallions, 3, chopped
Butter, 3 tablespoons
Frying Chicken, 1 or 2 quartered
Flour, 2 tablespoons
Salt, 1 teaspoon
Pepper, ⅛ teaspoon
Sherry, dry, ½ cup
Water, ½ cup
Milk, ½ cup
Cream, ½ cup

Cook scallions in butter until soft. Dredge chicken in flour, sprinkle with seasonings. Brown lightly in butter. Add sherry and water, cover tightly and simmer 30 minutes or until tender. Remove to hot platter. Add milk and cream to skillet, scrape up drippings in pan, heat thoroughly but do not boil, and pour over chicken.

To serve 4

BRAISED CURRIED CHICKEN

Proceed as for Braised Chicken in Sherry above. Add 2 teaspoons curry powder with the sherry.

CHICKEN PAPRIKA

Onions, 3 medium
Butter, 4 tablespoons
Paprika, 1 tablespoon
Black Pepper, ⅛ teasp.
Sugar, ½ teaspoon

Chop onions and cook slowly in butter until golden. Add seasonings.

Frying Chicken, 1 or 2 quartered
Salt, 1 teaspoon
Flour, 3 tablespoons
Chicken Stock or **Bouillon,** 1 cup
Sour Cream, 1 cup

To serve 4

Shake chicken in paper bag with salt and flour. Brown on all sides in onion mixture. Add broth, cover and simmer 40 minutes, or until tender. Stir in sour cream, heat, but do not boil.

COMPANY CASSEROLE

Butter, 3 tablespoons
Onion, chopped, 1 cup
Garlic, 1 clove, minced
Frying Chickens, 2, cut up
Flour
Salt, 2 teaspoons
Pepper, ⅛ teaspoon
Chicken Stock or **Bouillon,** 1 cup

Melt butter in top-of-the-stove casserole; lightly cook onion and garlic until soft. Coat chicken with flour, salt and pepper and add to casserole. Brown on all sides. Pour stock over chicken, cover.

Oven, moderate, 325°
Potatoes, 6–8, medium
Frozen Peas, 1 package, cooked
Pimiento, few slices

To serve 6 to 8

Bake 40 minutes. Pare and quarter potatoes and add to casserole. Continue baking 20 minutes, or until potatoes are tender. Add peas to casserole. Garnish with slices of pimiento.

Arroz con pollo

CHICKEN NOODLE CASSEROLE

Frying Chicken, cut up
Salt, 2 teaspoons
Onions, 1, sliced
Garlic, ½ clove, minced
Carrot, 1, quartered
Celery Leaves, few

Simmer chicken with salt, onions, garlic, carrot and celery leaves in a little water until tender. Remove meat from bones, cut in pieces. Strain broth; when cool, skim off fat; reserve.

Celery, ¼ cup, sliced
Green Pepper, chopped, ¼ cup
Flour, 2 tablespoons

Sauté celery and pepper slowly in chicken fat until lightly browned. Stir in flour. Add broth slowly and enough water to make 2 cups. Cook until thickened; stirring constantly. Add chicken.

Noodles, 8-ounce package, cooked
Sharp Cheese, grated, 1 cup

Combine chicken and noodles in casserole. Sprinkle cheese on top.

Oven, moderate, 375°

Bake 40 minutes or until lightly browned.

To serve 4 to 6

CHICKEN AND SPAGHETTI

Frying Chicken, cut up
Garlic, 1 clove
Parmesan Cheese, grated
Olive Oil, 3 tablesps.
Chicken Broth, 1½ cups
Sherry, ⅓ cup
Salt, 1 teaspoon
Pepper, ⅛ teaspoon
Flour, 2 tablespoons

Rub chicken with cut garlic, sprinkle with cheese, cook lightly in oil, about 5 minutes. Add broth, sherry, salt and pepper, bring to boil, cover and simmer over low heat, 40 minutes or until tender. Mix flour in a little cold water and add to mixture, cooking until slightly thickened.

Spaghetti, 8-oz., cooked

Place spaghetti in a deep dish, pour chicken and sauce over top. Serve with Parmesan cheese on the side.

To serve 4

CHICKEN WITH OLIVE-AND-CAPER SAUCE

Frying Chicken, cut up
Flour, ¼ cup
Salt, 1 teaspoon
Pepper, ⅛ teaspoon
Butter, 3 tablespoons

Shake chicken pieces in paper bag with flour, salt and pepper. Cook, covered slowly in butter, 40 minutes.

Olives, Stuffed, ½ cup, sliced
Capers, 2 tablespoons
Caper Liquid, 1 tablesp.
Water, 2 tablespoons
Parsley, ¼ cup, chopped

Add remaining ingredients and heat thoroughly.

To serve 4

GINGERED CREAMED CHICKEN

Frying Chicken, 1 or 2 quartered
Flour, 3 tablespoons
Salt, 1 teaspoon
Pepper, ⅛ teaspoon
Ginger, 1 teaspoon
Butter, 3 tablespoons
Chicken Bouillon, ¾ cup

Shake chicken in paper bag with flour and seasonings. Brown in butter, add any remaining flour mixture. Add bouillon, bring to boil, cover and simmer 30 minutes, or until tender.

Cream, ½ cup

Add cream, heat but do not boil.

To serve 4

STEWED CHICKEN WITH DUMPLINGS

Fowl, 6 pounds, cut up
Water, 6 cups
Pickling Spice, 1 tablesp.
Salt, 2 teaspoons
Onions, 8 small white
Carrots, 4, sliced
Celery, 4 stalks, cut up

Put chicken in pot with seasonings and water. Bring to boil, cover and simmer over low heat for 1 hour. *Never boil.* Add onions and simmer 30 minutes longer. Add carrots and celery and cook until chicken and vegetables are tender.

Flour, ½ cup
Water, ½ cup
Dumpling Batter (see below)

Mix flour and water into paste and add to kettle. Stir until thickened. Drop spoonfuls of batter on chicken and cover tightly; simmer 15 minutes. Serve at once.

To serve 4

DUMPLINGS

Flour, 1 cup, sifted
Baking Powder, 1 teasp.
Salt, ¾ teaspoon
Mace or **Nutmeg,** ⅛ teaspoon
Onion, 1 teasp., minced
Egg Yolks, 2
Milk, ⅓ cup

Sift dry ingredients together. Add onion. Beat eggs with milk and blend into dry mixture. Drop spoonfuls of batter on chicken and cover tightly. Simmer 15 minutes without removing cover. Serve at once.

To serve 4

CHICKEN PIE

Stew chicken as described above, with vegetables added; thicken gravy. Pour into casserole and top with pastry (see page 180). With sharp knife, make slits in pastry. Bake in hot oven, 425°, until crust is golden brown.

BOK YOU GUY

Stewing Chicken, cut up
Water, 4 cups
Soy Sauce, 3 tablesps.

Simmer chicken in water with soy sauce about 2 hours or until tender. Place chicken on platter.

Cornstarch, 2 tablesps.

Thicken liquid with cornstarch, mixed with a little cold water. Pour over chicken.

To serve 4

CHICKEN POT PIE

Stewing Chicken,
  cut up
Onions, 2, cut up
Salt, 1 tablespoon
Pepper, ¼ teaspoon

Simmer chicken, onions and ·
seasonings in water to cover
about 2 hours or until tender.
Remove from kettle and pour
stock into a saucepan. Meanwhile make crust as follows:

Lard, ½ cup
Flour, 2 cups, sifted
Salt, 1 teaspoon
Water

Combine lard, flour and salt
until crumbly, cutting it
together with 2 knives or a
pastry blender. Add enough
very cold water to make a ball,
not enough to be sticky. Roll it
out very thick and cut into
easily handled pieces.

Arrange layer of chicken in
kettle, cover with layer of pastry,
sprinkle lightly with flour.
Repeat until chicken and pastry
are used up, finishing the top
with pastry. Heat stock to
boiling point and pour over
chicken and pastry. There
should be enough to cover the
top crust; if not, add boiling
water. Cover kettle tightly and
simmer 30 minutes without
lifting lid.

To serve 4 to 6

CHICKEN WITH BROCCOLI

Stewing Chicken,
  quartered
Water, 3 cups
Salt, 1 teaspoon
Frozen Broccoli, 2 pkgs.

Simmer chicken in water with
salt until tender. Remove meat
from bones in large pieces.
Cook broccoli until just done.
Drain well. Place broccoli in
casserole and cover with slices
of chicken.

Butter, 2 tablespoons
Flour, 2 tablespoons
Chicken Broth, 1 cup
Milk, 1 cup

Melt butter in skillet, stir in
flour. Add broth from cooking
chicken and milk to make 2 cups
in all. Stir while it cooks until
thickened.

Sherry, 2 tablespoons
Parmesan Cheese, ¼ cup

Add sherry. Pour over chicken
and broccoli. Sprinkle with
grated cheese.

Oven, Hot, 400°

Bake 10 minutes or until lightly
browned.

To serve 4

CHICKEN IN BÉCHAMEL SAUCE

Béchamel Sauce, 2 cups
  (page 90)
Stewed Chicken, 3 cups,
  cut up
Parsley, 2 tablespoons

In top of double boiler make
Béchamel Sauce. Add cut up
chicken. Mix lightly and heat
thoroughly. Serve on crisp
toast, and garnish with finely
chopped parsley.

To serve 4

Chicken with broccoli

CHICKEN GUMBO

Stewing Chicken,
  1, cut up
Water, 4 cups

Simmer chicken in large kettle about 2 hours or until tender.

Okra, 6 pods
Tomatoes, 3 medium
Celery, 4 stalks
Green Pepper, 2 medium
Onion, 2 medium
Parsley, 2 tablespoons
Salt, 2 teaspoons
Pepper, 1/8 teaspoon
Thyme, 1/2 teaspoon
Marjoram, 1/2 teaspoon
Rice, 1 cup, raw

To serve 4

Remove chicken, separate meat from bones and return meat to kettle. Chop vegetables in small pieces and add to chicken with seasonings. Simmer until vegetables are tender. Cook rice separately and serve with Gumbo poured over it in soup plates.

BRUNSWICK STEW

Stewing Chicken,
  4 pounds, cut up
Water, 4 cups
Salt, 2 teaspoons
Pepper, 1/4 teaspoon
Potato, 1 large, diced
Okra, frozen, 1 package
Whole-kernel Corn,
  frozen, 1 package
Lima Beans, frozen,
  1 package
Onions, 2 medium,
  quartered
Tomatoes, 28-ounce can
Sugar, 2 teaspoons

To serve 4 to 6

Place chicken, water, salt and pepper in large kettle, cover; bring to boil and simmer over low heat about 2 hours or until meat falls off bones. Discard bones. Cut chicken in small pieces and return to stock. Add remaining ingredients, bring to boil, simmer 30 minutes. Taste for additional salt and pepper.

CHICKEN LIVERS WITH CARROTS AND PEAS

Frozen Peas and **Carrots,**
  1 package, cooked
Chicken Livers, 1 pound
Flour in Shaker
Butter, 1/2 cup

Put drained peas and carrots in shallow casserole. Reserve liquid. Dredge chicken livers with a little flour, brown lightly in butter on all sides in skillet. Remove and arrange over vegetables.

Flour, 2 tablespoons
Chicken Bouillon Cube, 1
Vegetable liquid
Cream, 1/2 cup
Salt and **Pepper,** to taste

Blend flour with butter in skillet, add chicken bouillon cube, dissolved in water vegetables were cooked in, and cream. Cook until slightly thickened, stirring constantly. Pour over livers. Season to taste.

Oven, moderate, 350°

To serve 4

Bake 15 minutes.

CHICKEN TETRAZZINI

Stewing Chicken, cut up
Salt, 1 teaspoon
Garlic, 1 clove
Bay Leaf, 1
Water, 4 cups

Simmer chicken in water adding salt, garlic and bay leaf, about 2 hours or until tender. Remove meat from bones and cut in pieces. Strain and reserve stock.

Mushrooms, 1/2 pound,
  fresh, sliced
Onion, 1 cup, chopped
Celery, 1/4 cup, chopped
Butter or **Chicken Fat,**
  2 tablespoons
Flour, 2 tablespoons

Cook mushrooms, onion and celery in fat until lightly browned. Blend in flour, add stock, and cook until slightly thickened, stirring constantly. Add salt and pepper to taste.

Spaghetti, 8-ounce
  package, cooked
Parsley, 1/4 cup, chopped
Cheese, freshly grated
  Parmesan, 1/2 cup

Combine chicken, mushroom mixture, spaghetti and parsley in baking dish. Sprinkle with cheese.

Oven, moderate, 350°

To serve 4 to 6

Bake 30 minutes.

See the recipes in the section Leftovers, page 92, for the many ways to use cooked chicken.

BAKED CHICKEN WITH HERBS

Frying Chicken
Butter, 3 tablespoons
Flour, 3 tablespoons
Milk, 2 1/2 cups
Salt, 1 teaspoon
Pepper, 1/4 teaspoon
Thyme, 1/2 teaspoon
Rosemary, 1/2 teaspoon
Chives, chopped,
  1 tablespoon
Parsley, chopped,
  1 tablespoon

Brown chicken in butter in skillet. Place it in casserole. Add flour to skillet, stirring in thoroughly over low heat. Add milk and other ingredients and cook until slightly thickened, stirring constantly. Pour over chicken.

Oven, moderate, 325°

To serve 4

Bake, covered, 40 minutes or until tender.

CHICKEN IN LEMON BUTTER

Butter, 4 tablespoons
Lemon, 2 tablespoons
Water, 2 tablespoons
Salt, 1 teaspoon
Pepper, 1/8 teaspoon
Instant Garlic, 1/4 teasp.
Capers, 1 tablespoon
Broiler, 1, cut up

Combine all ingredients in skillet, bring to boil, turn heat low and simmer, tightly covered, 30 minutes or until tender.

To serve 4

CHICKEN FRICASSEE DE LUXE

Stewing Chicken,
  cut in pieces
Flour, 3 tablespoons
Salt, 1 teaspoon
Pepper, 1/8 teaspoon
Butter or **Chicken Fat,**
  3 tablespoons
Onion, 1 medium
Water, 2 cups
Celery, 2 stalks with
  leaves
Parsley, 2 sprigs
Thyme, 1/2 teaspoon
Egg Yolk, 1
Cream, 1/2 cup

To serve 4 to 6

Put chicken pieces, flour, salt and pepper in paper bag. Shake until chicken is well coated. Melt fat in heavy skillet, add onion and cook until soft. Add chicken and brown lightly on all sides. Add water and seasonings and bring to boil. Turn down heat and simmer gently until chicken is tender, 2 hours or longer, depending on the bird. Remove chicken to platter. Mix cream and egg yolk and add to liquid in kettle. Cook until slightly thickened, adding milk if greater quantity of gravy is desired. Pour over chicken.

If a pressure cooker is used, brown chicken first in cooker, then add water and seasonings and pressure cook according to directions with cooker. Remove chicken and make gravy in cooker, as described above.

ROAST DUCKLING

Prepare duck for cooking as directed for Poultry on page 55.

Stuff duck, if desired, with your favorite stuffing (see page 72). Place duck, breast side down, on rack well above bottom of roasting pan so that it will not rest in the fat drippings. Roast at 325°, allowing 20 to 25 minutes per pound for medium to well done. An oven thermometer should register 165° for medium, 185° for very well done. Pour off fat if too much accumulates.

Make gravy according to directions on page 56.

ROAST DUCK WITH ORANGE

Roast duck as in directions above without stuffing, until brown and crisp. Or the duck may be split in two, and placed skin up on the rack. Serve with the following sauce:

Orange Sauce

Orange Peel, 1 orange
Water, 1 cup

Cook peel in boiling water 3 minutes. Remove peel, discard white membrane and cut peel in thin strips. Return to water.

Duck Drippings,
  3 tablespoons
Flour, 3 tablespoons
Orange Juice, 1 cup
Mandarin Oranges, 1 can
Currant Jelly, 2 tablesps.

Pour off all fat in roasting pan except 3 tablespoons. Blend in flour and add water and peel slowly, stirring over low heat. Add orange juice and mandarin oranges with juice. Add jelly and continue cooking, stirring all the while, until jelly is melted and sauce thickened.

ROAST DUCK WITH TANGERINES

The above recipe may be varied by substituting 1 can of frozen tangerine juice for the orange juice, and 2 tangerines, separated into sections, for the canned mandarin oranges.

SPICED DUCK

Cinnamon
Clove
Nutmeg
Ginger
Duck, cut in quarters
Salt and **Pepper,** to taste

Combine an equal quantity of each spice in a salt shaker. Brush each piece of duck, each side, with butter; sprinkle with spices and salt and pepper. Place on rack in roasting pan, skin side up.

Oven, moderate, 350°
To serve 4

Roast 45 minutes, or until done. Serve with Orange Sauce, above.

TOP-OF-THE-STOVE ROAST DUCK

Duck, 4 to 5 pounds
Onion, 1 med., chopped
Salt, 1 teaspoon
Pepper, 1/4 teaspoon
Instant Garlic, 1/4 teasp.

To serve 4

In heavy kettle, brown duck slowly on all sides. Pour off fat. Put rack under duck and add onion and seasonings. Simmer tightly covered 1 1/2 hours, or until tender. Make gravy according to directions on page 56.

HAWAIIAN DUCKLING

Duck, cut in serving
  pieces
Soya Sauce, 1/4 cup
Ground Ginger, 1/2 teasp.
Garlic, 1 clove, minced
Cooking Oil, 2 tablesps.
Mushrooms, 4-oz. can
Pineapple Chunks,
  8-ounce can

Brush duck with soya sauce and ginger. Sauté in skillet with garlic until golden. Arrange duck in casserole. Add drained mushrooms, canned pineapple and juice to skillet and heat; stirring up any browned juices. Pour over duck.

Oven, moderate, 350°
To serve 4

Bake 1 hour or until tender.

MARINATED DUCK

Duck, quartered
Red Wine, 1 cup
Onion, 1/2 cup, minced
Rosemary, 1 teaspoon
Basil, 1 teaspoon
Anchovies, 2 chopped
Pepper, 1/8 teaspoon

Put duck in deep bowl. Mix all ingredients into a marinade, pour over duck and marinate several hours, basting frequently. Drain duck; save marinade.

Butter, 3 tablespoons

To serve 4

Brown duck in Dutch oven until golden brown. Add marinade and simmer until tender.

See the section on Leftovers for ways to use leftover duck.

BRAISED DUCK WITH MUSHROOMS
AND SHERRY

Follow directions for Top-of-the-Stove Roast Duck. Fifteen minutes before duck is finished, add ½ pound of fresh mushrooms sliced in half, and ¼ cup dry sherry.

ROAST TURKEY

Prepare turkey for roasting according to the directions for roasting Poultry, page 55.

Place turkey on rack in shallow roasting pan and brush with butter. Wrap the ends of the legs with pieces of foil so that they do not get done before the rest of the bird, and dry out. Place a square of foil loosely over the breast, so that the breast will not get brown before the bird is done. Or cover with a piece of cheesecloth dipped in melted butter.

Roast in a 325° oven (see timetable page 69). If you have a meat thermometer, insert it in the thigh muscle next to the body. Roast to 190°. When done, drumstick will move up and down easily. Forty-five minutes before bird is done, remove foil from breast, brush with melted butter, and finish roasting, then breast will be nicely browned. Remove to platter and let stand ½ hour before serving. Meanwhile make gravy (page 56).

FOIL-ROASTED TURKEY

Another way to cook a turkey, particularly if time is too short for slow roasting, is to wrap it in foil. This will give the bird a different flavor from dry-heat roasting, as foil roasting is the equivalent of a pot roast; the bird cooks in moisture and steam. Place the unstuffed bird in the center of a large square sheet of foil, or in 2 sheets joined together with a tight double fold. Bring sides of foil up over breast and fold tightly on top. Bring ends up and make tight fold. Place in roasting pan and roast in hot oven, 450°, for about 15 minutes per pound. About 20 minutes before roasting time is up, open foil to let bird brown, and let juices run into the pan for gravy.

TURKEY GIBLET GRAVY

Simmer giblets and neck in salted water to cover, with an onion and some celery leaves, for 2 hours or until very tender. Remove from stock, discard neck bones, chop meat fine, and return to stock.

When turkey is done, remove from pan and pour off all but 3 tablespoons of the fat. Add 3 tablespoons of flour and blend well, over very low heat. Add the giblets and stock and cook, stirring constantly, until gravy thickens. Scrape up all the browned bits in the roasting pan to flavor and color the gravy. If the gravy is not rich enough in color, add a little bottled brown coloring. Add salt and pepper to taste.

Roast duck can be served with apricots or apple sauce

TIMETABLE FOR ROASTING STUFFED TURKEY

Ready-to-cook Weight Before Stuffing	*Approximate Time in 325° Oven*
4–6 pounds	2½–3 hours
6–8 pounds	3½–4 hours
8–10 pounds	4–4½ hours
10–12 pounds	4½–5 hours
12–16 pounds	5–6 hours
16–20 pounds	6–7 hours
20–24 pounds	7–8 hours

Remember that these times are only approximate. The age and variety of the turkey will cause a variation in cooking time. Your safest guide is your thermometer.

OVEN-FRIED TURKEY

Shake young (up to 4 pounds) cut-up turkey in bag with 4 tablespoons flour, 1 teaspoon salt and ¼ teaspoon pepper. Brown in heavy skillet in fat ½-inch deep. Place turkey pieces one layer deep in shallow pan. Cook in moderate oven (350°) until turkey is tender, about 40 to 60 minutes. Baste several times during cooking with butter mixed with an equal quantity of hot broth. Turn turkey once during cooking.

OVEN-FRIED CHICKEN: The above method may also be used for cooking chicken, cutting the oven time to about 30 minutes.

BROILED TURKEY

Broil a young turkey, up to 4 pounds in weight. Have it split in half lengthwise. Fold wing tips under wings and skewer legs firmly to body. Brush with melted fat and sprinkle with salt and pepper. Place in broiler pan, skin side down, Broil slowly 5 to 7 inches from heat. Brush with fat several times during cooking and turn to brown each side evenly. Total cooking time about 50 to 60 minutes. Test for doneness with point of knife in thigh. When done it cuts easily and no pink color is visible. Serve on hot platter.

Turkey may be rubbed with lemon and thoroughly coated with the juice before broiling, if desired.

See the recipes in the section Leftovers, page 92, for the many ways to use cooked turkey.

Roast turkey garnished with spiced crabapples and water cress

STUFFED CORNISH HENS

Rock Cornish Hens,
  4, frozen
Butter, 1/4 cup
Salt and **Pepper**

Thaw hens, remove giblets, stuff as desired (see page 73). Put in roasting pan, brush with melted butter, sprinkle with salt and pepper. Baste with butter once or twice while roasting.

Oven, moderate, 350°
To serve 4

Roast 1 hour or until tender. Glaze if desired. (See page 58.)

GINGERED GAME HENS AND PILAU

Rock Cornish Hens,
  4, frozen
Butter, 2 tablespoons
Garlic, 1 clove, minced
Onion, 1 med., chopped
Ginger, 1/2 teaspoon
Fennel Seeds, 1/2 teasp.
Cardamon Seeds,
  1/4 teaspoon
Water, 2 cups

Thaw hens for 1 hour. Remove giblets. In heavy kettle sauté in butter until browned on all sides. Add garlic, onion, ginger, fennel seeds, cardamon seeds and water. Cover kettle and simmer 20 minutes. Remove birds.

Rice, 1 cup, raw
Seedless Raisins, 1 cup
Saffron, 1/8 teaspoon

Mix rice, raisins and saffron with liquid in kettle. Place birds on top and bring to boil. Cover kettle, simmer over low heat about 20 minutes, or until rice is tender. Remove birds; serve rice in center of hot platter with birds arranged around rice.

To serve 4

ROAST GOOSE

Roast goose according to directions for Roast Duck on page 67. Roast at oven temperature of 325°, allowing 20-30 minutes per pound. After roasting 1 hour, prick skin to permit melted fat to escape. Pour fat out of roasting pan if too much accumulates.

SALMIS OF GOOSE

Goose, cooked, cubed,
  4 cups
Lemon Juice, 2
  tablespoons
Worcestershire Sauce,
  1 tablespoon.
Goose Gravy, 2 cups
Ripe Olives, 12, sliced
Sherry, 1/4 cup

Add goose, lemon juice and Worcestershire Sauce to gravy and simmer over low heat about 20 minutes. Add olives and sherry and heat thoroughly. Serve at once on toast.

To serve 4 or 5

ROAST GUINEA HEN

Prepare guinea hen for roasting as in directions for Poultry. Stuff with highly-seasoned stuffing, if desired, or simply fill cavity with sliced onion. Truss and place on rack in roasting pan. Place strips of salt pork over bird. Roast at 325° about 30 minutes per pound, or until tender. Serve with giblet gravy. (See page 68.)

MENUS

For holidays or special occasions

Tomato Bouillon
Roast Turkey (page 68)
Oyster Stuffing · Giblet Gravy
Twice Baked Sweet Potatoes · Creamed Onions
Cranberry Jelly · Ripe and Green Olives
Hard Rolls · Butter
Mince Pie
Fruit · Nuts

Green Turtle Soup with Sherry (canned)
Roast Goose with Chestnut Stuffing
Brown Rice · Flemish Red Cabbage
Whole Cranberry Sauce · Celery
Hard Rolls · Butter
Plum Pudding with Lemon Sauce

Stuffed Cornish Hens
Baked Squash · Panned Brussels Sprouts
Cranberry-Orange Relish
Chocolate Bavarian

Gingered Game Hens and Pilau
Succotash
Tossed Green Salad with Tomato Wedges
Corn Sticks · Butter
Ambrosia

Roast Duck with Orange (page 67)
Mashed Sweet Potatoes · Panned Garden Greens
Celery and Radishes
Hard Rolls · Butter
Watermelon Sherbet

Spiced Duck (page 67)
Saffron Rice · Stewed Tomatoes and Corn
Cucumber Salad
Lemon Torte

GAME COOKERY

The success of game cookery is dependent first of all on the care the game has had after killing. Excessive gamey flavor develops when the carcass is not immediately bled, drawn and cooled.

Young, tender animals and birds can be cooked with dry heat, that is, by roasting or broiling, just as you would cook the tenderest cuts of meat or young poultry. Older, tougher game should be cooked by braising, pot roasting or stewing.

The unusual flavor of the game is due to the special diet of the animal or bird, and this flavor is concentrated in the fatty portions. Trimming off all possible fat will eliminate much of the gaminess. Necessary fat for cooking can then be added in the form of bacon, salt pork, or beef suet.

The following recipes can always be used for the "wild" game that is grown on game farms and sold in the markets. These birds and animals will be plumper and more tender than those shot in the field. Leftover meat can be used according to any of the recipes in the section on Leftovers. Curried dishes are particularly appropriate.

VENISON

The proper handling of game in the field is particularly important with venison. A carcass that has been correctly prepared will keep a long time; it can be skinned and quartered and allowed to dry naturally. At 35° it can be aged from 2 to 4 weeks, permitting it to develop its full flavor and tenderness. Wiping it occasionally with a clean cloth wrung out in vinegar will protect it from mold.

If you have no facilities for hanging game, your butcher may be willing to do it for you, and it will then be hung under ideal conditions.

BROILED VENISON

Broil chops from loin or leg of young deer. Brush with salad oil and cook under broiler 10 minutes on each side, or longer, if you prefer them very well done.

Venison may be served with a Barbecue Sauce, see page 56.

POT-ROASTED VENISON

Use a cut from leg or shoulder and follow directions for Pot Roast of Beef on page 30.

ROAST VENISON

Roast a piece of the loin from a young deer. If very lean, cover with slices of salt pork. Roast in 325° oven until meat thermometer registers 175–180°. This will require about 35 minutes to the pound. Make gravy from drippings in pan according to directions on page 22 for Beef Gravy.

VENISON STEW

Follow any of the recipes for Beef Stew.

RABBIT OR SQUIRREL

Always wear rubber gloves when handling wild rabbit or squirrel. These animals are carriers of tularemia, which can infect humans.

Soft ears and paws indicate the youth of the rabbit. These animals may be roasted, fried, fricasseed, or stewed, depending on their age, according to any chicken recipe.

HASENPFEFFER

Red Wine, or Wine Vinegar, 2 cups **Sugar,** 1 tablespoon **Onion,** 1 medium, sliced **Bay Leaf,** 1 **Garlic,** 1 clove, minced **Salt,** 1 teaspoon **Pepper,** 1/8 teaspoon **Parsley,** 2 tablespoons, chopped	Combine wine with sugar and seasonings and marinate rabbit overnight.
Rabbit, cut up **Butter,** 3 tablespoons **Flour**	Remove rabbit, dry and dredge with flour. Brown in butter in skillet. Strain marinade and pour over rabbit. Bring to boil and simmer, covered, over low heat, for about 1½ hours, or until tender. Thicken the sauce with a little flour mixed with a little cold water.
To serve 4	

RABBIT CASSEROLE

Rabbit, 2–3 lbs., cut up **Flour,** 3 tablespoons **Pepper,** ⅛ teaspoon **Salt,** 1 teaspoon **Fat or Oil,** ¼ cup **Onions,** 2, sliced **Consommé,** 1 can	Shake rabbit in paper bag with flour, salt and pepper. Brown in heavy skillet, in fat or oil. Arrange pieces in casserole. Cook onion in skillet until golden and add to casserole. Add consommé and cover.
Oven, moderate, 350°	Bake 1½ hours, or until tender. If gravy needs thickening, pour it into skillet and add 1 tablespoon flour mixed with a little water. Cook until thickened and pour back over rabbit.
To serve 4	

GAME BIRDS

Birds should be drawn immediately after killing to reduce any excessive gamey flavor. A bird may be aged under refrigeration for several days, never at room temperature. Birds should be dry plucked, or wax plucked; never scalded. To wax pluck, first pull off all the large feathers that come easily. Then paint the remainder with melted (not hot) paraffin. Let it harden, then finish plucking. If you are plucking a great many birds, the wax on the feathers may be melted, strained and re-used.

BROILED QUAIL, GROUSE, PARTRIDGE

Split bird in half. Brush with butter and sprinkle with salt and pepper. Broil 5–10 minutes on each side, depending on size. Serve with a tart jelly.

ROAST QUAIL, GROUSE OR PARTRIDGE

Season cavity with salt and pepper and a pinch of thyme. Wrap birds with bacon or strips of salt pork. Roast at 400° for about 30 minutes.

BROILED WILD DUCK

Wild ducks from the salt marshes are often served very rare to minimize the fishy flavor. To broil a small, young duck, split in half, rub with bacon fat and sprinkle with salt and freshly ground pepper. Put skin side down on rack under preheated broiler for 5 or 6 minutes each side. The meat will be firm but the juices, red. For medium doneness, allow 10 to 12 minutes to a side.

ROAST WILD DUCK

Roast only young birds. Fill the body cavity of the duck with slices of apple, onion, and celery, and a pinch of thyme. Sew up bird. Rub skin with bacon fat and roast at 400° for about 30 minutes, or until done rare, with red juices. This is how duck is preferred usually, but if desired medium done, roast at 350° for 1 hour.

ROAST PHEASANT

Prepare bird for cooking as described in section on Poultry.

Sprinkle cavity of bird with salt and pepper and fill with stuffing, if desired. Truss bird, brush with butter, sprinkle with salt and pepper, and place on roasting pan rack with breast down. Turn when half done; baste frequently with melted butter. Roast at 325° for about 1½ hours, or until tender. Make gravy from giblets (page 68).

PHEASANT FRICASSEE

Follow recipe for Chicken Fricassee (page 67).

ROAST SQUAB

Sprinkle body cavity of squab with salt and stuff with Wild Rice or Bread Stuffing. Brush bird with melted butter and roast uncovered in slow oven, 325°, for about 45 minutes or until tender. Baste with more butter while cooking. Allow one squab per person.

BROILED SQUAB

Split squab down the back and place on broiler rack, skin side up. Brush with melted butter and season with salt and pepper. Broil 10 minutes and turn; broil other side until browned. Turn back again and broil until done, about 25 to 30 minutes altogether.

GAME FISH

To retain the delicate flavor of fish, it must be cleaned promptly and kept cooled in fresh, cold water while you are fishing. Left in a warm creel it will become mushy and tasteless.

To cook game fish, follow the directions in the section on Fish.

STUFFINGS

A light and delicate bread stuffing is all that many people require in the way of an embellishment for a roast bird, but sometimes a more elaborate stuffing, containing, perhaps, chestnuts or oysters, is a welcome variation, particularly for a gala holiday meal. Also there are special stuffings that we traditionally associate with special birds: wild rice with game, for example.

Do not pack the bird too full—the stuffing will expand during cooking. Rather put a separate batch in a baking dish, if you are feeding a crowd, and bake it in the oven for an hour while the bird cooks.

BREAD STUFFING

Onion, 1 med., minced
Celery, ¼ cup, chopped
Butter, 3 tablespoons
Soft Bread Crumbs,
    3 cups
Salt, 1 teaspoon
Pepper, ¼ teaspoon
Thyme, ½ teaspoon or
Poultry Seasoning, 1
    teaspoon
Parsley, 2 tablespoons,
    chopped

Sauté onion and celery gently in butter in skillet until golden; remove from heat. Add bread crumbs and seasonings, mixing lightly with a fork.

Enough for 1 roasting chicken

SAGE STUFFING

Add 1 tablespoon dried sage, crumbled, to above recipe and omit thyme.

PECAN STUFFING

Onion, 1 med., chopped
Celery, ½ cup, chopped
Butter, ¼ cup
Salt, 1 teaspoon
Pepper, ¼ teaspoon
Soft Bread Crumbs,
    3 cups
Parsley, ¼ cup, chopped
Pecans, 1 cup, chopped

In large skillet cook onion and celery in butter until soft. Remove from heat. Add remaining ingredients and mix lightly.

Enough for 1 roasting chicken

OYSTER STUFFING

Oysters, 1 quart
Soft Bread Crumbs,
    8 cups
Salt, 2 teaspoons
Pepper, ⅛ teaspoon
Worcestershire, 2 teasp.
Bacon, 2 slices, chopped

Drain oysters, reserving liquid; cut in small pieces and mix with bread crumbs. Add remaining ingredients and toss together lightly. Use liquid in making gravy or add to soup.

Enough for a 10-pound turkey

MUSHROOM STUFFING

To above Bread Stuffing, add ½ cup chopped mushrooms sautéed with onions and celery.

GROUND MEAT AND GIBLET STUFFING

Chicken Giblets

Simmer giblets in a little water until tender; chop in small pieces, reserve liquid for gravy.

Ground Beef, ½ pound
Ground Pork, ½ pound
Onion, 1 med., chopped
Celery, 1 stalk, chopped
Butter, 4 tablespoons
Bread, 6 slices, crumbled
Salt, 1 teaspoon
Parmesan Cheese,
    ½ cup, grated
Egg, 1, beaten
Parsley, ¼ cup, chopped
Basil or **Rosemary,**
    1 tablespoon

Cook meat, onion and celery in butter until lightly browned. Turn off heat. Add giblets and remaining ingredients; mix thoroughly.

Enough to stuff 1 large roasting chicken

CHESTNUT STUFFING

Chestnuts, 2 pounds
Soft Bread Crumbs, 1 cup
Salt, 1 teaspoon
Pepper, ⅛ teaspoon
Butter, ¼ cup, melted
Stock or Bouillon, ½ cup
Onion, 1 tablesp., minced

Cook shelled chestnuts (page 138); put through ricer. Add bread crumbs and mix lightly with chestnuts. Add remaining ingredients and mix.

Enough for 1 roasting chicken

CLAM STUFFING

Salt Pork, 2 ozs., diced
Butter, ¼ cup
Onions, 2 med., minced
Soft Bread Cubes, 4 cups
Clams, minced, 10½-oz.
    can, drained
Thyme, ¼ teaspoon
Marjoram, ¼ teaspoon
Celery Seed, ½ teaspoon
Salt and Pepper, to taste

Brown salt pork in skillet. Add butter and onions and cook until onions are golden. Remove from heat, add remaining ingredients and mix well.

To make about 5 cups stuffing for poultry or fish

WILD RICE STUFFING

Wild Rice, 1 cup, washed
Water, 4 cups
Giblets, chopped
Salt, 1 teaspoon

Combine rice and water in saucepan, bring to boil, turn heat low; add giblets and salt. Simmer about 30 minutes, or until rice is nearly done. Drain and reserve liquid for gravy.

Onion, 1 med., chopped
Celery, 3 stalks, chopped
Butter, 3 tablespoons
Pepper, ¼ teaspoon
Thyme, ¼ teaspoon

In a skillet melt butter and sauté onion and celery until soft. Remove from heat, add rice mixture. Add pepper and thyme. Stuff bird.

To make 3 to 4 cups of stuffing

SAUSAGE STUFFING

Pork Sausage Meat, 1 lb.
Onion, 1 med., chopped
Soft Bread Crumbs, 10 cups
Parsley, 2 tablespoons, chopped
Salt and Pepper, if needed

Shape sausage meat into thin patties; sauté with onion until lightly browned, and pour off all but 4 tablespoons of the fat. Break sausage up into bits; add remaining ingredients and mix well. If sausage is mild, add seasonings.

Enough for a 10–12-pound turkey

PARSLEY STUFFING

When you want to flavor a bird without using a bread-type stuffing, wash a large bunch of parsley and remove the tough stems, season the inside of the bird with salt and pepper and stuff it with the whole bunch of parsley to impart a delicious flavor.

To vary this you might use a bunch of parsley with a cup of chopped celery, or a bunch of parsley with a cup of chopped onion.

See other sections of the book for special stuffings: Ham Stuffing for eggplant on page 141, Clam Stuffing for eggplant on page 141, stuffings for tomatoes and peppers on pages 156 and 148, and fish stuffings on pages 73 and 74

POTATO STUFFING

Onion, 1 med., minced
Butter, ¼ cup
Boiled Potatoes, chopped, 3 cups
Thyme, ¼ teaspoon
Parsley, 1 teaspoon
Salt and Pepper, to taste

Sauté onion in butter until golden. Add remaining ingredients and mix well.

To make 3½ cups stuffing for fish or poultry

APPLE-ONION STUFFING

Onion, 2 med., chopped
Butter, ¼ cup
Apples, tart, diced, 2 cups
Soft Bread Crumbs, 4 cups
Celery Seed, 1 teaspoon
Marjoram, ½ teaspoon
Salt and Pepper, to taste
Cider or Apple Juice, ½ cup

Cook onions in butter until golden. Add remaining ingredients and mix well.

To make about 4 cups stuffing for duck or pork

APPLE-SALT PORK STUFFING

Salt Pork, ¼ pound, diced
Celery, chopped, 1 cup
Onion, chopped, 1 cup
Parsley, chopped, ¼ cup
Apples, diced, 4 cups
Sugar, ½ cup
Dry Bread Crumbs, 3 cups
Salt, 1 teaspoon
Pepper, ¼ teaspoon

Fry salt pork until crisp, add celery, onion and parsley; cook until vegetables are soft. Add apples, sprinkled with sugar. Cook few minutes covered, then remove from heat. Add bread crumbs, salt and pepper, and mix well.

To make about 6 cups stuffing for venison

SEAFOOD

Aside from being a valuable source of protein, in a form that is easily digested, seafood fits into the meals-ready-in-thirty minutes category. Most fish and shellfish dishes are easy to prepare and short in cooking time.

FRESH FISH

Be sure to buy fresh fish—the signs are: clear protruding eyes, not dull or sunken; firm flesh; scales with a bright sheen; and no unpleasant odor. A generous serving is about one-half to three-quarters pound per person.

The fish dealer will scale and clean a fish for you, but if you have caught your own, proceed as follows: beginning at the tail, run the back of a knife against the scales, toward the head. Cut around the fins, and pull them off with a quick tug toward the head.

If preferred, you may skin the fish by slitting the skin the length of the backbone, then around the head near the gills. Strip it down toward the tail on one side; turn over and repeat the process.

Cut a dash in the abdomen and remove the entrails and the blood clot near the backbone. If you do not wish to cook the fish with head and tail on, cut them off.

HOW TO COOK A FISH

The important rule in cooking fish is not to overcook it. Cook it only until it is tender; longer cooking destroys its delicate flavor. It is done when the thick part of the flesh is no longer translucent. It cooks with very low heat.

Frozen fish should be thawed and cooked immediately. If cooked frozen, allow a little extra time.

The versatile fish may be cooked by poaching, steaming, baking, broiling, pan-frying and deep-fat frying, as described in the following sections.

POACHED FISH

To poach a fish is to *simmer* it gently in a seasoned stock, called "court bouillon." Never, never boil it, as this destroys the flavor.

Court Bouillon

Put 2 cups of water in the bottom of a roomy kettle, or large skillet. Add to it, 1 teaspoon salt, 1 sliced onion, several sprigs of parsley and celery leaves, 1 bay leaf, a few peppercorns and 1 cup of dry white wine. Bring to boil, reduce heat and simmer 5 minutes.

Add fish, cover and simmer gently about 10 minutes, or until fish flakes with a fork. Do not overcook. If desired, the fish may be placed on a square of cheesecloth so that it may easily be removed from the water after cooking.

It may be served immediately with one of the sauces on pages 90–91 or cooled in the broth, then chilled and served with a mayonnaise dressing (page 163).

Try these poached fish and sauce combinations:

Haddock with Dill Sauce

Salmon Steaks with Herb Mayonnaise

Flounder with Ravigote Sauce

Sole with Shrimp Sauce

Sea Bass with Sweet and Pungent Sauce

See sauces on pages 90–91, 163.

FILLETS OF SOLE MARGUERY

Court Bouillon (see left column)
Shrimp, ½ pound
Sole, 4 fillets

Bring court bouillon to a boil, add shrimp and cook a few minutes until the shells turn pink. Remove shrimp and add sole to court bouillon; poach 5 minutes, or until fish is flaky. Remove fish to heat-proof platter and keep warm in oven. Shell and devein shrimp, and add to platter.

Butter, 3 tablespoons
Onion, 1, sliced
Mushrooms, ¼ lb., sliced
Flour, 2 tablespoons
Sauterne, ¼ cup
Cream, ½ cup
Egg Yolk, 1, beaten
Parsley, 2 tablespoons, chopped

Meanwhile, melt butter in skillet, sauté thinly sliced onion and mushrooms until golden. Blend in flour and add wine and 2 cups of the court bouillon, strained. Simmer 5 minutes; add cream. Add a little of the mixture to the beaten egg yolk, then stir it back into the sauce. Heat, stirring constantly, for 1 minute, and pour over sole and shrimp. Heat briefly under the broiler. Garnish with chopped parsley.

To serve 4

Sole is sometimes hard to find, but flounder will make an excellent substitute in this dish. The recipe could also be used for any filleted fish.

KEDGEREE

Cod, 1 pound
Rice, cooked, 2 cups
Eggs, 4, hard-boiled, chopped
Cream, 1 cup
Salt and **Pepper**, to taste
Curry Powder, ½ teasp.

Poach cod until tender, and flake it. Add to remaining ingredients and heat all together, briefly.

To serve 4

FINNAN HADDIE KEDGEREE: Substitute finnan haddie for cod in the above recipe. First cover the fish with cold water, bring to boil and simmer 25 minutes, or until fish is flaky. Drain, then separate into flakes.

COD AND FRIED POTATOES

Potatoes, 1 pound
Onions, ½ pound
Butter or **Cooking Oil**
Cod Steak, 1 pound
Court Bouillon (page 75)
Parsley, 2 tablespoons
Tomatoes, Stewed

To serve 4

Peel and slice potatoes and onions, and fry until crisp and brown, and tender.

Meanwhile poach cod until flaky, drain and mix with potatoes and onions. Add parsley. Serve with stewed tomatoes on the side.

SALT MACKEREL FILLETS IN LEMON BUTTER

Salt Mackerel, 1 fillet
  per person

Soak mackerel in cold water overnight. Drain and cover with fresh cold water; bring to boil, pour off water and cover again with fresh water. Bring to boil and simmer a few minutes until tender. Remove to hot platter.

Butter, 1 tablespoon
  per fillet
Lemon Juice, ½ table-
  spoon per fillet

Melt butter in skillet, until frothy, add lemon juice, stir and pour over mackerel. Garnish platter with slices of lemon.

STUFFED FISH FILLETS

Butter, 3 tablespoons
Mushrooms, sliced, ½
  cup
Green Pepper,
  chopped, ¼ cup
Onions, chopped, ½
  cup
Salt, ½ teaspoon
White Pepper, dash

Sauté in butter the mushrooms, green pepper and onions until soft; add salt and pepper. Spread in bottom of shallow baking dish.

Butter, 2 tablespoons
Parsley, chopped, ¼
  cup
Sweet Basil, ¼
  teaspoon
Soft Bread Crumbs, 2
  cups
Salt, ½ teaspoon
Pepper, ⅛ teaspoon
Fillets of Flounder, 4

Melt butter in skillet, add parsley and basil and saute briefly; remove from heat and add bread crumbs, salt and pepper. Mix thoroughly. Place spoonful of mixture in center of each fillet, roll fish and secure with toothpicks. Place rolls in baking dish, brush with butter.

Oven, hot, 400°
White Wine, ½ cup

Bake 15 minutes. Remove Fish rolls from dish, add wine to vegetables in dish and heat. Pour over fish rolls and serve.

To serve 4

STUFFED BAKED FISH

Use a whole fish, cleaned but not split. The head and tail may be left on to help retain the stuffing. Stuff with an herb-flavored bread stuffing (page 73) and close with skewers or sew. Place in open pan, grease the top of the fish or spread with slices of salt pork. Sprinkle with minced onion, parsley, a pinch of thyme, and a pinch of instant garlic. Bake in moderate oven, 350°, until fish flakes with fork, about 15 minutes per pound.

Fish may also be baked without stuffing, and with head and tail removed. This will take a shorter cooking time than a stuffed fish.

If desired, the pan juices may be combined with a little lemon juice and a few tablespoons of water, simmered for a few minutes and poured over the fish; or any of the sauces on pages 90–91 may accompany it.

Try these baked fish and sauce combinations:

    Baked Cod with Mustard Sauce

    Stuffed Mackerel with Lemon Butter

    Halibut with Horse-radish Butter

    Baked Shad with Chive Butter

    Sea Bass with Anchovy-Parsley Butter

See sauces on pages 90–91.

SHRIMP-STUFFED RED SNAPPER

Red Snapper, 2½–3 lbs.
Salt and Pepper
Shrimp, ½ pound,
  cooked, chopped
Mushrooms, ½ pound,
  chopped
Marjoram, ¼ teaspoon
Parsley, 1 tablespoon,
  chopped
White Wine, ¼ cup
Butter

Have fish scaled, cleaned and boned. Leave head and tail on. Rinse to remove any clinging scales. Sprinkle cavity with salt and pepper. Stuff with shrimp, mushrooms, salt and pepper, marjoram, parsley and wine lightly mixed together. Sew up cavity. Brush with melted butter. Place on rack in shallow baking pan.

Oven, moderate, 350°

To serve 4 or 5

Bake 45 minutes or until flaky.

Any large whole fish may be substituted for red snapper.

FILLET OF FLOUNDER WITH PARSLEY SAUCE

Flounder Fillets, 2 lbs.
Salt and **Pepper,** to taste

Place fillets in wide baking pan, sprinkle with salt and pepper.

Butter, 4 tablespoons
Parsley, ½ cup, chopped
Lemon, 1, juice

Melt butter in skillet and when foaming, add parsley and lemon juice. Pour over fish.

Oven, moderate, 350°

Bake 15 or 20 minutes, or until tender.

To serve 4

POMPANO EN PAPILLOTTE

Pompano, 2
Salt, 1 teaspoon
Pepper, ¼ teaspoon
Lemon Juice, 2 tablesps.
Parchment or **Butcher Paper**

Cut pompano into 4 fillets. Place each in the center of a square of parchment or butcher paper which has been coated with salad oil. Sprinkle salt and pepper and a little lemon juice over each. Bring sides of paper up and make tight double fold over top of fish. Fold up the ends with a tight fold and clip each with a paper clip to hold it in place.

Oven, hot, 425°

Bake 20 minutes, or until paper is brown. Slit paper open and serve in paper.

To serve 4

Stuffed baked fish with lemon wedges and parsley

Stuffed fillets

BROILED FISH

Place fish on greased broiler rack and brush with melted butter or salad oil. Sprinkle with salt and pepper. Place whole fish about 3 inches from heat, split fish or fillets, 4 or 5 inches. Broil under medium heat, 4 or 5 minutes, turn fish over, spread with fat and broil 4 or 5 minutes, or until flaky. Serve on hot plates with lemon wedges, or with one of the sauces on pages 90–91.

Try these broiled fish and sauce combinations:

Red Snapper with Lemon Butter
Salmon Steaks with Savory Butter
Brook Trout with Chive Butter
Swordfish with Chili Sauce Butter
Scrod with Green Sauce
Flounder with Green Grape Sauce
Weakfish with Caper Butter

See sauces on pages 90–91.

FINNAN HADDIE

Finnan haddie is haddock that has been smoked and salted. It may be broiled and served with Lemon Butter. Or it may be baked in milk to cover, in a moderate oven for 1 hour, or until tender and flaky and served with Ravigote Sauce.

CREAMED FINNAN HADDIE

Finnan Haddie, 1½ lbs.
Milk, 2 cups
Instant Onion, ¼ teasp.

Soak finnan haddie in milk for 1 hour. Add onion and simmer 10 minutes.

Butter, 3 tablespoons
Flour, 3 tablespoons
Cream, ½ cup
Egg, 1, hard-cooked
Pimiento, 1 tablespoon, chopped

Add flour to melted butter in skillet over low heat. Slowly add milk strained from finnan haddie, stirring constantly; add cream and cook until thickened. Add fish, chopped egg and pimiento.

To serve 4

STEAMED FISH

Use a steamer, if you have one, or a small rack or colander in a covered kettle. Grease rack, arrange fish, sprinkle with salt and pepper. Add enough boiling water to kettle to come just below rack—it should not touch fish. Bring to boil, reduce heat and steam about 10 minutes to the pound, or until flaky. Do not overcook. Lift rack out so that you can remove fish without breaking it. Serve with melted butter or one of the sauces on pages 90–91.

Try these steamed fish and sauce combinations:

Cod with Egg Sauce
Whitefish with Anchovy Sauce
Swordfish with Cheese Sauce
Halibut with Hot Tartar Sauce
Hake with Oyster Sauce

See sauces on pages 90–91.

PAN-FRIED FISH

Cut large fish into portions, leave small ones whole. Before pan-frying, fish should have a protective coating. You may brush it with melted butter, then dredge it thoroughly with flour; or, bread it by dipping it first in a beaten egg diluted with 1 tablespoon of water and 1 tablespoon of lemon juice, then into fine bread crumbs or cornmeal. Fry in enough fat to cover bottom of skillet, over medium heat so that it does not splatter, until lightly brown on each side. Do not overcook. Serve immediately on hot plates, with lemon wedges or one of the sauces on pages 90–91.

Try these pan fried fish and sauce combinations:

Cod with Mornay Sauce
Smelts with Pimiento Butter
Fish Sticks with Soy Butter
Porgies with Brown Butter Sauce
Butterfish with Garlic Butter
Haddock with Sweet and Pungent Sauce

See sauces on pages 90–91.

DEEP-FAT FRIED FISH

Cut fish into serving size pieces and coat with egg beaten with a little water, then with bread crumbs or cornmeal. Fry a few pieces at a time in deep fat (370°) until golden brown. Drain on paper towels. Serve very hot with lemon wedges or one of the sauces on pages 90–91.

Deep-fat frying is particularly good for fish cakes, cutlets, and croquettes.

Try these deep-fat fried fish and sauce combinations:

Butterfish with Tartar Sauce
Porgies with Creole Sauce
Smelts with Olive Sauce
Perch with Horse-radish Sauce
Mullet with Chervil Butter

See sauces on pages 90–91.

FROGS' LEGS

Sprinkle frogs' legs with salt and pepper. Dip in egg and bread crumbs. Fry in deep fat (375°) for 3 minutes or sauté in skillet until brown. Allow ½ pound per serving.

FISH CROQUETTES

See page 92.

SHAD ROE

Shad roe may be broiled or sautéed. To broil, brush with melted butter and place in broiler 2 inches from heat, 4 or 5 minutes on each side. Season with salt and pepper, and sprinkle with finely chopped parsley. Serve with lemon wedges. Allow one roe per person.

Or sauté gently in butter until lightly browned on each side.

CODFISH CAKES

Salt Codfish, 1 pound **Potatoes,** mashed, 2 cups **Egg,** 1, beaten **Pepper,** ⅛ teaspoon **Deep hot fat**	Rinse codfish in cold water, or let soak 1 hour if very salty. Drain, add fresh water, bring to boil and simmer 15 minutes. Drain, shred, add mashed potatoes and mix; add egg and pepper and beat well. Drop by spoonfuls into hot fat (365°–380°) and fry until golden brown, 3 to 5 minutes. Drain on paper towels.

To serve 4

Codfish Cakes may be fried in a skillet with a little fat if preferred.

LOBSTER

Lobsters should be bought alive, unless you plan to broil them the day you buy them, when you may have the fish dealer split them for you.

"Chicken" lobsters weight just under 1 pound, medium-sized ones weight 18 ounces to 1 pound, and large, or, "Selects" weigh up to 2 pounds. For serving in the shell, allow one small, or one-half large lobster per person.

BOILED LOBSTER

Pick up live lobster just behind claws or use vegetable tongs and plunge it head first into a large kettle of rapidly boiling, salted water. (Add 1 tablespoon salt for each quart of water.) Cover, let water return to boiling, and boil 6 minutes to the pound. Boiling will change its color from green to red. Remove lobster and drop into cold water.

When cool enough to handle, twist off claws; turn lobster on its back. Cut thin undershell, with sharp knife or heavy scissors, from head to tail. Remove stomach sac just below head, and the dark vein that runs to end of tail. Do not remove the dark green liver, which is delicious, or the coral in the female lobster.

Lobster may be served hot, with side dishes of melted butter, and garnished with lemon wedges, or chilled, with mayonnaise or tartar sauce. Place claws on plate beside lobster and supply nutcrackers for opening them.

BROILED LOBSTER

Have your fish dealer split the live lobster the day you plan to use it, or do it yourself, as follows:

To kill the lobster, insert a sharp knife between body and tail shells, to sever the spinal cord. Place lobster on back; cut thin undershell lengthwise from head to tail. Force shell open as wide as possible, remove stomach sac and dark vein, and liver. Chop liver and mix with a few tablespoons of breadcrumbs; season with salt, pepper and instant onion, and replace in lobster cavity.

Lay lobster as flat as possible on broiler rack, brush meat with butter and sprinkle with salt and pepper. Broil slowly until delicately brown: 12 to 15 minutes for small lobsters, up to 18 minutes for larger ones.

ROCK LOBSTER TAILS

The so-called rock lobster is a crustacean whose meat is all in the tail. The tails are sold frozen, and weigh from 4 to 18 ounces a piece. 18 ounces would make 3 average servings. They may be boiled or broiled.

BOILED LOBSTER TAIL: Drop unthawed into boiling salted water and allow about 1 minute per ounce cooking time.

BROILED LOBSTER TAIL: Thaw. Cut away under-shell with scissors. Bend tail backward toward shell side to crack and prevent curling. Place shell side up on broiler rack and broil 5 minutes, 5 inches from heat. Turn over, spread with butter and broil 5 to 10 minutes longer, depending on size.

Serve in shell with melted butter and wedges of lemon or with Caper Butter. A little instant garlic may be sprinkled in tails before broiling if desired.

LOBSTER CHOWDER

Salt Pork, ¼ pound **Onion,** 1 tablespoon, finely chopped **Green Pepper,** 1 tablesp., finely chopped **Celery,** 1½ cups, finely chopped **Water,** 2 cups **Tomato Soup,** 1 can **Mushroom Soup,** 1 can **Lobster,** 1 can **Sherry,** ¼ cup	Fry salt pork until crisp and reserve. Sauté onion, green pepper, and celery lightly in pork fat. Add water; simmer until celery is tender. Add tomato soup, then mushroom soup, beating with rotary beater to make it smooth. Heat to boiling point. Add lobster in coarsely broken pieces; add sherry. Heat and serve.

To make about 6 cups

LOBSTER NEWBURG

Butter, 2 tablespoons **Flour,** 2 tablespoons **Milk,** 1 cup **Cream,** 1 cup **Salt,** 1 teaspoon **Lobster,** 2 cups, cooked, cut up **Sherry,** ¼ cup **Egg Yolks,** 2	In top part of double boiler combine melted butter, flour, milk, cream and salt. Stir until well blended over boiling water. Add lobster and sherry. Beat egg yolks, add a little of the mixture to them, and return to the sauce. Cook, stirring constantly, until just thickened.

To serve 4

Serve Newburg on toast or patty shells, garnished with paprika, or in individual casseroles, topped with buttered crumbs and browned under broiler.

Crab or Shrimp may be substituted for Lobster in the above recipe.

Lobster thermidor

*Lobster
Newburg
can be served
with waffles*

Rock lobster tails

LOBSTER THERMIDOR

Butter, 2 tablespoons
Flour, 4 tablespoons
Milk, 1 cup
Cream, 1 cup
Salt, 1 teaspoon
Paprika, ¼ teaspoon
Lobster, 2 cups, cooked,
 cut up
Sherry, ¼ cup
Grated Cheese

To serve 4

In top part of double boiler, over boiling water, combine melted butter with flour, add milk, cream, salt and paprika. Add lobster and sherry and cook, stirring constantly until thickened. Use mixture to fill lobster shells or individual baking dishes. Sprinkle tops with grated cheese, and brown lightly under broiler.

LOBSTER COCKTAIL

See page 244

SHRIMP

Shrimp are sold by the pound, and vary in size from very tiny to over an ounce in weight. The shells may be pulled off either before or after cooking, and the intestinal vein may be removed either before or after. This is the black line that runs the length of the shrimp. Actually it is harmless, but many consider it unappetizing.

Wash shrimp in cold water and drop into boiling salted water. Cover and cook about 5 minutes. Let cool in water. They will turn pink in the cooking. If desired the shrimp may be flavored by adding to the boiling water 2 bay leaves, a few sprigs of parsley, a stalk of celery, and an onion.

GRILLED SHRIMP

Jumbo Shrimp, 2 pounds
Garlic, 1 clove, minced
Butter, 3 tablespoons

To serve 4

Shell and devein shrimp. Heat garlic and butter together; dip shrimp in mixture and place on a hot broiler pan. Broil 3 minutes on each side. Serve piping hot with lemon wedges.

BUTTERFLY SHRIMP

Jumbo Shrimp, 6 or 8
 per person
Flour
Salt and **Pepper**
Egg, 1, beaten, per
 serving
Cracker Crumbs
Fat for Frying
Tartar Sauce (page 90)

Peel and devein uncooked shrimp; split without separating all the way and press flat to form the "butterfly." Dip in seasoned flour, then in beaten egg, then in fine cracker crumbs. Fry in deep hot fat (375°) until golden brown. Serve with Tartar Sauce.

SHRIMP CREOLE

Oil, 3 tablespoons
Onions, 2 medium, chopped
Green Pepper, 1 small, chopped
Celery, chopped, ½ cup
Garlic, 1 clove, minced
Salt, 1 teaspoon
Pepper, ⅛ teaspoon
Cayenne, dash
Tomatoes, canned, 2 cups
Shrimp, 1½ pounds, cooked

To serve 4

Cook onions, green pepper and celery in oil until soft, add garlic, seasonings and tomatoes. Simmer 20 minutes. Add shrimp, and heat but do not boil.

CURRIED SHRIMP CASSEROLE

Onions, 2 medium, chopped
Shrimp, raw, 1½ pounds, shelled
Butter, 2 tablespoons
Tomatoes, 16-ounce can
Rice, cooked, dry and fluffy, 2 cups
Curry, 2 teaspoons
Worcestershire Sauce, 1 teaspoon
Salt and **Pepper,** to taste
Bacon, 4 strips

To serve 4

Sauté onions and shrimp in butter gently until shrimp are pink. Add tomatoes, rice and seasonings. Pour into greased casserole; top with bacon strips.

JAPANESE FRIED SHRIMP
(Tempura)

Proceed as for Butterfly Shrimp (page 81), but substitute cornstarch for the flour and cracker crumbs. Serve with Mustard Sauce (page 90).

BATTER-FRIED SHRIMP

Shrimp, 2 pounds
Biscuit Mix, 1 cup
Milk, ¾ cup
Egg, 1, beaten
Fat for Frying

To serve 4

Remove shells and devein shrimp. Combine biscuit mix, milk and egg. Dip shrimp into batter and let set 10 minutes. Fry in deep fat (360°) until brown.

SHRIMP PILAF

Salt Pork, ¼ lb., diced
Onion, 1 med., chopped
Green Pepper, 1, chopped
Tomatoes, 16-ounce can
Rice, raw, 1 cup
Shrimp, 1 pound, cooked
Salt and **Pepper,** to taste

To serve 4

Fry salt pork until brown and crisp. Remove pork, cook onion and pepper in fat until golden. Add tomatoes and heat. Meanwhile cook rice until tender, drain. Add salt pork, onion and tomato mixture, and shrimp. Season to taste, and simmer 10 minutes.

SHRIMP COCKTAIL

See page 244.

See the Pantry Shelf section for additional shrimp recipes that may be used with fresh shrimp as well as canned or frozen. (Pages 11, 15, 16.)

Shrimp creole with rice

Deviled crabs (see page 84)

CRABS

Hard-shell crabs may be bought all year around. Soft-shell crabs are crabs that have molted, or shed their hard shell, and are available from June to September.

Buy alive and lively crabs. Wash them in several waters, handling them with kitchen tongs, to remove all external sand or dirt.

BOILED HARD-SHELL CRABS

Wash crabs and drop into rapidly boiling water, using 1 table-spoon of salt to each quart of water. Cover, bring to boil and boil for 10 minutes. The shell will turn a beautiful pink. Cool enough to handle in cold water. Break off claws and tail. Working at the tail end, force the shells apart. Remove any spongy or fibrous material, reserving only the meat which will flake away from the shell. Use a sharp-pointed knife or nut pick to retrieve all the meat. Use a nut cracker on the claws to obtain the claw meat also.

Crab sizes vary tremendously, depending on the region. The size crab you find in the market will depend on whether you live on the East Coast, in Florida, or in California.

Crab meat can also be bought frozen or in cans.

SOFT-SHELL CRABS

Wash the crabs in several waters. Place crab under side down and with sharp knife cut just behind the eyes. Lift up the tapered points on each side of the shell and remove the spongy material underneath. Turn crab on its back and with sharp knife remove "apron" that folds under body, and the spongy substance below it. Wash crabs again under running water. The soft shells of the crabs are edible, and they are usually fried.

FRIED SOFT-SHELL CRABS

Soft-Shell Crabs, 8–12	Prepare crabs as described
Egg, 1	above. Dip crabs in egg mixed
Water, 3 tablespoons,	with water, then in fine bread
Bread Crumbs	crumbs. Sauté in butter until
Butter, 3 tablespoons	golden brown, or in deep hot fat
Tartar Sauce (page 163).	(375°) 3 to 4 minutes. Serve
	with tartar sauce.

To serve 4

The size of soft-shell crabs varies so that the number you will need depends on the size and the appetites; 2 or 3 for each serving would be a usual amount.

CRAB MEAT COCKTAIL

See page 244.

CRAB CREOLE

Onion, 1, minced
Garlic, 1 clove, minced
Celery, 2 stalks, diced
Oil or **Salad Oil,**
  2 tablespoons
Basil, 1 teaspoon
Thyme, 1/4 teaspoon
Salt, 1 teaspoon
Cayenne, few grains
Worcestershire, 1 teasp.
Tomatoes, 16–ounce can
Crab Meat, 2 cups,
  cooked

Sauté onion, garlic and celery in oil in skillet until lightly browned. Add seasonings and tomatoes. Simmer over low heat for an hour. When ready to serve, add crab meat and heat thoroughly.

To serve 4

DEVILED CRABS

Thick White Sauce,
  1 cup (see page 90)
Egg, 1
Worcestershire, 1/2 teasp.
Tabasco, 1/4 teaspoon
Pepper, 1/8 teaspoon
Horse-radish, 1 teasp.
Parsley, 1 tablespoon,
  chopped
Dry Mustard, 1 teaspoon
Crab Meat, 1 1/2 cups,
  canned or cooked

Make white sauce; add beaten egg and seasonings. Add flaked crab meat and mix lightly. Turn into crab shells or individual casseroles. Brush tops with melted butter.

Oven, moderate, 375°

Bake until lightly browned.

To serve 4

CRAB CAKES

Crab Meat, 1 pound
Salt, 1/2 teaspoon
Pepper, 1/8 teaspoon
Worcestershire, 2 teasps.
Soft Bread Crumbs,
  1/2 cup
Egg, 1, beaten
Cream, 1 tablespoon
Fat for Frying

Melt all ingredients except fat together; shape into 8 cakes, and chill. When ready to cook, dredge cakes with flour and sauté in hot fat until golden brown.

To serve 4

OYSTERS

Oysters may be purchased from your fish market either in the shells or shucked. The small size is usually used for oyster stews, the large ones for frying.

If you are going to shuck the oysters yourself, first scrub the shells thoroughly and rinse. To open the shell, insert the point of a heavy, blunt knife into the hinge at the thick side. Twist the knife to pry shell open. Run the knife around the edge of the shell, cutting the muscle that holds it shut. Cut the muscle that holds the oyster to the shell, and empty it and the

MENUS

Six festive fish dinners

POACHED HADDOCK WITH DILL SAUCE
(page 90)

Baked Squash · Green Beans and Mushrooms
Rye Bread · Butter
Blueberry Crisp

KEDGEREE (page 75)

Hot Buttered Carrots and Green Peppers
Assorted Pickles
Melba Toast · Butter
Apple Pie

FILLET OF FLOUNDER WITH PARSLEY SAUCE (page 91)

Potato Rosettes · Green Peas Cooked with Lettuce
Watercress Salad
Coffee-Pecan Parfait Molds with Rum Cream

CRAB CREOLE

Saffron Rice
Hearts of Lettuce with French Dressing
Pecan Pie

DEVILED CRABS

French Fried Potatoes · Hot Cabbage Slaw
Dill Pickles
Whole-wheat Bread · Butter
Apricot-Orange Nectar

BAKED OYSTERS AND CROUTONS

Melba Toast · Butter
Green Salad · Blue Cheese Dressing
Melon Balls and Raspberries (frozen)

liquid into a bowl. Strain the liquid before using and inspect the oysters to make sure there are no shell fragments remaining.

FRIED OYSTERS

Large Oysters, 16
Eggs, 2, beaten
Fine Bread Crumbs or
  Cracker Crumbs

Dry oysters; dip in egg, then in crumbs. Let set 15 minutes. Fry in deep hot fat (375°) 2 to 3 minutes, or until golden brown. Drain on paper.

To serve 4

SAUTÉED OYSTERS

Prepare oysters for frying. Sauté in skillet with enough fat to cover bottom. Turn oysters, to brown evenly on both sides. Drain on paper towels.

Serve Fried or Sautéed Oysters with Tartar Sauce or one of the other fish sauces on pages 90–91.

OYSTERS ROCKEFELLER

6 large Oysters on the half shell per person	Remove oysters from shells, scrub and rinse shells and replace oysters. Place on broiler tray.
Frozen Chopped Spinach, 1 package **Onion,** 2 tablespoons, minced **Butter,** 2 tablespoons **Celery Salt,** ½ teaspoon **Pepper,** ¼ teaspoon **Anchovy Fillets,** 1 can	Thaw spinach; sauté onion in butter until soft and add spinach; add seasonings; cook, stirring, 5 minutes. Place spoonful of mixture on each oyster. Top with anchovy fillet.
Oven, hot, 450°	Bake 10 minutes or until oysters are plump. Serve on hot plates.

Buttered crumbs may be used as a topping instead of the anchovy if desired.

BAKED OYSTERS AND CROUTONS

Bread Cubes, 2 cups **Butter,** ¼ pound **Oysters,** 2 cups **Salt** **Pepper** **Onion Salt** **Cream,** ½ cup	Brown bread cubes lightly in butter. Cover bottom of small casserole with half the croutons. Add drained oysters and seasonings. Top with remaining croutons. Pour cream over top.
Oven, moderate, 325°	Bake 25 minutes.

To serve 4

OYSTERS IN CREAM SAUCE

Butter, 2 tablespoons **Flour,** 2 tablespoons **Salt,** 1 teaspoon **Pepper,** ⅛ teaspoon **White Wine,** ¼ cup **Cream,** 1 cup **Egg Yolks,** 2, beaten	In top part of double boiler melt butter; combine with flour, salt and pepper. Add wine and cream and cook, stirring, until thickened. Add a little of the mixture to the egg yolks, and return to sauce.
Oysters, Raw, 2 dozen **Paprika**	Meanwhile heat oysters in their liquid until edges begin to curl. Add oysters to sauce, with enough of the liquid to make the sauce a proper consistency. Heat but do not boil. Serve on toast or in tart shells. Garnish with paprika.

To serve 4

PANNED OYSTERS

In a shallow baking pan place oysters with a little of the oyster liquid. Sprinkle with salt and pepper. Bake in a hot oven (425°) for a few minutes, or until they are plump and hot. Serve oysters on hot buttered toast. Heat any remaining liquid, season and serve in cups.

OYSTER CASSEROLE

Stewing Oysters, 4 cups **Bread Crumbs,** dry, 2 cups **Salt** and **Pepper** **Butter** **Cream,** ½ cup	Pick over oysters to remove any bits of shell and drain thoroughly. Put alternate layers of oysters and bread crumbs in a casserole; sprinkle each layer with salt and pepper and dot with butter. Finish with a crumb layer. Pour cream over all.
Oven, moderate, 350°	Bake 25 minutes.

To serve 4

CLAMS

Clams can be bought in the shell or shucked. Clams in the shell should be alive, in which case the shell is tightly shut or closes when you touch it. There are two types—hard-shell and soft-shell. Small hard-shell clams, called littlenecks and cherry stones, are usually served raw. Larger ones are usually cut up and used for chowder. Soft-shell clams are small and are used chiefly for steaming, frying, or for stews, fritters, and other special dishes.

TO SHUCK HARD-SHELL CLAMS

Scrub clams, put in container with plenty of cold water and sprinkle handful of corn meal over surface. Let stand for several hours to rid them of sand and other black internal substances. Drain and cover again with clean water. The shells will open slightly; then hold gently and insert a strong knife between the shells. Cut through the muscle that holds the shells together, save the juice, and cut the clam loose from the shell.

CLAMS CASINO

Butter, 3 tablespoons **Anchovy paste,** ½ teaspoon **Cherrystone clams,** 3 dozen **Green Pepper,** finely chopped **Pimiento,** finely chopped **Bacon,** 8 or 9 slices **Rock salt**	Cream butter and anchovy paste together. Loosen clams. Put a dot of the anchovy butter in the shell under each clam. Top each clam with a pinch of green pepper and pimiento. Cover with a piece of raw bacon the size of the clam. Set clams firmly on a bed of rock salt in a shallow pan. Broil 3 inches from heat 6–8 minutes, turning bacon once, to broil both sides. Serve in shells.

Serves 6

Oysters Rockefeller

Clams Casino

STEAMED CLAMS IN DRAWN BUTTER

Soft Shelled Clams,
6 to 12 per person

Clams should be tightly closed or close when touched. Scrub with brush and rinse in running water to eliminate sand. Place in large kettle and add ½ cup boiling water to 8 quarts of clams. Cover tightly and simmer 5 to 10 minutes until shells open. Serve clams on hot platter, covered with napkins. Pour clam broth into cups to serve with clams. Serve individual small dishes of melted butter, seasoned with lemon juice, salt and pepper.

To eat clams, remove from shells, holding by neck, dip into butter, and eat all but neck.

FRIED CLAMS

Follow recipes for Fried Oysters and Sautéed Oysters on pages 84–85.

SCALLOPS

Scallops are bought shucked—either fresh or frozen. There are two types—bay scallops, which are small, and sea scallops, which are sometimes as large as 1½ inches in diameter. There is no waste.

SAUTÉED SCALLOPS

Butter, 2 tablespoons
Garlic, 1 clove, minced
Salt, ½ teaspoon
Pepper, ⅛ teaspoon
Scallops, 1¼ pounds
Parsley, 2 tablespoons
Lemon Wedges

Melt butter in skillet, add garlic and seasonings. Cook over low heat until garlic is soft. Add enough scallops to only cover bottom of pan. Sauté over medium heat until golden brown on all sides. Remove to hot platter and keep warm in oven if there are more scallops to cook. Repeat process with second batch. Serve with lemon and chopped parsley.

To serve 4

SCALLOPS IN SHERRY AND CREAM

Sauté scallops as described above. When all the scallops are cooked return them to the skillet; add ¼ cup of dry sherry and 1 cup of cream. Heat thoroughly and stir up browned drippings in bottom of pan; do not boil. Garnish with parsley.

MUSSELS

Mussels are purchased alive in closed shells—discard any shells that have opened. Scrub thoroughly and rinse in several waters. Trim off the beards which are not edible. Put mussels in kettle and add ½ cup boiling water. Cover tightly and steam over low heat 4 or 5 minutes, or until shells open, no longer. Serve on the bottom shell with melted butter and lemon wedges.

Sautéed bay scallops with lemon slices and carrot curls

SHORE DINNER CASSEROLE

Frying Chicken, 1, cut up
Butter, 3 tablespoons
Salt, 1 teaspoon

Brown chicken in butter in hot skillet. Put in large casserole.

Rice, ¾ cup
Bay Leaf, 1
Saffron, large pinch
Salt, 2 teaspoons
Pepper, ⅛ teaspoon
Cayenne, dash
Green Pepper, 1, sliced
Tomatoes, 2, quartered

Put raw rice into skillet and brown slightly. Add seasonings, green pepper and tomatoes and bring to boiling point. Pour over chicken.

Oven, hot, 425°
Sausage, smoked, ½ lb.
Littleneck Clams, 8
Shrimp, ½ pound
Lobster, 1 cup, cooked

Bake 25 minutes; reduce heat to 375°. Meanwhile, cut sausage in small pieces and fry until well browned. Add to casserole with clams, cooked, shelled shrimp and lobster. Bake, covered, 15 minutes longer or until rice is done.

To serve 4 to 6

SEA FOOD PANCAKES

Fish, 1½ pounds
(One, or several kinds may be combined, including lobster and shrimp)
Mornay Sauce (page 90)

Poach fish in court bouillon (see page 75). Drain fish well, chop and mix with half the Mornay sauce. Make 12 small pancakes.

Pancakes for Sea Food

Eggs, 3
Milk, 1½ cups
Butter, 2 tablespoons, melted
Salt, ½ teaspoon
Flour, Sifted, ⅞ cup

Combine ingredients in a blender, if you have one, or mix with a rotary beater, to make batter. Drop 2 tablespoons of batter in a 6-inch greased skillet; tilt pan until batter covers whole bottom. Turn when the edges look crinkled and golden.
Place each one separately in a warm oven—do not pile or they get soggy.

Parmesan Cheese, grated

Place some of the sea food mixture on each pancake, roll and arrange side by side, on a buttered baking pan. Sprinkle with cheese and cover with remainder of the sauce. Place under broiler a few minutes to brown. Serve immediately.

MUSSELS MARINIÈRE

Mussels, 3 dozen
Shallot or **Onion,** 1 minced
White Wine, ½ cup
Water, ½ cup

Put scrubbed and debearded mussels in kettle with shallots, wine and water. Cover tightly and boil 4 or 5 minutes, or until the shells open. Serve on half shells.

Butter, 1 tablespoon
Flour, 1 tablespoon
Salt and **Pepper,** to taste
Tabasco, 1 drop

Melt butter in small skillet, blend in flour. Strain liquid from cooking mussels and add to flour mixture, stirring constantly. Season to taste and serve as a sauce for the mussels.

To serve 4

SEAFOOD GUMBO

Salt Pork, ¼ pound, cut in cubes
Onions, chopped, ⅓ cup
Okra, sliced, 2 cups
Tomatoes, canned, 2 cups
Garlic, 1 clove, minced
Bay Leaf, 1
Paprika, ¼ teaspoon
Tabasco, dash
Worcestershire Sauce, 1 teasp.
Boiling Water, 3 cups

Render salt pork in skillet over low heat, then add onions and cook until they are soft. Add okra, tomatoes, garlic, bay leaf and seasonings. Add water and simmer for one hour.

Gumbo Filé, 1 teasp.
Crab Meat, cooked, 1 cup
Lobster, cooked, 1 cup
Shrimps, cooked, 1 cup

When ready to serve, add Gumbo Filé, Crab Meat, Lobster and Shrimps. Heat, and serve at once. More Gumbo Filé may be added if needed to make the mixture sufficiently thick and smooth.

To serve 4

TUNA

See the Pantry Shelf section for the many recipes using Tuna. Also the Leftovers section which contains recipes that are all good with cooked fish or canned.

See the Pantry Shelf section for many recipes using canned Crab, Lobster, Salmon and Shrimp. These are all good with fresh seafood too.

LEFTOVER FISH AND SEAFOOD

See the many recipes in the Leftovers section for using cooked fish and other seafood.

MENUS

SMELTS WITH PIMIENTO BUTTER (page 91)

Cheese, Potato and Mushroom Casserole
Cucumber Salad
Fresh Blackberry Whip

ASSORTED FRIED FISH (page 78)

Lemon Wedges · Tartar Sauce
Potato Chips
Tomato Salad
Watermelon

PORGIES WITH CREOLE SAUCE (page 78)

Grapefruit and Avocado Wedges on Watercress
French Dressing
Corn Sticks · Butter
Little Chess Pies

BAKED COD WITH MUSTARD SAUCE
(page 90)

Baked Potatoes·Creamed Onions and Mushrooms
Sweet and Sour Beet Shreds
Rye Bread · Butter
Pear Betty

SEAFOOD GUMBO

Fluffy Boiled Rice · Mixed Vegetables
Hard Rolls · Butter
Fruit Compote

SALMON STEAKS WITH SAVORY BUTTER
(page 91)

Sautéed Zucchini and Tomatoes
Endive Salad with French Dressing
Crisp Rolls · Butter
Lemon Chiffon Pie

SWORDFISH WITH CHEESE SAUCE

Spanish Lima Beans
Spring Salad
Hot Buttered Biscuits
Grape Parfait

SHORE DINNER CASSEROLE

Scallions · Celery
Assorted Buttered Rolls
Strawberry Meringues

**SALT MACKEREL FILLETS IN
LEMON BUTTER**

Home Fried Potatoes
Creamy Coleslaw
Cinnamon Cake

STEAMED CLAMS IN DRAWN BUTTER

French Fried Potatoes
Tomato and Cucumber Salad
Sliced Peaches

SAUCES

The sauce adds a touch of glamor to many dishes, but it must be the right sauce and it must be smoothly made. The latter is not so difficult as it sounds; the secret is to cook it over low heat so that you have ample time to blend the fat and flour and add the other ingredients with plenty of stirring before the thickening commences. It is high heat, making the flour expand too rapidly, that causes lumps. Make good use of your rotary beater, to smooth the sauce, and if it thickens too much more liquid may be added, a little at a time, until it is just right. In the list of sauces, we have indicated the type of food on which each may be used.

WHITE SAUCE

	Thin	*Medium*	*Thick*
Butter	1 tablespoon	2 tablespoons	3 tablespoons
Flour	1 tablespoon	2 tablespoons	3 tablespoons
Salt	½ teaspoon	½ teaspoon	½ teaspoon
Pepper	few grains	few grains	few grains
Milk	1 cup	1 cup	1 cup

To make 1 cup

In top of double boiler over boiling water, or in a saucepan over low heat, melt butter; add flour, salt and pepper; stir until blended. Add milk slowly stirring constantly. Cook until thickened.

Thin White Sauce is used for soups.
Medium White Sauce is used for vegetables, casseroles, sauces.
Thick White Sauce is used for croquettes, soufflés.

CREAM SAUCE

Substitute light cream for milk in the above recipes.

SAUCES WITH MEDIUM WHITE SAUCE BASE

ANCHOVY SAUCE: Omit salt and pepper. To one cup hot white sauce, add 1 teaspoon anchovy paste. Good with seafood.

BÉCHAMEL SAUCE: Substitute ½ cup chicken stock for ½ cup milk in white sauce recipe. Good with chicken croquettes and timbales.

CHEESE SAUCE: To 1 cup white sauce, add ¼ cup shredded cheese. Heat until melted. Good with eggs and vegetables.

CURRY SAUCE: To 1 cup white sauce, add 1 teaspoon curry powder, 1 teaspoon lemon juice. Good with leftover meats, poultry and eggs.

DILL SAUCE: To 1 cup white sauce, add 3 tablespoons minced dill. Use for creamed potatoes.

EGG SAUCE: To 1 cup white sauce, add 1 teaspoon prepared mustard, 1 diced hard-cooked egg. Good with vegetables and fish.

HORSE-RADISH SAUCE: To 1 cup hot white sauce, add, just before serving, 3 tablespoons prepared horse-radish. Good with tongue, corned beef, or boiled fresh beef.

HOT TARTAR SAUCE: To ¾ cup white sauce, add ¼ cup mayonnaise, 1 tablespoon lemon juice, 1 teaspoon minced onion, 3 tablespoons minced dill pickle, 2 tablespoons minced parsley. Salt and pepper to taste. Heat all together. Good with fried and broiled fish.

LOBSTER OR SHRIMP SAUCE: To 1 cup hot white sauce, add ⅓ cup minced cooked fresh or canned lobster or shrimp diced, 1 tablespoon lemon juice or 1 tablespoon white wine. Good with seafood.

MORNAY SAUCE: To 1 cup hot white sauce, add ½ teaspoon dry mustard, 2 tablespoons grated cheese, and a dash of cayenne. Good with fish or vegetables.

MUSTARD SAUCE: To 1 cup hot white sauce, add 2 tablespoons prepared mustard. Good with ham, tongue or corned beef.

RAVIGOTE SAUCE: To 1 cup hot white sauce, add 1 teaspoon each chopped chives, parsley and tarragon vinegar. Good with chicken or crab.

WORCESTERSHIRE WHITE SAUCE: To 1 cup hot white sauce add 2 teaspoons Worcestershire Sauce. Good on leftover meat or poultry.

The above sauces may also be made with a Cream Sauce Base.

BORDELAISE SAUCE

Butter, 2 tablespoons	Melt butter in skillet and stir in flour. Cook until browned, stirring constantly. Add stock gradually, stirring, until mixture thickens. Add tomato sauce, and sherry. Heat thoroughly.
Flour, 2 tablespoons	
Beef Stock or **Bouillon,** 1 cup	
Tomato Sauce, canned, ½ cup	
Sherry, ¼ cup	
To make about 1¾ cups	Good with steak.

MINT SAUCE FOR ROAST LAMB

Fresh Mint Leaves, 1 cup	Crush mint leaves with sugar. Add hot water; when dissolved add vinegar. Let stand about 2 hours before serving. The sauce should be thick with mint.
Sugar, 2 tablespoons	
Hot Water, ½ cup	
Cider Vinegar, ½ cup	
To make 1½ cups	

CAPER BUTTER SAUCE

To ¼ cup of melted butter add 2 tablespoons capers, 1 tablespoon lemon juice. Heat. Good with fish or steak.

SAUCE VELOUTÉ

Butter, 2 tablespoons
Flour, 2 tablespoons
Chicken or **Veal Stock,**
  1 cup
Salt and **Pepper,** to taste

Melt butter over low heat and stir in flour; gradually add stock, stirring constantly until mixture thickens and boils. Continue cooking few minutes and add seasonings.

To make 1 cup
Good with croquettes, baked or broiled fish.

OYSTER SAUCE

Sauté 6 large oysters in 1 tablespoon butter until edges curl. Remove from heat, chop; add to thin Cream Sauce.

BUTTER SAUCES

ANCHOVY-PARSLEY SAUCE: To ¼ cup melted butter, add 2 tablespoons minced anchovy, 1 tablespoon lemon juice, 2 tablespoons minced parsley. Good with baked or broiled fish, or steak.

BROWN BUTTER SAUCE: Brown ¼ cup butter slowly; do not burn. Add 2 teaspoons Worcestershire, 2 tablespoons lemon juice. Good with poached or baked fish, cauliflower, brains.

CHERVIL BUTTER: To ¼ cup melted butter add 2 tablespoons chervil. Good with fish or vegetables.

CHILI SAUCE BUTTER: To ¼ cup melted butter; add 2 table-spoons chili sauce and 1 tablespoon lemon juice. Good with fish or hamburgers.

CHIVE BUTTER: To ¼ cup melted butter add 2 tablespoons chives. Good with vegetables, poached, broiled or baked fish.

GARLIC BUTTER: To ¼ cup melted butter add ¼ teaspoon instant garlic. Good with fish, vegetables or hot breads.

GREEN GRAPE SAUCE: Heat 1 cup seedless grapes in pan with 1 tablespoon butter until they steam. Add 1 tablespoon lemon juice and 2 tablespoons chopped parsley. Good on poached fish.

GREEN SAUCE (Sauce Verte): To ¼ cup melted butter add 2 tablespoons watercress, chopped fine. Good with fish, boiled potatoes.

HORSE-RADISH BUTTER: To ¼ cup melted butter, add 1 table-spoon horse-radish, 1 teaspoon paprika. Good with fish.

LEMON BUTTER: Combine ¼ cup melted butter with 1 table-spoon lemon juice. Good with fish, steak.

PARSLEY BUTTER: To ¼ cup melted butter add 2 tablespoons parsley. Good with fish, potatoes, steak.

PIMIENTO BUTTER: To ¼ cup melted butter, add ¼ cup minced pimiento. Good with fish.

SAVORY BUTTER: To ⅓ cup soft butter add 1 tablespoon chopped chives, 1 tablespoon chopped celery leaves, 1 table-spoon chopped parsley, ½ teaspoon salt, ½ teaspoon sage, dash garlic salt. Beat until fluffy. Serve cold on hot fish.

SOY BUTTER SAUCE: Heat 3 tablespoons butter with 3 table-spoons soy sauce. Good on fish, liver, brains.

HOLLANDAISE SAUCE

Butter, ½ cup
Lemon Juice, 1 tablesp.
Egg Yolks, 2
Boiling Water, 1 tablesp.
Salt and **Pepper,** dash

Melt butter in small pan. In top of double boiler, over 1-inch of hot, not boiling, water, mix lemon juice and egg yolks; cook over low heat beating constantly with a wire whisk; add butter gradually. Beat until sauce is thick and creamy. Add boiling water a few drops at a time. Remove from heat and season to taste.

To make about ¾ cup
Good with cooked vegetables or eggs.

BÉARNAISE SAUCE: To basic Hollandaise Sauce add 1 teaspoon each onion juice, chopped parsley and chopped fresh tarra-gon, and 1 tablespoon white wine. Good with grilled steaks and chops.

SAUCE MOUSSELINE: To basic Hollandaise Sauce, when cool, fold in ½ cup whipped cream. Good with cooked fish, eggs or vegetables.

BLENDER HOLLANDAISE

Butter, ½ cup
Egg Yolks, 3
Lemon Juice, 2 tablesps.
Salt, ¼ teaspoon
Pepper, a dash

Melt butter to bubbling point. Do not brown. Into the blender put egg yolks, lemon juice, salt and pepper. Flick motor on at high speed. Turn off. Remove cover, turn on high and add butter gradually.

To make about 1 cup

RAISIN SAUCE

Seedless Raisins, 1 cup
Water, 1 cup
Sugar, ¼ cup
Cornstarch, 2 teaspoons
Salt, ¼ teaspoon
Butter, 1 tablespoon
Lemon Juice, 1 tablesp.

Add water to raisins and simmer 10 minutes; combine sugar, cornstarch and salt and add to raisins; cook and stir until slightly thickened. Add butter and lemon juice. Keep warm until ready to serve.

To make about 2 cups

Use with ham, corned beef, tongue.

SWEET AND PUNGENT SAUCE

Vinegar, ⅓ cup
Brown Sugar, ⅔ cup, packed
Water, 1 cup
Dry Mustard, 1 teaspoon
Salt and **Pepper,** to taste
Cornstarch, 1½ tablesps.

Combine vinegar, sugar, water, mustard, and salt and pepper, and bring to boil. Add corn-starch mixed with a little cold water. Cook over low heat, stirring, until thickened.

TOMATO SAUCE

See pages 125 and 141

LEFTOVERS

The term "leftovers" doesn't do justice to the many delicious dishes that require cooked meat or poultry as their basic ingredient. Instead, when buying a roast, the day after should be part of one's planning so that the remains of the roast need never present a problem. This point of view also permits us to buy a larger roast, which is sometimes a greater economy. It isn't necessary to use the meat up on successive days—if wrapped in foil or Saran wrap to prevent its drying out, it will keep several days in the refrigerator, or it may be stored in the freezer until you are in the mood for that particular meat again.

The following recipes are good with any cooked meat, poultry or seafood, although in the recipes we have used the term "meat" to cover them all.

CROQUETTES

Butter, 4 tablespoons
Flour, 4 tablespoons
Milk, 1 cup
Egg, 1, beaten
Onion, 1, minced
Lemon Juice, 1 tablesp.
Cooked Meat, 1½ cups, ground

In top part of double boiler, over, but not touching boiling water, melt butter, stir in flour until well blended, then add milk, a little at a time, stirring constantly. Cook, stirring until very thick. Add egg, onion and lemon juice, and stir. Add meat with salt and pepper to taste, cool.

Fine Dry Crumbs
Egg, 1, beaten
Fat

Shape cold mixture into 4 croquettes. Chill thoroughly. Dip croquettes in crumbs, then in egg with 2 tablespoons water added, then in crumbs. Let stand ½ hour. Fry in deep hot fat (390°) until brown.

To serve 4

MONDAY À LA KING

Butter, 3 tablespoons
Green Pepper, 1 small, chopped
Mushrooms, ¼ pound, sliced
Flour, 4 tablespoons
Milk, 2 cups
Cream, 1 cup
Cooked Meat, cubed, 3 cups
Pimientos, 2, chopped
Worcestershire, 1 teasp.
Salt and **Pepper**, to taste

Sauté peppers and mushrooms over low heat in butter until just tender. Blend in flour, then add milk and cook until thickened, stirring constantly. Add cream, meat, pimientos and Worcestershire. Heat thoroughly, but do not boil. Season to taste.

Serve on crisp, hot toast.

To serve 4 or 5

À LA KING IN POPOVERS

Make popovers following the recipe on page 179. Split and fill with the à la King mixture.

TUESDAY GOULASH

Onions, sliced, 1 cup
Butter, 3 tablespoons
Cooked Meat, cubed, 2½ cups
Gravy or **Bouillon**, 1½ cups
Marjoram, 1 teaspoon
Sherry, ¼ cup
Noodles, Fine, 8-ounce package, cooked

Sauté onions over low heat in butter until soft. Add meat and marjoram. Add gravy or bouillon slowly, stirring constantly. Add wine and simmer 10 minutes. If sauce needs thickening, add 1 tablespoon flour mixed in a little cold water. Serve with cooked noodles.

To serve 4

CURRY

Onion, 1 med., chopped
Butter, 3 tablespoons
Flour, 3 tablespoons
Curry Powder, 1 tablesp.
Salt, 1 teaspoon
Bouillon Cubes, 2
Water, 2 cups, boiling
Cream, 1 cup
Cooked Meat, 2 to 3 cups
Lemon Juice, 1 tablesp.

Sauté onion in butter over low heat until soft. Blend in flour, and seasonings. Add bouillon cubes dissolved in boiling water, a little at a time, stirring constantly. Stir in cream; cook until thickened. Add meat and lemon juice; heat.

Rice, 1 cup raw

Meanwhile cook rice to serve with the curry.

To serve 4

Have a collection of garnishes, served in individual dishes, to eat with curry. These might include chopped green pepper, chutney, tiny onions, grated coconut, chopped nuts, raisins.

Let taste be your guide in the use of curry powder. Some like it hot, some like less. If you are new to curry, start with a small amount to try.

CURRIED PIE

Prepare Curry, according to above recipe. Cover with pastry. Bake in hot oven, 425° for 10 minutes, or until pastry is golden brown.

Monday
à la King

CASSEROLES WITH NOODLES

Tomato Paste, 6-oz. can
Water, 3 cups
Garlic, 1 clove, minced
Bay Leaf, 1
Instant Onion, 1 teasp.
Salt, 2 teaspoons
Pepper, ⅛ teaspoon
Noodles, 1 8-oz. pkg.
Cooked Meat, cubed,
   2 to 3 cups
Parmesan Cheese, grated

To serve 4 or 5

Combine tomato paste, water and seasonings and bring to boil. Add noodles and cook until tender, adding more water if needed, to make sure sauce covers noodles while cooking. Add meat, heat thoroughly. Pour into casserole; sprinkle with grated cheese. Put under broiler for 5 minutes, or until cheese is lightly browned.

CASSEROLES WITH RICE

Rice, 1 cup
Mushroom Soup, 1 can
Milk, 1 can
Frozen Peas, 1 package
Worcestershire, 1 teasp.
Cooked Meat, cubed,
   2 to 3 cups

Cook rice as directed on package and put into casserole. Combine soup, milk, onion, peas and leftover meat and pour over rice.

Oven, moderate, 375°
To serve 4 or 5

Bake 30 minutes, or until golden brown and bubbly.

RICE CASSEROLE PARMESAN: Sprinkle casserole with grated Parmesan cheese, if desired.

An attractive variation of this dish is to bake it in a greased ring mold. To serve, unmold on platter and fill center with one green vegetable.

DAY-BEFORE-PAYDAY PAPRIKA

Onions, 2 large, sliced
Garlic, 1 clove, minced
Butter, 2 tablespoons
Tomato Purée, 1 can
Bouillon, 1 cup
Cooked Meat, cubed,
   2 cups
Paprika, 1 tablesp. or
   more accg. to taste
Sour Cream, 1 cup

To serve 4

Sauté onions and garlic in butter until golden. Add tomato purée, bouillon, paprika and meat. Simmer over low heat for 15 minutes. Stir in sour cream remove from heat before it boils, and serve at once, over rice or noodles.

CHOW MEIN

Oil, 3 tablespoons
Onion, 1 medium, sliced
Celery, sliced, 1 cup
Mushrooms, ½ lb.
Bouillon, 1 can
Water, ½ can
Cooked Meat, diced,
   2 cups
Bean Sprouts, 1 can,
   drained
Soy Sauce, 3 tablespoons
Salt and **Pepper,** to taste
Cornstarch, 1 tablespoon
Chow Mein Noodles,
   1 can

To serve 4

Sauté onion, celery and mushrooms in oil until soft. Add bouillon and water and simmer 5 minutes. Add meat, bean-sprouts and seasonings, mix cornstarch with a little cold water and add. Cook until just slightly thickened. Serve with chow mein noodles.

93

SALAD MIX-UP

Leftover Meat, 2 cups
Onions, minced, ¼ cup
Celery, chopped, 1 cup
Cheddar Cheese, diced,
   ½ cup
Lemon Juice, 1 tablesp.
Capers, 2 tablespoons
Mayonnaise, ½ cup
Salt and **Pepper**, to taste

Combine ingredients and mix
thoroughly.

Lettuce or **Watercress**
Cucumber or **Tomato**

Serve on individual plates of
crisp lettuce or watercress.
Garnish with slices of cucumber
or tomato wedges.

To serve 4

SALAD STRETCHERS: If leftover meat or poultry is on the short
side, cooked macaroni, rice or kidney beans may be substituted.

SUNDAY NIGHT SANDWICHES

Slice leftover meat or poultry thin, spread bread with butter,
mayonnaise or other sandwich spread. Fill sandwich with
sliced meat and one of the following:

Thin slices of onion
Pickle relish
Swiss or Mozarella cheese

Chili sauce
Catsup
Chopped watercress

EGG FOO YOUNG

Eggs, 4, beaten
Cooked Meat, diced,
   ¾ cup
Scallions, 3, chopped
Bean Sprouts, 1 cup,
   drained

To serve 4

Pour ¼ of beaten eggs into
small greased skillet. Combine
meat with vegetables and
sprinkle ¼ of mixture over egg.
Cook 1 minute, turn over and
lightly brown other side. Fold
over and set aside on warm
platter, while making the next.
When 4 are cooked, served with
Egg Foo Young Gravy.

EGG FOO YOUNG GRAVY

Chicken Broth or
   Consommé, 1½ cups
Soy Sauce, 1 tablespoon
Cornstarch, 1½ tablesps.
Sugar, 1 teaspoon

Boil ingredients together,
stirring until sauce is clear and
slightly thickened. Spoon over
Egg Foo Young.

SOUFFLÉS WITH MEAT

See Soufflés, page 117.

JAMBALAYA

See "Easy Jambalaya", page 18. Cooked, shelled, fresh or
frozen shrimp may be substituted for canned, if desired.

PENNYPINCH POT PIE

Fat, 3 tablespoons
Flour, 3 tablespoons
Meat Stock or **Bouillon,**
    2 cups
Milk, ½ cup
Cooked Meat, cubed,
    3½ cups
Frozen Mixed Vegetables,
    1 package, cooked
Pastry

Oven, hot, 425°

To serve 4

Melt fat in saucepan over low heat, blend in flour. Add meat stock and milk; cook, stirring constantly, until thickened. Add meat and heat thoroughly. Add cooked vegetables and pour into baking dish; or arrange an equal amount of the vegetable and meat in individual baking dishes, with a portion of sauce in each. Cover tops with pastry.

Bake 10 to 15 minutes, until pastry tops are browned.

BAKED HASH

Onions, 2 medium, sliced
Butter, 2 tablespoons
Cooked Meat, diced,
    2 cups
Potatoes, cooked, diced,
    2 cups
Parsley, 1 tablespoon
Marjoram, ¼ teaspoon
Worcestershire, 1 teasp.
Gravy or **Bouillon,** 1 cup
Salt and **Pepper,** to taste

Oven, moderate, 350°

To serve 4

Sauté onions in butter until soft. Add meat, potatoes and seasonings; brown lightly. Add gravy and mix; pour into greased casserole.

Bake 30 minutes.

TETRAZZINI

Spaghetti, 8 ounces
Frozen Peas, 1 package

Butter, 3 tablespoons
Flour, 3 tablespoons
Turkey or **Chicken Stock,**
    2 cups
Milk, 1 cup
Salt and **Pepper**
Leftover Poultry, 3 cups
Pimientos, 2 tablespoons,
    chopped
Parmesan Cheese

Oven, moderate, 375°

To serve 4

Cook spaghetti in boiling salted water according to directions on package. Cook peas separately.

Meanwhile, over low heat melt butter in skillet, blend in flour, add stock, stirring constantly. Add milk and stir until thickened. Add meat and pimiento and season to taste; heat thoroughly. Combine with spaghetti and peas in casserole. Sprinkle top with Parmesan Cheese.

Bake 20 minutes, or until lightly browned on top.

This dish is especially good with leftover turkey or chicken, but could be made with other leftover meats.

HOT SANDWICHES

Heat leftover gravy in skillet. If gravy is in short supply it can be extended with canned bouillon, or a bouillon cube dissolved in boiling water, or with canned gravy. Slice leftover meat in uniform slices and heat thoroughly, but do not boil, in gravy. Serve on plain bread or toast.

READY-QUICK RAGOÛT

Fat, 2 tablespoons
Onion, 1 large, chopped
Cooked Meat, cubed,
    2–3 cups
Salt, 1 teaspoon
Pepper, ¼ teaspoon
Worcestershire, 1 teasp.
Stock, Bouillon or
    Gravy, 1 cup
Mushrooms, 1 6-oz. can
Sour Cream, ½ cup.

To serve 4

Brown onions gently in fat in skillet. Add veal and brown lightly. Add seasonings and stock, cover and bring to boil and simmer 30 minutes. Add mushrooms and sour cream, heat thoroughly but do not boil.

This dish is especially good with veal.

SHEPHERD'S PIE

Cooked Meat, cubed,
    2 cups
Leftover Vegetables,
    1½ cups, or
Frozen Mixed Vegetables,
    1 package
Onions, 1 can, drained
Gravy, 2 cups

Mashed Potatoes, left-
    over or frozen, 2 cups
Egg Yolk, 1

Oven, hot, 425°

To serve 4

Combine meat, vegetables and gravy, heat, and season to taste. Pour into casserole.

Beat egg yolk into mashed potatoes, make border with pastry tube or spoon around edge of mixture in casserole.

Bake 25 minutes, or until potatoes are golden brown.

SCALLOPED MEAT AND POTATOES

See recipe for Scalloped Potatoes on page 149. Add 2 cups of chopped cooked meat, sprinkling it over each layer of potatoes.

MEAT FRITTERS

See recipe for Corn Fritters on page 140.

OMELETS WITH COOKED MEAT

See Filled Omelets, page 114.

Combine leftover meat and vegetables in casseroles with noodles or spaghetti

HAM AND SPAGHETTI CASSEROLE

Spaghetti, 1½ cups
Butter, 2 tablespoons

Flour, 2 tablespoons
Milk, 1 cup

American Cheese, grated, 1 cup
Salt, 1 teaspoon
Catsup, 2 tablespoons
Horse-radish, 1 tablespoon
Ham, cooked, diced, 2 cups
Peas, cooked, 1 cup
Bread Crumbs, fresh, ¼ cup
Butter, melted, 1 tablespoon

Serves 4

Cook 1 8-oz. pkg. spaghetti as directed; drain.

Melt butter in saucepan over low heat; blend in flour. Gradually add milk. Stir until thickened and remove from heat.

Add cheese, stirring until melted. Add spaghetti, salt, catsup, horse-radish, ham, peas. Put in 1½ quart casserole. Top with combined bread crumbs and melted butter. Bake, uncovered, 30 minutes, or until crumbs are browned.

GINGER CURRIED POULTRY

Butter, 5 tablespoons
Onions, minced, ½ cup
Flour, 6 tablespoons
Curry Powder, 2½ teaspoons
Salt, 1½ teaspoons
Ginger, ground, ¼ teaspoon

Chicken Bouillon, 1 cup
Milk, 2 cups

Turkey or chicken, cooked, diced, 4 cups
Lemon Juice, 1 teaspoon
Rice, cooked 3 cups

Serves 6–8

Melt butter in double boiler top over direct heat. Add onions, simmer until tender. Stir in flour and seasonings.

Gradually stir in bouillon and milk. Cook over boiling water, stirring until thickened.

Add turkey and lemon juice. Heat and serve in rice ring.

96

Curried turkey served in a rice ring

Shepherd's pie

STUFFED TOMATOES AND PEPPERS

Peppers, 4 large or **Tomatoes,** 4 large	Cut tops off peppers, scoop out seeds, boil in water 3 minutes. Cut tops off tomatoes; scoop out centers. Stuff with one of the following mixtures:

Bread Stuffing

Onion, 1 med., chopped **Fat,** 2 tablespoons **Cooked Meat,** minced, 2 cups **Parsley,** 1 tablespoon, chopped **Soft Bread Crumbs,** 1 cup **Worcestershire,** 1 teasp. **Prepared Mustard,** 1 tablespoon **Gravy,** 1 cup **Salt** and **Pepper,** to taste	Sauté onion in fat until soft. Add remaining ingredients, moistening with a little of the gravy. Season with salt and pepper. Put remaining gravy in casserole and place stuffed vegetables in it.
Oven, moderate, 375°	Bake 25 minutes.

Chili-Rice Stuffing

Cooked Meat, ground, 1 cup **Rice,** cooked, 1 cup **Egg,** 1, beaten **Butter,** 1 tablespoon **Salt,** ½ teaspoon **Pepper,** ⅛ teaspoon **Chili Powder,** ½ teasp. **Grated Cheese,** ¼ cup	Combine all ingredients and fill peppers.

SPENDTHRIFT MUSHROOMS AND SHERRY

Mushrooms, ½ lb., sliced **Butter,** 2 tablespoons **Instant Onion,** 1 teasp. **Leftover Gravy,** 1 cup **Leftover Roast Meat,** 8 slices **Sherry,** 2 tablespoons **Salt** and **Pepper,** to taste	Sauté mushrooms in butter until golden brown. Add remaining ingredients and heat thoroughly over low heat, seasoning to taste.

To serve 4

TOASTED TRIFLES

On broiler rack arrange slices of toast. Spread slices of roast meat with prepared mustard or salad dressing and arrange on toast; add 2 or 3 canned asparagus spears, then a thin slice of Cheddar cheese. Place under the broiler, but far enough from it so that the food can heat thoroughly without burning.

SOUP

The basis of all soups is "stock," the essence extracted from meat, poultry or fish, or, in some cases, vegetables alone. The old-fashioned way of making soup was to begin with meat and bones, simmered for hours into a rich brew. Today we have a quicker method with the pressure cooker and we also have delicious canned or dehydrated soups at hand. In by-gone days the thrifty cook, who had a coal range always warm, utilized her leftover steak and roast bones to keep a soup stock going, and added to it her wilted greens or left-over vegetables and cereals. With a modern stove this may not be an economy today, but because the flavour of good homemade soup is hard to beat, it might still be a good practice.

If you use a pressure cooker, follow the recipe for ingredients, browning them first in the pressure cooker, if the recipe calls for it, then process according to the instructions that came with your own cooker.

BROWN SOUP STOCK

Beef Shin, 4 pounds
Fat, 1 tablespoon
Cold Water, 12 cups
Onion, ¼ cup, chopped
Carrot, ½ cup, chopped
Parsley, 2 sprigs
Celery Tops, 2
Salt, 2 teaspoons
Pepper, ⅛ teaspoon
To make about 8 cups

Have a butcher chop bone and meat into pieces. Brown in fat lightly in kettle. Add water; heat slowly to boiling point. Skim, cover and simmer 3 hours, removing scum from time to time. Add vegetables and simmer ½ hour longer. Strain through fine sieve or cheesecloth. Cool and skim off fat.

To remove fat: Cool and skim off as much as possible with a spoon. To remove the last small globules of fat, float sheets of paper toweling on the surface, removing them quickly as they take up the grease.

BOUILLON

Bouillon is clarified Brown Soup Stock.

To clarify: Add slightly beaten egg white and broken egg shell to strained cold soup stock. Heat to boiling point, stirring constantly. Remove from heat, let it partially cool, strain through 2 thicknesses of cheesecloth.

CONSOMMÉ

Consommé is clarified Brown Soup Stock, but made with half knuckle of veal substituted for half of the beef shin.

BEEF BROTH

Beef Broth is Brown Soup Stock served in its unclarified state.

MIMOSA SOUP

Bouillon, 4 cups
Green Beans, cut in small pieces, 2 cups
Onion, sliced, ¼ cup
Egg Yolks, hard-cooked, 2
To make about 4 cups

Bring bouillon to boil, add string beans and onions, and cook until beans are tender, about 12 minutes. Pour into serving dishes and top each with a sprinkling of finely crumbled egg yolk.

FRENCH ONION SOUP

Onions, sliced, 3 cups
Butter, 4 tablespoons
Beef Stock, 4 cups
Salt and **Pepper,** to taste

Brown onions in butter in heavy kettle. Add stock, bring to boil and simmer ½ hour or until onions are tender. Season to taste.

French Bread, small slices, toasted
Grated Parmesan Cheese
To make about 4 cups

Serve in one large or individual casseroles. Top with toasted bread, sprinkled with cheese.

TOMATO BOUILLON

Combine canned tomato juice with an equal amount of bouillon and heat. Season with a little lemon juice; add a dash each of sugar and basil. Add instant onion, if you like the onion flavor in it. Top each portion with a little chopped parsley or a thin slice of lemon.

WHITE SOUP STOCK

Follow procedure in Brown Soup Stock, but for beef shin substitute 4 pounds knuckle of veal, cracked into pieces; or, a 4-pound stewing chicken. Or you might use a combination of both.

CHICKEN BROTH

Make a soup stock using only chicken; a 4-pound stewing chicken cut up. Proceed as in Brown Soup Stock. Strain and serve hot.

If desired 2 tablespoons of rice or barley that has been soaked overnight, may be added to broth and simmered until tender.

The chicken meat may be used in salads or creamed dishes.

CHICKEN CONSOMMÉ

Clarify the Chicken Broth following the directions under Bouillon.

JELLIED SOUPS

Bouillon and Consommé may be chilled and served in a jellied form as appetite-stimulating hot-weather soups. Garnish them with lemon slices.

*Consommé,
hot or jellied*

COCK-A-LEEKIE SOUP

Stewing Chicken, 1,
  cut up
Salt, 1 tablespoon
Water, 10 cups
Garlic, 1 clove, minced
Parsley, few sprigs
Leeks, 1 dozen, white
  parts only, cut up
Potatoes, 8, peeled and
  diced
Salt and Pepper, to taste
Cream, ½ cup

Simmer chicken and seasonings 3 hours or until chicken is tender. Remove meat from bones, cut in small pieces. Skim fat from stock. Add leeks, potatoes and chicken. Cover and simmer 30 minutes. Season to taste. Add cream and serve at once.

To make about 12 cups

CHINESE EGG DROP SOUP

Cornstarch, 2 tablesps.
White or Chicken Stock,
  6 cups
Eggs, 2, beaten
Salt and Pepper, to taste

Mix cornstarch in well-flavoured cold stock in saucepan. Bring to boil and simmer until clear, stirring occasionally. Gradually stir in eggs, check seasoning, and serve at once.

To make about 6 cups

MULLIGATAWNY

Onions, 3, chopped
Celery, chopped, ½ cup
Garlic, 1 clove, minced
Apple, 1, chopped
Curry Powder, 1 tablesp.
Salt, 2 teaspoons
Pepper, ¼ teaspoon
Stewing Chicken, 1, cut up
Water, 8 cups

In soup kettle sauté onions, celery, garlic and apple until golden. Add seasonings, chicken and water. Bring to boil, simmer 2 hours, or until tender.

Hot Boiled Rice

Serve with bowl of hot rice, to be eaten in the soup.

To make about 6 cups

PHILADELPHIA PEPPER POT

Veal Bone
Stewing Veal, 1 pound,
  cut up
Tripe, ½ lb., cut up
Thyme, ¼ teaspoon
Salt, 2 teaspoons
Whole Black Pepper,
  ½ teaspoon
Water, 8 cups
Onions, 2, chopped
Potatoes, 2, diced
Carrots, 2, diced
Celery, ½ cup, diced
Parsley, few sprigs,
  minced

Put veal bone, veal, tripe, thyme, salt, pepper and water in large kettle. Bring to boil and simmer 2 hours. Remove bone, add vegetables and simmer 30 minutes more. Add more salt and pepper if needed.

To make about 8 cups

SCOTCH BROTH

Breast of Lamb or
  Mutton, 3 lbs.,
  chopped in pieces
Barley, ½ cup
Salt, 1 tablespoon
Pepper, ¼ teaspoon
Water, 10 cups

Put lamb, barley, seasonings and water in kettle. Bring to boil, simmer for 2 hours, or until meat is tender. Remove meat from bones; trim off fat. Cool broth and skim fat. Return meat to kettle.

Onions, 2, chopped
Carrots, ½ cup, diced
Turnips, ½ cup, diced
Parsley, ¼ cup, chopped

Add vegetables, bring to boil, simmer ½ hour. Add more salt if necessary.

To make about 10 cups

BEAN SOUP

Dried Marrow, Navy, or
  Pea Beans, 1 pound
Water, 20 cups
Leftover Ham Bone
Onions, 2, chopped
Celery, 1 cup, diced
Garlic, 1 clove, minced
Bay Leaf, 1, crumbled
Salt and Pepper, to taste

Wash beans, cover with water; let soak overnight. Add ham bone with some meat on it; simmer, covered, 2 hours or until beans are soft and meat leaves bone. Remove bone and cut up meat. Add vegetables and seasonings; simmer 1 hour.

To make about 16 cups

BLACK BEAN SOUP

Follow directions for making Bean Soup. When cooked it can be puréed if desired by using a sieve or blender. Serve very hot and add 1 tablespoon of sherry in each bowl. Garnish with lemon slices or minced hard-cooked egg.

SPLIT PEA SOUP

Follow directions for making Bean Soup, substituting split peas for the beans. Remove bone and meat after cooking. Purée by putting soup through a sieve or blender. Serve with croutons or tiny sausage balls fried crisp. Good also with frankfurter slices.

LENTIL SOUP

Follow directions for making Bean Soup, substituting lentils for beans. Serve garnished with thin slices of lemon.

CORN CHOWDER

Salt Pork, ½ lb., diced
Onions, 2, chopped
Celery, ½ cup, chopped
Flour, 2 tablespoons
Water, 4 cups
Corn, 16-ounce can,
  cream style
Milk, 2 cups, evaporated
Salt and Pepper, to taste
Parsley, few sprigs,
  chopped

Cook salt pork in kettle until crisp. Remove pork and all but 3 tablespoons of fat. Add onions and celery to kettle and cook few minutes until soft. Blend in flour, add water. Cover and simmer 20 minutes. Add corn, milk and pork, heat thoroughly. Season to taste. Serve garnished with parsley.

To make about 8 cups

MINESTRONE

Salt Pork, ¼ lb., diced
Onions, 2 medium, sliced
Garlic, 1 clove, minced
Celery, ½ cup, sliced
Carrot, ½ cup, sliced
Parsley, ¼ cup, chopped
Cabbage, 1 cup, chopped
Water, 6 cups
Chick Peas, 16-ounce can
Tomatoes, 16-ounce can
Basil, ½ teaspoon
Thyme, ¼ teaspoon
Spaghetti, ½ cup, broken
Salt and **Pepper,** to taste

Parmesan Cheese, 1 cup, grated

To make about 10 cups

Brown salt pork and onion in large kettle. Add garlic and fresh vegetables; cook 10 minutes. Add water, chick peas, tomatoes and seasonings. Bring to boil, simmer 30 minutes. Add spaghetti, salt and pepper to taste. Simmer until spaghetti is tender.

Serve with a dish of grated cheese.

QUICK VEGETABLE SOUP

Onions, 2 medium
Green Pepper, 1
Carrots, 2
Celery Stalks, 2
Cabbage, ⅛ head
Butter, 3 tablespoons
Lima Beans, ½ cup
Green Beans, ½ cup
Tomatoes, 16-ounce can
Tomato Paste, 1 tablesp.
Bay Leaf
Salt and **Pepper,** to taste
Beef Bouillon, 3 cans
Water, 3 cans

To make about 10 cups

Slice onions, pepper, carrots, celery and cabbage. Melt butter in kettle, add onions and cook until golden in color. Add all remaining vegetables but tomatoes, and cook gently over low heat 5 minutes. Add tomatoes and paste, seasonings, bouillon and water. Cover, bring to boil and simmer until vegetables are tender, about 30 minutes.

Minestrone, a hearty nourishing soup

MUSHROOM SOUP

Mushrooms, 1 pound, chopped
Onion, 1 small, grated
Butter, 4 tablespoons
Flour, 4 tablespoons
Salt, 1 teaspoon
Pepper, ⅛ teaspoon
Milk, 4 cups
Chicken Stock, 2 cups
Sherry, ¼ cup
Parsley, ¼ cup, chopped

To make about 6 cups

Cook mushrooms and onion in butter until golden brown. Blend in flour and seasonings. Add milk and stock; cook until slightly thickened, stirring constantly. Add sherry. Serve and garnish with parsley.

CREAM OF POTATO SOUP

Leeks, 4
Butter, 2 tablespoons
Potatoes, 4 med., diced
Salt, 1 teaspoon
Milk, 2 cups
Cream, ½ cup
Pepper, ¼ teaspoon
Butter
Parsley, chopped

To make about 4 cups

Chop white part of leeks fine and cook in butter until soft and golden. Add potatoes, salt and boiling water to just cover. Cook until potatoes are soft. Mash them with potato masher. Add milk and cream and pepper and heat thoroughly, but do not boil. Pour into bowls; garnish with ½ teaspoonful of butter and sprinkle with chopped parsley. If smoother soup is desired, put potatoes and leek mixture through sieve or in blender.

Mushroom soup garnished with slivered raw mushrooms

FRESH PEA SOUP

Fresh Peas, 2 pounds
Water
Milk

Wash peas, shell and reserve ½ cupful. Put remaining peas and shells in water to just cover and boil about 30 minutes or until peas are mushy. Strain and reserve liquid. Press peas (and as much of the pod pulp as you can) through sieve or food mill. Combine with liquid and measure. Add an equal quantity of milk.

Butter, 3 tablespoons
Flour, 3 tablespoons
Egg, 1, beaten

Melt butter in deep saucepan, blend in flour, add soup mixture slowly, stirring constantly. Add reserved ½ cup of peas. Simmer, covered, over low heat 15 minutes. Add a little of the mixture to the egg, blend, and return to the pot. Heat and serve.

To make about 4 cups

CREAM OF SPINACH AND POTATO

Potato, 1 large
Onion, 1 large
Water
Frozen Spinach, 1 pkg.
Milk, 5 cups
Instant Garlic, ¼ teasp.
Celery Salt, ½ teasp.
Salt and Pepper, to taste

Cut up potato and onion, cover with water and cook slowly until tender. Add spinach, cook until thawed. Drain vegetables and put through blender or food mill, with half the ½ cup of milk. Do this twice. Reheat vegetable mixture and add remaining milk slowly, stirring constantly until hot. Add seasonings.

To make about 6 cups

BORSCH

Cooking Oil, 3 tablesps.
Onions, 4 large, sliced
Beets, 6 medium
Water, 8 cups, boiling
Salt, 1 teaspoon
Pepper, ¼ teaspoon
Celery Salt, ½ teaspoon
Basil, ½ teaspoon
Onion Salt, ½ teaspoon
Tomatoes, 16-ounce can
Sour Cream
Potatoes, hot boiled

Cook onions in oil in a large skillet until golden. Scrub and slice beets thin without peeling, and add to onions. Cook 10 minutes, stirring occasionally. Add water, seasonings, and tomatoes. Simmer slowly 30 minutes. Put through sieve or purée in blender. Reheat and serve with a dollop of sour cream on top of each bowl of soup; and pass potatoes to eat in the soup.

To make about 8 cups

This may be served chilled, if desired.

CREAM OF SPINACH WITH SHRIMP

Frozen Spinach, 1 pkg.

Cook spinach and purée in blender or food mill.

Butter, 3 tablespoons
Onion, 1 tablespoon, minced
Flour, 2 tablespoons
Beef Bouillon, 1 cup
Cream, thin, 2 cups
Shrimp, 1¼ cups, cooked or canned
Salt and Pepper, to taste
Sherry, ¼ cup

Sauté onion in butter until golden, blend in flour and bouillon, cook until it starts to thicken. Add cream and heat; add shrimp and seasoning; heat thoroughly but do not boil. Add sherry and serve.

To make about 6 cups

FRESH CREAM OF TOMATO

Ripe Tomatoes, 6
Onion, 1 small, chopped
Basil, 1 teaspoon
Bay Leaf, 1

Chop tomatoes and simmer with onion, basil and bay leaf for 15 minutes or until soft. Put through sieve or purée in colander.

Thin White Sauce, 3 cups (page 90)
Salt and Pepper, to taste

Make white sauce, add hot tomato purée slowly while stirring. If mixture curdles, beat smooth with rotary beater. Add salt and pepper to taste.

To make about 6 cups

OYSTER STEW

Oysters, 3 dozen, with liquid
Butter, ½ cup
Worcestershire, ¼ teasp.
Milk, 3 cups, hot
Light Cream, 3 cups, hot
Salt and Pepper, to taste
Paprika

Pick over oysters to remove any bits of shell. Put in large saucepan with liquid, butter and Worcestershire. Cook until edges of oysters begin to curl. Add milk and cream; heat, but do not boil. Add salt and pepper, sprinkle with paprika.

To serve 4

CLAM STEW: Substitute 3 dozen shucked clams with liquid for oysters.

LOBSTER STEW: Substitute 2 cups diced cooked lobster meat for oysters.

CLAM BROTH

Scrub clam shells and rinse in several waters. Put in kettle and add ½ cup of water for each quart of clams. Cover tightly and cook until shells open, about 10 minutes. Let stand 10 minutes, so that sediment will settle. Strain carefully and reserve cooked clams for clam chowder, or chop them for a canapé.

MANHATTAN CLAM CHOWDER

Salt Pork, ¼ lb., diced
Onion, 1 large, sliced
Celery, diced, ½ cup
Parsley, chopped,
  2 tablespoons
Carrot, diced, ½ cup
Potato, diced, 2 cups
Salt, 1 teaspoon
Water, 2 cups
Clams, 2 cups, with
  liquid
Tomatoes, 28-ounce can
Basil, ¼ teaspoon

Brown pork in kettle. Pour off all but 2 tablespoons fat and lightly brown onion and celery. Add carrot, potatoes, salt and water to kettle. Chop hard part of clams and add to kettle, reserving soft parts. Simmer 20 minutes or until potatoes are tender but not mushy. Add tomatoes, basil and soft part of clams to soup. Bring to boil, simmer few minutes.

To make 8–10 cups

NEW ENGLAND CLAM CHOWDER

Salt Pork, ¼ lb., diced
Onion, 1 large, sliced
Celery, 1 stalk, diced

Clams, 2 cups, with liquid
Potatoes, diced, 2 cups
Water, 1 cup
Milk, 3 cups
Salt and **Pepper,** to taste
Oyster Crackers

Brown salt pork in kettle. Pour off all but enough fat to cook onion and celery until soft but not brown.

Mince hard part of clams and add with liquid to kettle, reserving soft part. Add potatoes and water; bring to boil, cover, and simmer 20 minutes or until potatoes are tender. Add soft part of clams to soup; cook few minutes. Scald milk and add to soup. Season to taste, and serve at once with oyster crackers.

To make 6–8 cups

New England clam chowder can be made with a choice of seasonings

Cioppino and Bouillabaisse are two names for the same sort of seafood stew. In San Francisco you'll find Cioppino, and in New Orleans, Bouillabaisse. Both are traditional dishes in the lands surrounding the Mediterranean Sea, and in no two places are they made precisely alike, so you too may use your favorite fish and shellfish for these dishes.

FISHERMAN'S WHARF CIOPPINO

Olive Oil, 3 tablespoons
Onions, 2 med., chopped
Celery, 2 stalks, chopped
Parsley, 2 tablespoons, chopped
Thyme, ¼ teaspoon
Bay Leaf, 1, crumbled
Garlic, 2 cloves, minced
Salt, 1 teaspoon
Pepper, ¼ teaspoon
Tomatoes, 16-oz. can
Dry White Wine, 1 cup

Heat oil in skillet and cook onions, pepper and celery until soft but not brown. Add seasonings and tomatoes. Simmer 1 hour, covered. Add wine, simmer 5 minutes longer.

Small Clams, 12
Oysters, 12
Lobster Tails, 4, cracked
Crabs, 2, cracked

Scrub and rinse shellfish and put unshelled in large kettle. Pour sauce over, cover and simmer 20 minutes.

To serve 4 to 6

BOUILLABAISSE

Olive Oil, 4 tablespoons
Leeks, 3, chopped
Garlic, 2 cloves, minced
Fennel Seed, ½ teasp.
Cayenne, ⅛ teasp.
Tomatoes, 4, peeled
White Wine, ½ cup
Water or **Fish Stock,** 3 cups

Heat oil and cook leeks until soft but not brown. Add seasonings and tomatoes. Simmer 30 minutes. Just before cooking fish, add wine and water, and simmer 5 more minutes.

Fish, 3 pounds, assorted
Lobster Tails, 2 large, cut in pieces
Shrimp, 1 pound, shelled
Clams in shells, 1 dozen, scrubbed

Meanwhile prepare fish by cutting in pieces and removing as many bones as possible. Add fish, lobster, shrimp and clams to sauce, bring to boil, lower heat and simmer, covered, 15 minutes.

To serve 4

LOBSTER BISQUE

Milk, 3 cups
Cream, 1 cup
Salt, 1 teaspoon
Paprika, ¼ teaspoon
Instant Onion, ¼ teasp.
Flour, 3 tablespoons
Lobster, 6½-ounce can, chopped
Sherry, 2 tablespoons

With rotary beater combine milk, cream, salt, paprika, onion and flour in top part of double boiler and cook over rapidly boiling water 15 minutes, stirring frequently. Turn heat low and add lobster. Heat slowly 15 minutes. Add sherry. Serve hot or chilled.

To make about 5 cups

CRAB BISQUE

Follow the recipe for Lobster Bisque, but substitute 1 can crab meat for lobster.

CHICKEN OYSTER GUMBO

Stewing Chicken, 1, cut up
Water, 12 cups
Salt, 1 tablespoon

Simmer 3 hours or until chicken is tender. Remove meat from bones. Cut in small pieces. Discard bones and skin. Skim fat from broth.

Bacon Fat, 3 tablesps.
Garlic, 1 clove, minced
Onions, 3, chopped
Green Pepper, 1, chopped
Flour, 2 tablespoons
Tomatoes, 16-ounce can
Thyme, ¼ teaspoon
Parsley, few sprigs, chopped
Rice, ¼ cup
Worcestershire Sauce, 1 teaspoon
Gumbo Filé, 1–2 teasps.
Okra, 16-ounce can
Oysters, 2 cups

In fat in skillet, cook garlic, onions and pepper a few minutes until soft. Blend in flour. Add tomatoes, thyme, parsley and rice. Add to chicken and broth, and simmer ½ hour or until rice is tender. Add Worcestershire Sauce, Filé, okra and oysters. Cook until edges of oysters begin to curl. Serve at once.

To make about 12 cups

VELVETY SHRIMP BISQUE

Shrimp, 1 pound
Salt, 1 teaspoon
Bay Leaf, 1
Carrot, 1, sliced
Onion, 1, sliced

Remove shells and drop shrimp into boiling salted water, add seasonings. Simmer 5 minutes over low heat. Drain; devein shrimp and break in pieces.

Butter, 3 tablespoons
Celery, chopped, 1 cup
Onion, 1, minced
Flour, 4 tablespoons
Worcestershire, 1 teasp.
Salt, ½ teaspoon
Paprika, ½ teaspoon
Milk, 4 cups
Heavy Cream, 1 cup
Sherry, 3 tablespoons

Melt butter in skillet; sauté celery and onion until soft but not brown. Put into blender or through food chopper with shrimp. Return to saucepan; add flour and seasonings. Stir in milk and cook slowly until slightly thickened. Add cream, heat but do not boil. Add sherry and serve at once.

To make about 8 cups

106

Fish chowder may be garnished with sliced mushrooms

EASY FISH CHOWDER

Water, 4 cups
Salt, 1 teaspoon
Pepper, ¼ teaspoon
Cod or **Haddock,** 2 lb.
  or other fish in season

Bacon fat, 1 tablespoon
Onions, 2, chopped
Potatoes, 2 cups, diced
Milk, 2 cups scalded
Oyster Crackers
To make about 8 cups

Bring water and seasonings to boil; add fish, simmer 10 minutes. Remove fish and break into pieces. Strain liquid and reserve.

Cook onion in kettle with fat until soft. Add fish liquid and potatoes. Simmer 15 minutes or until tender. Add fish and milk. Heat thoroughly but do not boil. Serve with oyster crackers.

EASTERN SHORE CRAB SOUP

Onion, 1 med., chopped
Butter, 2 tablespoons
Crab, 2 6-ounce cans
Milk, 2½ cups
Heavy Cream, 1 cup
Scotch Whisky, 3 table-
  spoons

To make about 5 cups

Sauté onion in butter until soft. Pick over crab meat to remove any bits of shell and add to onion. Simmer over low heat 10 minutes; stir from time to time. Add milk and continue simmering 5 minutes, stirring constantly. Add cream, heat thoroughly but do not boil. Add Scotch and serve at once.

Some like it hot and some like it cold, but either way these soups, mainly from cans, with a little something added, are easy to prepare.

Try these combinations also with the delicious soup mixes that are now available in packages.

EASY SHRIMP BISQUE

Frozen Shrimp Soup, 2 cans
Milk, 2 cans
Sherry, 1/4 cup
Parsley, 2 tablespoons, chopped
Whipped Cream

To make about 5 cups

Combine soup and milk. Heat and beat with rotary beater until smooth. Add sherry. Serve with topping of whipped cream sprinkled with parsley.

CHILLED TOMATO-SHRIMP BISQUE

Tomato Soup, 1 can
Milk, 1 can
Shrimp, 4 1/2-ounce can
Lemon Juice, 1 tablesp.
Salt and Pepper, to taste
Chives, 1 tablespoon, chopped

To make about 4 cups

Beat soup and milk together until smooth. Add shrimp, broken into pieces. Add lemon juice; season to taste, chill. Garnish with chopped chives.

TOMATO CRAB BISQUE: Crab meat may be substituted for shrimp, or a combination of the two may be used.

CREAMY CELERY AND POTATO SOUP

Leftover Mashed Potatoes, 1/2 cup
Cream of Celery Soup, 1 can
Milk, 2 cups
Salt and Pepper, to taste
Chives or Parsley, 2 tablesps., chopped

To make about 4 cups

Combine in a blender or beat in a bowl, the potatoes, adding milk a little at a time until they are of a semi-liquid consistency. Then add the soup and balance of milk, beating all together. Season with salt and pepper. Chill thoroughly. Serve garnished with chives or parsley.

This may be served hot, too, if desired.

EASY CRAB BISQUE

Tomato Soup, 1 can
Pea Soup, 1 can
Milk, 1 can
Cream, 1 can
Crab Meat, 1 6-oz. can
Sherry, 1/4 cup

To make about 6 cups

Combine soups, milk and cream, and heat to boiling point. Add crab and sherry. Heat and serve.

SNOW DROP SOUP

Chicken-Rice Soup, 2 cans
Water, 2 cans
Onions, 1 med., chopped
Lemon Juice, 2 tablesps.
Sugar, 1 tablespoon
Eggs, 2, separated
Parsley, 2 tablespoons, minced

To make about 6 cups

Combine soup, water and onion, lemon juice and sugar in a saucepan, bring to boil and simmer 10 minutes. Stir a little of the soup into the beaten egg yolks, then add them to the soup. Let it simmer a few minutes. Beat the egg whites stiff and drop by spoonfuls on top of soup. Continue simmering 10 minutes. Serve with minced parsley, garnishing with the "snow drops".

APRICOT SOUP

Ripe Apricots, 1 pound
Water, 4 cups
Lemon Juice, 1 lemon
Stick Cinnamon, 1 small piece
Sugar, to taste
Sherry, 2 tablespoons
Sour Cream

To make about 5 cups

Pit apricots and put in saucepan with water and lemon juice, and cinnamon. Cook slowly until apricots are tender. Remove cinnamon, purée apricots in blender or sieve. Add a little sugar depending on acidity of fruit. Add sherry, heat until sugar melts. Chill thoroughly and serve with a dollop of sour cream on each portion.

This soup is good also made with plums, peaches, or sour cherries.

CHICKEN MEDLEY

Leeks, 2 sliced white part only
Bacon Fat, 2 tablesps.
Celery, 1/2 cup, sliced
Rice, raw, 1/4 cup
Chicken Broth, 2 cans
Water, 2 cans

Mushrooms, 1/4-pound, sliced
Butter, 1 tablespoon
Smoked Ham, 3/4 cup, thin strips
Chicken, Cooked, 1 cup, thin strips
Salt and Pepper, to taste
Leeks, 2, green tops only

To make about 7 cups

Sauté leeks lightly in bacon fat in kettle. Add celery and rice and stir over low heat 3 or 4 minutes. Add broth and water, bring to boil and simmer gently until celery and rice are nearly done, about 15 minutes.

Sauté mushrooms lightly in butter, then add to soup. Add ham strips and simmer 5 minutes. Add chicken strips just before serving and season to taste. Garnish with leek tops chopped fine.

ICED TOMATO BOUILLON

Bouillon, 1 can
Tomato Juice, 3 cups
Onion, 1, grated
Celery, 1 cup, diced
Green Pepper, 1, minced
Parsley, 2 tablespoons
Salt, 1 teaspoon
Garlic, 1 clove

Combine bouillon, tomato juice, vegetables and seasonings. Cover and chill several hours.

Lemon Juice, 3 tablesps.

Just before serving, remove garlic, add lemon juice. Put a cube of ice in each serving.

To make about 6 cups

TOMATO ICE

Tomatoes, 6, ripe
Green Onions, 2
Parsley, handful
Salt and **Pepper,** to taste

Put peeled tomatoes, onions and parsley into a blender or grind onions and parsley and put tomatoes through a ricer or food mill. Season and put in refrigerator tray to frappé. Serve with lemon wedges.

To serve 4

CHILLED CREAM OF TOMATO-AND-CUCUMBER SOUP

Tomato Soup, 1 can
Water, 1 can
Cucumber, ½, grated
Green Onions, ¼ cup, chopped
Salt, 1 teaspoon
Pepper, ⅛ teaspoon
Heavy Cream, 1 cup
Parsley

Combine soup, water, vegetables and seasonings. Chill for several hours. Strain. Add cream and chill. Garnish with chopped parsley.

To make about 4 cups

HOT CURRIED CONSOMMÉ

Apple, 1, tart
Onion, 1 medium
Consommé, 2 cans
Water, 2 cans
Salt and **Pepper,** to taste
Sherry, ¼ cup
Curry Powder, 1 teasp.

Peel and dice apple and onion and simmer in consommé and water over low heat until soft. Cool, then purée in electric blender or food mill. Return to stock, add salt and pepper, then the sherry and curry powder. Heat to boiling point and serve. Garnish each bowl with twist of lemon peel.

To make about 5 cups

CHILLED TARRAGON CHICKEN SOUP

Cream of Chicken Soup, 1 can
Chicken Broth, 1 can
Heavy Cream, 1 cup
Fresh Tarragon, 1 teasp.

Combine ingredients in electric blender or beat with rotary beater until mixture is smooth. Chill thoroughly.

To make about 4 cups

ITALIAN-STYLE BLACK BEAN SOUP

Black Bean Soup, 2 cans
Beef Bouillon, 1 can
Water, 1 cup
Dry Red Wine, ½ cup
Salami, 1½ cups, cubed

Mix soup and liquids and heat thoroughly. Add cubed salami; heat 5 minutes longer before serving.

To make about 6 cups

Chilled soup made with sour cherries

GAZPACHO

Tomatoes, 4, ripe
Bouillon, 1 cup
Water, 1 cup
Olive Oil, ¼ cup
Lemon Juice, ¼ cup
Garlic, 2 cloves, minced
Tray of Ice Cubes
Green Onions, 2, sliced
Cucumber, 1, sliced
Green Peppers,
   1, chopped
Celery, ½ cup, diced
Bread Crumbs, dry, 2
   cups, or tiny croutons

Scald and peel tomatoes; purée in blender or food mill. Add bouillon, water, olive oil, lemon juice, and garlic and pour over ice cubes in a deep bowl. Add the vegetables and stir. Let the bowl sit until the ice is nearly all melted. Serve while icy cold, in individual bowls, and sprinkle bread crumbs on the top, or toast dry bread into half-inch squares.

To make about 8 cups

This Spanish soup might almost be called a salad-soup, and can take the place of both in a summer meal.

MAINE FISH CHOWDER

Salt Pork, ¼ pound,
   cut in ½" cubes
Potatoes, raw, diced,
   4 cups
Onions, 2 medium, sliced
Boiling Water, 2 cups

Cook pork slowly in chowder kettle until fat is rendered out. Remove crisp pieces of pork and reserve. Add potatoes, onions and boiling water to pot and cook 10 minutes, or until potatoes are tender but firm.

Haddock or **Cod,**
   2 pounds, skinned
Cold Water

Meanwhile cut fish in pieces, and in separate pan combine fish with cold water to just cover it and bring to boil. Simmer 10 minutes. Remove bones and add fish and liquid to potato mixture. Reheat but do not boil, and add scalded milk, salt and pepper and butter.

Milk, 4 cups, scalded
Salt and **Pepper** to taste
Butter, 3 tablespoons.

Serve in chowder bowls with a large bowl of oyster crackers on the side. Crisp pork bits may be used as garnish. The chowder may be reheated, but never let it boil.

TOMATO MADRILENE

Prepare Tomato Bouillon (page 109). For each cup of soup add ½ envelope of gelatin. Soften gelatin in ¼ cup of cold water and dissolve in a cup of hot soup. Add it to the remainder of the soup; stir thoroughly and chill until nearly firm. Break up slightly with a fork. Serve in bouillon cups with lemon wedges.

VICHYSSOISE

Leeks, 4 large
Onion, 1
Butter, ¼ cup
Potatoes, 4 med., peeled
Chicken Stock or **Canned
   Chicken Consommé,**
   4 cups

Chop white part of leeks, and onion, very fine. Cook gently in butter until soft, without browning. Slice potatoes very thin and add with stock to onion mixture. Bring to boil and simmer, covered, 30 minutes. put through fine sieve or blender; return to kettle.

Cream, 2 cups
Salt and **Pepper,** to taste
Chives, ½ cup, chopped

Add cream to soup mixture, bring to scalding point, remove from heat. Season to taste. Chill thoroughly. Serve in chilled bowl with 1 tablespoon of chives sprinkled on each serving.

To make about 6 cups

WATERCRESS SOUP

Follow the above recipe for Vichyssoise and add one bunch of well-washed chopped watercress to the onion mixture at the same time the potatoes are added. Continue with recipe as given. When serving, garnish each bowl of soup with a sprig of watercress.

HEARTY BEEF AND VEGETABLE SOUP

Ground Beef, ¾ pound
Vegetable Oil,
   3 tablespoons
Onions, 2 medium,
   chopped
Garlic, one clove,
   chopped fine
Tomatoes, 28-ounce can
Tomato Juice, 1 cup
Peas, 16-ounce can
Salt, 2 teaspoons
Pepper, ⅛ teaspoon
Basil, dried, ½ teaspoon
Thin Spaghetti, broken
   1-inch pieces, 1 cup
Grated Cheese, Romano
   or **Parmesan,** 1 cup

In the soup pot, lightly brown the beef, breaking it apart with a fork. Add vegetables and seasonings, mixing all together. Cover and simmer over low heat for 30 minutes, stirring from time to time.

Add spaghetti and simmer an additional 15 minutes. Thin with additional hot tomato juice or hot water, if needed. Serve in soup bowls and top each serving with grated cheese.

EGGS

Eggs are a high source of protein and contain many of the vitamins and minerals that the body requires. So that none of these nutrients are lost, eggs should be refrigerated from the time they are laid. Buy only refrigerated eggs and get them home and into your own refrigerator quickly. Store them, without washing, large end up in a covered container. When possible, buy eggs that are government graded for quality and size. Government quality grades are US grade AA, A, B and C. Size grades are Jumbo, Extra Large, Large, Medium, Small and Peewee.

Many of these egg dishes can substitute for meat at dinner, and they make quickly prepared lunch and supper dishes. See also the cheese dishes in the following section that combine with eggs to make an even more nourishing meal.

SOFT-COOKED EGGS

When eggs are to be cooked in their shells, remove from refrigerator and let them come to room temperature. Icy cold shells are apt to break in cooking.

Put eggs in saucepan with enough cold water to completely cover tops. Cover, bring to hard boil; remove from heat. Let stand in hot water 2 minutes for very soft eggs; 3 minutes for medium; and 4 minutes for eggs with very firm whites but soft yolks.

Serve in shells in egg cups, with the end cracked; or remove from shells into dish. Sprinkle with salt and pepper.

HARD-COOKED EGGS

Follow directions for soft-cooked eggs, but let eggs stand for 15 minutes. Drain and cool at once in cold water, to aid in removing shells. To peel egg, tap entire surface to crack it; loosen shell starting at large end.

DEVILED EGGS

Eggs, 4, hard-cooked
Mayonnaise, 2 tablesps.
Prep. Mustard, ½ teasp.
Paprika, ¼ teasp.
Celery Seed, ¼ teasp.
Salt, ¼ teaspoon
White Pepper, dash

Shell eggs and cut in half lengthwise. Remove yolks, set whites aside. Mash yolks with fork, add mayonnaise and seasonings and mix well. Fill whites, letting the mixture form a mound. Garnish top with slice of stuffed olive.

CURRY DEVILED EGGS: To the above recipe add ¼ teaspoon curry powder.

ANCHOVY DEVILED EGGS: Follow the above recipe for Deviled Eggs, but omit mustard and salt. Add 1 tablespoon anchovy paste.

EGGS BENEDICT

Ham, 8 slices, baked or ready-to-fry
English Muffins, 4
Eggs, 8, poached
Hollandaise Sauce (page 91)

To serve 4

Fry ham gently; when done put on top of muffins that have been split, toasted and buttered. Top each with poached egg and cover with sauce.

EGGS IN CREAM SAUCE

Medium White Sauce, 2 cups
Eggs, 6, hard-cooked
Bread Crumbs or **Grated Cheese,** optional

To serve 4

Make medium white sauce in top of double boiler (see page 90). Slice hard-cooked eggs and add. Serve on crisp toast; or, pour into baking dish and top with buttered bread crumbs or grated cheese. Heat under broiler until top is lightly browned.

EGGS IN CHEESE SAUCE

Add 6 sliced hard-cooked eggs to 2 cups of Cheese Sauce (page 90). Serve on toast. To serve 4.

CURRIED EGGS

Add 6 sliced eggs to 2 cups Béchamel Sauce (page 90). Blend in 1 teaspoon curry powder. Serve on toast. To serve 4. More curry may be added to suit the taste.

EGGS AU GRATIN

Eggs, 6, hard-cooked
Sharp Cheddar Cheese, 1 cup, diced
Béchamel Sauce, 1 cup (see page 90)
Heavy Cream, ½ cup
Bread Crumbs, ⅓ cup, soft
Butter, 2 tablespoons

Oven, moderate, 375°
To serve 4

Combine sliced eggs, cheese, sauce and cream in baking dish. Melt butter and combine with soft bread crumbs, to top baking dish.

Bake 15 minutes, or until golden brown.

EGGS DE LUXE

Chicken Livers, ½ lb.
Mushrooms, ¼ pound
Butter, 2 tablespoons
Béchamel Sauce, 1½ cups (see page 90)
Egg, 1, beaten
Eggs, 4, hard-cooked, quartered

To serve 4

Cut chicken livers in several pieces and slice mushrooms: sauté in butter until lightly browned. Add sauce and heat well. Mix a little of the sauce with beaten egg, and add back to sauce. Add hard-cooked eggs. Serve on patty shells or toast.

Poached eggs on toast

SHIRRED (BAKED) EGGS

Butter individual baking dishes or custard cups. Break one or two eggs into each. Season with salt and pepper. Bake in slow (325°) oven 10 to 15 minutes, or until egg is done to your taste.

For a variation, season shirred eggs with a pinch of rosemary and a teaspoon of sherry.

EGGS IN TOMATO CUPS

Tomatoes, 4 Basil Oven, moderate, 350°	Cut off stem end of tomatoes and scoop cut-out cores. Turn upside down to drain. Place in baking dish, sprinkle with a pinch of basil and bake 10 minutes.
Eggs, 4 Salt and Pepper, to taste Instant Onion Cheese, 2 tablespoons, grated Bread Crumbs, 2 tablesps. *To serve 4*	Break an egg into each tomato. Season with salt and pepper, and a pinch of onion. Combine cheese and crumbs and sprinkle on top. Bake 10 minutes longer or until golden brown.

TOP-OF-THE-STOVE SHIRRED EGGS

Break eggs into individual buttered baking dishes and set in a skillet containing a half-inch of boiling water. Cook on top of stove until eggs are set. If you want the yolks to be veiled cover the skillet.

POACHED EGGS

Use an egg poacher according to directions; or fill a skillet with enough water so that eggs will be covered, bring to a boil and lower heat so that water is barely simmering. Add ½ teaspoon salt. Break egg into saucer and slide gently into water. Several eggs may be poached at once. Simmer 3 to 5 minutes, or until whites are set and yolks done as desired. Use slotted spoon to remove from water; drain well. Serve on toast.

Poached eggs may be topped with Cheese Sauce (page 90) or Hollandaise Sauce (page 91) if desired.

EGGS POACHED IN CREAM

Follow above recipe for poached eggs, using ½ inch of cream in skillet instead of water. Keep it just under the boiling point. Poach eggs to desired doneness.

CORNED BEEF HASH AND POACHED EGG

Sauté slices of canned corned beef hash and serve topped with poached egg.

SPINACH AND POACHED EGG

Serve mounds of cooked, well-drained spinach topped with poached egg.

FRIED EGGS

Butter, 1 tablespoon Eggs, 4	In 8-inch skillet melt butter; add eggs, breaking each one in a saucer and sliding it into the pan. Cover and cook over very low heat until whites are set.

EGGS "OVER" WITHOUT TURNING: Cook as above but add 1 tablespoon of water to pan before covering. The water will "veil" the yolks.

EGGS WITH BROWNED BUTTER

Fry eggs gently in butter as above. Remove eggs and keep warm. Add an extra tablespoon of butter to skillet and let brown. Add 1 tablespoon of lemon juice; beat, and pour over eggs.

BACON AND EGGS

Bacon, 8 slices
Eggs, 8

Fry bacon in 10-inch skillet until crisp. Drain on paper towels and set in warm place. Pour off all but two tablespoons of the fat. Break eggs one by one in a cup and slide into skillet, doing as many at one time as the skillet will comfortably hold. Cover and cook over low heat until whites are set. Turn, if you like them easy over, with a pancake turner, or add a tablespoon of water which will "veil" the yolks.

To serve 4

HAM AND EGGS

Smoked Ham Slice, 1 lb.
Eggs, 8

Cut ham into serving pieces and fry in skillet until brown on both sides. Use a little of the outside fat on the ham to grease the skillet. Remove ham to warm platter and keep in warm place while cooking eggs according to recipe for Bacon and Eggs.

To serve 4

SCRAMBLED EGGS

Eggs, 8
Milk, 1/2 cup
Salt, 1/2 teaspoon
Pepper, 1/8 teaspoon
Butter, 3 tablespoons

Break eggs into large bowl, add milk, salt and pepper, and beat until foamy. Melt butter in large skillet, pour in eggs and cook slowly. Use the edge of your pancake turner to push back mixture from edges as it cooks, letting liquid mixture take its place. Finished eggs should have a fluffy appearance, and be slightly moist. Serve at once on warm plates.

To serve 4

EGGS COUNTRY STYLE

Potatoes, 2, medium
Butter, 1 tablespoon

Pare potatoes and slice very thin. Sauté in butter until brown, stirring frequently. Spread evenly in shallow baking dish.

Eggs, 4
Salt and **Pepper,** to taste
Milk, 1/4 cup

Break eggs carefully over potatoes. Season with salt and pepper. Add milk.

Oven, moderate, 350°

Bake 10 minutes or until eggs are set.

To serve 4

SCRAMBLED EGGS WITH TOMATO

Eggs, 6, beaten
Tomatoes, 1 cup, canned, undrained
Salt, 1/2 teaspoon
Pepper, 1/8 teaspoon
Basil, 1/4 teaspoon
Butter, 1 tablespoon

Combine eggs, tomatoes and seasonings in skillet in which butter is melted. Cook over medium heat, stirring up from the bottom occasionally, until mixture is thick. Serve at once.

To serve 4

SCRAMBLED EGGS WITH CHEESE AND ONION

Follow above recipe for scrambled eggs adding 1 tablespoon minced onion and 1/2 cup grated cheese to egg mixture.

DOUBLE BOILER EGGS

Eggs, 4
Salt, 1/2 teaspoon
Pepper, 1/8 teaspoon
Milk, 1 1/3 cups
Chives, 1 teaspoon, chopped

Beat eggs until very light, add other ingredients and pour into well-buttered top of double boiler. Cover and cook over 1 inch of simmering water 20–25 minutes, or until set. Do not uncover for 20 minutes.

To serve 4

PLAIN OMELET

Butter, 1 tablespoon
Eggs, 6
Milk, 3 tablespoons
Salt, 1/2 teaspoon

Melt butter in 10-inch skillet. Beat eggs, milk and salt together until foamy and pour into hot skillet. Cook over low heat, lifting cooked edges all around with spatula and tilting pan so that liquid egg can flow under. When bottom is well set, but top still creamy, loosen one side with a pancake turner and fold over. The ideal omelet is lightly brown on the outside, soft in the center.

To serve 4

Omelets may be accompanied by slices of crisp bacon, ham or fried sausages.

Omelets may be flavored with herbs, such as chives or parsley.

FLUFFY OMELET

Eggs, 6, separated
Milk, 6 tablespoons
Salt, 1/2 teaspoon
Pepper, 1/8 teaspoon
Butter, 1 tablespoon

Beat egg yolks with milk and seasonings. Beat egg whites stiff, but not dry. Fold yolks into whites, and turn into hot, buttered 10-inch ovenproof skillet. Cook over low heat until omelet is puffy and lightly browned on bottom.

Oven, moderate, 350°

Place in preheated oven 10 minutes, or until top springs back when pressed with finger. Crease lightly across center, loosen one side from bottom with spatula and fold over. Serve at once on hot platter.

To serve 4

FRENCH OMELET

Eggs, 4
Water, 1 tablespoon
Butter, 1 tablespoon

Beat eggs until just blended. Melt butter in 10-inch skillet. When hot enough that a drop of water will sizzle, pour eggs into pan. Cook over low heat, lifting edges with spatula to let liquid egg run to bottom of the pan. When set on bottom, but still soft on top, fold over, using a cake turner, season, and serve at once.

This amount will make 2 large servings. It is better not to cook too many eggs at once, but to make 2 omelets if more servings are needed.

FILLED OMELETS

Make a French Omelet as described above. Before folding spread with one of the following fillings: ½ cup of any cooked, chopped meat, fish, or poultry; mushrooms; cooked or diced sausage meat; strained canned tomatoes, or other cooked vegetable; grated cheese or cottage cheese; jelly or preserved fruits. Sweet omelets may be dusted with powdered sugar, if desired.

Creasing center of fluffy omelet

Folding fluffy omelet

Steps in making a French omelet

FRESH PEACH OMELET

Follow the recipe for French Omelet.

Meanwhile put a cup of sliced, sugared peaches in a saucepan and let them heat briefly, but not actually cook. When omelet is set and ready to turn out, add peaches to one half of it, fold other half over, and serve at once.

For variation in the above recipe, use fresh strawberries or raspberries. Canned peaches may be used when fresh are not in season.

SPANISH OMELET

Butter, 2 tablespoons **Green Pepper,** 1 medium, chopped **Onion,** 1 med., chopped **Garlic,** ½ clove, minced **Salt,** ½ teaspoon **Pepper,** ⅛ teaspoon **Parsley,** 1 tablespoon, minced **Thyme,** ⅛ teaspoon **Tomatoes,** 1 cup, canned drained	Melt butter in skillet and sauté pepper, onion and garlic until soft. Add seasonings and tomatoes; simmer 10 minutes.
Eggs, 6, beaten	Add eggs to mixture in skillet; cook over medium heat. Lift edges of omelet to let uncooked egg flow under. When set, fold over. Serve at once on warm platter.
To serve 4	

MENUS

Eggs enhance any menu: they are the mainstay of a hearty breakfast or Sunday brunch, they are festive enough for a company lunch, a satisfying substitute for meat in an occasional dinner, and can be quickly prepared for a late supper.

CREAMED EGGS AND HAM ON WAFFLES

Maple Sugar Baked Apples

SCRAMBLED EGGS

Shad Roe · Crisp Bacon Slices
Popovers · Butter
Oranges with Strawberries

HAM-FILLED OMELET

Toast · Currant Jelly
Stewed Plums · Cinnamon Coffee Cake

CHEESE SOUFFLÉ

Melba Toast · Raspberry Jam
Melon Bowl

SPANISH OMELET

Corn Fritters
Fresh Fruit Salad

FRIED CHICKEN

Baked Hominy · Eggplant Parmigiania
French Bread · Butter
Vanilla Soufflé

CHEESE

The secret in cooking with cheese is to always use a low temperature to melt it. High temperatures will make the cheese stringy, or cause it to curdle. To keep the natural cheeses from drying out, keep them tightly wrapped in waxed paper or plastic wrap, in the refrigerator. Cream and cottage cheese are as perishable as milk, and should receive the same care.

A bit of cheese adds a tang to many cooked dishes—cooked vegetables, casseroles of meat or vegetables, egg dishes, and it is particularly useful to eke out leftovers. Use up dry ends of cheese by grating them and storing in a tightly covered jar for future flavoring.

POPULAR CHEESES AND THEIR POPULAR USES

AMERICAN CHEDDAR: An all-purpose yellow or white "store" cheese used in cooking for soufflés, fondues, or in sandwiches, or with desserts.

BLUE (AMERICAN) BLEU (DANISH): Serve with crackers, or in salad dressings.

BEL PAESE: Serve with fruit or crackers.

BRICK: Use for sandwiches or on crackers.

BRIE: Serve with fruit, crackers, or in sandwiches.

CAMEMBERT: A soft dessert cheese; serve it on crackers with fruit.

COTTAGE: American unripened soft cheese; use as relish, in salads, or cheese cake.

CREAM: Often used as recipe ingredient, with sandwich filling mixture, or served with desserts.

EDAM: Hard, round cheese; serve with fruit or crackers.

GOUDA: Similar to Edam, and smaller.

GORGONZOLA: Serve with fruit or add to tossed salad.

GRUYÈRE: Serve with crackers or dessert.

LIEDERKRANZ: Serve with crackers as dessert or accompaniment to fruit or salad.

LIMBURGER: Good for snack sandwiches or pumpernickel or other dark bread to serve with beer.

MUENSTER: Good for dark bread sandwiches or with crackers.

NEUFCHATEL: Unripened soft cheese; use as sandwich spread with crackers or salad; also in some cheese cakes.

PARMESAN: Too hard to slice; use grated in soufflé, on spaghetti dishes or in Italian soup.

RICOTTA: An Italian "cottage cheese."

ROQUEFORT: Use in salads or salad dressings or with crackers.

SWISS: Use with plate of cold cuts or in sandwiches.

CHEESE SOUFFLÉ

Thick White Sauce, 1 cup **Sharp Cheddar Cheese,** 1 cup, diced	In top of double boiler make thick white sauce (see page 90). Add cheese and stir until it melts. Remove from heat.
Egg Yolks, 4 **Egg Whites,** 4	Beat egg yolks until thick and creamy and add to cheese sauce, stirring constantly. With clean beater, beat whites until stiff and glossy, but not dry. With rubber scraper, fold cheese mixture into whites. Pour into buttered 2-quart straight-sided baking dish.
Oven, moderate, 375°	Bake 40 to 45 minutes, or until firm. Serve at once.

To serve 4

HAM SOUFFLÉ

Follow above recipe for Cheese Soufflé, but add 1 extra egg white, and substitute 1 cup ground cooked ham for the cheese.

LOBSTER SOUFFLÉ

Follow above recipe for Cheese Soufflé, but add 1 extra egg white, and substitute 1 cup of finely chopped cooked lobster for the cheese.

CLAM SOUFFLÉ

Follow above recipe for Cheese Soufflé but add 1 extra egg white, and substitute 1 cup minced clams for the cheese.

TOP HAT SOUFFLÉ

Follow the recipes for Soufflé, above. After the soufflé is poured into the casserole, with a teaspoon dip into the soufflé about 2 inches in from the edge of the casserole and scoop a circle around the top. The center of the top, inside the circle, will rise higher than the rest of the soufflé, to form the "top hat."

Cheese soufflé

Roquefort cheese

Swiss cheese

Tamale cheese pie

WELSH RABBIT

Cheddar Cheese, 1 lb., cut up
Butter, 1 tablespoon
Mustard, prepared, 1 teaspoon
Beer, ½ cup
Eggs, 2, slightly beaten
Toast, 8 slices

To serve 4

Heat cheese and butter in top of double boiler over boiling water until cheese is melted. Add mustard. Mix beer with eggs; add slowly to cheese, stirring constantly and cook until smooth and thick. Serve on toast and garnish with paprika.

QUICHE LORRAINE

Pastry for 8-inch pie

Line a pie plate with pastry.

Bacon, 4 slices
Onion, 1, chopped
American Cheddar, grated, 1 cup
Eggs, 4, lightly beaten
Cream, 2 cups
Salt, ½ teaspoon
Pepper, ⅛ teaspoon

Sauté bacon until crisp; drain on paper. Pour off all but 1 tablespoon of fat and add onion to skillet. Cook until soft; remove from heat. Sprinkle crumbled bacon, onion and cheese in pie plate. Combine eggs, cream and seasonings, and pour over the cheese mixture.

Oven, hot, 450°

Bake at 450° for 10 minutes, reduce heat to 325° and bake 30 minutes longer, or until custard is set and a knife inserted comes out clean.

To serve 4 to 6

GOLDEN BUCK

Butter, 2 tablespoons
Milk, ½ cup
American Cheddar, ½ pound, cut up
Salt and **Pepper**
Worcestershire, 1 teasp.
Toast
Eggs, 4, poached

To serve 4

Heat butter, milk and cheese in top of double boiler over boiling water until cheese is melted. Season to taste and cook until thickened. Serve on toast and top each portion with poached egg.

SWISS FONDUE

Swiss Cheese, ½ pound, grated
Flour, 1 teaspoon
White Wine, ½ cup
Salt and **Pepper**
Instant Garlic, few grains
Kirsch, 1 ounce

To serve 3 or 4

Mix cheese with flour. Pour wine into chafing dish and heat over low flame until almost boiling. Add cheese, slowly, stirring until melted. Add seasonings and kirsch.

This is the Swiss dunking fondue which guests eat with pieces of French bread or cubes of toast held on a fork and dunked into the chafing dish.

BAKED CHEESE FONDUE

Milk, 1½ cups
Soft Bread Crumbs, 2 cups
Sharp Cheddar Cheese, 1½ cups, shredded
Eggs, 3, separated
Salt, 1 teaspoon
Paprika, ⅛ teaspoon
Cayenne, dash

Pour milk over bread crumbs, add cheese, well-beaten egg yolks and seasonings. Beat egg whites stiff and fold in. Turn into greased baking dish.

Oven, moderate, 350°

Bake 30–40 minutes until a knife inserted comes out clean.

To serve 4

RINKTUM DITTY

American Cheddar, ½ pound, cut up
Tomato Soup, 1 can
Water, ½ can
Salt, ½ teaspoon
Worcestershire, 1 teasp.
Cayenne, dash
Eggs, 2, beaten

To serve 4

In top part of double boiler, over boiling water, heat cheese, tomato soup and water until cheese is melted, stirring occasionally. Add seasonings. Blend in well-beaten eggs. Serve on toast or toasted crackers.

TAMALE CHEESE PIE

Salt Pork, ½ pound, diced
Onion, 1 medium-sized, sliced

Fry pork; add onion and brown slightly.

Tomatoes, 16-ounce can
Corn, 1 cup canned kernels
Yellow Cornmeal, ½ cup
Salt, 1 teaspoon

Boil tomatoes, corn, cornmeal and salt 5 minutes, stirring constantly.

Olive Oil, ½ cup
Chili Powder, 1 tablespoon
Hominy, 1 cup canned, chopped

Add salt pork and onion, oil, chili powder and hominy, stirring well, then cool.

Egg, 1 slightly beaten
Milk, ½ cup
Olives, 1 cup chopped
Cheese, 1 cup sharp cheddar, shredded

Combine egg and milk; stir into tomato-corn mixture; add olives and turn into casserole. Bake, covered, 45 minutes. Remove cover, top with cheese and bake 15 minutes more, or until cheese is melted and bubbling.

Oven, moderate 350°

To serve 4–6

RICE

A versatile and nourishing food that can be served at breakfast, lunch or dinner; for main courses, or desserts. Vary your rice dishes with unpolished brown rice, for its higher vitamin content. And when you haven't time for long cooking, try the pre-cooked kind.

Most rice today is sold packaged, and the package has on it the exact directions for one or more methods of cooking that particular type. Some are quick cooking, but the old-fashioned type requires long cooking, 20 minutes or so. Be sure you read the label.

For the long-cooking types we prefer the following method:

BOILED LONG-COOKING RICE

This method of cooking retains all the nutrients—nothing is poured away. Never wash rice either before or after cooking.

Bring 2 cups of water with 1 teaspoon salt to a boil in a heavy saucepan; shake 1 cup of rice in it slowly so as not to disturb boiling. Cover and cook over slow heat until liquid is absorbed. White rice requires 20 to 25 minutes; brown rice, 40 to 50. If rice becomes too dry before it is tender, add a little more boiling water. When rice is done uncover and shake over low heat a few minutes to separate and fluff grains.

Bouillon or stock may be substituted for water if desired. Salt may be omitted.

One cup of raw rice makes about 3 or 4 cups of cooked rice,

To keep white rice white, a little lemon juice may be added to water.

QUICK PARSLEY RICE

Pre-cooked Rice, 1½ cups	Prepare rice according to directions on package in water
Salt, ½ teaspoon	to which turmeric has been
Boiling water, 1½ cups	added. When cooked, add
Turmeric, ¼ teaspoon	parsley and combine lightly
Parsley, ¼ cup, chopped	with fork.

To serve 4

SAFFRON RICE

Follow the recipe for boiled or steamed rice, adding a pinch of saffron for its bright yellow coloring and delicate flavor. If saffron is unobtainable at your store, ¼ teaspoonful turmeric may be substituted to give the rice a yellow color but no flavor.

SPANISH RICE

Bacon Fat, 3 tablespoons	In bacon fat sauté rice until
Rice, 1 cup, raw	golden brown. Add onion and
Onion, 2, sliced	pepper and continue cooking
Green Pepper, 1, chopped	until they are golden. Add
Tomatoes, 16-ounce can	tomatoes, seasonings and water,
Salt, 1 teaspoon	and bring to boil; simmer until
Paprika, 1 teaspoon	rice is tender. Add a little more
Water, 1 cup	water if it becomes too dry.

To serve 4

ITALIAN RICE

Olive or Cooking Oil, ¼ cup	Heat oil in skillet and add rice; cook and stir until golden; add
Rice, 1 cup, raw	onion and continue cooking
Onion, 2, chopped	until onion is soft. Add boiling
Beef Stock or Bouillon, 2½ cups	stock, bring to boil and simmer until rice is tender, about
Parmesan Cheese, ½ cup, grated	20 minutes. All the liquid should be absorbed. Uncover and shake over heat few minutes to separate grains. Put into serving dish and sprinkle with cheese.

To serve 4

A pinch of saffron may be added to this dish if desired.

SHRIMP PILAF

Onion, 1 med., chopped	Sauté onion and pepper in
Green Pepper, 1, chopped	butter until soft, add tomatoes
Butter, 3 tablespoons	and bring to boil. Add rice
Water, ¾ cup	slowly so as not to interrupt
Tomatoes, 16-oz. can	boiling. Add salt. Cover tightly
Rice, ¾ cup, raw	and simmer 20 or 25 minutes,
Salt, 1 teaspoon	until tender. Add shrimp and
Shrimp, cooked, sliced lengthwise, 1 cup	heat.

To serve 4

LOBSTER PILAF: Substitute 1 cup of cooked lobster for shrimp.

WILD RICE

Wild rice is often served with game. Follow directions on the package; or if there are none, wash rice and pour off any foreign bits that float to the surface. Add ½ cup of wild rice to 3 cups of boiling water, adding slowly so that water continues to boil. Cook 45 minutes, over low heat, until tender and water is absorbed. Shake rice occasionally to prevent sticking. Uncover and shake a few moments over heat to separate grains.

WILD RICE AND MUSHROOMS

Sauté ½ pound of mushrooms, sliced, in 2 tablespoons butter until golden brown. Combine with cooked rice lightly with a fork.

Spanish rice

Curried rice

122

Tarragon chicken and rice

CURRIED RICE

For each cup of boiled rice melt 1 tablespoon of butter. Sauté over low heat 1 small white onion, chopped, until soft and golden yellow; stir in ¼ teaspoon curry powder; add 2 tablespoons raisins and heat until soft. Combine with the rice and 1 tablespoon slivered almonds or salted peanuts if desired.

TARRAGON CHICKEN AND RICE

Butter, 3 tablespoons
Frying Chicken, 1, quartered

Melt the butter and brown the chicken in it over low heat, turning once.

Salt and **Pepper**
Tarragon, 1 teaspoon
White Wine, dry, 1 cup

Remove to a casserole, season and sprinkle with tarragon. Pour the wine into the frying pan, scrape up all the glaze and pour over the chicken. Cover tightly and cook 30 minutes in moderate oven.

Rice, 3 cups cooked

Add the rice and let it absorb the gravy before serving.

Oven, moderate 350°

To serve 4

CHILI RICE

Follow recipe for Spanish Rice, but add 1 teaspoon of chili powder, or more, if you like it hot.

RICE CAKES

To each cup of cooked rice add 1 beaten egg. Drop by the spoonful into a skillet greased with a little butter. Brown lightly on each side.

RICE CROQUETTES

See general recipe for croquettes on page 92. Substitute 1½ cups of cooked rice for the cooked meat in this recipe.

LAMB PILAF

Lamb Shoulder, 2 lbs., cut in cubes	Brown lamb on all sides in hot skillet. Pour off rendered fat.
Salt, 2 teaspoons	Add seasonings and tomatoes.
Pepper, ¼ teaspoon	Bring to boil and simmer 1½
Basil, ½ teaspoon	hours, or until tender. Remove
Garlic, 1 clove, minced	celery tops and parsley. Add
Onion, 1, chopped	rice; cover and simmer 30
Celery Tops, few sprigs	minutes more, or until rice is
Parsley, few sprigs	tender and liquid is absorbed.
Tomatoes, 16-ounce can	(A little additional water may
Rice, ½ cup, raw	be necessary for cooking the
To serve 4	rice.)

A teaspoon or more of curry powder may be added to the above recipe if desired.

CHICKEN LIVER PILAF

Follow recipe for Shrimp Pilaf on page 82, substituting 1 cup of sautéed and broken chicken livers for the shrimp.

QUICK SPANISH RICE

Bacon Drippings, ¼ cup	Brown rice lightly in bacon
Pre-cooked Rice, 5-ounce package	drippings, add other ingredients. Bring to boil and simmer
Onion, 2 tablespoons, minced	5 minutes.
Green Pepper, 2 tablesps., minced	
Tomato Sauce, 2 8-oz. cans, and	
Hot Water, 1½ cups or	
Tomatoes, 28-ounce can	
Prepared Mustard, ½ teaspoon	
Salt and **Pepper**	
To serve 4	

Also try the very good packaged mix now on the market.

RICE FRITTERS

See recipe for Corn Fritters on page 140.

PASTA AND SAUCES

Pasta is the Italian name for the family of wheat products that include macaroni, spaghetti, noodles and their many cousins of all shapes and sizes. Use them with melted butter or a delicious sauce, as a substitute for potatoes, or in combination with other foods, for a hearty all-in-one-pot meal.

BOILED MACARONI, SPAGHETTI OR NOODLES

Boil an 8-ounce package of macaroni, spaghetti or noodles according to the directions on the package. Drain well. Season with salt and pepper, and pour 2 or 3 tablespoons of melted butter over it.

If preferred, the butter may be flavored with a little garlic powder. Or grated cheese may be sprinkled over the top, or stirred into the cooked pasta. American cheese or Parmesan may be used.

To serve 4

ITALIAN SPAGHETTI

The thin, long spaghetti used for those spaghetti dishes served with delicious sauces that you eat in Italian restaurants can be found loose or packaged in the larger markets or Italian food stores. It is sold by the pound, which will serve 4 people a good-sized main dish portion. Cook it in plenty of water in a large kettle, with a tablespoon of salt to the pound of spaghetti. Drop the spaghetti into the boiling water, letting the ends project above the water if they are too long. As the water softens the spaghetti, fold it over gently with a fork, until all of it is under water. Stir it with the fork a few times during cooking, so that the strands do not stick together. Test a strand from time to time until it is done just right—in Italy this means tender, but still slightly resistant to chewing.

When the spaghetti is done drain it at once and divide it into individual portions on hot plates. Serve with melted butter and freshly grated cheese, with butter flavored with garlic, or with one of the following sauces, with meat balls added, if desired.

TOMATO-MEAT SAUCE

Onion, 1, minced
Garlic, 2 cloves, minced
Olive Oil, ¼ cup
Ground Beef, 1 pound
Tomatoes, 28-ounce can
Tomato Paste, 6-oz. can
Salt, 2 teaspoons
Sugar, 1 teaspoon
Basil, ½ teaspoon
Thyme, ½ teaspoon
Bay Leaf, 1
Red Wine, ½ cup
Water, 1 cup

Cook garlic and onion in oil until golden. Add beef and brown lightly. Add remaining ingredients. Simmer 1 hour. Add more water if necessary.

To serve 4

TOMATO SAUCE

Onion, minced, ¼ cup
Garlic, 1 clove, minced
Olive Oil, ¼ cup
Carrot, minced, ¼ cup
Celery, minced, 1 cup
Basil, 1 teaspoon
Salt and Pepper, to taste
Tomato Paste, 2 6-ounce cans
Water, 3 cans

Sauté onion and garlic in oil until golden. Add carrot, celery, sweet basil, salt and pepper, and continue cooking until vegetables are wilted. Add tomato paste and water and simmer 45 minutes.

To serve 4

HOT TUNA SAUCE

To Tomato Sauce (above) add the following ingredients:

Tuna, 2 7-ounce cans, broken up
Black Olives, pitted and chopped, ½ cup
Capers, 2 tablespoons
Anchovies, 2-ounce can, cut in halves
Black Peppers, ¼ teasp.
Chili Pepper, 1, crushed

Continue cooking 5 minutes longer.

To serve 4 to 6

CHICKEN LIVER-MUSHROOM SAUCE

Chicken Livers, 1 cup
Mushrooms, chopped, 1 cup
Butter, 3 tablespoons

Garlic, 1 clove, chopped
Onion, 1 large, chopped
Tomatoes, 16-ounce can
Tomato Paste, 6-oz. can
Bouillon, 1 can
Water, 1 soup can
Sugar, 1 teaspoon
Thyme, 1 teaspoon
Bay Leaf, 1, crumbled
Cloves, ⅛ teaspoon
Salt and Pepper, to taste

Break chicken livers up into pieces and sauté with mushrooms in butter until lightly browned. Remove from skillet.

Sauté onion and garlic in skillet until soft; add tomatoes, tomato paste, bouillon and water; seasonings and spices. Simmer 45 minutes. Add chicken livers and mushrooms, heat 10 minutes.

To serve 4 to 6

125

*Spaghetti
with Italian
meat sauce*

Lasagne baked with cheese and tomato sauce (basil is optional)

Stuffed tufoli

STUFFED TUFOLI

Tufoli, ½ pound	Cook in rapidly boiling salted water until tender, but not soft.
Ricotta Cheese, ½ pound **Parmesan Cheese,** grated, ¼ cup **Eggs,** 1 **Parsley,** finely chopped, 2 tablespoons	Blend the ricotta with the Parmesan, eggs and parsley. Stuff the tufoli with this mixture, using a pastry tube or a teaspoon.
Tomato-Meat Sauce (page 125) **Mozzarella Cheese,** thinly sliced, ½ pound **Parmesan Cheese,** grated, ¼ cup	Arrange a layer of stuffed tufoli in a casserole, add a layer of tomato-meat sauce, then a layer of Mozzarella. Sprinkle with Parmesan. Repeat for one or two more layers, covering the top with sliced Mozzarella arranged in overlapping concentric circles.
Oven, moderate, 350°	Bake for 1½ hours.

Serves 4

PIZZA

Active Dry Yeast, 1 pkg. **Warm Water,** ½ cup **Shortening,** ½ cup **Sugar,** 2 teaspoons **Salt,** 2 teaspoons **Boiling Water,** 1¾ cups **Flour,** sifted, 6 cups	Soften yeast in warm water. Mix shortening, boiling water, sugar and salt in large bowl until shortening is melted; cool to warm. Add flour, ⅓ at a time, and beat until smooth. Divide dough into 4 parts and roll each one on floured board to fit 12-inch pizza pan. Let rise in warm place until light.
Anchovy Fillets, 2 2-ounce cans **Garlic,** 2 cloves, minced **Italian-style Tomatoes,** 2 28-ounce cans **Mozzarella Cheese,** thinly sliced, 1 pound **Parmesan Cheese,** grated, 1 cup **Oregano,** 1 teaspoon	Mix oil from anchovies with garlic and brush on dough. Cover with tomatoes and seasoning. Spread Mozzarella Cheese and anchovies over tomatoes and top with Parmesan Cheese and Oregano.
Oven, hot, 425°	Bake 15 to 20 minutes; cut in wedges and serve at once.

*Ravioli,
served with
extra cheese and
a tossed salad*

EASY PIZZA

Biscuit Mix, 2 cups
Water, ⅔ cup
Salad or **Olive Oil,**
 ¼ cup

Oven, hot, 450°

Tomatoes, fresh or
canned, 2 cups
Onion, 1 medium
Instant Garlic, ¼ teasp.
Oregano, 1 teaspoon
Parmesan Cheese, grated,
 ½ cup
Salt and **Pepper,** to taste
Anchovies

To make 8 servings

Mix biscuit mix with water. Roll out to cover 2 greased cake pans. Brush dough with half the oil.

Bake 10 minutes.

Sprinkle crust with remaining oil, tomatoes, onion and garlic; crumble oregano over all and sprinkle with cheese. Season with freshly ground black pepper and a little salt. Garnish with anchovies. Bake about 10 minutes longer in hot oven. Cut in wedges to serve.

LASAGNA

Lasagna Noodles,
 1-pound package
Salt, 2 teaspoons
Ricotta or **Cottage
 Cheese,** ½ pound
Egg, 1, beaten
Mozzarella Cheese,
 8 ounces, sliced
Parmesan Cheese,
 ½ cup, grated
Tomato-Meat Sauce

Oven, moderate, 325°

To serve 4 to 6

Cook in boiling salted water according to directions on package. Drain. Mix Ricotta or cottage cheese with beaten egg, arrange noodles in 3 alternate layers with the cheeses and sauce.

Bake 45 minutes.

RAVIOLI

Flour, 1½ cups
Salt, ½ teaspoon
Warm Water
Egg Yolk, 1
Filling

Sift flour and salt together in bowl, make depression in center, drop in egg yolk, mix and moisten with enough warm water, a little at a time, to make a stiff dough. Turn out on floured board, knead until smooth, cover and let stand 30 minutes. With rolling pin, roll out paper thin; cut into 3-inch strips 6 inches long. Put teaspoon of filling on half of each strip, fold over and press edges together.

Boiling Chicken Stock or **Salted Water**
Tomato Sauce, pages 125, 141
Parmesan Cheese, grated

Cook in boiling stock or water 20 minutes. Remove with slotted spoon, arrange in serving dish. Cover with Tomato Sauce and sprinkle generously with grated Parmesan Cheese.

To serve 4 to 6

RAVIOLI FILLING

Chicken, cooked, minced, ½ cup
Spinach, cooked, chopped, ½ cup
Bread Crumbs, ¼ cup
Parmesan Cheese, grated, ¼ cup
Parsley, few pieces, chopped
Garlic, ½ clove, chopped
Salt and **Pepper** to taste
Egg, 1 beaten

Mix together all ingredients but egg, then add egg to moisten and hold together. Drop by teaspoonfuls on strips of ravioli dough, and proceed as above.

Any desired variation of the meat and vegetable combination may be used. You might substitute veal or pork for the chicken, and use up leftover bits of cooked vegetables.

HOT CLAM SAUCE

Olive Oil, 2 tablespoons
Garlic, 1 clove, split

Cook garlic in hot oil until brown. Discard garlic.

Clams, 1 can minced
Butter, ¼ cup
Oregano, ½ teaspoon
Green Pepper, ½ chopped
Italian Tomatoes, canned, 2 cups
Salt, 1½ teaspoon
Pepper, ⅛ teaspoon
Parsley, ¼ cup chopped

Drain clams. Add liquid to oil in skillet with butter, oregano, green pepper, tomatoes, salt and pepper. Cook, uncovered, 30 minutes. Add clams and parsley; cook 3 minutes.

To serve 6–8

BAKED MACARONI AND CHEESE

Macaroni, 8-ounce package

Cook macaroni in boiling salted water until tender.

Thin White Sauce, 3 cups (see page 90)
Cheese, Sharp Cheddar, ½ pound, shredded

Mix macaroni with white sauce and cheese in baking dish. Reserve ½ cup of cheese for top layer.

Oven, moderate, 375°

Bake 30 minutes, or until lightly browned.

To serve 4 or 5

BAKED MACARONI WITH HAM: Mix 1 cup slivered cooked ham with macaroni and cheese.

Tongue or canned chopped ham are also good in this dish.

VEGETABLES

There are so many interesting ways to prepare vegetables that reluctant vegetable eaters can often be turned into enthusiasts when a new method of cooking is tried. It is important to select green vegetables that are as fresh as you can get them, store them in the refrigerator, then use them up quickly before they dry out and lose their flavor.

Vegetables also lose their vitamin content when they lie around and dry out, so be sure to buy those that look fresh and green, not wilted and limp. Buy leafy vegetables that are crisp bright green and with compact heads; potatoes with clear smooth skins, not spotted or sprouted; green beans that are crisp so that they snap easily; beans and peas with well-filled pods, but not so far developed that they will be tough; eggplant should be satiny and squash unspotted, with summer squash tender to the fingernail. Corn must be plucked the day you buy it, and you can easily tell whether it is fresh, if the kernels are tender to your fingernail.

If turnips, beets and carrots still have their leafy tops on when you buy them, remove at once—they rob the roots of their nutrients.

Prepare vegetables for cooking by washing thoroughly in several waters to remove all sand, strip off any wilted or yellowed leaves, cut away any woody, tough stems. (Consult cooking guide for special requirements for each vegetable.)

In general, cook vegetables with as little water as possible, then try to use the water that is left after cooking in soup or gravy. Don't drown your vegetables in quantities of water which you later pour away along with the nutrients it contains. Cook quickly in a tightly covered pan just long enough to make the vegetable tender but still slightly crisp.

Frozen vegetables can be cooked without thawing, or can be partially thawed so that the pieces separate more easily and cook more evenly. Follow the directions and time suggestions on the package, but cook them as briefly as possible; since they have been heated before freezing, they will require less time than fresh vegetables.

PANNED VEGETABLES

Panning is a cooking method used by the Chinese which conserves most of the color, flavor and food value of the vegetable. For this method, tough stems and ribs are removed, leafy vegetables are shredded, and green beans are sliced lengthwise. Put a tablespoon of oil or bacon drippings into a skillet, add the vegetable and stir around until heated. Put on a tight lid and cook over low heat until vegetable is just tender. Quick-cooking vegetables will contain enough moisture to prevent sticking, by this process, but for slower kinds a few tablespoons of water may be added. Season with salt and pepper before serving.

STEAMED VEGETABLES

Mild flavored vegetables can be cooked by steaming, and this conserves more of the nutrients than boiling. Prepare vegetables as for boiling and put in perforated part of steamer, or in a colander placed over boiling water and covered tightly. Allow 10 to 15 minutes more cooking time than boiling. Season and serve as you would a boiled vegetable.

BOILED VEGETABLES

Boil vegetables in as little water as possible (½ cup is ample for four servings). Bring water to boil with ½ teaspoon of salt. Add vegetables, cover, bring to boil again and time according to timetable on opposite page. Drain and reserve any remaining liquid for gravies or soups, since it contains valuable vitamins and minerals. Serve with melted butter, or with white sauce, cheese sauce, Hollandaise or mustard sauce. (See pages 90–91.)

OVEN-COOKED VEGETABLES

When you are using your oven for the balance of the meal, it is economical to cook your vegetables in it also. Place the vegetables in a covered casserole with butter, salt and a few tablespoonsful of water.

FRESH VEGETABLE PREPARATION AND TIMETABLE FOR BOILING

Note: If you are using a pressure cooker, follow the timetable that came with it. If using the following timetable, put vegetable into a small amount of boiling, salted water and begin timing when water returns to boil. *Cook all vegetables covered.*

Vegetable	Preparation	Approx. Cooking Time (after water returns to boil) in Minutes
Artichokes, Globe	Wash, remove discolored outer leaves, cut off stem.	35–45
Artichokes, Jerusalem	Scrub, pare thin. Boil like potatoes.	20–30
Asparagus	Cut off tough half of stalks, rinse thoroughly in several waters to remove sand; lay in wide skillet with 1-inch boiling water. They will cook to a uniform bright green. Tough ends may be cut in 1-inch lengths and cooked separately, 20 to 30 minutes.	10–20
Beans, Green or Wax	Break off both ends; cut into 1-inch pieces or in thin lengthwise strips.	10–30
Beans, Lima	Shell beans just before using.	20–30
Beets	Scrub and cook in skins. Cook fresh tops separately as a green.	Young 30; Old 45–90
Broccoli	Cut off large outer leaves and tough lower end of stem. If stems are thick split into several pieces. Soak in cold, salted water 15 minutes. Cook, covered, in skillet.	8–20
Brussels Sprouts	Remove wilted leaves; wash well, soak in cold, salted water 15 minutes. For uniform color cook in wide skillet in a single layer.	10–18
Cabbage, green	Remove wilted outer leaves, wash, cut in quarters to shred to cut cooking time.	quartered 10–20 shredded 3–10
Cabbage, red	Prepare as above and shred.	8–12
Carrots	Cut off tops, scrape; cut in quarters lengthwise, slice or dice.	10–20
Cauliflower	Remove leaves and stalks. Wash and soak head down in cold salted water. Boil whole or in separate flowerets until just tender.	10–15
Celery	Separate stalks, remove leaves and roots, wash. Slice or dice.	15–20
Corn on Cob	Remove husks, strip off silk, cut off undeveloped tips. Cook in boiling water to cover. Do not put salt in the water, as salt toughens corn.	5–8
Greens: Kale, Collards, Beet, Turnip, Mustard	Cut off roots and wilted leaves; wash thoroughly in 5 or 6 waters.	20–30
Kohlrabi	Wash, pare, and cut into small cubes or slices or quarters.	quarters, 20–25
Leeks	Cut off green tops within an inch of white.	15–20
Onions	Wash and peel, or cook unpeeled and peel after cooking. Cook whole.	30–35
Parsnips	Wash and scrape; cook whole or in halves, or quarter lengthwise.	quarters 20; whole 30
Peas	Shell peas just before cooking to conserve flavor. Older peas may be improved by adding 1/4 teaspoon sugar to the pound.	8–20
Potatoes, White	Scrub and rinse; peel, or cook in skins. Boil in salted water to barely cover. Save water for gravies or soups.	quartered 15 whole 25–40
Potatoes, Sweet	Follow procedure for White Potatoes.	quartered 15; whole 25–30
Spinach and Swiss Chard	Cut off tough stems and wilted leaves. Wash several times in large quantities of cold water. Lift from last water, place in kettle; cook without additional water.	5–10
Squash, Winter	Wash, cut in quarters, remove seeds and pulp. Pare off rind, cut in pieces. After boiling, mash and season with salt and pepper, and butter.	Hubbard 20–30 Acorn 10–20
Squash, Summer	Use young squash with very tender skins. Wash but do not pare. Slice or cube for cooking.	10–20
Tomatoes	Blanch in boiling water 1 minute; drain, slip off skins, cut out stem ends; cook in own juice.	7–10
Turnips	Yellow, or rutabagas are stronger flavored than white. Scrub and pare; cook diced or in quarters, or whole if small.	cubes 15–20 whole 30

A wealth of vegetables are yours for the choosing

ARTICHOKES

Artichokes, 1 med.-sized per person

Cut off stems and bottom leaves and scissor-trim the brown tips of all other leaves. Wash well and stand upright in saucepan.

Salt, ½ teaspoon
Salad Oil, 1 teaspoon each
Garlic, 1 clove, minced

Add garlic and salad oil to each artichoke, fill saucepan one-third of the way with boiling salted water and simmer 45 minutes or until tender. Drain and serve with small individual dishes of melted butter or Hollandaise sauce (page 91).

To eat, dip individual leaves in sauce, eating only soft bottom part and discarding hard top. When leaves are all removed, cut out hairy "choke" and eat choice bottom "heart" beneath.

JERUSALEM ARTICHOKES

The Jerusalem artichoke is a tuber somewhat like the potato. To prepare, scrub and scrape them and put into rapidly boiling water for 20 minutes, or until tender. Do not over-cook as they become tough. Drain and serve with melted butter and chopped parsley, or with a medium white sauce, or with vinegar.

ASPARAGUS OVALS

When you wish to use just the asparagus tips for one meal, the lower part of the stalks can be used later and be most delicious. Slice the stalks thinly on the diagonal, drop them into boiling water to just cover, and boil for about 5 minutes, or until tender. Drain, sprinkle with salt, and serve with butter or Hollandaise (page 91).

ASPARAGUS PARMESAN

Asparagus Spears, 2 cans
Parmesan Cheese, grated

Lay asparagus in row in shallow baking pan; sprinkle generously with Parmesan cheese. Put under broiler until cheese is melted.

To serve 4 to 6

Fresh cooked asparagus may be used if preferred.

SPANISH LIMA BEANS

Frozen Baby Limas, 1 package

Cook according to directions on package.

Butter, 1 tablespoon
Onion, 1 tablespoon, chopped
Green Pepper, ½ cup, chopped
Tomatoes, canned, 1 cup
Bread Cubes, Toasted, 1 cup

Heat fat and brown onion and pepper in skillet. Add tomatoes and simmer slowly about 10 minutes. Add drained beans and season to taste. Turn into serving dish and top with toasted bread cubes.

To serve 4

CURRIED BEANS AND ONIONS

Frozen Green Beans, 1 package
Onions, 1-pound can
Butter, 2 tablespoons
Curry Powder, 1 teasp.
Salt and **Pepper,** to taste

Cook beans according to directions on label; drain. Add onions, drained. Add butter and curry powder, and heat. Season to taste.

To serve 4 or 5

PANNED GREEN BEANS

Green or **Wax Beans,** 1 pound
Butter or **Bacon Fat,** 1 tablespoon

Slice beans diagonally into thin strips. Heat butter in skillet, add beans; cover to hold in steam and cook over low heat until beans are just tender, about 10 minutes. Stir occasionally to prevent sticking and if necessary add a few tablespoons of water.

To serve 4

LIMAS AND LEEKS

Frozen Limas, 1 package

Cook as directed on label. Drain, reserving liquid.

Leeks, several small
Butter, 2 tablespoons
Flour, 1 tablespoon
Salt and **Pepper,** to taste
Paprika, ¼ teaspoon

Slice leeks thin, cook gently in butter until golden in color. Blend in flour, add ½ cup bean liquid, and cook until thickened. Add beans and seasonings.

To serve 4 or 5

GREEN BEANS AND MUSHROOMS

Green Beans, 1 pound
Mushrooms, 1/4 pound
Butter, 2 tablespoons
Onion Powder, 1/4 teasp.
Salt and **Pepper,** to taste

Slice beans and mushrooms into thin strips. Cook, covered, in butter, over low heat. Stir occasionally to prevent sticking and add a little water if necessary. Add seasonings.

Sour Cream, 1/2 cup

Add sour cream and remove from heat; do not let boil. Serve at once.

To serve 4 or 5

JULIENNE BEANS WITH BACON

Bacon, 2 slices

Fry bacon gently until crisp; set aside. Pour off all but 2 tablespoons of fat.

Green Beans, 1 pound
Onion Flakes, 1/2 teasp.
Salt and **Pepper,** to taste
Basil, 1/2 teaspoon
To serve 4

Cut beans into thin strips, add seasonings and cook covered in bacon fat over low heat until just tender. Crumble bacon and mix with beans.

GREEN BEANS WITH CREAM

Green or **Wax Beans,**
 1 pound
Salt and **Pepper,** to taste
Sugar, 2 teaspoons
Cream, 1/4 cup

Pan-cook beans as described above, until just tender. Remove from heat, add remaining ingredients and serve at once.

To serve 4

DRIED BEANS

When houses had coal stoves in the kitchen the bean pot could simmer along for 24 hours. Now we can try to shorten the baking time by pre-soaking and pre-cooking. The pressure cooker comes in handy for this. If you have one, follow carefully the directions that came with it.

COUNTRY-STYLE BEANS

Marrow Beans, 1 pound

Wash beans and soak overnight. Drain.

Salt Pork, 1/2 lb., cubed
Onion, 1 medium, sliced
Carrots, 2 medium
Turnips, 2 small
Onions, 8 tiny
Cabbage, small head
Celery, 2 stalks
Tomatoes, 3 large
Salt, 2 teaspoons
Pepper, 1/4 teaspoon

Sauté pork in skillet until brown, put in kettle with beans. Pour off all but 2 tablespoons fat in skillet and sauté onion. Add to beans. Cover beans with water and simmer until tender, 2 hours or more. Cut up carrots, turnips, onions, celery and tomatoes; shred cabbage and add vegetables to beans; add seasonings; simmer until all are tender.

To serve 4

This dish may be made with whatever vegetables are in season.

GARLIC GREEN BEANS

Olive Oil, 2 tablespoons
Green Beans, 1 pound
Garlic, 1 clove, minced

Heat olive oil in skillet, add beans and garlic, and cook over low heat, covered, until just tender. Add a little water if necessary.

Capers, 2 tablespoons
Anchovies, 2 tablespoons, chopped
Salt and **Pepper,** to taste

Add capers and anchovies and mix thoroughly. Season to taste and serve at once.

To serve 4

NEW ENGLAND BAKED BEANS

Pea Beans, 1 pound
Water, to cover
Molasses, 1/4 cup
Salt, 1 teaspoon
Dry Mustard, 1 teasp.
Salt Pork, 1/2 pound

Wash beans, cover with water and bring to boil. Let beans soak overnight, if possible, or at least one hour. Then bring to boil and simmer until nearly tender. Drain beans, reserve liquid; put beans in bean pot. Add molasses and seasoning and enough bean liquid to nearly fill crock. Score rind of salt pork, place on top of beans. Cover pot.

Oven, slow, 275°

Bake 6 to 8 hours. Add more liquid if necessary during baking.

CHILI BEANS

Red Kidney Beans, 1 lb.
Onion, 1, chopped
Garlic, 1 clove, chopped
Bacon, 1/4 lb., chopped
Chili Powder, 2 teasps.
Salt, 1 teaspoon
Red Wine, 1 cup
Water, 3 cups
Tomatoes, 16-ounce can

Wash beans, cover with water and soak overnight. Drain and put in kettle with remaining ingredients, except tomatoes. Simmer gently until beans are tender, and sauce thick and rich, about 4 hours. Add a little more water if needed. Add tomatoes the last hour of cooking.

To serve 4 to 6

TOMATO-LIMA CASSEROLE

Lima Beans, 1 pound
Onion, 1 medium, sliced
Bacon Fat, 2 tablesps.
Salt, 1 teaspoon
Pepper, 1/8 teaspoon
Sugar, 1 teaspoon
Tomatoes, canned, 3 cups
Parmesan Cheese

Soak lima beans in water to cover overnight. Simmer until tender; drain. Place in casserole with onion sautéed in fat, seasonings and tomatoes. Top with grated cheese.

Oven, moderate, 350°

Bake 35 minutes or until lightly browned.

To serve 4 to 6

Asparagus served with
Hollandaise sauce

Green beans garnished with onion rings

KIDNEY BEAN SALAD

See page 162.

SWEET AND SOUR BEET SHREDS

Butter, 1 tablespoon
Vinegar, 1 tablespoon
Sugar, 1 tablespoon
Salt and **Pepper,** to taste
Shredded Beets,
   16-ounce can

To serve 4

Combine butter, vinegar and sugar in saucepan and heat to boiling point. Add beet shreds and stir lightly with fork. Heat thoroughly. Season to taste.

This recipe may be used for canned diced beets if shredded are not available. It is also very good made with fresh beets. If finely shredded they will cook in 5 minutes and are a gorgeous color.

YALE BEETS

Butter, 2 tablespoons
Cornstarch, 2 teaspoons
Orange Juice, ½ cup
Sugar, 1 tablespoon
Beets, canned or cooked,
   2 cups, sliced
Beet Water, ½ cup

To serve 4

Combine all ingredients but beets in saucepan and cook over slow heat until slightly thickened. Add beets and heat thoroughly, but do not boil.

HARVARD BEETS

Butter, 2 tablespoons
Cornstarch, 2 teaspoons
Vinegar, ¼ cup
Beet Water, ¾ cup
Sugar, 2 tablespoons
Beets, canned or cooked,
   2 cups, sliced

To serve 4

Combine all ingredients but beets in saucepan and cook over slow heat until slightly thickened. Add beets and heat thoroughly, but do not boil.

BROCCOLI WITH BLUE CHEESE

Frozen Broccoli, 2 pkgs.

Cook according to package directions. Place in serving dish.

Salad Oil, 3 tablespoons
Vinegar, 2 tablespoons
Sugar, 1 tablespoon
Paprika
Blue Cheese, 2 ounces

To serve 4

Combine oil, vinegar and sugar in small saucepan and heat to boiling point. Remove from heat and crumble cheese into mixture. Pour over broccoli. Sprinkle paprika on top.

This dish is good also with Brussels Sprouts.

PANNED CABBAGE

Cabbage, small head
Butter or **Bacon Drippings,** 2 tablespoons
Salt and **Pepper**

To serve 4

Shred cabbage. Heat fat in heavy skillet, add cabbage and ¼ cup of water. Cover tightly and cook 10 minutes or until tender. Season with salt and pepper.

CREAMED CABBAGE

Prepare cabbage as above and serve mixed with one cup of medium white sauce. Or mix with one cup of sour cream. Top with a sprinkling of paprika.

CABBAGE CASSEROLE

Cabbage, 1 medium
Eggs, 2, beaten
Butter, 1 tablespoon
Salt, ½ teaspoon
Pepper, ⅛ teaspoon
Cream, ½ cup

Oven, moderate, 375°

To serve 4

Combine cooked, drained cabbage with other ingredients in greased casserole and bake until lightly browned, about 25 minutes.

FLEMISH RED CABBAGE

Onion, 1
Bacon Fat, 2 tablespoons
Red Cabbage, 1 can
Apple Slices, 1 can
Lemon Juice, 1 tablesp.
Salt and **Pepper,** to taste

To serve 4 to 6

Chop onion and cook in bacon fat until golden in color. Add cabbage and apples; heat thoroughly over low heat. Add lemon juice and seasonings.

HOT CABBAGE SLAW

Cabbage, 1 medium
Butter, 1 tablespoon
Water, ¼ cup
Salt, ½ teaspoon
Pepper, dash

Chop cabbage and combine with butter, water and seasoning in heavy pan; cook until tender, about 10 minutes, over low heat.

Egg Yolks, 2, beaten
Sugar, ½ cup
Vinegar, ¼ cup
Light Cream, 1 cup

To serve 4 to 5

Combine ingredients, pour over cabbage and heat thoroughly but do not boil. Taste and correct for seasoning if necessary.

GLAZED CARROTS

Carrots, 2 cups, cooked, sliced
Brown Sugar, ½ cup
Butter, ¼ cup
Hot Water, ¼ cup

Oven, moderate, 375°

To serve 4

Combine sugar, butter and water, and cook 5 minutes. Pour syrup over cooked carrots in baking dish.

Bake 20 minutes or until browned, basting with syrup occasionally.

QUICK CARROTS

Carrots, 1 bunch
Butter, 2 tablespoons
Water, ¼ cup
Salt and **Pepper,** to taste

Scrape carrots and shred into thin strips. Combine with butter and water in pan. Cook, tightly covered, 5 minutes, or until tender. Season with salt and pepper.

Broccoli may be served with Hollandaise sauce as a separate course

BAKED CARROTS

Prepare carrots as in recipe for Quick Carrots above, and put with the same ingredients into a baking dish. Cover and bake until tender, about 20 minutes, in moderate oven.

CARROTS AND GREEN PEPPERS

Carrots, 1 bunch **Green Peppers,** 2 medium **Butter,** 1 tablespoon **Salt** and **Pepper,** to taste	Scrape and dice carrots, cook in boiling water to barely cover for 10 minutes. Chop peppers and add to carrots; continue cooking 5 minutes, or until vegetables are tender. Drain and place in serving dish, add butter and seasonings.

To serve 4

BAKED BABY CARROTS

Tiny Carrots, 1 pound	Scrape carrots and cook in boiling salted water until nearly tender. Drain and place in baking dish.
Butter, ¼ cup **Dry Bread Crumbs,** ½ cup **Minced Onion,** 1 teasp.	Mix ingredients together and spread crumb topping over carrots.
Oven, moderate, 350°	Bake 15 minutes, until golden brown.

To serve 4

CARROT SOUFFLÉ

See Spinach Soufflé, page 153.

CREAMED BEANS AND CARROTS

Carrots, 2 small **Frozen Lima Beans,** 1 package **Salt,** 1 teaspoon **Butter,** 1 tablespoon **Cream,** ½ cup	Scrape and dice carrots, put in pan with lima beans and enough boiling salted water to just cover. Cook for 10 minutes, or until vegetables are tender. Drain and add butter and cream. Heat again, but do not boil.

To serve 4 or 5

This combination is good also with a thin white sauce.

CAULIFLOWER AU GRATIN

Boil medium-sized head of cauliflower as described on page 131. Put into buttered baking dish with 1 cup of medium white sauce (page 90). Top with ¼ cup grated Cheddar cheese. Put under broiler until cheese melts and browns a little.

To serve 4

CELERIAC

Celeriac, or celery root, is a variety of celery with a large knobby root. It can be served raw, seasoned with salt and vinegar. To cook, remove leaves and pare root. Dice and cook in boiling water 15 minutes or until just tender. Serve with melted butter or white sauce.

Braised celery

BRAISED CELERY

Celery, 1 bunch
Butter, 3 tablespoons
Bouillon Cube, 1
Water, ½ cup, boiling

Cut celery stalks into 2-inch pieces and sauté in butter in heavy skillet until golden brown. Add bouillon cube dissolved in water and continue cooking slowly until celery is tender.

To serve 4 to 6

CREAMED CELERY

Braise celery as in above recipe, adding a little water instead of bouillon. When celery is tender, add 1 cup of cream. Heat, but do not boil. Season with salt and pepper.

Or follow same procedure but add 1 cup of white sauce instead of cream. Add 1 teaspoon of chopped parsley before serving.

CHAYOTE

Chayotes are a type of squash grown in Mexico and South America. They are pear-shaped, greenish white, with white, firm flesh. Follow recipe for squash, in preparing them.

CHESTNUTS

To shell chestnuts, slit shells with sharp knife, place in heavy skillet with a little salad oil and stir over heat for about 10 minutes or bake in very hot oven for about 20 minutes. Or slit shells and drop into boiling water to cover and cook for 20 minutes. Remove shells and skins.

Chestnuts can be used as a vegetable. Cook them in boiling water to cover, after they are shelled, until tender, about 12 to 15 minutes. Mash or rice and serve with salt, pepper and butter. Or serve with white sauce.

BOILED CORN ON THE COB

Use only freshly picked, tender corn. Test for tenderness—your thumb nail should easily puncture a grain. Cook, covered in boiling water, 5 to 8 minutes. Do not overcook, and do not put salt in the water, it will make the corn tough. Serve immediately with salt, pepper and butter.

CORN OFF THE COB

Cook corn as above. With sharp knife cut kernels off the cob and keep them hot in top part of double boiler with hot water below. Dress with melted butter, salt and pepper to serve.

STEAMED EARS OF CORN

Turn back husks on tender ears of corn and remove silk. Replace husks over cob and tie ends. Let stand in cold water for 30 minutes. Drain, place in heavy kettle, cover, and heat kettle. Turn heat low and cook 15 minutes. Serve with butter, salt and pepper.

CORN-ZUCCHINI CASSEROLE

Onion, 1 medium
Green Pepper, 1
Butter, 3 tablespoons
Zucchini, 6 small
Whole-kernel Corn,
  8-ounce can
Tomatoes, 16-ounce can
Salt and **Pepper,** to taste
Parmesan Cheese, ½ cup

Chop onion and pepper and sauté in butter until golden in color. Add washed zucchini, sliced thin, and simmer 10 minutes, or until tender. Add tomatoes, corn drained and seasoning and heat thoroughly. Pour into casserole and top with grated cheese. Place under broiler for few minutes to brown.

To serve 4

ROASTED CORN EARS

Pull back husks from ears of corn and remove silk; replace husks and tie in place. Bake in a hot oven (425°) for 15 or 20 minutes, or until husks are browned. Remove husks and serve with butter, salt and pepper.

SUCCOTASH

Lima Beans, 1½ cups,
  shelled
Corn, 1½ cups, cut from
  cob, uncooked
Cream, ½ cup
Butter, 2 tablespoons
Salt and **Pepper,** to taste

Cook lima beans, in boiling water to barely cover, until just tender. Add corn and cook 3 minutes longer; liquid should be nearly cooked away. If not, drain off all but ¼ cup. Add cream, butter and seasonings. Reheat, but do not boil.

To serve 4 to 6

TOP-OF-THE-STOVE CORN PUDDING

Eggs, 4
Salt, 1 teaspoon
Pepper, ⅛ teaspoon
Milk, 1⅓ cups

Corn, 4 ears

Grease top of double boiler, add eggs, seasonings and milk and heat slightly.

Slit kernels on cob lengthwise with sharp knife and scrape pulp out with back of knife. Add to egg mixture. Cover and cook over boiling water 30 minutes, or until set.

To serve 4 to 6

CORN FRITTERS

All-purpose Flour,
  1¾ cups
Baking Powder, 2 teasps.
Salt, 1 teaspoon
Milk, ¾ cup
Egg, 1, beaten
Fat, 1 tablespoon, melted
Corn, 1 cup, canned,
  cream-style

Sift dry ingredients together, add milk, egg, corn and melted fat; mix well and quickly. Drop by spoonfuls into deep, hot fat (360°) 4 or 5 minutes, or until golden brown; drain on paper towels. Serve with red currant jelly.

To make about 12 fritters, depending on size.

CHEESE FRITTERS: Substitute 1 cup of chopped sharp cheese for corn.

CLAM FRITTERS: Substitute 1 cup of minced clams for corn.

MEAT AND POULTRY FRITTERS: Substitute 1 cup of minced cooked meat or poultry for corn. Add 1 teaspoonful of instant onion.

FRIED CORNMEAL MUSH

Buy cornmeal mush in pans from your butcher, or cook the cornmeal according to the directions on the package, until thick. Pour thick mush into a loaf pan to mold. When firm and cold, cut into ½-inch slices, dredge with flour and fry in bacon fat or butter until lightly brown and crisp on both sides. Serve hot with syrup as an accompaniment to sausage or bacon.

BAKED HOMINY

Onion, 1, minced
Green Pepper, ½, minced
Butter, 3 tablespoons
Flour, 3 tablespoons
Salt, 1 teaspoon
Dry Mustard, ½ teasp.
Cayenne, large dash
Milk, 1½ cups
American Cheese, ¾ cup,
  crumbled

Cook onion and green pepper in skillet until golden. Stir in flour and seasonings. Add milk and cheese. Cook slowly, stirring constantly until slightly thickened.

Whole Hominy,
  24-ounce can
Bread Crumbs, ¾ cup
Butter, 3 tablespoons

Drain hominy and pour into shallow casserole. Mix sauce with it. Mix bread crumbs with melted butter and spread over top.

Oven, moderate, 375°

Bake 30 minutes.

To serve 4 to 6

FRIED HOMINY

Hominy grits may be prepared in the same manner as Cornmeal Mush above.

SCALLOPED CORN

Corn, 2 cups, cut from
  cob, uncooked
Eggs, 2
Milk, ¾ cup
Salt, ½ teaspoon

Place corn in greased baking dish. Combine beaten eggs, milk and salt and pour over corn.

Dry Bread Crumbs, 1 cup
Butter, 2 tablespoons

Add bread crumbs to melted butter and arrange on top of corn.

Oven, moderate, 325°

Bake 30 minutes.

To serve 4

MEXICAN CORN

Corn, 16-ounce can,
  whole kernel
Butter, 2 tablespoons
Green Pepper, chopped,
  1 tablespoon
Pimiento, 1, chopped
Salt, ½ teaspoon
Chili Powder, ½ teasp.

Combine all ingredients and simmer 10 minutes, stirring occasionally.

To serve 4

STEWED CUCUMBERS

Cucumbers, 6 small
Flour in Shaker
Butter, 2 tablespoons
Bouillon Cube
Water, 1 cup, boiling
Salt, 1 teaspoon
Pepper, ⅛ teaspoon

Cut cucumbers into thick slices, sprinkle with flour, and sauté in butter until lightly browned. Dissolve cube in water and add to cucumbers with seasoning. Cover and simmer 5 minutes.

To serve 4

A cup of canned tomatoes may be substituted for the bouillon, and a teaspoon of minced onion added.

CUCUMBERS AU GRATIN

Cucumbers, 6 small
Butter, 2 tablespoons
Medium White Sauce,
  1 cup
Grated Cheese, ¼ cup

Cut cucumbers in slices and sauté in butter until lightly browned. Add hot white sauce to cucumbers and pour into baking dish. Top with grated cheese and put under broiler a few minutes until cheese melts and browns a little.

To serve 4 or 5

DASHEEN

Dasheens are white-fleshed vegetables grown chiefly in the Caribbean area. They may be prepared by any of the recipes for potatoes, but cook in slightly less time. They have a nutty flavor when cooked, and are white to pale violet in color.

FRIED EGGPLANT

Eggplant	Cut eggplant in slices ½ inch thick and peel each slice. Dip slices in milk, dredge with flour, and spread on platter to dry for 15 minutes. Fry gently until crisp and brown, and season with salt and pepper.
Milk, 1 cup	
Flour in Shaker	
Vegetable Oil to cover bottom of skillet	
Salt and Pepper, to taste	

BREADED EGGPLANT

Eggplant	Prepare eggplant as above. Dip slices in egg and water mixed together, then dip in bread crumbs. Set aside for 15 minutes, then fry as above.
Water, 2 tablespoons	
Egg, 1, beaten slightly	
Dry Bread Crumbs, or Cornmeal	
Vegetable Oil to cover bottom of skillet	

EGGPLANT AU GRATIN

Prepare Scalloped Eggplant (page 143); place on top of it thin slices of cheese, or a layer of grated cheese. Bake as for Scalloped Eggplant.

EGGPLANT AND TOMATO SCALLOP

Tomatoes, canned, 1 cup	Proceed as for Scalloped Eggplant (page 143) but substitute tomatoes for milk and combine with the eggplant and onion, and add also the basil and Worcestershire.
Basil, ½ teaspoon	
Worcestershire, ½ teasp.	

EGGPLANT PARMIGIANA

Eggplant, 1 large	Cut eggplant in ½-inch slices and peel each slice. Dredge each slice with flour and fry in cooking oil until lightly browned. Arrange in baking dish alternate layers of eggplant, thin slices of cheese and tomato sauce. Top with sauce and grated cheese.
Cooking Oil, 3 tablesps.	
Flour in shaker	
Mozzarella Cheese, ½ lb.	
Tomato Sauce	
Parmesan Cheese, ½ cup, grated	
Oven, moderate, 375°	Bake uncovered 20 minutes, or until browned.

To serve 4

Tomato Sauce

Tomatoes, 16-oz. can	Combine ingredients in saucepan, bring to boil, simmer 30 minutes over low heat.
Tomato Paste, 6-oz. can	
Garlic, 1 clove, minced	
Onion, 1, chopped	
Sugar, 2 teaspoons	
Salt, 1 teaspoon	
Pepper, ¼ teaspoon	
Oregano, ½ teaspoon	
Parsley, 2 sprigs, chopped	

STUFFED EGGPLANT

Eggplant, large	Cut eggplant in half lengthwise and parboil 10 minutes. Scoop out center to within ½ inch of skin, chop fine and set aside.

Stuff eggplant skins with one of the following combinations:

Ham Stuffing

Ham, cooked, ¾ cup, diced	Combine chopped eggplant with ham and onion and stuff the shells. Melt butter and mix with bread crumbs. Sprinkle on top of eggplant. Place in shallow baking dish.
Onion, ¼ cup, chopped	
Dry Bread Crumbs, 1 cup	
Butter, 1 tablespoon	
Oven, hot, 400°	Bake 15 minutes.

Clam Stuffing

Onion, 1, minced	Sauté onion in 2 tablespoons butter until it is golden, remove from heat; add eggplant, egg, drained minced clams, parsley, seasoning, and enough soft bread crumbs to stiffen the mixture. Stuff the eggplant shells and sprinkle more bread crumbs on top. Dot with butter.
Butter, 2 tablespoons	
Egg, 1, beaten	
Clams, fresh or canned, 1 cup, minced	
Parsley, 1 tablespoon, minced	
Salt and Pepper, to taste	
Soft Bread Crumbs	
Butter, 1 tablespoon	
Oven, moderate, 375°	Bake for 30 minutes.

BULGARIAN EGGPLANT

Onion, 1 small	Chop onion and brown lightly in fat in heavy skillet. Peel eggplant and cut into cubes; sprinkle with flour and brown in skillet. Remove and set aside.
Fat, 2 tablespoons	
Eggplant	
Flour in Shaker	
Lamb, 1 pound, ground	Add lamb and seasonings to skillet, brown lightly. In casserole arrange alternate layers of eggplant and lamb.
Salt, 1 teaspoon	
Pepper, ¼ teaspoon	
Paprika, 1 teaspoon	
Egg Yolks, 2, beaten	Mix egg yolks, sour cream and flour together and pour over mixture in casserole. Arrange slices of tomato over top.
Sour Cream, ½ cup	
Flour, 2 tablespoons	
Tomatoes, 2 or 3	
Oven, moderate, 350°	Bake 30 minutes.

To serve 4

CREOLE EGGPLANT

Butter, 1 tablespoon	Chop onion and brown gently in butter. Peel and cube eggplant and add to onion. Chop pepper and add to mixture. Add tomatoes, cover and simmer 10 minutes or until eggplant is tender. Season to taste.
Onion, 1 medium	
Eggplant, 1 medium	
Green Pepper, 1 medium	
Tomatoes, 2	
Salt and Pepper, to taste	

To serve 4

Three ways of cooking eggplant to accompany a hearty stew:
fried, stuffed, or fried and topped with melted cheese

SCALLOPED EGGPLANT

Eggplant, 1 medium	Pare and dice eggplant, parboil few minutes and drain well.
Onion, 1 medium **Butter,** 1 tablespoon **Soft Bread Crumbs,** ¾ cup **Butter,** 2 tablespoons **Milk,** ½ cup **Salt** and **Pepper,** to taste	Sauté onion in butter until soft, and add to eggplant. Place mixture in casserole with alternate layers of bread crumbs mixed with melted butter. Season with salt and pepper. Pour milk over all.
Oven, moderate, 375°	Bake 30 minutes.

To serve 4

FRENCH FRIED EGGPLANT STICKS

Cut eggplant into julienne strips; dip in egg seasoned with salt and pepper and then into cracker crumbs. Fry in deep fat (370°) until golden brown.

FRENCH FRIED CAULIFLOWER: Separate cauliflower into individual flowerettes and proceed as for French Fried Eggplant Sticks.

BRAISED ENDIVE

Endive, 8 small heads **Butter,** 2 tablespoons **Consommé,** ¼ cup **Salt** and **Pepper,** to taste	Melt butter in skillet, add endive, brown lightly; add consommé and seasoning, cover tightly and cook over low heat 15 minutes, or until tender. Broth or bouillon may be substituted for consommé.

To serve 4

PANNED GARDEN GREENS

Bacon Drippings, or
  other fat, 2 tablesps.
Greens (beet, cabbage,
  escarole, chard,
  lettuce, romaine,
  spinach, dandelion or
  mustard)
Salt and **Pepper,** to taste
	Cook greens quickly in fat in large heavy skillet. Cook over low heat and use tight lid to keep in steam. Stir occasionally to prevent sticking, and, if necessary, add a few tablespoons of water. Season to taste and serve with melted butter, or sour cream and chives, or Hollandaise. Or garnish with crisply fried bacon, crumbled.

4 to 6 cups of shredded greens will serve 4

Panned greens

KALE

Follow recipes for Greens and Spinach, allowing longer cooking time. Serve kale with cream sauce or cheese sauce.

KOHLRABI

Remove leaves, wash, pare and cut into pieces. Cook covered in boiling salted water for 30 minutes, or until just tender; drain, season with salt and pepper and serve with white sauce or hollandaise sauce.

LETTUCE

To cook lettuce, follow recipe for Panned Greens. Heads may be cut into sections, or pulled apart into individual leaves. Another method is to steam them in just the amount of water that clings to the leaves after washing. Cook tightly covered 5 to 10 minutes, or until just tender. Drain and season with salt, pepper and butter.

LENTILS ODETTE

Lentils, 1 pound **Onion,** 1 large, chopped **Carrot,** 1 medium, chopped **Bay Leaves,** 2 **Salt,** 1 teaspoon	Buy quick-cooking lentils and boil according to directions on package, adding the onion, carrot and bay leaves. Cook until just tender, not mushy. Drain and cool.
Shallots, 2, chopped **Parsley,** chopped, 1 tablespoon **Pepper,** ⅛ teaspoon, freshly ground **Vinaigrette Dressing,** page 159	Combine lentils with shallots, parsley, pepper and vinaigrette dressing and marinate over night. Serve thoroughly chilled on a bed of crisp lettuce as an appetizer, or as a main course vegetable.

MUSHROOMS

Never soak mushrooms in water; if they need cleaning, wipe them with a damp cloth. Young caps do not need peeling; if skin is old and tough it can be peeled off with the edge of a knife. If stems are tender break off and use with the caps; discarded stems may be used for flavoring soups and sauces. If used, cut off discolored end.

Mushrooms may be cooked in a very little water 5 to 10 minutes, or until just tender. Season them with salt, pepper and butter, or serve with a white sauce.

SAUTÉED MUSHROOMS

Sauté mushrooms slowly in butter until tender, allowing 1 tablespoon of butter to ¼ pound of mushrooms. Use caps whole or sliced, and stems, if tender. Season to taste and sprinkle with lemon juice.

CREAMED MUSHROOMS

Follow recipe for Sautéed Mushrooms. When tender, stir cream in gradually, allowing ½ cup to ¼ pound of mushrooms. Heat over low heat, but do not boil. Scrape up browned butter from bottom of pan to flavor cream. Flavor with chopped parsley, a little garlic, or Worcestershire, or with a tablespoon of sherry.

STUFFED MUSHROOMS

Mushrooms, 16 large	Wipe mushrooms, cut stems from caps, and chop stems. Invert caps in buttered baking dish.
Onion, 1 medium **Butter,** 1 tablespoon **Garlic,** 1 clove, minced **Marjoram,** ¼ teaspoon **Ground Beef,** ½ pound **Salt,** ½ teaspoon **Pepper,** ⅛ teaspoon **Grated Cheese,** 3 tablesp.	Chop onion, sauté in butter until soft, remove from heat; add stems, garlic, marjoram, salt and pepper and beef. Combine thoroughly and put a portion on each mushroom, packing it gently into cap. Sprinkle a little cheese on each.
Oven, hot, 400°	Bake in preheated oven 20 minutes.

To serve 4

MUSHROOM NEWBURG

Mushrooms, 1 pound fresh young caps, if available **Butter,** 3 tablespoons **Sherry,** ¼ cup **Salt and Pepper,** to taste	Wipe mushrooms, remove stems; or, if large mushrooms are used, slice through caps and stems and leave all in one. Cook gently in butter until golden brown. Add sherry and simmer 5 minutes. Season and remove from heat.
Cream, 1 cup **Egg Yolk,** 1	Beat egg yolk and add to cream, combine with mushroom mixture and reheat. Do not boil. Serve on crisp toast.

To serve 4

MUSHROOM AND HAM SOUFFLÉ

Thick White Sauce, 1½ cups **Parsley,** 1 tablespoon, chopped **Worcestershire,** 1 teasp. **Mushrooms,** ½ pound, chopped **Ham,** cooked, ¾ cup, chopped **Eggs,** 4, separated	To white sauce add parsley, Worcestershire, mushrooms and ham. Add egg yolks and mix well; then fold in stiffly beaten whites. Turn into a buttered casserole and set in pan of hot water.
Oven, moderate, 350°	Bake 30 to 40 minutes, or until lightly browned. Serve at once.

To serve 4 or 5

PANNED OKRA

Okra, 1 pound **Butter,** 2 tablespoons **Salt and Pepper**	Wash okra and cut off stems. Slice large pods; leave small ones whole if desired. Melt butter in heavy pan, stir in okra, cover tightly, and cook over low heat 10 minutes or more, until tender. Season with salt and pepper.

GUMBO

Onions, 2 sliced
Green Peppers,
2, chopped
Bacon Drippings,
2 tablespoons
Okra, 1 lb., small pods
Tomatoes, 3 large, peeled
Corn, cut, 1 cup
Salt and **Pepper,** to taste

Sauté onions and green pepper in bacon drippings until soft; cut stems from okra and add with tomatoes; simmer 10 minutes, stirring frequently. Add corn and cook about 6 minutes longer. Test kernel for doneness. Season.

To serve 4 or 5

OKRA-TOMATO SAUTÉ

Onion, 1 medium
Green Pepper, 1 medium
Bacon Fat, 2 tablespoons
Tomatoes, 16-ounce can
Okra, 1 pound, sliced
Rosemary, ½ teaspoon
Cornstarch, 2 teaspoons
Water, 1 tablespoon

Chop onion and green pepper and sauté in fat until soft. Add tomatoes, seasonings and okra; simmer over low heat until okra is tender. Blend cornstarch with water, stir into mixture and cook until slightly thickened.

To serve 4 to 6

CREAMED ONIONS

Small White Onions,
16 to 20
White Sauce, 2 cups
Parsley, ⅓ cup, chopped
Paprika, ⅛ teaspoon

Peel onions and cook, or cook in their skins, in boiling water until tender; drain and peel. Add to white sauce. Garnish with parsley and paprika.

To serve 4

Cheese Sauce may be substituted for White Sauce.

CREAMED ONIONS AND MUSHROOMS

Creamed Onions
Mushrooms, ½ pound
Butter, 2 tablespoons

Prepare Creamed Onions as above; sauté mushrooms in butter until golden brown and add to onions.

ONION SOUFFLÉ

Onions, 10 small white

Boil onions in their skins until very tender, drain and skin; purée them by putting through fine sieve, or with a blender. This should make a cup of purée.

Thick White Sauce, 1 cup
Eggs, 4, separated
Salt and **Pepper,** to taste
Parsley, 1 tablespoon,
chopped

When sauce is smooth and hot, stir in onions. Reduce heat and stir in beaten egg yolks. Cook 1 minute until mixture thickens. Add seasonings and let mixture cool. Beat egg whites stiff and fold them lightly into the onion mixture. Turn into ungreased baking dish.

Oven, moderate, 350°

Bake 45 minutes, or until puffed high and golden brown. Serve at once.

To serve 4

FRENCH FRIED ONIONS

Onions, large, 1 per
person
Milk, ½ cup
Flour, ¼ cup
Salt, ½ teaspoon

Cut onions in crosswise slices, put slices in bowl and cover with milk. Combine salt with flour, drain each slice and dip in flour. Fry in hot fat (360°) until lightly browned. Drain on paper towels.

FRENCH FRIED ONION RINGS

Follow recipe above for French Fried Onions, but separate the slices into individual rings.

SAUTÉED ONIONS

Onions, 8 medium-sized
Bacon Fat or **Butter,**
3 tablespoons
Salt and **Pepper,** to taste

Peel onions under running water; slice very thin. Sauté in heavy skillet over low heat until golden yellow and tender, stirring frequently to keep from burning. Season and serve at once.

To serve 4

BAKED ONIONS

Onions, 1 large one per
serving
Salt and **Pepper,** to taste
Sugar, ¼ teaspoon per
1 onion
Butter, as needed

Peel onions and cut crosswise in halves; place side by side in buttered baking dish. Season each one with a little salt, pepper, sugar and a dab of butter.

Oven, moderate, 325°

Bake 1 hour, or until tender.

The large Spanish onions are delicious prepared in this way.

GLAZED ONIONS

Small White Onions,
16 to 20
Salt, 1 teaspoon

Peel onions and boil, or boil in their skins, until tender; drain, cool and remove skins.

Butter, 3 tablespoons
Sugar, 1 tablespoon
Salt, ¼ teaspoon

Heat butter and add sugar and salt; add onions and cook slowly, stirring and turning onions till they are golden brown.

To serve 4

GRILLED ONIONS

Onions, 3 large, mild
Butter, ¼ cup
Salt and **Pepper,** to taste

Peel onions, cut in slices; place on broiler pan, one layer deep. Brush each slice with melted butter and sprinkle with salt and pepper. Broil 5 minutes, turn slices and repeat on other side.

To serve 4 or 5

QUICK CREAMED ONIONS

Celery Soup, 1 can **Milk,** ½ can **Onions,** 16-ounce can, drained	Mix all together and bring to boiling point. Simmer few minutes.

To serve 4

QUICK CREAMED CARROTS: Substitute 1 can tiny carrots for the onions in above recipe.

QUICK CREAMED ONIONS AND POTATOES

Celery Soup, 1 can **Milk,** ½ can **Potatoes,** 16-ounce can **Onions,** 16-ounce can **Instant Onion,** 1 teaspoon	Blend soup and milk together in saucepan over medium heat. Drain potatoes and onions and add to soup. Add onion seasoning.

To serve 4

SHERRIED ONIONS

Small White Onions, 16 to 20 **Cream,** 1 cup **Sherry,** ¼ cup **Salt,** ½ teaspoon **Pepper,** ⅛ teaspoon	Peel onions and boil, or boil in their skins until just tender; drain, peel onions, and arrange in buttered baking dish. Combine cream, sherry, salt and pepper, and pour over onions. Heat under broiler for few minutes or until lightly browned.

To serve 4

GREEN ONIONS AND PEAS

Green Onions, 1 bunch **Fresh Peas,** 2 pounds **Salt,** 1 teaspoon	Cut white part of onions in small pieces and combine with shelled peas in saucepan with boiling water to barely cover. Add salt and cook covered for 10 minutes, or until vegetables are tender. Serve with butter or white sauce.

To serve 4

ONIONS, CARROTS AND GREEN BEANS

Small White Onions, 8 to 12 **Green Beans,** ½ pound **Carrots,** 3 young **Salt** and **Pepper** **Butter**	Peel onions, cut beans in pieces, and carrots in thin slices. Cook onions, in boiling water to barely cover, 5 minutes, then add beans and carrots. Continue cooking until vegetables are just tender. Season to taste, and serve with butter.

To serve 4

BAKED PARSNIPS

Parsnips, 1 pound **Butter,** 2 tablespoons **Brown Sugar,** ½ cup	Scrape parsnips and cook in a little boiling water 30 minutes, or until tender. Cut in halves or quarters and place in baking dish. Brush with melted butter and sprinkle with brown sugar.
Oven, hot, 400°	Bake 20 minutes.

To serve 4

FRENCH FRIED PARSNIPS

Cut boiled parsnips (page 131) crosswise into ½ inch slices. Dip in slightly beaten egg, then in flour; fry in deep hot fat (380°) 3 to 5 minutes, or until lightly browned. Drain on absorbent paper; salt lightly and serve at once. Allow 2 medium-sized parsnips per portion.

GREEN PEAS COOKED WITH LETTUCE

Fresh Peas, 3 pounds **Butter,** 3 tablespoons **Water,** ½ cup **Lettuce,** several leaves	Melt butter in heavy saucepan, add peas and boiling water. Cover peas with lettuce leaves, pressing them down closely over the peas. Cook, tightly covered, over low heat until tender, 10 to 15 minutes. The lettuce leaves may be removed, or chopped up and served with the peas. Dress with melted butter, or stir in ½ cup of cream.

To serve 4

MINTED PEAS

A little fresh mint, or dried mint leaves, may be added to peas while cooking, or to the melted butter or cream which is served with them.

FRESH PEAS AND NEW POTATOES

New Potatoes, 1 pound **Fresh Peas,** 2 pounds **Salt,** 1 teaspoon **Pepper,** ⅛ teaspoon **Cream,** 1 cup	Peel potatoes and cook in boiling salted water to just cover until nearly tender; if potatoes are tiny, leave whole, otherwise cut in pieces. Shell peas and add to potatoes; continue cooking until vegetables are tender. Drain, add cream, heat but do not boil. Dress with pepper.

To serve 4

SAUTÉED GREEN PEPPERS AND TOMATOES

Green Peppers, 2 large **Butter,** 2 tablespoons **Tomatoes,** 4 quartered **Salt,** ½ teaspoon **Pepper,** ⅛ teaspoon **Sugar,** ½ teaspoon	Cut peppers in pieces, removing centers, and cook in butter for 3 minutes. Add tomatoes and seasonings, cover skillet and cook over low heat until peppers are tender. Stir occasionally.

FRENCH FRIED PEPPER RINGS

Green Peppers, approx. 1 per serving **Egg,** 1 **Water,** 1 tablespoon **Fine Dry Breadcrumbs,** 1 cup **Salt**	Wash peppers, cut in thin slices and remove centers. Dip in egg mixed with water, then in crumbs. Fry in deep hot fat (380°) until nicely browned. Do a few at a time and drain on absorbent paper.

BRAISED RADISHES

Wash, remove tops, and slice radishes; parboil, in water to barely cover, 5 minutes; drain. Sauté slowly in butter 5 minutes; add a little cream and continue cooking over very low heat until tender.

Peas and onions, a classic combination which may be lightly flavored with curry

*Green peppers with
savory stuffing
and corn*

SALSIFY (OYSTER PLANT)

Wash and scrape salsify and put at once into water to prevent discoloration. Drain and cover with boiling water, cook 10 to 15 minutes, or until tender. Drain and serve seasoned with salt and pepper, and butter or white sauce.

STUFFED PEPPERS

Green Peppers, 1 per serving	Leave peppers whole and remove stem end and seeds, or cut in half lengthwise and fill each half. Rub butter on outside skin of peppers, and stuff with any of the following mixtures.
Oven, moderate, 350°	Bake 30 minutes, or until top of mixture is lightly browned.

Savory Stuffing

Celery, ¼ cup, chopped Onion, 1 medium, sliced Butter, 2 tablespoons Soft Bread Crumbs, 4 cups Salt, 1 teaspoon Pepper, ⅛ teaspoon Marjoram, ½ teaspoon Parsley, 1 tablespoon Milk, ½ cup	Sauté celery and onion in butter until soft. Add bread crumbs, and seasonings and mix well. Moisten stuffing with milk and fill peppers.

To fill 4 large peppers

Tomato Stuffing

Onion, 1 med., chopped Butter, 2 tablespoons Tomatoes, 1 cup canned Soft Bread Crumbs, 2 cups Celery, 1 cup, chopped	Combine ingredients, fill peppers, dot top with butter. (Corn optional.)

To fill 4 large peppers

Hamburg Stuffing

Onion, 1 med., chopped Hamburg, 1 pound Tomato Sauce, ½ can Salt and Pepper, to taste Soft Bread Crumbs, ½ cup	Combine ingredients and fill peppers. Top with dabs of butter.

To fill 4 large peppers

Recipes for Stuffed Tomatoes and Stuffed Eggplant may also be used.

BOILED POTATOES

Scrub potatoes and pare, or cook in their skins, if preferred. It is best to cook them whole so that less nutrients are lost. Cover with boiling salted water and boil 20 to 30 minutes, or until fork tender. Potatoes cooked in their skins may be peeled after cooking, or served in their jackets, dressed with butter, salt and pepper. The skins of new potatoes make good eating. Be sure to save the water in which potatoes were cooked, as well as all other vegetable water, for making soups or gravies—it contains valuable minerals and vitamins.

PARSLEY POTATOES

Cook small potatoes in their skins, as directed above; peel. Dip in melted butter; sprinkle with finely chopped parsley.

NEW POTATOES IN OLIVE OIL

Boil new potatoes in jackets. When done roll in olive oil to coat lightly and dust with salt.

POTATOES IN SOUR CREAM

Boil potatoes as in above recipe; when tender cut in cubes and return to saucepan with 2 tablespoons of the potato water. Reheat and add ½ cup of sour cream for each 4 medium potatoes; do not boil, but mix lightly over heat. Pour into hot serving dish and sprinkle finely chopped parsley over top.

SAVORY POTATOES

Peel small equal-sized old potatoes. Melt butter in skillet and move potatoes around in it until well coated and golden in color. Add ½ cup of consommé or bouillon and simmer, covered, over low heat until potatoes are tender. Consommé should simmer down and potatoes be browned when finished.

GOLDEN BROWN NEW POTATOES

New Potatoes, 1 pound, boiled Butter, 2 tablespoons Salt, 1 teaspoon Pepper, ⅛ teaspoon *To serve 4*	Peel boiled potatoes, dip in butter, then sprinkle with seasonings. Put in single layer in baking pan and bake in hot oven (425°) for 10 or 15 minutes, or until crisp and lightly browned.

PAN-ROASTED POTATOES

Pare medium-sized potatoes and boil in salted water for 10 or 12 minutes. Drain and place in pan with roasting meat. Baste with fat drippings from the roast. Bake 40 minutes, or until tender, turning occasionally so that all sides are browned.

Potatoes can always be cooked in this way with fat drippings saved from a previous roast.

MASHED POTATOES

Wash and peel potatoes; if large, cut in half. Cook covered in boiling salted water to just cover, until tender. Drain thoroughly. Mash with potato masher or ricer, or beat in electric mixer. Add a little butter melted in a little hot milk. Beat until fluffy and season to taste. Old potatoes mash more smoothly than new ones. If you like a creamy mashed potato you will find that the potatoes will absorb quite a bit of milk with constant beating. Should they become too liquid, set the pan over low heat for a few minutes until a little of the liquid evaporates. Then fluff up once more with a fork and serve.

DUCHESS POTATOES

Mash or rice potatoes as in preceding recipe. To each 2 cups of seasoned mashed potatoes, add 1 beaten egg yolk. Shape in mounds on baking sheet, brush with melted butter, and bake in hot oven (400°) until lightly browned.

ROSETTES

Prepare Duchess Potatoes by the above recipe. Put into pastry bag and squeeze out little round shapes onto a buttered baking sheet. Brush with beaten egg and bake in hot oven (425°) until golden.

GOLDEN MOUNTAINS

Prepare Duchess Potatoes by the above recipe. Arrange small portions on a buttered baking sheet, and form them into cone shapes. Sprinkle thickly with grated cheese and place in very hot oven (450°) for 5 minutes, or until golden brown.

CHEESE POTATOES

Prepare Duchess Potatoes according to the above recipe. Form into balls and put on buttered baking sheet. Press a ½-inch cube of sharp cheese into the center of each. Brush with egg and bake in hot oven (425°) for 5 minutes, or until golden.   Serve at once.

POTATO CAKES

Leftover Mashed Potatoes, 2½ cups	Fluff up potatoes with an egg beater and mix in egg and
Egg, 1, beaten	seasonings. Shape into 8 flat
Instant Onion, 1 teasp.	cakes, and brown slowly in a
Salt and **Pepper,** to taste	little fat in skillet, turning until
Fat	each side is done evenly.
To serve 4	

If potatoes are too soft to handle, drop them by the tablespoonful into the skillet.

CRISP BAKED POTATOES

Scrub potatoes thoroughly, and dry. Rub skins with a little butter and roll in salt until lightly crusted. Arrange on cookie sheet in very hot oven (450°) and bake 45 minutes or until tender. Cut the skin on top of each potato, press potato gently to loosen, fluff gently with fork without breaking potato apart, and top with a pat of butter.

Baked potatoes are delicious served with a side dish of sour cream flavored with chopped chives.

The salty skins make delicious eating, but if a soft skin is preferred, simply rub the skins with butter and omit the salt.

BAKED POTATOES ON THE HALF SHELL

Bake potatoes as in the above recipe. When tender, cut in half lengthwise; scoop potato out of skins into a bowl. Mash, add butter melted in a little hot milk, and seasonings. Beat lightly with a fork until fluffy, pile lightly into potato shells, brush with melted butter and brown lightly in hot oven (400°).

Seasonings can be varied for this dish; you may use onion salt, instant garlic, parsley, fresh ground pepper, or Worcestershire sauce. The potatoes may be topped with grated cheese before the final baking.

CREAMED POTATOES

Cook potatoes in their skins, as in recipe for Boiled Potatoes, then dice and add to white sauce (see page 148). Or, peel and dice potatoes, cook 10 minutes in ½ cup of water. When tender, add ½ cup of milk and cook until slightly thickened, stirring carefully to prevent sticking. Season to taste and garnish with finely chopped parsley. This amount of liquid will prepare about 4 medium potatoes.

SCALLOPED POTATOES WITH CUCUMBER

Potatoes, 4 cups, sliced	In greased baking dish, arrange
Cucumber, 1 medium, sliced	alternate layers of thinly-sliced potatoes and cucumbers with a
Flour, 2 tablespoons	sprinkling of flour, salt and
Salt, 1 teaspoon	pepper, and put a little butter
Pepper, ⅛ teaspoon	with each layer. Heat milk and
Butter, 2 tablespoons	pour over all.
Milk, 2 cups	
Oven, moderate, 375°	Bake, covered, 30 minutes, then uncover and bake 15 or 20 minutes more, or until potatoes are tender and top is lightly
To serve 4	browned.

POTATOES AU GRATIN

Proceed as with Scalloped Potatoes above, but add ½ pound of crumbled sharp cheese to potato layers. Onions may be substituted for the cucumber.

SCALLOPED POTATOES AND HAM

Follow the above recipe for Scalloped Potatoes with Cucumber and add 2 cups of chopped cooked ham, sprinkle a little over each layer of potatoes.

POTATOES AND HAM AU GRATIN

Combine sliced boiled potatoes, and cubed cooked ham, with white sauce (see page 90) and pour into baking dish. Top with grated cheese and brown under broiler for a few minutes.

QUICK CREAMED POTATOES

Combine canned potatoes with canned cream of celery soup; garnish with chopped parsley.

LYONNAISE POTATOES

Fat, 3 tablespoons	Melt fat in frying pan, add
Onions, 3 medium	chopped onions and sauté until
Potatoes, 6, cooked	they are soft. Slice potatoes and
Salt and **Pepper,** to taste	add to onions. Season and cook slowly until potatoes are brown on one side. Turn over and
To serve 4	brown on other side.

French fried potatoes

O'BRIEN POTATOES

Cooked Potatoes, 2 cups, diced
Flour, 1 tablespoon
Onion, 1 small, chopped
Green Pepper, 1 small, chopped
Cheddar Cheese, ¼ pound, grated
Milk, 1 cup
Salt and **Pepper,** to taste
Dry Bread Crumbs

Combine ingredients in a greased casserole, topping lightly with fine bread crumbs.

Oven, moderate, 350°

Bake 20 minutes or until lightly browned.

To serve 4

CHEESE-POTATO-MUSHROOM CASSEROLE

Potatoes, 4 medium
Mushrooms, 1 pound
Cheese, ½ cup, grated
Parsley, 2 tablespoons, chopped
Onion, 1 small, chopped
Salt and **Pepper,** to taste
Cream, 1½ cups

Pare and slice potatoes, and slice mushrooms. Place in alternate layers in a buttered casserole with a sprinkling of cheese, parsley, onion, salt and pepper on each layer. Pour the cream over all.

Oven, moderate, 375°

Bake about 35 minutes or until potatoes are fork tender.

To serve 4

HASHED BROWN POTATOES

Potatoes, 3 cups, diced
Onion, 1 med., chopped
Salt, ½ teaspoon
Pepper, ⅛ teaspoon
Fat, 3 tablespoons

Mix raw potatoes, onion and seasoning together. Heat fat in skillet; spread mixture in skillet and flatten it with broad spatula. Sauté over low heat until bottom of mixture is brown. Turn whole cake over, in one piece if possible, or in two halves, and cook until brown on other side and done. Serve piping hot.

To serve 4

POTATO RAGOÛT

Celery, 2 stalks
Onion, 1 medium
Garlic, 1 clove, chopped
Cooking Oil, ¼ cup
Potatoes, 3 large
Salt Pork, 1 slice
Tomatoes, 16-ounce can
Salt, ½ teaspoon
Pepper, ⅛ teaspoon
Parsley, 2 sprigs
Marjoram, ½ teaspoon

Sauté celery, onion and garlic in oil until soft; slice potatoes thin and add with salt pork, cut in cubes, to onions. Continue cooking until potatoes are lightly brown, stirring to prevent sticking. Add tomatoes and seasonings. Cover and simmer 15 minutes.

To serve 4

POTATO AND ONION SAUTÉ

Fat, 3 tablespoons
Potatoes, 4 medium
Onions, 4 medium
Salt and **Pepper**

Melt fat in heavy skillet and add sliced potatoes and onions. Cook slowly, occasionally turning up the bottom layer with a spatula so that all becomes browned. Cook 20 to 30 minutes, or until potatoes are tender. Season to taste.

To serve 4

POTATO PANCAKES

Potatoes, 5 medium
Egg, 2, beaten
Salt, 1 teaspoon
Onion, 1 tablespoon, chopped
Butter, 2 tablespoons

Peel and grate raw potatoes; add other ingredients. Melt butter in skillet and drop potatoes by spoonfuls into pancake shape. Brown on both sides.

To serve 4

FRENCH-FRIED POTATOES

Wash and peel potatoes; cut into lengthwise slices, then into strips, ¼ inch thick. Soak a few minutes in ice-cold water, and dry. Meanwhile heat to 375°, on a hot-fat thermometer, enough fat to cover potatoes. Drop potatoes into hot fat, cook until tender and brown. Drain on absorbent paper. Sprinkle with salt and serve immediately.

French-Fried Potatoes become soggy very soon and cannot be reheated successfully, so they should be served as soon as cooked.

TWICE-FRIED POTATOES

Prepare potatoes as in recipe for French-Fried Potatoes. Put potatoes into 375° fat and fry for about 10 minutes, or until only partly cooked. Remove potatoes from fat and drain. This is best done with a frying-basket that can be raised up and will drip off. Remove fat from heat until ready for second frying, just before you are ready to serve. Then heat fat to 385°, return potatoes to fat, and fry until brown. Drain potatoes on paper towels, sprinkle with salt and serve at once.

This method permits you to partially cook the potatoes ahead of time, saves you time later.

POMMES SOUFFLÉES

Cut potatoes in lengthwise slices ⅛-inch thick. Soak in cold water for 10 minutes. Drain and dry on paper towels. Heat 2 deep frying kettles of fat—one at moderate temperature (360°) and the other very hot (400°). Place a few slices in frying basket in moderate fat; let cook until they rise to the surface and the edges look somewhat puffy. When this first sign of puffing appears, quickly transfer basket to hot kettle. Cook until puffed and brown. Drain on absorbent paper and sprinkle with salt. If desired the potatoes may be partially cooked ahead of time, then given a final cooking in very hot fat just before serving.

The choice of potato is important in this dish—do not use Idaho baking potatoes or new potatoes of any kind.

POTATO DUMPLINGS
Kartoffelkloesse

Potatoes, 6 medium **Flour,** ½ cup, sifted **Salt,** 1 teaspoon **Eggs,** 2, slightly beaten	Peel potatoes and cook in boiling salted water until tender. Cool and put through ricer or sieve. Let stand several hours uncovered, until dry. Add flour, eggs and salt and mix well. Form into 1-inch balls and drop them into a large kettle of gently boiling salted water. Boil uncovered for 15 minutes.

To serve 4

Kartoffelkloesse are traditional with Sauerbraten; also very good with any kind of roast beef.

PANNED SPINACH

Spinach, 2 pounds **Bacon Drippings,** 2 tablespoons **Salt** and **Pepper,** to taste **Butter**	See preparation of spinach on page 131. Melt fat in large, heavy skillet, add spinach, cook over low heat and cover tightly to keep in steam. Stir occasionally to avoid sticking, and cook until just tender, 5 to 10 minutes. Drain, season, and serve with melted butter or hollandaise sauce. Garnish, if desired, with hard-boiled eggs, sliced or quartered.

To serve 4

CREAMED SPINACH

Spinach, 2 pounds	Clean spinach and cook, as above, until tender; drain, chop fine, or put through a ricer or blender.

Thick White Sauce, 1 cup
   (see page 90)
Onion, 1 tablespoon,
   minced
Salt and **Pepper,** to taste
	Add spinach and onion to hot white sauce and cook together for 2 minutes until heated and well blended. Season with salt and pepper.

To serve 4

WILTED SPINACH

Bacon, 4 slices	Fry slowly until crisp, remove from pan. Pour off all but 2 tablespoons of fat.
Vinegar, ¼ cup **Sugar,** 1 tablespoon **Salt,** 1 teaspoon **Pepper,** ⅛ teaspoon **Water,** ¼ cup **Spinach,** 2 pounds	Add vinegar, sugar, salt, pepper and water to bacon fat in skillet; bring to boil. Add spinach, stir in and heat thoroughly, covered, about 3 minutes. Drain and place in serving dish; crumble bacon on top.

To serve 4

SPINACH CHANTILLY

Creamed Spinach	Follow recipe for Creamed Spinach.
Whipping Cream, ½ cup **Salt,** ⅛ teaspoon **Horse-radish,** 1 teasp.	Whip cream until stiff and fold in salt and horse-radish. Spread over creamed spinach in baking dish. Brown lightly under broiler.

To serve 4

SPINACH AND BLUE CHEESE CASSEROLE

Prepare Creamed Spinach according to recipe above. To the spinach and white sauce mixture add 2 ounces of blue cheese crumbled. Turn mixture into buttered casserole, top with sliced hard-cooked eggs, cover and bake 20 minutes in 350° oven.

To serve 4

MOLDED SPINACH RING

Onion, 1 medium
Butter, 2 tablespoons
Cooked Spinach,
   2½ cups, chopped
Thick White Sauce,
   2 cups
Salt, ½ teaspoon
Pepper, ⅛ teaspoon
Mace, ⅛ teaspoon
Eggs, 2, separated
	Mince onion and sauté in butter until soft. Remove from heat; add spinach, white sauce, slightly beaten egg yolks, and seasonings, and mix well. Fold in stiffly beaten egg whites. Turn into buttered ring mold, place in pan of hot water.

Oven, moderate, 375°	Bake 30 minutes, or until firm.

To serve 4

SPINACH TIMBALES

Spinach, 2 cups,
   chopped, cooked
Butter, 2 tablespoons,
   melted
Eggs, 2 slightly beaten
Cream, ½ cup
Milk, ½ cup
Onion Salt, ½ teasp.
Pepper, ⅛ teaspoon
	Frozen chopped spinach, thawed, may be used. Drain well. Combine ingredients and pour into a buttered mold or baking dish. Set in pan of hot water.

Oven, slow, 300°	Bake about 30 minutes, or until a silver knife inserted will come out clean. Turn out on platter to serve.

To serve 4

SPINACH SOUFFLÉ

Eggs, 3, separated	Beat egg yolks until foamy and
Thick White Sauce, 1 cup	lemon colored. Stir into white
Onion Salt, 1/4 teaspoon	sauce; add spinach and onion
Spinach, 1 cup, cooked, chopped, drained	salt. Fold in stiffly beaten egg whites. Turn into ungreased baking dish.
Oven, moderate, 350°	Bake 35 to 40 minutes, or until lightly risen and golden brown.

To serve 4

CARROT SOUFFLÉ: Substitute 1 cup of cooked mashed carrots for spinach.

CORN SOUFFLÉ: Substitute 1 cup of whole corn kernels for spinach.

SUMMER SQUASH

Summer squash includes a number of thin-skinned varieties, such as the white disc-shaped or patty-pan, straight yellow, zucchini, or crooknecked. They are best when young and tender, and can be tested with the finger-nail; if you can cut the skin easily with your nail, it is tender. Squash with tender skins do not need peeling; the skins are edible. Squash may be boiled (see page 131) and served either mashed or sliced, with butter and salt and pepper.

PANNED SUMMER SQUASH

Fat, 2 tablespoons	Melt butter or other fat in
Squash, 3 or 4 cups, cut up	skillet; add squash to fat; cover, and cook over low heat for
Salt, 1/2 teaspoon	10 minutes or until tender. Stir
Pepper, to taste	to prevent sticking, and add a little water if needed. Season with salt and pepper.

SQUASH WITH CREAM

Prepare squash and cook as in recipe for Panned Squash. When squash is tender add 1/4 cup of cream and season to taste. Heat thoroughly, but do not boil again.

SQUASH AND GREEN BEANS

Prepare Panned Squash recipe and add 1/2 pound of green beans, cut in thin slivers, cooking them along with the squash.

BAKED SUMMER SQUASH

Cut squash into cubes and put into buttered baking dish. Sprinkle with melted butter, salt and pepper. Bake in 350° oven for 20 minutes, or until tender. They may also be cut in half and baked in their skins.

For variation, squash may be seasoned with a little onion, or instant garlic, or with cinnamon or mace.

ZUCCHINI AND ONIONS

Butter, 3 tablespoons	Melt butter in skillet and cook
Onions, 3 medium, sliced	onions over low heat until soft.
Salt and **Pepper,** to taste	Add zucchini; cover and cook
Zucchini, 3 cups, sliced	8 or 10 minutes, or until tender stirring frequently. Add seasonings.

To serve 4

When possible, buy small young zucchini for their superb flavor.

ZUCCHINI AND TOMATOES

Zucchini, 3 to 4 cups, sliced	Sauté zucchini and garlic in butter over low heat for
Garlic, 1 clove, minced	5 minutes, stirring frequently.
Butter, 2 tablespoons	Add tomatoes and simmer for
Canned Tomatoes, 1 cup, or fresh, if preferred	5 minutes. Add seasoning.
Salt and **Pepper,** to taste	

To serve 4

ZUCCHINI, TOMATOES AND CHEESE

Prepare Zucchini and Tomatoes above, add 1 cup of soft crumbs, pour into baking dish, top with grated cheese, and brown quickly under hot broiler.

WINTER SQUASH

Winter Squash are the tough-skinned late varieties such as Hubbard, acorn, or Des Moines. They may be boiled (see page 131), then mashed and served with salt, pepper and butter; they may be used in pies or fritters, or baked.

BAKED WINTER SQUASH

Pare squash, remove seeds, and proceed as for Baked Summer Squash. Longer baking time will be required, possibly an hour. They may also be cut in half and baked in their skins.

STEAMED ACORN SQUASH

Cut squash in half, remove seeds and pulp. Place cut side down on broiler rack over 1/2 inch of boiling water. Bake in hot oven (400°) for 30 minutes, or until tender. Turn squash upright, season with salt, pepper and butter, and leave in oven for a few minutes longer.

BAKED SWEET POTATOES OR YAMS

Allow one medium potato for serving. Scrub well, dry and bake in hot oven 30 to 40 minutes, or until fork tender. Slit skin on top and insert pat of butter in each.

CANDIED SWEET POTATOES

Sweet Potatoes, 4 med., boiled, or 1 can	Skin and split potatoes and arrange in casserole; sprinkle
Cinnamon, 1 teaspoon	with cinnamon-sugar mixture.
Sugar, 2 tablespoons	Pour syrup over potatoes and
Dark Corn Syrup, 1/3 cup	dot with butter.
Butter, 2 tablespoons	
Oven, moderate, 350°	Bake 30 minutes.

To serve 4

CANDIED YAMS: Follow the above recipe.

MAPLE CANDIED SWEET POTATOES

Follow recipe above for Candied Sweet Potatoes, but substitute 1/3 cup Maple Syrup for corn syrup.

Zucchini and onions combined with cheese sauce

SWEET POTATOES AND ORANGES WITH COINTREAU

Sweet Potatoes, 4, med.
Oranges, 2
Brown Sugar, ¼ cup
Butter, 2 tablespoons
Cointreau, ¼ cup

Boil potatoes in jackets until nearly tender. Skin, slice and put in alternate layers with slices of unpeeled oranges with seeds removed. Sprinkle layers with sugar and dot top with butter. Pour Cointreau over mixture.

Oven, moderate, 350°
To serve 4

Bake for 30 minutes, or until well browned.

Brandy or sherry may be substituted for Cointreau.

BAKED SWEET POTATOES WITH SHERRY

Sweet Potatoes, 4 med.

Bake in moderate oven or until tender.

Butter, 2 tablespoons
Sherry
Nuts, 2 tablespoons, chopped (almonds or pecans)

Split potato, scoop out insides and mash, adding butter, beating in enough sherry to moisten. Refill skins. Sprinkle nuts on top.

Oven, hot, 420°

To serve 4

Bake 5 minutes, until crisp on top.

Baked mashed sweet potatoes

MASHED SWEET POTATOES

Mash boiled or baked sweet potatoes and season with salt and pepper and a pat of butter. For 4 sweet potatoes add about ⅓ cup of hot milk and beat until light and fluffy. Add more milk if more moisture is desired.

BAKED MASHED SWEET POTATOES: Turn mashed sweet potatoes into shallow baking pan. Dot with butter and sprinkle with a dash of nutmeg. Bake in moderate oven (350°) 30 minutes.

STEWED TOMATOES

Tomatoes, 2 pounds, firm, ripe	Dip tomatoes in boiling water for 1 minute, plunge in cold
Or Canned Tomatoes, 1 large can	water, then slip off skins. Remove stem ends and cut in
Onion, 1 small, minced	quarters; cook in their own
Salt, 1 teaspoon	juice over moderate heat until
Pepper, ⅛ teaspoon	tender. Add onion and season-
Basil, ½ teaspoon	ings while cooking. Pour into
Sugar, 1 teaspoon	serving dish and top with
Croutons, 1 cup	croutons.

To serve 4

2 green peppers may be sliced and added to the above.

SCALLOPED TOMATOES

Follow recipe for Stewed Tomatoes above, but place ingredients in buttered baking dish, adding 1 cup soft crumbs to mixture and topping with ½ cup grated cheese. Bake in moderate oven (375°) 30 minutes.

BROILED TOMATO HALVES

Remove hard stem end of tomatoes and cut in halves. Place on baking sheet and season with salt, pepper and instant onion or garlic, or top with fresh or dry crushed herbs such as rosemary, basil, dill, or thyme. Broil under moderate heat. Do not overcook. Broiled tomatoes may be garnished with chopped parsley, crisp bacon, anchovies, or mayonnaise, or with sliced mushrooms that have been sautéed in butter.

TOMATO PIE

Pie Shell, 9-inch, baked	Fill pie shell with sliced
Tomatoes, 6, underripe	tomatoes and sprinkle with salt,
Salt, 1½ teaspoons	pepper and garlic. Top with
Pepper, ⅛ teaspoon	grated cheese.
Instant Garlic, ¼ teasp.	
Parmesan Chesse, ½ cup, grated	
Oven, moderate, 350°	Bake 20 minutes, or until browned.

To serve 4

BAKED STUFFED TOMATOES

Cut slice from stem ends of tomatoes and scoop out centers. Reserve centers to combine with other ingredients in the following recipes. After filling tomatoes, place in baking dish and bake in moderate oven, 375°, about 25 minutes.

Rice Stuffing

Precooked Rice, 5-ounce package
Tomato Juice
Instant Garlic, ¼ teasp.
Parsley, 1 tablespoon, chopped
Tomato Centers
Salt and **Pepper,** to taste
Butter

Prepare rice according to package directions, substituting tomato juice for water; add garlic and parsley. Chop and add reserved tomato centers. Season to taste with salt and pepper. Fill tomatoes with mixture; dot with butter. Bake as directed above.

Curried Rice Stuffing

Follow recipe for Rice Stuffing, but substitute ½–1 teaspoon curry powder for garlic.

Anchovy Stuffing

Soft Bread Crumbs, 1 cup
Tomato Centers, chopped
Anchovies, 3, chopped
Basil, ½ teaspoon
Instant Garlic, ¼ teasp.
Parmesan Cheese, ¼ cup

Mix centers with bread crumbs, anchovies and seasonings. Salt tomatoes lightly and fill. Top with grated cheese.

To fill 4 large tomatoes

Spinach Stuffing
(Tomatoes Florentine)

Chopped Frozen Spinach, 1 package
Instant Garlic, ¼ teasp.
Salt and **Pepper,** to taste
Worcestershire, ½ teasp.
Butter, 1 tablespoon, melted
Mace, ¼ teaspoon
Parmesan Cheese, ¼ cup

Cook spinach according to directions on package. Drain. Combine with other ingredients and fill tomatoes with mixture. Sprinkle tops with cheese.

To fill 4 to 6 large tomatoes

See also, recipes for Stuffed Peppers and Stuffed Eggplant.

Tomatoes with stuffing

FRIED TOMATOES

Slice underripe or green tomatoes ½ inch thick and dredge with flour. Fry in butter or bacon fat, a few minutes on each side, until lightly browned. Season with salt and pepper, and a little sugar. Allow 1 tomato per portion.

SLICED TOMATOES HAITIAN

Firm Ripe Tomatoes
Salad Oil, 3 tablespoons
Vinegar, 1 tablespoon
Onion, 1, small, minced
Salt and **Pepper,** to taste

Slice tomatoes and arrange them in a ring around the edge of a platter. In the center of the platter place a bowl containing the dressing. There should be a server for the tomatoes and a spoon in the dressing, so that people may help themselves to both.

FRIED TOMATOES WITH MILK GRAVY

Tomatoes, 4 large, sliced
Salt, 1 teaspoon
Pepper, ⅛ teaspoon
Flour in shaker
Fat, 2 tablespoons
Milk, 1 cup

To serve 4

Dredge tomatoes with flour and season; sauté in fat until browned on both sides. Remove slices from skillet, add 1 tablespoon flour to skillet and blend with fat; add milk and cook until thickened. Taste for seasoning, and pour over tomatoes.

This dish can be made also without removing the tomatoes from the pan when the gravy is made. Simply blend the flour in with the tomatoes, stirring until the tomatoes are broken up and then adding the milk. The consistency will be more like stewed tomatoes.

Sliced tomatoes garnished with anchovy fillets

CHILLED HERB TOMATOES

Tomatoes, firm, ripe	Peel and slice chilled tomatoes.
Onion Salt	Sprinkle with the onion and
Celery Salt	celery salts, and crumbled
Dried Basil	basil. No additional dressing is required.

MARINATED TOMATOES

Tomatoes, 4	Cut firm, ripe tomatoes in slices
Garlic, 1 clove, cut in half	and arrange in shallow bowl.
Parsley, 1 tablespoon, chopped	Mix herbs with French Dressing and pour over tomatoes. Chill
Basil, 1 teaspoon	for several hours. Remove garlic
French Dressing, ¼ cup	before serving.

TRUFFLES

Truffles are used to add a touch of elegance, and in much the same way that we use mushrooms. Chop a few in small pieces to add to a special sauce for meat or poultry; or use them as a garnish.

MASHED TURNIPS

Boil turnips according to directions on page 131. Drain, mash, season with salt and pepper, and dress with butter.

CREAMED TURNIPS

Boil turnips according to directions on page 131. Follow recipe for Creamed Potatoes.

VEGETABLE DINNER
(Roumanian Ghivech)

In a very large shallow casserole combine as many fresh vegetables as you can find in the market. This might include one of the cabbage family: cauliflower, broccoli or brussels sprouts; potatoes, carrots, peas, onions, zucchini or eggplant, string beans, and celery. Prepare about 12 cups of cut-up vegetables for 4 people. Pour over the vegetables the sauce described below. Cover casserole with aluminium foil and bake in a moderate oven, 350°, for 40 minutes or until vegetables are tender.

Consommé or **Beef Broth,** 1 can	Combine all ingredients in saucepan; bring to boil,
Water, ½ cup	simmer 10 minutes.
White Wine or **Tomato Juice,** ½ cup	
Olive Oil, ¼ cup	
Garlic, 2 cloves, minced	
Fresh Herbs (Dill, Parsley, Tarragon), 2 tablespoons, chopped	
Salt, 1 tablespoon	
Pepper, ½ teaspoon	

SALAD DRESSINGS AND SALADS

Nearly all salads are served with one of three basic salad dressings to which are added other ingredients for variations. The basic dressings are French Dressing, Mayonnaise and Cooked Dressing, and in this chapter we have devoted separate sections to each basic dressing and its variations, then listed the salads which are best complemented by each one.

FRENCH DRESSING

On the list of controversial subjects, next to Martinis comes French Dressing, with the proportion of oil to vinegar the crux of the argument. Some say 2 to 1, some 3 to 1 and some 4 to 1. We have taken the middle course for our basic recipe. In general if you like an oily dressing, increase the amount of oil; if you like it tart, increase the vinegar. With a little experimenting you will find the proportion you like. You might also like to experiment with various kinds of vinegar—cider, wine or malt, or vinegar flavored with tarragon or other herbs.

BASIC FRENCH DRESSING

Vinegar, ¼ cup
Oil, ¾ cup (olive oil, salad oil, or a mixture of both)
Garlic, 1 clove, sliced
Salt, ½ teaspoon

Put all ingredients together in a jar with tightly fitting lid, and shake.

VARIATIONS

ANCHOVY DRESSING: To ½ cup French Dressing add 2 teaspoons anchovy paste, 1 tablespoon parsley.

CHIFFONADE DRESSING: To ½ cup French Dressing add 1 chopped hard-cooked egg, 1 teaspoon chopped onion or shallot, 1 teaspoon minced parsley, 1 tablespoon chopped pimiento, ⅛ teaspoon paprika.

CURRY DRESSING: To ½ cup French Dressing add ½ teaspoon curry powder.

DILL DRESSING: To ½ cup French Dressing add 1 teaspoon chopped fresh dill.

FRUIT SALAD DRESSING: Omit garlic in French Dressing, use lemon juice only, no vinegar, and add 1 tablespoon chopped mint.

HERB DRESSING: To ½ cup French Dressing add either dried herbs, ¼ teaspoon each of thyme, marjoram, rosemary; or, fresh herbs, 1 teaspoon of each.

HORSE-RADISH DRESSING: To ½ cup French Dressing add 1 tablespoon horse-radish.

HOT DRESSING: To ½ cup French Dressing add ½ teaspoon chili powder, ½ teaspoon dry mustard, dash cayenne.

MUSTARD DRESSING: To ½ cup French Dressing add 1 teaspoon dry mustard.

PIQUANTE DRESSING: To ½ cup French Dressing add 1 tablespoon chopped black olives, 1 teaspoon capers, 1 teaspoon chopped pimiento.

ROQUEFORT OR BLUE CHEESE DRESSING: To ½ cup French Dressing add ¼ cup cheese.

SOUR CREAM DRESSING: To ½ cup French Dressing add ¼ cup sour cream.

TARRAGON DRESSING: To ½ cup French Dressing add 1 tablespoon tarragon vinegar.

VINAIGRETTE DRESSING: To ½ cup French Dressing add 1 teaspoon chopped chives, 1 teaspoon parsley, 1 teaspoon chopped sour or dill pickles, 1 teaspoon chopped capers, 1 teaspoon grated onion, 1 chopped hard-cooked egg.

BOUGHT SALAD DRESSINGS

There are excellent commercial French Dressings on the market as well as Mayonnaise and Salad Dressing. These can be suited to the salad by adding the ingredients listed in the recipes.

TOSSED GREEN SALAD

This is the most popular and versatile of all salads. It is the perfect accompaniment to almost any meal, and need never become monotonous because of the large assortment of green growing things that can be used to make it. When you tire of Iceberg and Boston lettuce, try young raw spinach, watercress, endive, dandelion greens, mustard greens, bibb lettuce, escarole, romaine, chicory, or even young green cabbage, in any combination. Just be sure to buy them crisp and green, then keep them that way in the refrigerator crisper.

To prepare greens for use, wash them thoroughly under cold running water, shake off the excess and pat dry with linen or paper towels. Tear, don't cut, the greens into bite-size pieces, and heap lightly in a salad bowl. Cover and set bowl in refrigerator until ready to serve; then season with salt and freshly ground black pepper and dribble French dressing over the greens. Turn and toss lightly with your salad tools until each leaf is lightly coated (not dripping).

Be sure to add any fresh herbs that are available. Parsley is always good and can be relied upon if the exotic ones are hard to come by. Those who have room to grow a small herb garden can always have a supply of basil, summer savory, thyme, rosemary, etc. to add distinctive flavors to their salads.

For variation try one of the alternate French Dressings on page 159. Or, if your family doesn't like a highly seasoned dressing, serve cruets of oil and vinegar, and let them mix their own at the table.

Tossed salads may be varied also by adding any bits of fresh

Tossed green salad: lettuce, spinach and onion rings

Add raw vegetables to salad greens

vegetables that are in season, such as young scallions, chopped green pepper rings, young sliced carrots, chopped celery, cauliflower, radishes, cucumbers and/or slices of tomato and avocado.

To make a tossed salad more substantial, if the rest of the meal is light, shore it up with cubes of cooked ham, salami, frankfurters or sharp cheese; or blue cheese with strips of cooked turkey or chicken. With any of these mixtures, cubes of pineapple, apple, or orange sections can add an interesting flavor and texture.

SPRING SALAD

Scallions, 4
Young Carrots, 2
Radishes, 6
Cucumber, 1
Boston Lettuce, 2 heads
French Dressing
Salt and Pepper, to taste

Slice vegetables very thin, combine with Boston lettuce broken in pieces. Add French Dressing and toss lightly. Season with salt and pepper.

To serve 4

CARROT SALAD

Grate or shred young raw carrots and combine with enough French Dressing to moisten. Serve on a bed of lettuce or watercress.

CARROT AND GREEN PEPPER SALAD

Follow the recipe for Carrot Salad, but for each cup of grated carrots, add ¼ cup of chopped green pepper.

For other variations, add ¼ cup of seedless raisins, or ¼ cup crushed pineapple, drained.

COTTAGE CHEESE AND ORANGE SALAD

Salad Greens
Cottage Cheese, 1 cup
Oranges, 4 medium
Fresh Mint, few sprigs
Sour Cream Dressing

Arrange salad greens on individual plates. Place ¼ cup of cottage cheese in the center of each and surround it with thin crosswise slices of orange. Garnish with chopped mint and serve with Sour Cream Dressing.

To serve 4

DILLED CUCUMBER TOMATOES

Tomatoes, 4 medium
Cucumber, 1 large
Dill, fresh, 2 tablesps., chopped
French Dressing, 2 tablespoons

Blanch and skin tomatoes. Cut in slices and arrange on platter. Peel and slice cucumber, arranging slices on tomatoes. Sprinkle with dill and moisten with French Dressing. Chill in refrigerator before serving.

To serve 4

CHEF'S SALAD

Salad Greens
Ham or Tongue, cooked
Swiss Cheese
Chicken, cooked
Radishes
Cucumbers
Tomato
Hard-cooked Eggs
French Dressing or
  Roquefort Dressing

In a wide salad bowl, or in individual bowls, if preferred, arrange a bed of mixed salad greens. In the center place thin strips of ham, cheese and chicken. Around the edge arrange radish, cucumber and tomatoes slices and quartered eggs. Sprinkle all with salt and freshly ground pepper. Serve with a sauce boat of French Dressing or Roquefort Dressing. (See page 159.)

GREEN BEAN AND POTATO SALAD

Potatoes, 2 cups, cooked, diced
Green Beans, 2 cups, cooked, sliced
Onion, 1 tablespoon, minced
French Dressing
Salad Greens
Anchovies

Combine potatoes with beans and minced onion and mix with French Dressing. Serve on a bed of lettuce or other salad greens and garnish with anchovy fillets.

To serve 4

Kidney bean salad (page 162)

KIDNEY BEAN SALAD

Kidney Beans, 16-oz. can
Onion, 1 medium
Cucumber, 1 medium
Green Pepper, 1
Carrot, 1
Herb French Dressing
Salad Greens

To serve 4

Drain kidney beans and add onion, cucumber, pepper and carrot, all cut in very thin slices. Season with salt and pepper. Arrange on salad greens and moisten with Herb French Dressing. Toss lightly.

RAINBOW SALAD

Tomatoes
Carrots
Wax Beans
Broccoli
Baby Beets
Salad Greens
Herb Dressing or
   Vinaigrette (p. 159)

Any combination of fresh vegetables may be used, selected because of their colors. Cook separately those that require it; leave tomatoes and greens raw. Dress each kind of vegetable separately with Herb or Vinaigrette Dressing and arrange in individual piles on greens around the edge of a platter with a bowl of additional dressing in the center.

EGG AND ANCHOVY SALAD

Eggs, 3
Salad Greens
Salt and **Pepper,** to taste
Anchovy Dressing

To serve 4

Hard-cook eggs and put them through ricer, or grate. Arrange salad greens in bowl and sprinkle eggs on top. Add Anchovy Dressing and toss lightly. Season with salt and pepper.

SPANISH ONION SALAD

Cut large sweet Spanish onions in thin slices and combine with Sour Cream Dressing. (See page 159.) Season to taste with salt and pepper.

Combine ripe tomato slices with the onion slices and marinate in Herb Dressing. (See page 159.) Season to taste with salt and pepper.

ROAST BEEF AND POTATO SALAD

Leftover Roast Beef, cut
   in thin strips, 2 cups
Potatoes, 4, cooked
Tomatoes, 2, large
Pickle Relish, 2 tablesps.
Chili Sauce, ¼ cup
Horse-radish Dressing
Salt and **Pepper,** to taste
Salad Greens

To serve 4

Dice potatoes and tomatoes and add to roast beef. Add relish and chili sauce and enough dressing to moisten, add seasonings. Serve on a bed of salad greens.

LAMB AND CUCUMBER SALAD

Lamb, cooked, diced,
   2 cups
Cucumber, 2 medium
Onion, 1 medium
Salt and **Pepper,** to taste
Curry French Dressing
   (page 159)
Salad Greens
Sour Cream

To serve 4

Add lamb to thinly sliced cucumber and minced onion. Season to taste and moisten mixture with Curry French Dressing. Serve on greens with a bowl of sour cream.

SHRIMP-CUCUMBER PLATE

Shrimp, 2 boxes, frozen

Cook shrimp according to directions on box and chill.

Cucumber, 1 large
Salad Greens
Horse-radish Dressing
   (see page 159)

To serve 4

Cut chilled cucumber into 8 lengthwise sections; arrange 2 greens on individual salad plates with a row of shrimp between 2 sections cucumber. Serve the sauce on the side.

WILTED LETTUCE

Boston or **Leaf Lettuce,**
   2 heads
Chives, 2 tablespoons,
   chopped
Bacon Fat, 3 tablespoons
Vinegar, 3 tablespoons
Sugar, 1 teaspoon
Salt and **Pepper,** to taste

To serve 4

Arrange lettuce leaves in bowl, top with chives. Heat fat, add vinegar and seasonings. When very hot, pour over lettuce. Toss and serve at once.

Salad preparation

TROPICAL CHEF'S SALAD

Lettuce, ½ head
Endive, 2 small heads
Watercress, ½ bunch
Chicken, cooked, diced, 1 cup
Sharp Cheddar Cheese, ½ cup, diced
Pineapple Chunks, ¾ cup
Orange Sections, ¾ cup
Sour Cream Dressing, ½ cup (page 159)
Salt and **Pepper,** to taste

To serve 4

Wash, dry and arrange salad greens in salad bowl. Add remaining ingredients and toss lightly. Season with salt and pepper.

CAESAR SALAD

Garlic Powder, pinch
Butter, 2 tablespoons
Bread, 2 slices, cubed

Romaine, 1 large head
Salt, ½ teaspoon
Fresh-ground Black Pepper
Parmesan Cheese, ½ cup
French Dressing (made with lemon juice), ½ cup
Anchovies, 2 tablespoons, minced
Egg, 1, coddled 1 minute

To serve 4

Add garlic powder to melted butter in skillet and sauté bread cubes until crisp and golden.

Break romaine into a bowl well rubbed with fresh garlic. Sprinkle with salt, pepper and Parmesan cheese. Add French Dressing and anchovies. Break egg over salad. Toss vigorously to combine all ingredients.

WATERCRESS SALAD

Watercress, 2 bunches
Eggs, 2, hard-cooked, sliced
Scallions, 2 or 3, chopped
Salt and **Pepper,** to taste
Olive Oil
Wine Vinegar

To serve 4

Break watercress into bite-size pieces in salad bowl. Top with eggs and scallions.

Serve with salt, pepper mill and cruets of olive oil and wine vinegar.

MAYONNAISE

Mustard, ½ teaspoon
Salt, ½ teaspoon
Sugar, ½ teaspoon
Egg, 1
Lemon Juice, or **Vinegar,** or mixed, 2 tablesps.
Olive Oil or **Salad Oil** 1 cup
Have all ingredients at room temperature

Combine dry ingredients in bowl. Add egg and beat to mix thoroughly. Add 1 tablespoon of lemon juice, slowly, beating as you add. Add oil, beginning with a teaspoon at a time, beating all the while, until ½ cup is added. Add remaining juice and oil in small quantities alternately. The mixture will thicken as you beat.

Store Mayonnaise in the warmest area of the refrigerator. If a little oil rises to the top after storage, pour it off.

VARIATIONS

CREAM MAYONNAISE: Fold ½ cup of heavy cream, whipped, into ½ cup Mayonnaise; or use half cream and half sour cream.

CUCUMBER MAYONNAISE: To ½ cup Mayonnaise add ¼ cup grated cucumber.

CURRY MAYONNAISE: To ½ cup Mayonnaise add ½ teaspoon curry powder.

GREEN GODDESS DRESSING: To 1 cup of Mayonnaise add ¼ cup minced parsley, ¼ cup chopped chives, ¼ teaspoon tarragon, ¼ teaspoon dry mustard, ¼ teaspoon instant garlic, 2 teaspoons anchovy paste, ⅛ teaspoon pepper, ¼ cup sour cream.

HERB MAYONNAISE: To ½ cup Mayonnaise add 1 teaspoon each fresh parsley, chives, tarragon and marjoram, all finely chopped.

HORSE-RADISH MAYONNAISE: To ½ cup Mayonnaise add ½ cup sour cream, 1 tablespoon horse-radish.

PIQUANTE MAYONNAISE: To ½ cup Mayonnaise add 1 tablespoon each of minced green pepper, minced red pepper, minced dill pickle, and a dash of garlic powder.

REMOULADE SAUCE: To ½ cup Mayonnaise add 1 hard-cooked egg yolk, minced; ½ tablespoon chopped capers, ½ teaspoon anchovy paste, 1 teaspoon each chopped chives and parsley, ½ teaspoon dry mustard, and 1 teaspoon tarragon.

ROQUEFORT OR BLUE CHEESE MAYONNAISE: To ½ cup Mayonnaise add ½ cup sour cream, 2 tablespoons minced parsley, ¼ cup cheese, crumbled.

RUSSIAN DRESSING: To ½ cup Mayonnaise add ¼ cup chili sauce.

SAVORY MAYONNAISE: To ½ cup Mayonnaise add 1 teaspoon Worcestershire, 1 teaspoon prepared mustard.

SOUR CREAM MAYONNAISE: To ½ cup Mayonnaise add ½ cup sour cream.

TARTAR SAUCE: To ½ cup Mayonnaise add 2 teaspoons chopped pickles, 1 teaspoon chopped parsley, 2 teaspoons chopped olives, 1 teaspoon chopped capers, 1 teaspoon grated onion.

THOUSAND ISLAND DRESSING: To ½ cup Mayonnaise add ¼ cup chili sauce, 1 tablespoon each chopped chives, chopped green peppers, chopped pimientos, ¼ teaspoon paprika.

SHRIMP SALAD

Prepare 2 packages of frozen shrimp according to the directions on the package, or cook fresh if you prefer. Chill until serving time. Mix the shrimp with Thousand Island Dressing (see page 163), enough to coat each one and serve on a bed of watercress. Good also with Horse-radish Mayonnaise (page 163).

STUFFED TOMATOES

Allow 1 tomato per person. Cut slice from stem end of each, scoop out pulp and turn upside down to drain. Stuff with any one of the following mixtures and serve on lettuce.

Fresh fruit salad

TOMATOES STUFFED WITH CURRIED COTTAGE CHEESE

Cottage Cheese, 1 cup
Curry Powder, ½ teasp.
Chives, 1 tablespoon, chopped
Salt and **Pepper**, to taste
Piquante Mayonnaise

To fill 4 tomatoes

Combine cottage cheese with seasonings and Piquante Mayonnaise.

TOMATOES STUFFED WITH EGG SALAD

Eggs, 6, hard-cooked
Onion, 1 small, minced
Capers, 1 tablespoon
Salt and **Pepper**, to taste
Cucumber Mayonnaise

To fill 4 tomatoes

Combine chopped eggs and seasonings with tomato pulp and add enough Cucumber Mayonnaise to moisten. Fill tomato shells and add a small dab of Cucumber Mayonnaise on top.

TOMATOES STUFFED WITH TUNA FISH

Tuna Fish, 7-ounce can
Celery, ⅓ cup, chopped
Green Pepper, ⅓ cup
Herb Mayonnaise

To fill 4 tomatoes

Break up tuna with fork, mix in celery and pepper and the tomato pulp scooped from tomatoes. Moisten with Herb Mayonnaise. Fill tomato shells and serve with Herb Mayonnaise.

Sardines, salmon, crab or lobster may be substituted for tuna fish.

FRESH FRUIT SALAD

Any combination of fresh fruit makes a delicious salad, and one that can pinch-hit as a dessert. Peel firm ripe fruit and cut in bite-size pieces or wash carefully the kinds, such as berries, that need no peeling. Sprinkle with lemon juice those that have a tendency to discolor, such as bananas, apples, peaches and avocados.

Combine fruit with Fruit Salad Dressing (page 159) or Sour Cream Mayonnaise (page 163) and chill thoroughly. Serve in one bowl or on individual plates of greens with additional dressing on the side.

GARDEN SALAD BOWL

Cauliflower, 1 cup, small flowerettes
Tomatoes, 4, cut in wedges
Cucumber, 1, sliced
Green Pepper, ½, sliced
Scallions, 2, chopped
Eggs, 4, hard-cooked, sliced
Radishes, 4, sliced
Dill, fresh, few sprigs, chopped
Salt and **Pepper**, to taste
Mayonnaise, ⅓ cup
Lettuce
Bacon, 4 slices

To serve 4

Combine vegetables and eggs with mayonnaise. Add salt and pepper if necessary. Heap on bed of lettuce. Fry bacon crisp and crumble on top.

HEARTS OF LETTUCE WITH ROQUEFORT MAYONNAISE

Cut hearts of crisp lettuce into quarters and serve on individual serving plates with Roquefort Mayonnaise.

Russian Dressing or Thousand Island Dressing may be substituted for Roquefort Mayonnaise.

LOBSTER SALAD

Cooked Lobster, 2 cups
Celery, diced, ½ cup
French Dressing, ¼ cup
Eggs, hard-cooked, 4
Caviar

Combine lobster, cut in small pieces, with celery and marinate in French Dressing in refrigerator for 1 hour stirring occasionally. Serve on lettuce with Mayonnaise. Surround with slices of hard-cooked eggs topped with caviar.

To serve 4

CRAB SALAD

Crab Meat, flaked, 2 cups
Green Pepper, 2 tablesps., chopped
Capers, 1 tablespoon
Pimiento, 2, chopped
French Dressing, ¼ cup
Cucumber Mayonnaise

Combine crab meat with pepper, capers, pimiento, and French Dressing. Serve with Cucumber Mayonnaise on a bed of lettuce.

To serve 4

SHRIMP-STUFFED AVOCADOS

Frozen Shrimp, 2 boxes (or fresh, if preferred)

Avocados, 2 large
Lemon Juice, 2 tablesps.
Cucumber Mayonnaise (page 163)

Prepare shrimp as directed on the label. Chill.

Split and peel avocados and remove seeds; sprinkle halves with lemon juice. Fill centers with shrimp and arrange on individual plates of greens with extra shrimp around avocado.

Serve with Cucumber Mayonnaise.

To serve 4

CURRIED CHICKEN SALAD

Cooked Chicken, diced, 3 cups
Celery, diced, 2 cups
Almonds, ½ cup, slivered
Lemon, juice of 1
Onion, 1 tablespoon, minced
Curry Powder, 2 teasps.
Salt, 1 teaspoon
Pepper, ⅛ teaspoon
Mayonnaise, ¾ cup
Lettuce

Toss all ingredients together. Add Mayonnaise last and mix thoroughly. Serve on lettuce.

To serve 4 to 6

CHICKEN SALAD

Chicken, cooked, diced, 3 cups
Celery, 1 cup, diced
French Dressing, ¼ cup

Marinate chicken and celery in French dressing for 1 hour.

Mayonnaise, ½ cup
Salt and Pepper, to taste
Lettuce
To serve 4

Mix chicken and celery with mayonnaise. Season to taste and arrange individual portions on lettuce.

Cooked Dressing may be substituted for Mayonnaise.
For variation, add 1 cup tiny green grapes.

CHICKEN SALAD PIQUANTE

Chicken, cooked, diced, 3 cups
Celery, diced, 1 cup
French Dressing, ¼ cup
Capers, 1 tablespoon
Piquante Mayonnaise, ¾ cup
Salt and Pepper
Pimineto, 1

Combine chicken and celery with French Dressing and marinate several hours. Add capers and Mayonnaise, mix thoroughly, season to taste, and serve on a bed of greens. Garnish with strips of pimiento.

To serve 4

Use Chicken Salad as a stuffing for tomatoes or avocados.

This recipe may also be used for left-over lamb, veal or ham.

TURKEY SALAD: Follow the above recipe, increasing the amount of celery to 1½ cups.

COOKED SALAD DRESSING

Sugar, 2 tablespoons
Salt, 1 teaspoon
Dry Mustard, 1 teasp.
Flour, 1½ tablesps.
Egg, 1, beaten
Milk, ¾ cup
Vinegar, ¼ cup
Butter, 1 tablespoon

In top part of double boiler combine dry ingredients. Add egg and milk and mix well. Add vinegar a little at a time as you stir. Cook over hot water, stirring constantly, until thickened. Add butter and blend thoroughly. Cool.

COLESLAW

Coarsely grate a hard head of cabbage, or with a chopping knife cut it into fine shreds. To 4 cups of cabbage add 1 cup Cooked Salad Dressing (above). Add salt and freshly ground pepper to taste. Serve chilled, at room temperature, or hot, as desired.

Finely chopped red and green pepper will add sparkling color to the slaw. A teaspoon of celery seed adds interest.

To serve 4

QUICK COLESLAW

Prepare cabbage as above. Add to it ½ cup of Mayonnaise and ½ cup of Sour Cream combined. Flavor with ½ teaspoon of caraway seeds. Add a little sugar, salt and pepper, if needed.

To serve 4

CREAMY COLESLAW

In the above recipe for Quick Coleslaw, substitute ½ cup heavy cream for sour cream, whip it and fold it in.

WALDORF SALAD

Apples, 2 cups, diced
Celery, 1 cup, diced
Cooked Salad Dressing, 1 cup
Walnuts, ½ cup, broken

Combine apples, celery and Cooked Salad Dressing; chill thoroughly. When ready to serve, add nuts. Arrange salad on individual plates of lettuce, Boston preferably.

To serve 4

POTATO SALAD, HOT OR COLD

Potatoes, cooked, diced, 4 cups
Celery, ½ cup, diced
Onion, ¼ cup, minced
Cooked Dressing, 1 cup
Salt and **Pepper**, to taste

Combine vegetables with hot or cold Cooked Dressing and season to taste. Serve hot, at room temperature, or chilled, as preferred.

To serve 4

Diced cucumbers, ½ cup, may be added to this recipe.

HOT POTATO SALAD WITH CREAM

Potatoes, cooked, diced, 4 cups
Instant Onion, 1 tablesp.
Vinegar, 2 tablespoons
Heavy Cream, 1 cup
Salt and **Pepper**, to taste
Parsley, few sprigs

Return cooked, diced potatoes to saucepan; add onion and vinegar; mix and heat. Gently mix in heavy cream and continue heating but do not boil. Season with salt and pepper. Pour into serving dish and sprinkle with finely chopped parsley.

To serve 4

HOT MUSTARD POTATO SALAD

Bacon, 4 slices
Flour, 1 tablespoon
Vinegar, ¼ cup
Mustard, 1 tablespoon
Salt, 1 teaspoon
Pepper, ⅛ teaspoon
Milk, ¾ cup

Fry bacon until crisp; remove from pan. Blend flour in bacon fat, add vinegar and seasonings; bring to boil. Add milk slowly while stirring; heat but do not boil.

Potatoes, cooked, sliced, 4 cups
Onion, 1 med., chopped
Parsley, 2 tablespoons
Celery Seed, 1 teaspoon

Combine potatoes with onions, parsley and celery seed. Add dressing and mix. Top with crumbled bacon. Serve at once.

To serve 4

POTATO SALAD WITH SOUR CREAM

Potatoes, cooked, diced, 4 cups
Scallions, 4, chopped
Celery Seed, 1 teaspoon
French Dressing, ½ cup
Sour Cream, ¾ cup
Salt and **Pepper**, to taste
Paprika

Combine potatoes and seasonings with French Dressing and let marinate in refrigerator until ready to use and thoroughly chilled. When ready to serve gently mix in sour cream; season with salt and pepper. Sprinkle with paprika.

To serve 4

CURRIED POTATO SALAD: Follow recipe for Potato Salad with Sour Cream, but substitute Curry Dressing (page 163) for plain French Dressing.

Sliced hard-cooked eggs may be used as a garnish.

DILLED POTATO SALAD: Follow the recipe for Potato Salad With Sour Cream, but substitute 1 tablespoon fresh dill for the celery seed. Omit the paprika.

Hot potato salad

Jellied cold cuts

POTATO SALAD WITH SAVORY MAYONNAISE

Potatoes, cooked,
  diced, 4 cups
Onion, 1 med., minced
Celery, diced, ½ cup
Sweet Red Pepper, diced,
  ¼ cup
Salt, 1 teaspoon
Vinegar, 2 tablespoons
Sugar, ½ tablespoon
Mayonnaise, ¾ cup

Combine all ingredients but
Mayonnaise and mix thoroughly.
Add Mayonnaise and chill be-
fore serving.

To serve 4

To vary this recipe, 3 chopped hard-cooked eggs may be
added, or 1 cup of crumbled sharp cheese. Also good with
fresh dill.

QUICK POTATO SALAD

Potatoes, 2 cans
Onion, 1 medium
Celery Seed, 1 teaspoon
**Bottled Coleslaw
  Dressing,** ½ cup

Cut potatoes into cubes, chop
onion fine and add, with celery
seed, to bought dressing. Taste
and correct for seasoning if
needed. Chill thoroughly
before serving.

CUCUMBERS WITH YOGHURT

Cucumbers, 2 or 3
Fresh Mint, ¼ cup,
  chopped
Salt and **Pepper,** to taste
Plain Yoghurt, ½ pint

Peel cucumbers and slice thin.
Put them in a bowl with the
seasonings and yoghurt and
chill several hours. Serve in
individual lettuce cups.

To serve 4

WILTED CUCUMBERS AND ONIONS

Cucumber, 1 large
Onions, 2 medium
Salt

Peel and thinly slice cucumbers
and onions. Arrange alternate
layers in bowl, sprinkle lightly
with salt. Weight with saucer,
cover bowl tightly with plastic
and let stand in refrigerator one
hour. Drain.

Vinegar, ¼ cup
Sugar, 1 tablespoon
Pepper, ¼ teaspoon
Parsley, chopped

Add seasonings and mix
thoroughly. Garnish with
parsley.

To serve 4

JELLIED CUCUMBER RING WITH TOMATOES

Unflavored Gelatin,
  1 envelope
Water, ¼ cup, cold
Water, 1¼ cups, boiling
Green Coloring
Salt, ½ teaspoon
Lemon Juice, 1 tablesp.

Soften gelatin in cold water,
then add boiling water to
dissolve. Add salt, lemon juice
and a few drops of green
coloring to tint it just a pale
green. Chill in ring mold until
partially set.

Cucumber, 1 cup, thin
  slices
Onion, 1 small, minced
Tomatoes, 3 or 4
Salad Greens
**Horse-radish Mayon-
  naise**

Stir in cucumber and onion;
chill until firm. Unmold on
salad greens and fill center with
quartered ripe tomatoes. Serve
with Horse-radish Mayonnaise.

To serve 4

JELLIED CUCUMBER AND COTTAGE-CHEESE RING

Unflavored Gelatin,
1 envelope
Water, ¼ cup, cold
Water, 1 cup, boiling
Lemon Juice, 1 tablesp.
Salt, 1 teaspoon

Soften gelatin in cold water, then add boiling water to dissolve. Add salt, lemon juice. Chill until partially set.

Cottage Cheese, 1 cup
Cucumber, 1 cup, sliced
Onion, 1 small, grated
Horse-radish, 1 tablesp.
Thousand Island
Dressing

Combine ingredients and mix well with gelatin mixture. Continue chilling until firm. Unmold and serve with Thousand Island Dressing.

To serve 4

CURRIED CHICKEN ASPIC

Unflavored Gelatin,
1 envelope
Chicken Broth, 2 cups
Curry Powder, 1 teasp.
Chicken, cooked, 1 cup, diced
Celery, ½ cup, diced
Green Pepper, 2 table-spoons, minced
Salt, 1 teaspoon
Pepper, ⅛ teaspoon

Soften gelatin in cold chicken broth, add curry powder, heat until gelatin is dissolved. Chill gelatin until partially set, then add chicken, celery, green pepper and seasonings. Pour into individual molds. Chill until firm, allowing several hours at least.

Lettuce
Mayonnaise, ½ cup
Capers, 1 tablespoon

Unmold on lettuce. Serve with Mayonnaise mixed with capers.

To serve 4

TONGUE IN ASPIC: Substitute beef broth or bouillon for chicken broth in above recipe; substitute sliced or chopped tongue for chicken. Omit curry powder.

CHICKEN IN ASPIC

Stewing Chicken,
1, cut up
Water, 6 cups
Onion, 1, cut up
Celery, 2 stalks
Bay Leaf, 1
Salt, 1 teaspoon
Pepper, ⅛ teaspoon
Curry or Herb
Mayonnaise

Place chicken with other ingredients in kettle, cover, bring to boil, reduce heat and simmer 2 hours or until tender. Cool chicken, remove meat from bones, cut into pieces. Arrange pieces in 6 individual molds or 1 loaf pan. Remove fat from stock and strain. Reduce by boiling to 2 cups. Add additional salt and pepper, if needed, and pour into molds. Let set until cool, then chill until firmly molded. Serve with Curry or Herb Mayonnaise.

To serve 6

GREEN GODDESS SALAD

Combine mixed salad greens with cooked, deveined shrimp and quartered tomatoes. Serve with Green Goddess Dressing (page 163). Crab meat, flaked, fresh or corned, may be substituted for shrimp.

JELLIED TOMATO MOLD

Unflavored Gelatin,
2 envelopes
Tomato Juice, 3 cups
Lemon Juice, 1 tablesp.
Celery Salt, 1 teaspoon
Instant Onion, 1 teasp.
Pepper, ⅛ teaspoon
Worcestershire, 1 teasp.
Salt, to taste
Mayonnaise or Sour
Cream

Soften gelatin in ¼ cup of tomato juice; add ¾ cup tomato juice to it and heat until gelatin is dissolved. Add remaining tomato juice, lemon juice and seasonings. Add additional salt if needed. Stir well, pour into mold and chill until firm; or pour into individual molds if preferred. Unmold onto salad greens. Serve with mayonnaise or sour cream.

To serve 4

For variation, finely diced vegetables such as cucumber, onion, celery, or green pepper may be used. They may be added when the tomato mixture is partially set; or added for flavor to the juice and simmered for 10 minutes, then strained before the gelatin is added.

The jellied tomato may be made in a ring mold, then unmolded and the center filled with tuna fish, chicken, or other salad.

JELLIED LOBSTER RING

Unflavored Gelatin,
1 envelope
Cold Water, ¼ cup
Boiling Water, ½ cup
Lobster Meat, 2 cups, cooked, diced
Celery, ¼ cup
Stuffed Olives, ¼ cup, chopped
Chili Sauce, ¼ cup
Mayonnaise, ½ cup

Soften gelatin in cold water and add boiling water to dissolve it. Cool. Add remaining ingredients. Mix well and pour into ring mold. Chill until firm.

Mixed Greens
French Dressing

Unmold ring on serving plate. Fill center with greens moistened with French Dressing and put a few greens around the outside of the mold for decoration.

To serve 4

JELLIED CRAB-MEAT RING

Follow recipe for Jellied Lobster Ring, but substitute 2 cups cooked crab meat for the lobster.

JELLIED SHRIMP RING

Follow recipe for Jellied Lobster Ring, but substitute 2 cups cooked shrimp for the lobster, cutting it into small pieces.

JELLIED SALMON SALAD

Follow recipe for Jellied Lobster Ring, but substitute 1 1-pound can of salmon, drained, for the lobster.

If canned seafood is used in the above recipes, it must be well drained; drain well after cooking, too.

Tuna mousse

CHICKEN MOUSSE

Chicken Stock, ¾ cup
Milk, 1 cup
Unflavored Gelatin,
   2 envelopes
Egg Yolks, 2, slightly
   beaten
Salt and **Pepper,** to taste
Parsley, few sprigs,
   chopped
Chicken, 2 cups, ground
	Combine cold chicken stock and
	milk in saucepan; add gelatin,
	allowing few minutes for it to
	soften. Add egg yolks. Then
	cook over slow heat, stirring
	constantly until mixture is
	slightly thickened. Add chicken
	and parsley to mixture. Cool
	until partly set.

Heavy Cream, ¾ cup	Whip cream until stiff, fold into mixture. Put in mold and chill until firm. To serve, unmold on chilled platter.

To serve 4 to 6

TUNA MOUSSE: Tuna may be substituted for chicken in the above recipe.

SEAFOOD MOUSSE: Lobster, crabmeat or shrimp may be substituted for chicken in the above recipe.

Try some of the variations of mayonnaise (page 163) with these mousses.

HAM MOUSSE

Unflavored Gelatin, 1 envelope **Water,** ¼ cup	Soften gelatin in cold water.
Egg Yolks, 2 **Salt,** ½ teaspoon **Pepper,** ⅛ teaspoon **Mustard,** ½ teaspoon **Bouillon,** 1 cup	In top part of double boiler combine egg yolks and season- ings and beat until thick and lemon-colored. Add bouillon and cook over hot water until mixture thickens, stirring constantly. Remove from heat, add gelatin and stir until dissolved. Cool.

Onion, 1 tablespoon,
   minced
Ham, cooked, minced,
   2 cups
Mayonnaise, ¼ cup
Heavy Cream, ½ cup
	Stir in onion, ham, and mayon-
	naise; whip cream and fold in.
	Pour into mold and chill until
	firm. Unmold on bed of water
	cress.

To serve 4

A good recipe for leftovers; substitute any other cooked meat, poultry or fish.

RELISHES

Relishes are the spice of the meal. They are especially chosen to complement the main dish, and in many cases they contain a particular enzyme which helps in the digestion of that particular food. Such relishes have become traditional so that we quite unconsciously think of cranberry sauce with turkey, or applesauce with pork. There is still much to be said for the homemade product over the store-bought variety.

RAW VEGETABLE RELISHES

Raw vegetables not only add a crisp touch to the meal, they bring us vitamins and minerals in full measure without any loss of content through cooking. Serve such things as celery, carrots, radishes or cucumbers whenever possible, either alone as a relish or in a salad.

CARROT STICKS OR CURLS: Slice carrots lengthwise into thin sticks, or shave with slicer. Crisp in ice water for 1 hour.

CELERY OR CUCUMBER STICKS: Slice the celery stalk or whole cucumber into lengthwise sticks.

RADISH ROSES: Leave 1 inch of stem on each radish. Cut a thin slice from root end and cut peel in uniform strips toward stem, but letting them remain connected to radish. Place radishes in ice water; the peel will curl back like petals.

PENNSYLVANIA PEPPER CABBAGE

Cabbage, 1 medium head	Shred cabbage and chop peppers
Sweet Red Pepper, 1	fine. Combine with other
Sweet Green Pepper, 1	ingredients and put into a
Celery Seed, 1 teaspoon	sterile jar or covered crock.
Mustard Seed, ½ teasp.	Keep in the refrigerator; it will
Salt, ½ teaspoon	last a week or two.
Sugar, 2 tablespoons	
Vinegar, ¼ cup	

To make about 4 cups

APPLESAUCE

Wash and quarter tart apples. Cook covered in their skins (the skins add flavor), with just enough water to keep from burning, until soft. Put through food mill. Add a few grains of salt and sugar to taste. Heat until sugar melts. If apples need more flavor, add a few slices of lemon rind, or a little cinnamon.

BLENDER APPLESAUCE: See page 215.

FRIED APPLE SLICES

Core tart unpeeled apples and slice into ½-inch thick slices. Sauté lightly in butter until tender but not mushy, turning once. Serve with sausage or ham.

WHOLE CRANBERRY SAUCE

Cranberries, 1 pound	Wash and pick over cranberries.
Sugar, 2 cups	Boil with sugar, salt and water
Boiling Water, 2 cups	10 minutes or until berries pop
Salt, dash	in the syrup. Skim and cool.

To serve 4 to 6

CRANBERRY JELLY

Cranberries, 1 pound	Wash and pick over cranberries.
Boiling Water, 2 cups	Cook in boiling water until soft
Sugar, 2 cups	and mash with potato masher.
Salt, ⅛ teaspoon	Put through strainer to remove
	skins. Return to saucepan, bring
	to boil, add salt and sugar and
	cook 2 minutes. Mold and chill.

CRANBERRY AND ORANGE RELISH

Wash 2 cups cranberries; cut 1 orange in pieces with skin on, and remove seeds. Put cranberries and oranges through food chopper with coarse blade. Add 1 cup of sugar, mix thoroughly, and let stand at room temperature for about 20 minutes before refrigerating.

MARINATED EGGPLANT

Eggplant, 1 medium	Peel and dice eggplant and place
Onion, 1 medium,	in colander over boiling water.
minced	Cover and steam for 10 minutes,
Green Pepper, 1, chopped	or until tender. Cool, add
Salad Oil, 2 tablespoons	remaining ingredients and toss
Vinegar, 1 tablespoon	lightly together. Keep in
Salt, 1 teaspoon	covered dish and chill several
Paprika, ¼ teaspoon	hours before serving.

PICKLED MUSHROOMS

Button Mushrooms, ½ pound	Drop into boiling water, drain at once and place in quart jar.
Salad Oil, 3 tablespoons	Mix remaining ingredients, pour
Salt, 1 teaspoon	over mushrooms. Chill at least
Vinegar, ¼ cup	24 hours before using.
Garlic, 1 clove, sliced	
Paprika, ¼ teaspoon	

BEET AND HORSE-RADISH RELISH

Baby Strained Beets, 4¾-ounce jar	Mix all ingredients together. Cover and store in refrigerator.
Horse-radish, 1 tablesp.	
Onion Flakes, ½ teasp.	
Celery Seed, ¼ teasp.	
Worcestershire, 1 teasp.	

Also see pickles and relishes in the Canning section.

BREAD

It is sad that so many homemakers are out of the habit of baking their own bread, for the commercial feather-soft, air-filled loaf really has no relationship to the home-baked, gold-crusted product with its yeasty aroma. Baking bread is not a difficult job and it can establish you as a great cook in your family's eyes. Moreover there is a magical pleasure in the handling of yeast dough, in watching it rise; and the smell of good bread baking is a rare perfume indeed.

Once you get your hand in, you will want to try the whole-grained flours for their greater nutritional value and zesty flavors.

INGREDIENTS

Bread is made of a few simple ingredients:

Yeast—Either the dry packaged type or the compressed cake may be used interchangeably. The former does not need refrigeration, but the cake is perishable. It can be kept in the refrigerator about a week, or in the freezer for several months. Dissolve yeast in liquid of the correct temperature.

Liquid—Either water or milk or a combination of both. It is used warm, but not hot, to dissolve the yeast which is added to it. The correct temperature for yeast cake is luke-warm (80° to 90°), for dry yeast, warmer (105° to 115°).

Sugar—It adds flavor and helps color the crust.

Salt—A little gives flavor; too much retards the yeast action.

Shortening—It improves flavor, keeps bread fresh longer and makes it brown well.

Flour—The all-purpose kind, which is a blend of hard and soft wheats. Use unbleached white flour which is richer in nutrients.

HOW TO MAKE A LOAF OF BREAD

1. Assemble all utensils: mixing bowl, spoon, loaf pans, standard measuring cup and spoons, board, brush, clean cloth.

2. Assemble all ingredients specified in recipe.

3. Sift flour before measuring. Sift a large quantity of flour onto a large plate or sheet of waxed paper. Then spoon it lightly into your measuring cup, never packing it down or jarring the cup. If a second sifting is required, empty the flour from the measuring cup into the sifter, which is placed over your mixing bowl.

Whole-grain flours should be stirred with a fork, but not sifted.

4. Provide liquid at correct temperature: lukewarm for compressed yeast, slightly warmer but not hot, for the dry yeast. Crumble the cake in the liquid or sprinkle the dry yeast in it, in a large mixing bowl. Let it stand 5 minutes; stir until dissolved. Add sugar and salt, and dissolve.

5. Add soft shortening.

6. Add half of flour, beat with spoon until smooth and well mixed. Add remaining flour and work in with your hand until it is stiff and forms a ball.

7. Turn out on lightly floured board and knead: fold dough in half toward you and push away from you with heels of hands. Give dough a quarter turn, repeat; repeat until dough is smooth and elastic, in about 5 minutes.

8. Shape into ball and place in lightly greased bowl. Apply light film of oil or butter to top with brush. Cover with clean damp cloth; put to rise in a warm (80° to 85°) place out of drafts until double in bulk (about 1½ to 2 hours). Press top with finger and if it holds the impression it has risen enough. Do not let it more than double or it will fall and make a coarse loaf.

9. Punch in center, fold edges over and turn over in bowl. Let rise a second time until almost double, about 30 to 40 minutes.

10. Place dough on board. Divide for loaves and let rest 10 minutes. Knead each one until smooth and free of large air bubbles. Fold ends of dough to center and place in greased loaf pans with the folded seam down, smooth side on top.

11. Brush top of loaves with salad oil, cover with towel and set in warm place (85°). Let rise until sides of dough have reached top of pan and center is well rounded. At this stage your finger impression will remain on the top.

12. Bake in preheated oven according to directions in recipe. The loaf is done when well-browned, shrinks from sides of pan, and sounds hollow when tapped. If you bake in glass rather than metal pans, use a 25° lower temperature—glass browns loaves much faster than metal.

13. Remove loaf from pan as soon as baked. If a soft crust is desired apply a film of soft butter. If you want the crust crisp, do not grease.

14. Cool bread uncovered on cake racks out of drafts.

Bread will rise more quickly if the yeast content is doubled but a better quality product will result with slow rising.

TWO LOAVES OF WHITE BREAD

Water, 1½ cups, warm
(see page   )
Yeast, Cake or **Packaged
Active Dry,** 1
Milk, ¾ cup, scalded
and cooled to luke-
warm
Sugar, ¼ cup
Salt, 2 teaspoons
Shortening, 2 tablesps.
All-Purpose Flour, sifted,
6 cups

Oven, hot, 425°

Put water in large mixing bowl,
add yeast, let stand 5 minutes.
Add milk and stir in sugar and
salt until dissolved. Add soft
shortening. Add half of flour
and beat with spoon until
smooth and well mixed. Add
remaining flour and work in
until it is stiff and forms a ball.
Follow directions above for
kneading and rising. Put into 2
greased 9″ x 5″ loaf pans for
final rising.

Bake 25 to 30 minutes.

FOUR LOAVES OF WHITE BREAD: Double above recipe to fill
4 loaf pans.

WHOLE WHEAT BREAD

To the above recipe for Two Loaves, add 1½ cups of whole
wheat flour, and ½ cup molasses in place of sugar. Bake at
375°.

RYE BREAD

In the above recipe for Two Loaves, substitute 3 cups of rye
flour for 3 cups of white. Rye bread requires a longer time
to rise than white; it need not quite double in bulk.

QUICK RISING CINNAMON ROLL

Follow the above method for making bread, but double the
quantity of yeast. After the first rising punch dough down
and turn out on a board. Let rest for 10 minutes. Divide
dough into loaf portions and roll each section flat into a
rectangle about ¼-inch thick. Brush with slightly beaten
egg and sprinkle with a combination of sugar and cinnamon,
in the proportion of 1 teaspoon cinnamon to ¼ cup sugar.
Roll like jelly roll and place in loaf pans with seam down.
Brush tops with melted butter and let rise in warm place
until center is slightly higher than sides of pan. Bake 1 hour
in preheated 400° oven.

ROLLS

Follow recipe for Two Loaves of Bread and instead of making
loaves, form into one of the following shapes. Let rise until
double in bulk and bake in hot (400°) oven 15 to 20 minutes.

PARKER HOUSE ROLLS: Roll dough out ¼-inch thick. Cut
into 2-inch rounds with biscuit cutter. Make crease across
dough, off-center; brush with melted butter and fold smaller
side over on larger portion. Press ends of crease together and
place rolls 1 inch apart on baking sheet.

CLOVER LEAF ROLLS: Shape dough into small balls, dip in
melted butter, and put 3 together in greased muffin pan.

PAN ROLLS: Cut small uniform pieces of dough and shape into
round balls. Place close together on baking sheet with
smoothest side on top; they will rise tall and be soft.

CRUSTY ROLLS: Shape dough into small round balls, place
1 inch apart on baking sheet or so that they will not touch
when risen.

RAISED BISCUITS: Roll dough ¼ inch thick; cut out with
biscuit cutter; brush half the rounds with butter, top with
the remaining ones. Put on baking sheet to rise.

BRIOCHE

Milk, ¾ cup
Butter, ⅓ cup
Salt, 1 teaspoon
Sugar, ¼ cup
Yeast, Cake or **Packaged
Active Dry,** 1
Eggs, 2, beaten
Flour, sifted, 3 cups

Scald milk and add butter to
melt; add salt and sugar and
stir until dissolved. Cool to
lukewarm and add yeast; stir
until dissolved. Add eggs and
mix. Add sifted flour and beat
to make a soft smooth dough.
Cover with cloth and set in
warm place (85°) to rise until
double in bulk. Refrigerate
12 hours.

Turn dough onto lightly floured
board; shape 18 balls to fill
greased muffin tins ⅓ full.
Shape remaining dough into
18 1-inch balls and press into
tops of first batch. Let rise in
warm place 1 hour.

Oven, hot, 425°

Bake about 15 minutes or until
done. Remove from pans at
once.

BASIC SWEET DOUGH

Yeast, Cake or **Packaged
Active Dry,** 2
Water, ½ cup, warm
(see page   )
All-Purpose Flour, sifted,
5 cups
Sugar, ½ cup
Salt, 2 teaspoons
Milk, ¾ cup
Eggs, 2

Soften yeast in water in large
mixing bowl. Combine half the
flour with other dry ingredients.
Add milk and eggs and beat until
smooth. Gradually add enough
of remaining flour to make soft
dough. Turn out on floured
board; knead 5 minutes (see
directions above) or until
smooth and elastic.

Put in greased bowl and lightly
grease top. Cover with cloth and
stand in warm place (80° to 85°)
to rise until double in bulk,
about 1½ hours. Punch down,
cover and let rise 30 minutes.
Turn out on floured board,
shape into coffee cake as
desired, cover and let rise until
doubled, about 45 minutes.

Oven, moderate, 350°

Bake 20 to 30 minutes.

Coffee cake: basic sweet dough with pecans and sugar frosting

SWEET ROLLS

Follow the recipe for Basic Sweet Dough above. Shape the dough into squares, and cut half the squares diagonally to make triangles. Put a spoonful of filling into the centers of the squares and fold the 4 corners up to form envelopes. Put filling in the triangles, then roll up and shape into crescents. Or roll ropes of dough and coil to form snails.

Almond Paste Filling

Almonds, ¼ pound	Blanch and grind the almonds
Sugar, ⅓ cup	and mix with sugar. Add egg
Egg, 1, slightly beaten	and mix until smooth.

Prune Filling

Prunes, ½ cup, puréed	Purée prunes in sieve or blender,
Almonds, ground, ¼ cup	add almonds and orange rind.
Orange Rind, 1 teaspoon, grated	

Cheese Filling

Cottage Cheese, 1 cup	Combine all ingredients
Egg, 1, well beaten	thoroughly.
Sugar, 2 tablespoons	
Butter, 1 tablespoon, melted	
Salt, ⅛ teaspoon	
Nutmeg, ¼ teaspoon	

HOT CROSS BUNS

Prepare Sweet Rolls above, shaping dough into large biscuits and placing them side by side in greased pan, 1 inch apart. Cover and let rise in warm place until double in bulk. Make a deep cross in center of each and brush with beaten egg yolk. Bake in moderate (350°) oven, 20 to 30 minutes. While warm, glaze with 1 egg white beaten with ½ cup confectioner's sugar.

CINNAMON BUNS

Roll Basic Sweet Dough to ¼ inch thickness. Spread with softened butter; sprinkle with a mixture of ½ cup brown sugar, 2 teaspoons cinnamon and ½ cup seedless raisins. Roll up and cut into 1½-inch lengths. In 2 well-buttered 9-inch square baking pans pour 1 cup of light or dark corn syrup. Stand buns in syrup, cover with cloth and let rise until double in bulk. Bake in moderate (350°) oven about 45 minutes. Turn out of pan immediately. To make about 24 buns.

Preparing cinnamon buns

KUCHEN

Roll Basic Sweet Dough into rectangle ½ inch thick and fit into 9-inch square baking pans. Cover and let rise until double in bulk. Brush with the white of 1 egg slightly beaten with 1 tablespoon of water. Sprinkle with chopped nut meats and raisins. Bake in moderate oven (375°) 20 to 25 minutes. To make 2 square cakes.

Step 1: combining milk and dry ingredients

Step 2: completing the mixture

Step 3: cutting on a floured board

Step 4: frying in deep fat

RAISED DOUGHNUTS

Milk, 1 cup, scalded	Dissolve shortening and salt in
Shortening, ¼ cup	milk in large bowl and cool to
Salt, ½ teaspoon	lukewarm. Add yeast, soften and
Yeast, Cake or **Packaged**	stir until dissolved. Sift to-
Active Dry, 1	gether flour, sugar and spices
All-Purpose Flour, sifted,	and add half gradually to yeast
4 cups	mixture, beating thoroughly.
Sugar, ¾ cup	Add eggs, then remaining flour
Cinnamon, 1½ teasps.	mixture to make a dough.
Nutmeg, ¼ teaspoon	Knead well on lightly floured
Eggs, 3, well beaten	board; put in bowl and let rise
	until double in bulk.

Turn out on lightly floured board. Roll dough 1 inch thick; cut with floured doughnut cutter, or shape into rounds, bars, or twists. Cover and let rise until double in bulk.

Deep, hot fat, 360°–370°

Drop into fat, raised side down. Fry 2 or 3 minutes or until lightly browned. Drain on paper towels. Cool.

To make about 30

Doughnuts may be dusted with confectioners' sugar, or a mixture of sugar and cinnamon; or glazed (page 202).

FRENCH CROISSANTS

Milk, 1 cup
Lard, 1 tablespoon
Sugar, 1 tablespoon
Salt, ½ teaspoon
Yeast, Cake or **Packaged Active Dry,** 1
All-Purpose Flour, sifted, 2½ cups (about)

Scald milk, add lard, sugar and salt; stir until lard is melted, and cool until lukewarm. Add yeast and dissolve. Stir in flour, enough to make a soft dough. Turn out on lightly floured board and knead until smooth and elastic. Place in greased bowl, cover with cloth and put in warm (85°) place to rise until double in bulk. Place in refrigerator to chill thoroughly.

Butter, 1 cup

Cream butter until fluffy. Roll out dough into a rectangle, ¼ inch thick. Spread dough with one-quarter of butter, and fold it over in thirds. Swing the right end of the folded dough toward you and once again roll it out until it is ¼ inch thick. (Work quickly so that dough does not become warm, or chill it after each folding.)

Spread with butter, fold, and repeat process twice more, or four times in all, using all the butter. Cover dough and chill for 2 hours. Roll the dough out once more, ¼ inch thick. Cut it into squares, and cut each square diagonally to form triangles. Form each triangle into a roll, starting with the wide side and ending up with the point. Curve the rolls into crescents and place on baking tin. Chill them for 30 minutes.

Oven, hot, 400°

Bake 10 minutes, decrease heat to 350°, bake 15 minutes longer, or until golden brown.

To make 24 crescents

HUSH PUPPIES

Cornmeal, 3 cups
Baking Powder, 2 teasps.
Flour, 2 tablespoons
Salt, 1½ teaspoons
Eggs, 1, beaten
Milk, 2 cups
Onion, 1 med., chopped
Deep Hot Fat

Mix cornmeal, baking powder, flour and salt together. Add egg, milk and onion; mix well. Mold into small cakes and fry in deep hot fat (375°) until golden brown. Or fry in fat in frying pan, if desired, to brown both sides. Drain on paper towels and serve hot.

QUICK BREADS

Quick breads are made with baking powder and/or baking soda instead of yeast. They are delicious when fresh but do not have the keeping qualities of yeast bread, or its satisfying nature.

If you use glass rather than metal loaf pans, use a 25° lower temperature than that specified in recipes—glass browns much faster than metal.

BRAN BREAD

All-Purpose Flour, 1½ cups
Baking Powder, 3 teasps.
Baking Soda, ½ teasp.
Salt, 1 teaspoon
Sugar, ½ cup
Bran, 1 cup
Raisins, ½ cup
Egg, 1, well-beaten
Milk, ¾ cup
Molasses, ¼ cup
Salad Oil or **Melted Fat,** ¼ cup

Sift together flour, baking powder, salt and sugar; stir in unsifted bran and raisins. Mix egg, milk and molasses, and add to flour mixture; stir only until mixed. Add shortening. Pour into greased 9 × 5-inch loaf pan.

Oven, moderate, 350°   Bake about 1 hour.

BANANA BREAD

All-Purpose Flour, sifted, 2 cups
Soda, 1 teaspoon
Salt, ½ teaspoon

Sift dry ingredients together.

Butter, ½ cup
Sugar, 1 cup

Eggs, 2
Banana, 1½ cups
Nuts, ½ cup, chopped

In a large mixing bowl cream room-temperature butter and sugar together until very fluffy. Add eggs one at a time beating after each one. Add sifted dry ingredients alternately with banana purée. Add chopped nuts. Pour into greased 9 × 5-inch loaf pan.

Oven, moderate, 350°

Bake 55 to 60 minutes or until cake tester, or toothpick, comes out clean.

BOSTON BROWN BREAD

Rye Flour, 1 cup
Cornmeal, 1 cup
Baking Soda, 2 teaspoons
Salt, 1 teaspoon
Whole Wheat Flour, 1 cup
Seeded Raisins, 1 cup
Molasses, ¾ cup
Sour Milk or **Buttermilk,** 2 cups

Sift together rye flour, cornmeal, soda and salt; stir in unsifted whole wheat flour. Add raisins. Combine milk and molasses and add to dry ingredients, stirring only until just mixed. Fill well-greased molds ⅔ full, cover tightly and steam 2 to 3 hours, depending on size of molds.

One pound baking powder cans with their tight-fitting lids make excellent molds for Boston Brown Bread, or heavy foil may be securely tied on any can.

Sally Lunn bread can be baked in a kugelhopf pan

NUT BREAD

All-Purpose Flour, 2 cups Baking Powder, 3 teasps. Salt, ½ teaspoon Sugar, ⅓ cup Nuts, 1 cup, chopped Eggs, 2, well-beaten Milk, 1 cup Salad Oil or Melted Fat, ¼ cup	Sift together flour, baking powder, and salt and sugar; stir in chopped nuts. Mix eggs and milk and add to flour mixture; stir only until mixed. Add shortening. Pour into greased 9 × 5-inch loaf pan.
Oven, moderate, 350°	Bake 40 to 45 minutes.

Good served with whipped butter or cream cheese.

CORN BREAD

All-Purpose Flour, sifted,
    ¾ cup
Yellow Cornmeal,
    1½ cups
Baking Powder, 3 teasps.
Salt, 1 teaspoon
Eggs, 2, well-beaten
Milk, 1¼ cups
Salad Oil, or Melted Fat,
    ¼ cup
	Sift dry ingredients together. Combine eggs and milk and add flour mixture; stir until just mixed. Stir in oil. Pour into greased 11½ × 7½-inch or 9-inch square pan.

Oven, hot, 400°	Bake about 30 minutes.

CORN BREAD STICKS

All-Purpose Flour, sifted,
    1½ cups
Yellow Cornmeal, ¾ cup
Baking Powder, 3 teasps.
Salt, 1 teaspoon
Sugar, 3 teaspoons
Egg, 1, well-beaten
Milk, 1 cup
Salad Oil or Melted Fat,
    ¼ cup
	Sift dry ingredients together. Combine egg, milk and salad oil. Add dry ingredients; stir just enough to moisten. Pour into well-greased hot corn stick pans, ⅔ full.

Oven, hot, 425°	Bake about 25 minutes.

To make about 15 corn bread sticks

SALLY LUNN

All-Purpose Flour, sifted,
    2 cups
Baking Powder, 3 teasps.
Salt, ½ teaspoon
Sugar, ¼ cup
Eggs, 2, separated
Milk, ½ cup
Salad Oil or Melted Fat,
    ½ cup
	Sift dry ingredients together. Combine beaten egg yolks and milk. Add dry ingredients. Stir just enough to mix. Add salad oil. Fold in stiffly beaten egg whites. Pour into greased 9-inch square pan.

Oven, moderate, 350°	Bake about 30 minutes.

SPOON BREAD

Milk, 2 cups Salt, 1 teaspoon Cornmeal, 1 cup Baking Powder, 2 teasps. Eggs, 2, separated	Scald milk in top of double boiler and add salt. Stir in corn-meal gradually and cook over hot water until thick, stirring until smooth. Remove from heat, cool slightly; add baking powder and well-beaten egg yolks. Fold in stiffly beaten egg whites and pour into greased casserole.
Oven, moderate, 350° *To serve 4*	Bake about 30 minutes or until set. Serve hot with main course.

JOHNNY CAKE

White Cornmeal, 1 cup Salt, 1 teaspoon Water, boiling, 1 cup Milk, ½ cup Salad Oil or Melted Butter, 2 tablespoons	Mix salt with cornmeal; stir in boiling water; add milk, then oil. The batter should be soft but not watery. Bake on a griddle, or spread batter in shallow cake pan and bake in medium oven until crisp. Serve with butter or syrup, or as a base for a creamed dish.

DUMPLINGS

All-Purpose Flour, 1 cup Baking Powder, 1½ teaspoons Salt, ½ teaspoon Shortening, 1 tablesp. Milk, ½ cup	Sift flour, baking powder and salt. Cut in shortening. Stir in milk with fork slowly, using only enough to keep dough stiff. Drop by spoonfuls on simmering stew, letting it rest on meat or vegetables—not settle into the liquid. Cover tightly, cook 15 minutes without raising cover.

Dumplings may be flavored with 1 tablespoon finely chopped parsley, or 1 teaspoon dried thyme or other herbs, or 1 tablespoon chopped chives.

BISCUITS

In spite of the good biscuit mixes on the market today, there is still something to be said for the fluffy lightness of the made-from-scratch biscuit. Though this is a very old favorite, it is very modern to freeze an extra batch while you are making them, either before or after baking (see page 274).

On the thickness of the dough will depend whether you have thin crisp biscuits or thick soft ones, a matter of preference. To make the former, roll the dough out to ¼ inch in thickness; ½ inch for taller, softer ones.

FEATHER-LIGHT BAKING POWDER BISCUITS

Cake Flour, sifted, 2½ cups
Baking Powder, 2½ teaspoons
Salt, 1¼ teaspoons
Shortening (half butter), ⅓ cup
Milk, ⅔ cup

Sift together the dry ingredients. With pastry blender, cut in room-temperature shortening; blend well with fork to make a soft dough. Flatten dough on lightly floured board and fold into thirds, then pat out again. Cut biscuits with floured 2-inch cutter and put on baking sheet. Fit leftover bits of dough together and pat into biscuits.

Oven, hot, 450°

Bake 12 minutes.

MUFFINS

Muffins are probably the easiest of the hot breads to make. They require only a light touch and a scant blending of the ingredients; just enough to moisten the flour. The batter will be lumpy. Peaks and tunnels in the finished muffins are caused by over beating. Use ingredients at room temperature.

All-Purpose Flour, sifted, 2 cups
Baking Powder, 3 teasps.
Salt, 1 teaspoon
Sugar, 3 tablespoons
Shortening, 3 tablesps.
Egg, 1
Milk, 1 cup

Grease muffin tins. Sift together dry ingredients in mixing bowl. Add room-temperature shortening: with a pastry blender, mix only enough to blend. Add egg and milk, stirring just enough to blend; batter will be lumpy. Fill muffin tins ⅔ full.

Oven, moderate, 400°

Bake 20 to 25 minutes, or until golden brown.

To make 12 muffins

You can have an endless variety of muffins; after cutting shortening into the sifted dry ingredients add one of the following:

BLUEBERRY MUFFINS: ¾ cup fresh blueberries.

NUT MUFFINS: ½ cup coarsely chopped nuts.

CRANBERRY MUFFINS: ½ cup chopped cranberries mixed with 2 tablespoons sugar.

RAISIN MUFFINS: ½ cup seedless raisins.

WHOLE WHEAT MUFFINS

Substitute brown sugar for white, and 1 cup unsifted whole wheat flour for 1 cup All-Purpose Flour.

BRAN MUFFINS

Substitute 1 cup of bran for 1 cup of All-Purpose Flour. Increase baking powder to 3½ teaspoons. Beat egg before adding.

PANCAKES

Pancakes are made the world around and are as old as the ancient Chinese. They are cooked unleavened; with or without eggs; or risen, with yeast, soda, or baking powder. They can be served for any meal of the day; as a main dish, rolled with cottage cheese, meat, poultry or fish (page 88), or as a dessert with fruit and liqueur sauces.

SOUR MILK OR BUTTERMILK PANCAKES

All-Purpose Flour, sifted, 2 cups
Soda, 1 teaspoon
Salt, 1 teaspoon
Eggs, 2 separated
Sour Milk, or **Buttermilk,** 2 cups
Salad Oil or **Melted Fat,** 2 tablespoons

Sift dry ingredients together. Combine well-beaten egg yolks and milk; add flour mixture and beat until just smooth. Add shortening; mix briefly. Fold in stiffly beaten egg whites. Bake on lightly greased griddle.

To make about 12 good-size pancakes

NEW ENGLAND GRIDDLE CAKES

All-Purpose Flour, sifted, 2 cups
Baking Powder, 3 teasps.
Salt, 1 teaspoon
Eggs, 2, well-beaten
Milk, 1½ cups
Salad Oil or **Melted Fat,** 2 tablespoons

Sift dry ingredients together. Combine eggs and milk; add flour mixture and beat until just smooth. Add shortening; mix briefly. Bake on lightly greased griddle. If a thick cake is desired, use a little less milk.

To make about 12 medium-size griddle cakes

Serve with butter and maple sugar sprinkled on each cake while hot, or with maple syrup.

BUCKWHEAT CAKES: Substitute 1 cup buckwheat flour for 1 cup All-Purpose Flour; add 3 tablespoons sugar. Increase milk if necessary.

CORNMEAL CAKES: Substitute ¾ cup cornmeal for ¾ cup All-Purpose Flour.

BLUEBERRY PANCAKES: Add 1 cup fresh blueberries to batter. Serve with Blueberry Sauce (page 234).

BLINTZES

Crêpes, 16

Make crêpes according to above recipe.

Cottage Cheese, 2 cups
Egg, 1, beaten
Salt, ¼ teaspoon
Sugar, 2 tablespoons
Cinnamon, ½ teaspoon
Butter, melted
Sour Cream

Combine ingredients, put a spoonful in each crêpe and roll up. Place side by side in shallow baking pan, brush with melted butter, and place under broiler for few minutes until lightly browned. Turn each one over, brush with melted butter and brown lightly. Serve with a dish of sour cream.

YEAST PANCAKES

Milk, 1½ cups
Yeast, Cake or **Packaged Active Dry,** 1
Salt, 1 teaspoon
Sugar, 2 teaspoons
Salad Oil, or **Melted Fat,** 2 tablespoons
All-Purpose Flour, 2 cups
Egg, 1, well-beaten

Scald milk and cool to luke-warm; dissolve yeast. Add salt, sugar, shortening, flour and egg. Beat thoroughly and set in warm place to rise. When double in bulk, stir again. Cook at once on hot griddle.

WAFFLES

Modern waffle irons usually require no greasing; however, follow the manufacturer's directions for breaking in or seasoning a new iron. To bake, heat it until drops of water sprinkled on the surface will skitter across it. Clean it by wiping off the outside with a damp cloth and brushing the inside, when cool, with a stiff brush to loosen any clinging particles.

All-Purpose Flour, 2 cups
Baking Powder, 3 teasps.
Salt, 1 teaspoon
Sugar, 2 teaspoons
Eggs, 2, separated
Milk, 1¼ cups
Vanilla, ½ teaspoon (optional)
Salad Oil, or **Melted Butter,** 2 tablespoons

Sift dry ingredients together. Combine well-beaten egg yolks with milk and vanilla; add to flour mixture, blending in quickly. Do not over-mix, the batter should have a pebbly look. Add shortening, and mix briefly. Fold in stiffly beaten egg whites. Bake in hot waffle iron, pouring batter into center of iron until iron is about half covered.

To make about 6 waffles

BUTTERMILK WAFFLES: Substitute ¾ teaspoon soda for 1 teaspoon baking powder, and 1½ cups buttermilk or sour milk for sweet milk.

GINGER WAFFLES: Add 2 teaspoons ginger to Buttermilk Waffles. Serve as a dessert waffle with vanilla ice cream, or with applesauce.

CINNAMON TOAST

Butter thin slices of toast and sprinkle with a mixture of cinnamon and sugar in the proportion of 1 teaspoon of cinnamon to ½ cup of sugar.

For interesting variations, spread toast with butter, then with orange marmalade, then sprinkle with cinnamon; or spread with honey butter, then sprinkle with cinnamon.

CRÊPES SUZETTE

Crêpes Suzette are thin French pancakes which provide an excuse for eating a very delectable sauce.

The Pancakes

Eggs, 2
Milk, ¾ cup
Shortening, 1 tablesp., melted
All-Purpose Flour, sifted, ¾ cup
Salt, ½ teaspoon
Sugar, 1 teaspoon

Beat eggs until foamy; add milk and shortening. Add sifted dry ingredients to eggs; beat with rotary beater until smooth. (The mixture should have the consistency of cream. If too thick, add milk.) Heat a 7-inch skillet and grease lightly. Add a large spoonful of batter. Tilt pan so that it spreads all over the bottom evenly. Cook quickly, and when brown on one side, turn over and brown other side. Stack crêpes and keep warm until all are finished.

To make about 16 crêpes

The Sauce

Butter, ½ cup
Grated Rind of Lemon and **Orange,** 1 each
Orange Juice, ½ cup
Sugar, 2 tablespoons
Cointreau or **Curaçao,** ¼ cup
Cognac, ¼ cup
Kirsch, ¼ cup

In a skillet or chafing dish melt butter. Add grated rind, orange juice and sugar; heat and stir until sugar is melted. Add Cointreau, cognac and kirsch, and touch with lighted match to flame it. Dip crêpes in sauce and fold into quarters. Set each to one side of the pan, as you fold the next.

Cognac, ¼ cup

When all are bathed in the sauce, pour the cognac over all, flame it and spoon the flaming sauce over the crêpes. Serve at once.

POPOVERS

Success with popovers is dependent on the correct oven temperature and on baking them long enough. Don't be misled because they seem raised and golden brown ahead of time. Let them stay in the oven for the full time the recipe indicates. Grease only the bottom of the pan so that the popover may cling to the sides in rising. Use ingredients at room temperature.

All-Purpose Flour, sifted, 1 cup
Salt, ½ teaspoon
Eggs, 2
Milk, 1 cup

Grease bottoms only of muffin tins or custard cups. Put all ingredients together in a bowl and beat with rotary beater until smooth. Fill muffin tins or cups ¼ full.

Oven, hot, 425°

To make 8 popovers

Bake 35 to 40 minutes or until popovers are firm and golden brown.

CROUTONS

Cut stale bread into ½ inch cubes. Bake in slow oven (300°) 10 to 15 minutes, stirring occasionally to brown evenly. Or sauté cubes in small amount of butter, turning frequently to brown evenly; or fry cubes in deep hot fat (375°) about 40 seconds and drain on paper towels. Serve with soup.

MARJ'S SOUR DOUGH STARTER

Making bread, pancakes and the like from a sour dough starter was a method invented in a day when yeast was hard to come by, for it permitted you to carry over some of your original yeasty mixture for future bakings. When handled properly the yeast starter can be perpetuated from baking to baking, and Marj says she has had her Starter going for several years. She advises not to try to start in extremely hot weather since it is somewhat temperamental and seems to prefer a moderately warm temperature to ferment properly. With the method described below you save out a cup of Starter at each baking, and this becomes the new starter.

Actually there are two steps involved, as follows:

Step 1. In a large glass or ceramic bowl dissolve a yeast cake in ½ cup of warm water (about 110°). Add 2 teaspoons of sugar and beat in 2½ cups of flour and 2 cups of warm water, alternately a little at a time. Cover bowl with damp cloth and secure it with a rubber band. Stir it down once daily and at the end of 4 days add ¼ cup of flour and ¼ cup of warm water. Beat it well and let it sit one more day.

Step 2. At the end of the fifth day add 2 cups of flour and 2 cups of milk. Mix well and let it stand at room temperature for at least 12 hours, or until it is light and bubbly.

At this point you can take out one cup of the brew which now becomes your new Starter. Put it in a covered jar that hold 2 cups. The extra space in the jar will permit it to rise and then settle without running over. Store it in the refrigerator until you are ready to use it again. When you are ready for your next baking, begin with Step 2, above. Then remove one cup to save, and so on. Never use a metal container or metal lid. Put a piece of plastic over the jar top to separate the lid from the Starter.

After removing your cup of Starter, use the remainder in the following recipes:

SOUR DOUGH WAFFLES

Starter, as described above
Egg, 1, well beaten
Salt, 1 teaspoon
Soda, 1 teaspoon
Sugar, 2 teaspoons
Butter or **Oil,** 1 tablespoon

Combine the starter with the other ingredients and mix well. Bake on your waffle griddle as with regular waffles.

SOUR DOUGH PANCAKES

The above recipe for Waffles can also be used for Pancakes, but a little additional milk may be used if a thinner pancake is desired.

WHITE BREAD

After saving out one cup of your Starter, as described above, proceed as follows:

Milk, 1 cup
Butter or margarine, 2 tablespoons
Sugar, 3 tablespoons
Salt, 1 teaspoon
Starter as described above
Flour, 5 to 6 cups, all-purpose

Combine milk, soft butter or margarine, sugar, and salt in a saucepan and heat until warm (110°). Add Starter and beat in one cup of flour, or enough to make a thick batter. Then stir in enough additional flour to make a soft dough and form a ball. Place on a lightly floured board and knead until smooth, about 5 minutes. Place in greased bowl, cover with a damp cloth and set in a warm place to rise until double in bulk, about 1 to 1½ hours.

Punch down dough and turn out on floured board. Divide in two and let rest 15 minutes. Knead each half well, sprinkling a little extra flour on it if it is too sticky to handle. Form each half into a loaf and place in 9″ × 5″ loaf pans. Cover pans with a cloth and let rise in a warm place until bulk is not quite doubled, about 30 to 45 minutes.

Oven, hot, 400°

Bake in preheated oven 30 minutes, or until well-browned. Remove bread from pans and allow to cool away from drafts.

STORE-BOUGHT BREADS GO FANCY

GARLIC LOAF: Spread slices of bread with ½ cup of soft butter mixed with ¼ teaspoon instant garlic. Put loaf back together and stand up in loaf pan. Heat 10 minutes in 400° oven. This method can be used for ready-sliced loaves or by slicing French or Italian loaves.

ONION ROLLS: Slice rolls in half and spread with butter seasoned with instant onion. Replace halves, wrap in foil, and heat in oven.

CHEESE LOAF: Spread slices of bread with soft butter and sprinkle with Parmesan cheese. Put loaf back together and heat in 400° oven for 10 minutes.

POPPYSEED BISCUITS: Separate a package of ready-made biscuits. Brush the top of each with melted butter and sprinkle with poppy seed. Bake as directed. And for variety try sesame seed.

PASTRY

The secret of tender flaky pastry is a light touch and as little handling as possible. The hydrogenated fats, butter, or lard are all suitable for making pastry, but lard will give you the "shortest" crust, one that will shatter when you bite into it.

HOW TO MAKE PIE CRUST

1. Combine your favorite shortening with sifted All-Purpose Flour and salt by cutting it in either with a pastry blender or two knives. The mix should have a texture somewhere between coarse cornmeal and small peas.

2. Add very cold water, a little at a time, stirring with a fork until portions of the dough are just moist enough to stick together. Set these aside and moisten the remainder. Too much water makes a crust hard and brittle, not tender. Too little makes it difficult to handle. Roll dough into a ball, wrap in wax paper and chill 15 minutes.

3. Roll dough out on a lightly floured board or pastry cloth to ⅛ inch in thickness. Roll from the center toward the edges.

Press rim of pie pan gently on dough to gauge size circle you will need and cut it 1½ inches larger all around to allow for edging. Lift dough up with wide cake turner and slide pie pan under it. Or fold dough over in half, then in quarters, and lift.

If it breaks apart just piece it together in the pan; this is usually a sign that it will be a tender crust.

4. Press edge with finger or fork to form a fluting. If two crusts are used, press the top and bottom crusts together and flute to form the edge. Trim off any excess.

5. Bake in center of oven according to the directions in the recipe.

measure the flour and shortening

combine with pastry blender

add cold water until dough is just moist

wrap and chill

roll dough and slide pie pan under it

flute edges

seal two crust edges together

STANDARD PIE CRUST

All-Purpose Flour, sifted, Follow above method for
  2¼ cups   mixing.
Salt, 1 teaspoon
Shortening, ¾ cup
Cold Water, about ⅓ cup

Will make two 9-inch pie shells or one 2-crust pie

HOT-WATER PIE CRUST

Shortening, ¾ cup   In mixing bowl pour boiling
Boiling Water, ¼ cup   water over shortening and whip
All-Purpose Flour, sifted, with fork until mixture is like
  2 cups   whipped cream. Sift in flour and
Salt, 1 teaspoon   salt. Stir quickly until dough
                              clings together and leaves sides
                              of bowl clean. Chill, then roll
To make two 9-inch crusts   out.

SALAD OIL PIE CRUST

Flour, sifted, 2 cups   Sift flour and salt together.
Salt, 1 teaspoon   Combine oil and water and add
Salad Oil, ½ cup   to flour. Mix with fork and form
Ice Water, 5 tablesps.   into balls.

Enough for two 9-inch pie crusts

LATTICE CRUST FOR FRUIT PIES

Place lower crust in pie pan and fill with fruit.

Roll remaining dough into a rectangle and with knife or
pastry wheel cut it into ½-inch strips. Place strips on top of
fruit in opposite directions with spaces in between to form
lattice. Press strips tightly against edges of bottom crust to
hold them in place.

If desired a lattice may be woven on waxed paper, chilled
thoroughly, then transferred to the pie.

TURNOVERS

Roll out Pie Crust. Using small plate as pattern, cut out circles
of pastry. Cover half of circle with apples or other fruit,
sprinkled with sugar. Fold other half of dough over fruit and
press edges together firmly. Prick top with fork. Bake 30
minutes, or until lightly browned.

TARTS

Make recipe for Pie Crust above. Divide dough into 12 parts
and roll each one out to fit over back of 3½-inch tart pans.
Bake in hot oven, 425°, 10 minutes. Cook and remove from
pans. Fill with any cooked, chilled pie filling, or just before
serving, fill with ice cream and top with chocolate sauce,
preserves, or fresh fruit.

CRUMB CRUST

Graham Cracker,
  Gingersnap, Zwieback
  or Cooky Crumbs,
  1½ cups
Sugar, ¼ cup
Cinnamon, ⅛ teaspoon
Butter, ¼ cup, melted

Crush crackers or cookies fine with a rolling pin, if not available packaged ready to use. Mix with other ingredients and press firmly on bottom and sides of 9-inch pie pan.

Oven, slow, 300°

Bake 10 minutes.

To make one 9-inch crust

APPLE PIE

Pie Crust, two 9-inch
Apples, 6 to 8, tart
Sugar, ½ cup
Cinnamon, 1 teaspoon
Lemon Juice, 1 tablesp.
Butter, 1 tablespoon

Line a pie plate with pastry. Fill heaping with apples peeled and sliced. Sprinkle with sugar and cinnamon mixed together, and lemon juice; cover with dots of butter. Cover with top crust and press edges together. Make slits in crust.

Oven, hot, 425°

Bake 40 to 50 minutes, or until apples feel tender to the point of a knife, and crust is nicely browned.

PEACH PIE: Substitute 5 cups peaches for apples. Use less sugar if peaches are sweet.

Preparing an apple pie

APPLE CRUMB PIE

Follow recipe for Apple Pie, using only a bottom crust. Top the apples with a crumb mixture made with ¼ cup melted butter, ½ cup sugar, ¼ cup flour, 1 teaspoon cinnamon, combined lightly with a fork.

The above topping may be used also for Peach or Cherry Pie.

RHUBARB LATTICE PIE

Rhubarb, 5 cups
Sugar, 1¼ cups
Salt, ¼ teaspoon
Flour, 3 tablespoons
Orange Juice, ¼ cup
Pie Crust, one 9-inch and
  lattice strips

Cut rhubarb stalks in 1-inch pieces. Mix with sugar, salt and flour. Add orange juice and turn into bottom crust. Place lattice strips on top of rhubarb, pressing ends to edge of bottom crust.

Oven, hot, 450°

Bake 10 minutes and reduce heat to 350°. Bake about 30 minutes more, or until rhubarb looks juicy between lattice.

GOOSEBERRY PIE: Substitute 4 cups of gooseberries for rhubarb, and increase sugar to 2 cups.

FRESH DEEP-DISH CHERRY PIE

Cherries, red, sour,
  4 cups
Sugar, ¾ cup
Cornstarch, 3 tablesps.
Salt, ⅛ teaspoon
Water, ½ cup
Pastry for One Crust Pie

Pit cherries and combine with sugar, cornstarch, salt and water. Pour into an 8-inch square baking dish or a glass casserole. Cover with pie crust. Make slits in crust.

Oven, hot, 425°

Bake 40 to 45 minutes or until crust is brown.

Blackberries, blueberries, apples or peaches may be substituted for cherries, use about ½ cup of sugar and a little cinnamon.

CHERRY PIE: To make a regular 9-inch pie, use half the quantities above, put crust on bottom and top with lattice strips (page 181).

RASPBERRY DREAM

Frozen Raspberries,
  10 oz. package
Sugar, 1 cup
Lemon Juice,
  1 tablespoon

Thaw raspberries and save a few whole ones. Combine the remainder with sugar and lemon juice and beat by hand or puree in blender.

Egg Whites, 2,
  at room temperature
Salt, ⅛ teaspoon
Whipping Cream, 1 cup,
  whipped
Baked Pastry Shell,
  9 inch

Add salt to egg whites and beat until stiff. Fold into mixture. Fold in whipped cream and pile lightly in pastry shell. Freeze until firm and garnish with reserved raspberries.

Individual pecan pies baked in muffin tins

PECAN PIE

Eggs, 3
Butter, 2 tablespoons, melted
Flour, 2 tablespoons
Vanilla, 1 teaspoon
Salt, 1/8 teaspoon
Sugar, 1/2 cup
Dark Corn Syrup, 1 cup
Pecans, 1 1/2 cups
Unbaked Pie Crust, 9-in.

Beat together all ingredients but pecans. Spread pecans over bottom of pie crust; pour syrup mixture over them.

Oven, moderate, 325°   Bake about 45 minutes.

CHOCOLATE-PECAN PIE: Follow above recipe but add 2 squares unsweetened chocolate, melted, to syrup mixture.

MINCE PIE

Pie Crust, two 9-inch
Mincemeat, commercial or homemade, 3 cups
Rum, Brandy or **Whiskey,** 1/4 cup

Moisten mincemeat with brandy or whiskey, pour mixture into bottom crust and cover with top crust. Gash top crust with knife in several places.

Oven, hot, 400°   Bake 30 minutes, or until well browned.

Orange juice or cider may be substituted for the rum, brandy or whiskey.

MINCEMEAT

Lean Beef, 2 pounds
Water, 3 cups
Suet, 1 pound
Apples, 4 pounds, tart
Raisins, seedless, 2 lbs.
Currants, 1 pound
Salt, 1 tablespoon
Brown Sugar, 2 cups
Molasses, 1 cup
Cinnamon, 1 tablespoon
Allspice, 1 teaspoon
Clove, 1 teaspoon
Lemon Juice, 3 tablesps.
Brandy or **Cider,** 1 pint

To make about 24 cups

Cut beef in small pieces, add water, bring to boil and simmer, covered, 2 hours or until tender. Reserve stock; put meat through food chopper with suet and pared and cored apples, and put in large kettle. Add raisins, currants, salt, sugar, molasses, spices and beef stock. Simmer, covered, over low heat for 1 hour, stirring frequently. Add lemon juice and brandy and heat few minutes. Cover tightly and store in a cool place.

GLAZED CURRANT TARTS

Fresh Currants, 4 cups
Water, 1/2 cup
Sugar, 3/4 cup
Salt, dash
Cornstarch, 2 tablesps.

Remove stems from currants and set aside 3 cups to fill tart shells. Combine remaining currants with water, sugar, salt and cornstarch. Cook, stirring constantly, 5 minutes or until thickened. Cool.

Tart Shells, Baked, 6 to 8
Cream Cheese, 8-ounce package

Soften cream cheese at room temperature and spread a layer on bottom of each tart shell. Fill shells with currants and pour cornstarch mixture over top. Add dab of cream cheese to top of each. Chill.

STRAWBERRY GLACÉ

Sugar, 3 tablespoons
Cornstarch, 1 1/2 tablesps.
Water, 1 1/2 cups
Red Coloring

Combine sugar and cornstarch with water and cook until mixture boils and begins to thicken. Add few drops of red coloring. Cool.

Strawberries, large, 4 cups
Baked Pie Crust, one 9-inch

Wash and hull berries and place them in pie crust with points up, filling nearly level with top. Cut berries in half to fill spaces in between, if necessary. Pour glaze over berries and chill several hours. Before serving top with sour cream or whipped cream. Serve same day it is made.

Lemon chiffon pie

LEMON SPONGE PIE

Egg Yolks, 3
Sugar, ½ cup
Lemon, 1, juice and rind
Salt, pinch
Water, hot, ¼ cup

Beat egg yolks until thick and add sugar, lemon juice, rind, salt and water. Cook in double boiler until thick.

Egg Whites, 3
Sugar, ½ cup
Unbaked Pie Crust,
  one 8-inch

Beat egg whites stiff, gradually adding sugar, and fold in cooked mixture. Pour into pie crust.

Oven, moderate, 325°

Bake 20 minutes or until pie is light brown.

LEMON CHIFFON PIE

Unflavored Gelatin,
  1 envelope
Sugar, ½ cup
Salt, ½ teaspoon
Egg Yolks, 4, beaten
Lemon Juice, ⅓ cup
Water, ⅓ cup
Lemon Rind, 2 teasps.,
  grated

With rotary beater combine ingredients in top of double boiler; cook over boiling water, stirring constantly, until gelatin is thoroughly dissolved and mixture coats a metal spoon. Remove from heat, add rind; cool, and chill until partially set.

Egg Whites, 4
Sugar, ½ cup
Baked Pie Crust, 9-inch
Heavy Cream, 1 cup,
  whipped

Beat egg whites until stiff, adding sugar gradually. Fold in gelatin mixture. Pour into pie crust. Chill until firm; top with whipped cream.

LIME CHIFFON PIE

Follow recipe for Lemon Chiffon Pie but substitute ¼ cup of lime juice for lemon juice, and grated lime rind for lemon rind.

CUSTARD PIE

Milk, 2 cups
Sugar, ½ cup
Salt, ½ teaspoon
Vanilla, ½ teaspoon
Nutmeg, ¼ teaspoon
Eggs, 3
Pie Crust, 9-inch

Scald milk; add sugar, salt, vanilla and nutmeg. Beat eggs slightly and gradually pour hot mixture over them, stirring constantly. Strain into pastry-lined pie pan.

Oven, moderate, 350°

Bake 50 minutes, or until knife inserted in center comes out clean. Cool before serving.

COCONUT CUSTARD: Add ⅔ cup of shredded coconut to custard.

CHESS PIES

Butter, ½ cup
Sugar, 1 cup
Egg Yolks, 2
Egg Whites, 2, stiffly
  beaten
Walnuts, chopped, 1 cup
Seedless Raisins,
  chopped, 1 cup
Vanilla, 1 teaspoon
Tart Shells, 8, baked

Cream butter, gradually adding sugar. Beat egg yolks until thick and add to butter-sugar mixture. Fold in egg whites; then nuts, raisins and vanilla. Divide filling among tart shells.

Oven, hot, 400°

Bake 5 minutes; reduce temperature to 350° and bake another 15 to 20 minutes or until tops are a rich brown. Cool; serve with scoops of vanilla ice cream.

To make 8 tarts

BLACK BOTTOM PIE

Chocolate Cookies, 1 pkg.
Butter, ¼ cup

Crush enough chocolate cookies with rolling pin to make 1½ cups of crumbs. Mix with melted butter and press on bottom and sides of deep 9-inch pie pan to form crust.

Unflavored Gelatin,
  1 envelope
Milk, 1⅔ cups
Egg Yolks, 4
Sugar, ½ cup
Salt, ½ teaspoon
Cornstarch, 1 tablesp.

Soften gelatin in cold milk and heat in top part of double boiler, stirring until dissolved. Beat egg yolks with sugar, salt and cornstarch. Add milk slowly, stirring constantly. Return to double boiler and cook, stirring constantly for few minutes or until custard coats a metal spoon. Divide custard in half and chill one-half.

Unsweetened Chocolate,
  2 squares

Melt chocolate and blend with remaining half of custard. Pour into crust and chill until firm.

Rum, 3 tablespoons
Egg Whites, 4
Sugar, ¼ cup
Heavy Cream, 1 cup
Confectioners' Sugar,
  2 tablespoons

When other half of custard is partially set, add rum. Beat egg white stiff, gradually adding sugar. Fold in custard and pour over chocolate mixture. Chill until firm. Top with cream whipped with confectioner's sugar. Decorate with shavings of remaining chocolate. Chill thoroughly.

COCONUT CREAM PIE

Sugar, ⅔ cup
Flour, ½ cup
Salt, ½ teaspoon
Milk, 2 cups, scalded
Egg Yolks, 3, beaten
Coconut, shredded,
  ½ cup
Vanilla, 1 teaspoon
Pie Crust, 9-inch, baked

In top of double boiler, mix together sugar, flour and salt; gradually stir in milk, and cook over boiling water, stirring constantly, until mixture thickens. Pour a little of the mixture into egg yolks, then return to pan and continue cooking for 2 minutes, or until thickened. Add coconut and vanilla; cool until lukewarm. Pour into crust.

Egg Whites, 3
Sugar, ⅓ cup

Beat egg whites stiff, gradually adding sugar. Spread over pie filling.

Oven, hot, 400°

Bake 5 to 8 minutes, or until meringue is delicately browned.

PUMPKIN PIE

Pumpkin, 2 cups, cooked
  or canned
Sugar, ½ cup
Eggs, 2, slightly beaten
Salt, ½ teaspoon
Cream, 1½ cups
Butter, 2 tablespoons,
  melted
Ginger, ¼ teaspoon
Cinnamon, 1 teaspoon
Nutmeg, ½ teaspoon
Unbaked Pie Crust, 9-in.

Combine all ingredients. Pour into pie crust.

Oven, moderate, 400°

Put into 400° oven and reduce heat to 350°. Bake 45 minutes or until knife inserted in center comes out clean.

If desired, 2 tablespoons of brandy may be added.

SWEET POTATO PIE: Substitute 1½ cups mashed sweet potatoes for pumpkin in the above recipe.

SQUASH PIE: Substitute 2 cups of cooked, drained winter squash for pumpkin in the above recipe.

LEMON MERINGUE PIE

Lemon Juice, ½ cup
Lemon Rind, grated,
  1 teaspoon
**Sweetened Condensed
  Milk,** 1 can
Egg Yolks, 2
Baked Pie Crust,
  8-inch, chilled

Combine lemon juice and lemon rind and gradually stir in condensed milk. Add egg yolks and beat until well blended. Pour into chilled crust.

Egg Whites, 2
Cream of Tartar,
  ¼ teaspoon
Sugar, ¼ cup

Beat egg whites with cream of tartar until fluffy. Add sugar gradually, beating until stiff. Pile lightly on pie filling.

Oven, slow, 325°

Bake until lightly browned, about 20 minutes. Cool.

CHOCOLATE CHIFFON PIE

Unflavored Gelatin,
  1 envelope
Water, ¼ cup
Coffee, ½ cup
Semi-Sweet Chocolate,
  6-ounce package
Egg Yolks, 4, well beaten
Sugar, ¼ cup
Salt, ¼ teaspoon
Vanilla, 1 teaspoon

Soften gelatin in cold water for 5 minutes. Heat coffee and chocolate together until chocolate is melted, stirring constantly. Add gelatin and stir until dissolved. Combine egg yolks, sugar, salt and vanilla with chocolate mixture. Chill until partially thickened.

Egg Whites, 4
Sugar, ¼ cup
Baked Pie Crust, 9-inch

Beat egg whites until stiff, gradually adding sugar. Fold into chocolate mixture. Turn into pie crust. Chill until firm.

STRAWBERRY CHIFFON PIE

Unflavored Gelatin, 1 envelope
Water, ¼ cup, cold
Water, ½ cup, boiling
Sugar, ¾ cup
Salt, ⅛ teaspoon
Strawberries, puréed, 1 cup

Soak gelatin in cold water, add boiling water and stir until dissolved. Add sugar, salt, strawberry purée (put strawberries through sieve or blender). Chill until mixture is partially set.

Egg Whites, 2
Sugar, ¼ cup
Heavy Cream, ½ cup, whipped
Baked Pie Crust, 9-inch
Whipped Cream
Whole Strawberries

Fold in egg white beaten stiff with sugar. Fold in whipped cream. Turn into pie crust and chill. Garnish with whipped cream and strawberries.

NESSELRODE CHIFFON PIE

Unflavored Gelatin, 1 envelope
Milk, 1½ cups
Salt, ¼ teaspoon
Sugar, ¼ cup
Egg Yolks, 3, slightly beaten

In top of double boiler combine gelatin, milk, salt, sugar and beaten egg yolks. Cook until gelatin is dissolved and mixture will coat a metal spoon. Chill until mixture begins to stiffen.

Maraschino Cherries, ¼ cup, chopped
Sweet Chocolate, 3 tablespoons, shaved
Rum, 2 tablespoons
Egg Whites, 3
Sugar, ¼ cup
Baked Pie Crust, 9-inch
Heavy Cream, ½ cup, whipped

Stir cherries, chocolate and rum into gelatin mixture. Beat egg whites stiff, gradually adding sugar. Fold into gelatin mixture. Chill in baked pie crust until firm. Top with whipped cream.

PASTRY BITS

Don't waste left-over bits of pastry, however small. Piece them together, sprinkle with a mixture of sugar and cinnamon and roll up. Bake 10 minutes.

PUFF PASTE

Sift together 3½ cups of All-Purpose Flour and 1 teaspoon salt. Cut in ¼ pound butter until mixed in coarse particles; add ice water in small quantities with fork until just moist enough to form a ball. Chill thoroughly.

Cream ¾ pound butter until soft and smooth; chill. Divide dough in half and roll each half on lightly floured board into ⅛ inch thick rectangle. Roll butter out thin and place between the two sheets of dough. Fold dough into thirds, press edges together, fold in thirds again, in the opposite direction, and chill about 1 hour.

When chilled, roll out dough on lightly floured board, but do not permit butter to break through. Fold in thirds; and fold again the opposite way. Chill thoroughly and repeat rolling and folding process twice more. When ready to use, roll ¼ inch thick, cut in desired shapes, and place on baking sheet. Paste may be stored in refrigerator several days before using, if desired.

Bake in very hot oven, 450°, about 8 minutes, or until paste has risen its full height; reduce to 350° and bake 10 to 20 minutes, or until lightly browned.

PATTY CASES: Roll Puff Paste ¼ inch thick; cut in 3-inch rounds with cutter; cut centers out of half the rounds with smaller cutter; moisten undersides of rings with cold water, and press down on solid rounds to form sides of case. Chill thoroughly. Bake as directed above. Bake small rounds for lids.

To make 18 patty cases

NAPOLEONS: Divide Puff Paste in two. Roll each into an oblong about 9″ × 14″. Cut in strips 3″ × 14″ and put on cooky sheets, lined with brown paper. Prick paste with fork and cover with another cooky sheet to keep flat. Bake at 450° for 5 minutes; reduce heat to 350° and bake 15 minutes longer. Remove top cooky sheet and bake 15 minutes longer, or until pastry is dry and brown. Make 2 piles of 3 layers, with Vanilla Filling between the layers. Chill and cut each crosswise into pieces 2 inches wide. Spread sugar glaze on top and dribble lines of chocolate frosting across glaze (page 202).

To make 14 Napoleons.

CHEESE STICKS

All-Purpose Flour, sifted, 1¼ cups
Salt, ½ teaspoon
Shortening, 3 tablespoons
Grated Cheese, ⅓ cup
Cold Water, 3 tablesps.

Sift flour and salt together in mixing bowl; add shortening and cheese and cut in with pastry cutter until like coarse corn meal. Add just enough cold water to make particles cling together to form dough. Roll dough ¼ inch thick; cut into strips 3″ × ¼″. Place on ungreased baking sheet.

Oven, hot, 475°
To make about 60 sticks

Bake about 10 minutes.

CREAM PUFFS

Water, 1 cup
Butter, ½ cup
Salt, ¼ teaspoon
All-Purpose Flour,
  sifted, 1 cup
Eggs, 4

Heat water, butter and salt in saucepan to full rolling boil. Reduce heat; quickly add flour all at once, stirring vigorously with a wooden spoon until mixture forms a ball which leaves sides of pan clean. Beat in eggs, one at a time, and continue beating until mixture is smooth. With metal tablespoon place mixture on greased baking sheet, making mounds 2 inches apart—round for cream puffs, or oblong for eclairs.

Oven, hot, 400°

Bake 45–50 minutes, until puffed, golden and dry. Cool on racks away from drafts. Split each and fill with Vanilla Filling, ice cream, or whipped cream. Top cream puffs with confectioners' sugar.

To make 12 large puffs

ECLAIRS: Fill oblong shells and top with Chocolate Frosting (page 203).

MINIATURE PUFFS: Use above recipe, but drop mounds of dough with teaspoon. To make about 30. Bake about 30 minutes.

Vanilla Filling

Milk, 3 cups
Sugar, ¾ cup
Cornstarch, 6 tablesps.
Salt, ½ tablespoon
Eggs, 3, beaten
Vanilla, 2 teaspoons

Scald milk in top of double boiler over boiling water. Mix sugar, cornstarch and salt, and stir into milk. Cook, stirring until thick. Cook 10 minutes longer, covered. Add small amount of hot mixture to eggs and return to double boiler; cook 5 minutes. Add vanilla. Put in bowl and sprinkle top with a little confectioners' sugar to prevent skin from forming. Chill.

CHOCOLATE FILLING: Follow recipe above and add 3 squares unsweetened chocolate melted in the milk. Beat until smooth.

Making cream puffs

STRUDEL

All-Purpose Flour,
  sifted, 3 cups
Water, 1 cup
Egg, 1, beaten
Salad Oil, 1 tablespoon
Salt, ½ teaspoon

Put flour into bowl and make a well in the center. Add remaining ingredients and stir until combined into a smooth dough. Turn onto floured board and knead 5 minutes. Cover with a warm bowl and let stand 30 minutes, in a warm place.

Cover a table at least the size of a card table with a tablecloth, lightly sprinkle with flour and rub in. Secure cloth with pins or Scotch tape so it will stay in place. Roll dough out with rolling pin into a circle. Then with well-floured hands begin stretching the dough in all directions until it is at least 30 inches square. As it reaches the side of the table, anchor it over the edge to hold it until it is all stretched. Trim off edges of dough neatly.

With a pastry brush, coat surface with salad oil or melted butter. Spread filling in an even line the full width of dough and about 3 inches from one end. Fold end of dough over the filling; fold sides up for few inches on each side, completely enclosing filling at end. Loosen tablecloth at end near filling and lift it to make the dough roll over on itself. Continue rolling until all dough is rolled. Slice the roll in half and roll each half onto a baking sheet.

APPLE STRUDEL FILLING

Dry Bread Crumbs,
  ½ cup
Apples, 2 pounds, tart,
  chopped
Raisins, ½ cup, seedless
Nuts, ½ cup, chopped
Currants, ¼ cup
Cinnamon, 1 teaspoon
Lemon Rind, 1, grated
Sugar, 1 cup

Oven, moderate, 375°

Confectioners' Sugar

Sprinkle line of bread crumbs across strudel dough, 3 inches from one end. Combine remaining ingredients and place on top of the crumbs. Roll strudel, cut in half and roll each half onto baking sheet.

Bake 30 minutes or until golden brown. Sprinkle with confectioners' sugar. Cut into slices and serve plain or with heavy cream, if desired.

PROFITEROLES

Make miniature cream puffs following recipe on page 187. Fill with whipped cream. Serve with hot chocolate sauce using recipe on page 235, omitting walnuts.

TORTILLAS

Cornmeal, 1 cup
Flour, 1 cup
Salt, 1 teaspoon
Warm Water

Mix cornmeal, flour and salt; add enough water to make a stiff dough, and set dough aside for 20 minutes. Dip hands in water and mold dough into small balls about an inch in diameter. Pat balls into paper-thin cakes, stretching the dough as you pat. Bake on a lightly greased griddle, lightly browning both sides.

To make about 12 tortillas

CAKES AND FROSTINGS

You often hear a woman say that she is a pretty good cook but can't bake a cake. Such a cook has been discouraged by failures that may be due to an inaccurate oven control, the wrong size cake pans, the wrong kind of baking powder or old baking powder that has lost its zip, or perhaps a type of flour other than the one specified in the recipe. In other words, cake making is practically an exact science, and if you provide the correct ingredients and follow exactly the directions in the recipe you will have successful cakes.

It is a good idea to check your oven's control with a portable oven thermometer to make sure the control is working properly. Check it set at 300°, 375° and 450°—it might be accurate at one temperature but not another.

USING THE MIXER

Some cakes, let's face it, take a lot of hard beating and the arm can get very tired. Without any question, the electric mixer simplifies the job. If you use a mixer, consult the directions that came with it for mixing speeds and times. Or, be guided by the directions in the recipe as to whether a batter requires a lot of beating or just a little. In general, beat the butter and egg mixture very thoroughly, at a medium speed. It is almost impossible to beat them too much. More care is required in adding the flour and milk, with just enough beating to combine the ingredients smoothly after each addition.

BAKING POWDER

In the following recipes double-acting baking powder is called for. This is the type most generally found on the market today. However, check the label on your can to make sure, and if by chance you have a tartrate type, use twice as much as called for in these recipes.

Do not use self-rising flours in these recipes, or in any recipe in this book. Only all-purpose or cake flours are specified. Baking powder and/or soda must always be added separately.

UTENSILS

Have a selection of cake pans so that you will have the size called for in the recipe you are using. Have standard measuring cups and spoons—use a nest of cups that can be leveled off evenly at the top to measure dry ingredients or fats. Use a cup with a lip for liquids.

If you use glass rather than metal for loaf cakes, use a 25° lower temperature than that specified in recipes—glass browns much faster than metal.

HOW TO MAKE A BUTTER CAKE

1. One hour before mixing, remove eggs, shortening and milk from refrigerator, setting them out to come to room temperature.

2. Prepare special ingredients: chopped nuts, fruits, shaved chocolate and the like. Assemble other ingredients and utensils.

3. Prepare cake pans of the size specified in the recipe (measure diameter at the upper edge); do not use larger pans; if you use smaller ones fill them only ⅔ full and use the balance of the batter for cup cakes. Either grease and lightly

Preparation of pans for cake baking

flour bottoms of pans or cut wax paper to fit. Grease paper but not sides of pans.

4. Place racks in center of oven. Preheat oven to temperature specified. Use a portable thermometer if oven has no heat control.

5. Measure accurately. Sift flour onto wax paper before measuring it; then with a spoon lightly fill measuring cup. Do not pack it down or tap the cup; let it overflow and level it with the edge of knife or spatula. Empty the amount needed for the recipe into the sifter with the other dry ingredients, ready to sift all together before adding to batter.

6. Measure the fat by pressing it down solidly into the cup with a spatula. Or if using butter, a quarter pound, or one stick, is equal to half a cup. Other fats may be used if preferred.

7. Cream fat and sugar together until light and fluffy, almost like whipped cream. (Fat must be at room temperature.) Use a mixer if you have one, or beat with a spoon, adding flavoring; or beat with rotary beater. You can't beat it too much.

8. Add the unbeaten eggs or yolks one by one and beat thoroughly after each. If recipe specifies adding whites separately, separate them from yolks carefully, making sure no speck of yolk gets into the white.

9. Add sifted dry ingredients alternately with liquid, stirring in a few tablespoons of each at a time and beating enough each time to make batter smooth. Do not overbeat. Use electric mixer at low speed.

10. If egg whites are added separately, this is the time to do it. Beat them to soft peaks, but not dry. (Be sure beater and bowl are grease-free.) Pour them onto batter and cut into batter with edge of spoon, bringing spoon up with some batter and turning it over the whites. Repeat until whites are distributed through batter.

11. Pour batter into pans, dividing it evenly and spreading it out to edges.

12. Place in pre-heated oven. Stagger the pans so that one is not directly above another.

13. Let cake bake minimum time required in recipe. Then open oven door and test by touching cake with finger. If it springs back, cake is done. If impressions remain in cake, bake a little longer.

14. Remove pans to cake rack and let stand 10 minutes. Loosen cake around edges with knife. Turn pans upside down on rack and lift off pans. Carefully peel paper. Let cool before frosting.

ONE EGG CAKE

Cake Flour, sifted, 2 cups **Baking Powder,** 2½ teaspoons **Salt,** ½ teaspoon	Sift flour, baking powder and salt together.
Butter, ⅓ cup **Sugar,** 1 cup **Vanilla,** 1 teaspoon **Egg,** 1 **Milk,** ⅔ cup	In a large mixing bowl, cream room-temperature butter and sugar together until fluffy; beat in vanilla and egg. Add flour mixture alternately with milk, beating smooth after each addition. Pour batter into 2 greased 8-inch layer pans, or one 9″ × 13″ pan.
Oven, moderate, 350°	Bake 30–35 minutes. Cool and frost with your favorite frosting.

This recipe will also make 14 cup cakes

CINNAMON COFFEE CAKE

Follow recipe for One Egg Cake. Sprinkle each pan of batter with sugar and cinnamon, combining 1 cup sugar with 2 tablespoons cinnamon. Serve the single layers as a breakfast cake.

Creaming shortening and sugar

Angel food cake decorated with chocolate bits

TWO EGG CAKE WITH CHOCOLATE SEVEN MINUTE FROSTING

Cake Flour, sifted, 2 cups **Baking Powder,** 2½ teaspoons **Salt,** ½ teaspoon	Sift flour, baking powder and salt together.
Butter, ½ cup **Sugar,** 1 cup **Vanilla,** 1 teaspoon **Eggs,** 2 **Milk,** ⅔ cup	In a large mixing bowl, cream room-temperature butter and sugar together until fluffy; add vanilla and beat in eggs, one at a time. Add flour mixture alternately with milk, beating smooth after each addition. Pour batter into 2 greased 8- or 9-inch layer pans.
Oven, moderate, 350° **Chocolate Seven Minute Frosting** (page 203)	Bake about 30–35 minutes. Cool cake and frost.

This recipe will also make 20 cup cakes

COCONUT FROSTED ORANGE CAKE

Follow recipe for Two Egg Cake, but substitute ⅔ cup orange juice for milk and 1 tablespoon grated orange rind for vanilla. Frost cake with Coconut Frosting (see page 203).

CARAMEL CAKE

Sugar, ½ cup **Boiling Water,** 1 cup	Melt sugar in heavy pan over low heat, stirring until liquid becomes golden brown. Remove from heat and gradually stir in boiling water; then simmer until caramel is dissolved; cool.
Cake Flour, sifted, 3 cups **Baking Powder,** 4 teasps. **Salt,** ¾ teaspoon	Sift together flour, baking powder and salt.
Butter, ¾ cup **Sugar,** 1½ cups **Vanilla,** 1 teaspoon **Egg Yolks,** 2	In large mixing bowl, cream room-temperature butter until soft and smooth; gradually add sugar, beating until fluffy. Beat in vanilla and well-beaten egg yolks. Add flour mixture alternately with caramel syrup, beating smooth after each addition.
Egg Whites, 2	Fold in egg whites beaten stiff but not dry. Pour into 2 greased 9-inch layer pans.
Oven, moderate, 350° **Caramel Frosting** (page 202)	Bake 25 to 30 minutes. Cool cake and frost.

FROSTED MOCHA CAKE

Unsweetened Chocolate, 2 squares	Melt chocolate and let cool.
Cake Flour, sifted, 3 cups **Baking Powder,** 3 teasps. **Soda,** ¼ teaspoon **Salt,** ¾ teaspoon	Sift dry ingredients together.
Butter, ¾ cup **Sugar,** 1½ cups **Eggs,** 2 **Cold Coffee,** 1 cup	In a large mixing bowl, cream room-temperature butter and sugar until light and fluffy. Add eggs, one at a time, beating thoroughly after each addition. Add cooled chocolate. Add sifted dry ingredients alternating with coffee, beating until smooth. Pour batter into 3 greased 9-inch layer pans.
Oven, moderate, 350° **Coffee Butter Cream Frosting** (page 202)	Bake for about 35 minutes. Cool cake and frost.

CHOCOLATE FROSTED POLKA DOT CAKE

Cake Flour, sifted, 2¼ cups **Baking Powder,** 3 teasps. **Salt,** 1 teaspoon	Sift dry ingredients together.
Butter, ⅓ cup **Sugar,** ¾ cup **Vanilla,** 1 teaspoon **Eggs,** 2 **Milk,** ⅔ cup **Semi-sweet Chocolate** pieces, 6-ounce pkg.	In a large mixing bowl, cream room-temperature butter and sugar until fluffy. Add vanilla, then eggs, one at a time, beating thoroughly after each addition. Add sifted dry ingredients alternately with milk. Pour half the batter into two 8-inch greased layer pans. Sprinkle with half the chocolate bits. Pour in remaining batter and sprinkle with remaining chocolate bits.
Oven, moderate, 350° **Chocolate Velvet Frosting** (page 202)	Bake about 30 minutes. Cool cake and frost.

THREE EGG CAKE WITH ORANGE FROSTING

Cake Flour, sifted, 2 cups
Baking Powder, 2 teasps.
Salt, ½ teaspoon

Sift flour, baking powder and salt together.

Butter, ⅔ cup
Sugar, 1¼ cups
Vanilla, 1 teaspoon
Egg Yolks, 3
Milk, ½ cup

In a large mixing bowl, cream room-temperature butter and sugar together until fluffy. Beat in vanilla and well-beaten egg yolks. Add flour mixture, alternating with milk, beating until smooth after each addition.

Egg Whites, 3

Beat egg whites stiff; fold into cake batter. Pour batter into 2 greased 9-inch layer pans.

Oven, moderate, 350°
Orange Frosting
 (page 203)

Bake 25–30 minutes. Cool and frost cake. Or fill layers with Orange Filling, if desired.

This recipe will also make 30 cup cakes

RUM AND ORANGE CAKE

Flour, sifted, 1 cup
Baking Powder, 2
 teaspoons

Sift flour and baking powder together 3 times.

Eggs, 3
Sugar, 1 cup
Orange Juice, 3
 tablespoons
Grated Rind of 2
 Oranges

Beat eggs until light; gradually beat in sugar and continue beating until mixture is thick and lemon-colored. (Use electric beater at high speed, if you have one.) Stir in orange juice and rind. Fold dry ingredients into mixture. Pour into buttered and floured 9″ springform pan.

Oven, moderate, 350°
Rum Frosting, (page
 203)

Bake about 30 minutes. Cool in pan. Remove from pan and frost.

WHITE CAKE WITH DREAMY CHOCOLATE FROSTING

Cake Flour, sifted, 2 cups
Baking Powder,
 2½ teaspoons
Salt, ½ teaspoon

Sift flour, baking powder and salt together.

Butter, ½ cup
Sugar, 1⅛ cups
Vanilla, 1 teaspoon
Milk, ⅔ cup,
 beaten
Egg Whites, 3 stiffly
 'beaten

In a large mixing bowl, cream room-temperature butter and sugar until fluffy; add vanilla. Add flour mixture alternately with milk, beating smooth after each addition. Fold in egg whites. Pour batter into 2 greased 8-inch layer pans.

Oven, moderate, 350°
Dreamy Chocolate
 Frosting (page 203)

Bake about 25–30 minutes. Cool cake and frost.

SPICE CAKE WITH BUTTER CREAM FROSTING

All-Purpose Flour,
 sifted, 2½ cups
Baking Powder,
 2½ teaspoons
Salt, ½ teaspoon
Cinnamon, 1 teaspoon
Nutmeg, ¾ teaspoon
Clove, ¼ teaspoon
Raisins, 1 cup

Sift dry ingredients together and then add raisins.

Butter, 1 cup
Sugar, 1½ cups
Eggs, 3
Milk, ½ cup
Fresh Orange Juice,
 ⅓ cup

In a large mixing bowl, cream room-temperature butter and sugar until fluffy. Beat in eggs one at a time. Alternately add ⅓ of flour mixture with milk and orange juice. Repeat until all are used up. Turn into greased 9″ × 5″ loaf pan.

Oven, moderate, 350°
Butter Cream Frosting
 (page 202)

Bake 1 hour and 15 minutes. Cool cake and frost.

Consult the section, How to Bake A Cake, at the beginning of this chapter before you tackle these recipes.

FOUR EGG CAKE WITH CHOCOLATE BUTTER CREAM FROSTING

All-Purpose Flour,
 sifted, 3 cups
Baking Powder,
 3½ teaspoons
Salt, ¾ teaspoon

Sift flour, baking powder, and salt together three times.

Butter, 1 cup
Sugar, 1½ cups
Egg Yolks, 4
Vanilla, 1 teaspoon
Milk, 1 cup

In a large mixing bowl, cream room-temperature butter and sugar together until fluffy. Beat in egg yolks, one at a time; add vanilla. Add flour mixture alternating with milk, beating until smooth after each addition.

Egg Whites, 4

Fold in egg whites beaten until stiff but not dry. Pour batter into greased 10-inch tube pan or 3 greased 9-inch layer pans.

Oven, moderate, 350°
Chocolate Butter Cream
 Frosting (page 202)

Bake tube about 1 hour, layers about 35 minutes. Cool and frost cake, or fill layers with Creamy Chocolate Filling, if desired.

GOLDEN FAVORITE

Butter, 1 cup
Cake Flour, sifted, 5 cups
Sugar, 3 cups
Baking Powder, 6 teaspoons
Salt, 2 teaspoons
Milk, 2 cups
Vanilla, 2 teaspoons
Eggs, 4

Into large mixing bowl put butter and sifted dry ingredients. Add half the milk and vanilla and mix until dry ingredients are moistened. Mix thoroughly by hand or 2 minutes at medium speed in the electric mixer. Add remaining milk and eggs, and repeat beating, scraping bowl thoroughly as you beat. Divide batter into two 13″ x 9″ pans, lined on bottom with wax paper.

Oven, moderate, 375°

Bake about 30 minutes; cool slightly; turn out on racks, peel off paper.

This is a many-purpose large cake, to be used as single layers frosted, or plain with fruit or ice cream; or as a layer cake if you prefer.

STRAWBERRY FAVORITE: Cut cake into squares and top with whipped cream and sugared strawberries. Or use both layers with strawberries and whipped cream between the layers, also.

MARBLE CAKE

Cake Flour, sifted, 2 cups
Salt, ¾ teaspoon
Baking Powder, 2 teasps.

Sift dry ingredients together.

Butter, ½ cup
Sugar, 1¼ cups
Vanilla, 1¼ teasps.
Milk, ½ cup
Egg Whites, 4, stiffly beaten

In a large mixing bowl, cream room-temperature butter and sugar until fluffy. Add vanilla. Add dry ingredients alternately with milk. Fold in egg whites. Divide batter in half.

Unsweetened Chocolate, 2¼ squares
Sugar, ¼ cup
Water, 3 tablespoons

Melt chocolate and add sugar and water and stir until thick; cool. Blend into half the batter. Alternate light and dark layers in greased 9″ x 5″ loaf pan. Run knife through batter several times to marbleize.

Oven, moderate, 350°
Shadow Frosting (page 203)

Bake about 1 hour. Cool and frost cake.

Marble cake with chocolate nut frosting

GOLD CAKE

Cake Flour, sifted, 2 cups
Baking Powder, 2 teasps.
Salt, ¾ teaspoon
Sugar, 1 cup

Sift dry ingredients together.

Butter, ½ cup
Egg Yolks, 5, unbeaten
Vanilla, 1 teaspoon
Milk, ¾ cup

In a large mixing bowl, cream room-temperature butter. Beat in egg yolks one at a time; add vanilla. Add flour mixture alternately with milk, beating as you add; beat 1 minute longer. Pour into greased 9″ x 5″ loaf pan or 2 greased 8-inch round layer pans.

Oven, moderate, 350°

Bake 40 to 60 minutes in loaf pan. Bake about 25 minutes in layer pans.

Sugar Glaze (page 202)

Cool and frost cake.

LORD BALTIMORE CAKE

Follow above recipe for Gold Cake, making two layers; cool. Spread Lord Baltimore Filling (page 204) between layers and cover with remaining Seven Minute Frosting.

*Pound cake baked
a fancy pan*

SILVER CAKE

Cake Flour, sifted, 3 cups
Baking Powder,
   3½ teaspoons
Salt, ¾ teaspoon

Sift flour, baking powder and
salt together.

Butter, ¾ cup
Sugar, 1½ cups
Milk, ½ cup
Water, ½ cup
Egg Whites, 6, stiffly
   beaten

In a large mixing bowl, cream
room-temperature butter and
sugar until very fluffy. Add flour
mixture alternately with milk
and water combined, beating
smooth after each addition.
Fold in stiffly beaten egg whites.
**Turn into 3 greased 9-inch layer
pans, or paper-lined tube pan.**

Oven, moderate, 350°

Bake in layer pans about
35 minutes. Bake in tube pan
about 55 minutes.

LADY BALTIMORE CAKE

Follow above recipe for Silver Cake; cool. Spread Lady
Baltimore Filling (page 204) between the layers and cover
with remaining frosting.

POUND CAKE

Butter, 1 pound
Sugar, 1 lb. (2¼ cups)
Egg Yolks, 10
Cake Flour, sifted,
   1 pound (4½ cups)
Egg Whites, 10,
   stiffly beaten
Mace, ¼ teaspoon

In a large mixing bowl, cream
room-temperature butter and
sugar until very fluffy. Beat egg
yolks until thick and lemon-
colored. Combine with butter
and sugar mixture and beat
hard until light and fluffy. Sift
flour and mace into mixture
alternately with stiffly beaten
egg whites, beating very smooth
after each addition. Turn into
2 buttered 9″ × 5″ loaf pans or
1 10-inch tube pan.

Oven, slow, 325°
Sugar Glaze (page 202)

Bake 1½ to 1¾ hours. Cool and
glaze.

MARBLE POUND CAKE: Melt 2 squares of melted chocolate;
divide batter in half and stir chocolate briefly into one half.
Put by spoonfuls into prepared pans, alternating dark and
light batters. Bake as above.

CHOCOLATE CAKES

There are three types of chocolate cakes: Devil's Food, which contains a considerable amount of soda, causing the cake to have a dark red color and an open grain; Fudge Cake, which contains less soda, is a dark chocolate color, moist and rich in chocolate flavor; and just Chocolate Cake, which is brown in color, with a velvety texture, and has a true chocolate flavor.

DEVIL'S FOOD CAKE

Cake Flour, sifted, 2 cups
Baking Soda, 1 teaspoon
Salt, ½ teaspoon

Sift flour, soda, and salt together.

Butter, ½ cup
Sugar, 1½ cups
Vanilla, 1 teaspoon
Egg Yolks, 3
Unsweetened Chocolate, 2 squares, melted
Sour Milk or **Buttermilk,** 1 cup

In large mixing bowl, cream room-temperature butter and sugar together until very smooth and fluffy; add vanilla and well-beaten egg yolks. Add melted chocolate. Add flour mixture alternately with sour milk or buttermilk.

Egg Whites, 3

Fold in stiffly beaten egg whites. Pour batter into 2 greased 9-inch layer pans.

Oven, moderate, 350°
Seven Minute Frosting (page 203)

Bake approximately 30 minutes. Cool cake and frost.

CHOCOLATE FUDGE CAKE

Cake Flour, sifted, 2 cups
Baking Powder, 1½ teaspoons
Baking Soda, ½ teasp.
Salt, ½ teaspoon

Sift flour, baking powder, soda and salt together.

Butter, ½ cup
Light Brown Sugar, 1¼ cups, packed
Vanilla, 1 teaspoon
Eggs, 2
Unsweetened Chocolate, 3 squares, melted
Milk, 1 cup

In a large mixing bowl cream room-temperature butter and sugar together until very fluffy; add vanilla and beat in thoroughly 1 egg at a time. Beat in melted chocolate. Add flour mixture alternately with milk. Pour into 2 greased 8-inch layer pans.

Oven, moderate, 350°
Chocolate Velvet Frosting (page 202)

Bake 25–30 minutes. Cool cake and frost.

NO-EGG CHOCOLATE CAKE

All-Purpose Flour, sifted, 1⅔ cups
Sugar, 1 cup
Cocoa, ½ cup
Soda, 1 teaspoon
Salt, ½ teaspoon

Sift dry ingredients together.

Buttermilk or **Sour Milk,** 1 cup
Shortening, ½ cup, melted
Vanilla, 1½ teaspoons

Beat in other ingredients and stir until smooth. Pour into greased 9-inch square pan.

Oven, moderate, 350°

Bake 30–40 minutes.

Devil's food cake

MARSHMALLOW FROSTED CHOCOLATE CAKE

Cake Flour, sifted,
 1½ cups
Soda, ¾ teaspoon
Salt, ¼ teaspoon
Cocoa, ⅓ cup

Sift dry ingredients together.

Butter, 6 tablespoons
Sugar, 1 cup
Vanilla, 1 teaspoon
Egg Yolks, 2
Milk, 1 cup

In a large mixing bowl, cream room-temperature butter and sugar until fluffy. Add vanilla, then egg yolks, one at a time, beating thoroughly after each addition. Add sifted dry ingredients alternately with milk, beating until smooth. Pour batter into 2 greased 8-inch layer pans.

Oven, moderate, 350°
Marshmallow Frosting
 (page 203)

Bake about 25 minutes. Cool cake and frost.

PARTY CHOCOLATE CAKE

Cake Flour, sifted,
 2¼ cups
Baking Powder, 3 teasps.
Salt, ½ teaspoon

Sift together flour, baking powder and salt.

Butter, 1 cup
Sugar, 1¾ cups
Vanilla, 1 teaspoon
Egg Yolks, 3
Unsweetened Chocolate,
 3 squares, melted
Milk, ¾ cup

In a large mixing bowl, cream room-temperature butter and sugar together until very fluffy, beat in vanilla and well-beaten egg yolks. Beat in melted chocolate. Add flour mixture alternately with milk.

Egg Whites, 3

Beat egg whites until stiff; fold into cake batter. Pour into 2 9-inch greased layer pans.

Oven, moderate, 350°
Butter Cream Frosting
 (page 202)

Bake about 30 minutes. Cool cake and frost.

CHIFFON CAKES

These extremely light-textured cakes are made with oil instead of butter or other shortening, and are easy to mix.

CHIFFON CAKE WITH SEAFOAM FROSTING

Cake Flour, sifted,
 2¼ cups
Sugar, 1½ cups
Baking Powder, 3 teasps.
Salt, 1 teaspoon
Salad Oil, ½ cup
Egg Yolks, 5, unbeaten
Cold Water, ¾ cup
Vanilla, 2 teaspoons

Sift dry ingredients together into large mixing bowl. Make a well and add, in order, salad oil, egg yolks, water, and vanilla. Beat all together with spoon until smooth.

Egg Whites, 7
Cream of Tartar,
 ½ teaspoon

Combine egg whites and cream of tartar in large mixing bowl. Whip until whites form very stiff peaks. Pour egg yolk mixture gradually over whipped egg whites, gently folding until just blended. Do not stir. Pour into ungreased 10-inch tube pan.

Oven, slow, 325°
Seafoam Frosting
 (page 203)

Bake 55 minutes, then increase heat to 350° for 10 to 15 minutes. Invert pan on funnel until cool. Remove cake from pan and frost.

BANANA CHIFFON: Reduce vanilla to 1 teaspoon; add ½ to ⅔ cup sieved fully ripe bananas (about 2 medium-sized) to the egg yolk mixture.

SPICY CHIFFON: Sift 1 teaspoon cinnamon, ½ teaspoon each nutmeg, allspice and cloves with dry ingredients.

ORANGE CHIFFON: Omit Vanilla. Substitute ½ cup orange juice for ½ cup water, and add 2 tablespoons grated orange rind.

CHOCOLATE CHIFFON CAKE

Water, boiling, ¾ cup
Cocoa, ½ cup

Combine water and cocoa and stir until smooth; cool.

Cake Flour, sifted,
 1¾ cups
Sugar, 1¾ cups
Baking Powder, 3 teasps.
Salt, 1 teaspoon
Salad Oil, ½ cup
Egg Yolks, 5, unbeaten
Cold Water, ¾ cup
Vanilla, 1 teaspoon
Cocoa Mixture

Sift dry ingredients together into large mixing bowl. Make a well and add, in order, salad oil, egg yolks, water and vanilla. Add cooled cocoa mixture. Beat with spoon until smooth.

Egg Whites, 7
Cream of Tartar
 ½ teaspoon

Combine egg whites and cream of tartar in large mixing bowl. Beat until whites form very stiff peaks. Pour egg yolk mixture gradually over beaten egg whites, gently folding until just blended. Do not stir. Pour into ungreased tube pan.

Oven, slow, 325°
White Mountain Frosting (page 203)

Bake 55 minutes, then increase heat to 350° for 10 to 15 minutes. Invert pan on funnel until cool. Remove cake from pan and frost.

SPONGE CAKES

True sponge cakes are made usually without fat and without baking powder; the object is to enclose as much air as possible in the batter. The other ingredients are folded into the stiff egg whites, not beaten. Use ingredients at room temperature.

LEMON SPONGE CAKE

Cake Flour, sifted, 1 cup — Sift flour 3 times.

Egg Yolks, 5
Lemon Rind, grated, 1 teaspoon
Lemon Juice, 1½ tablespoons

Beat egg yolks until thick and lemon-colored, add lemon rind and juice and continue beating until very thick.

Egg Whites, 5
Cream of Tartar, ½ teaspoon
Salt, ¼ teaspoon
Sugar, 1 cup

In large mixing bowl, using a clean beater, beat egg whites with cream of tartar until frothy; sprinkle salt over top and continue beating until stiff enough to form peaks, but not dry. Gradually beat in sugar, adding about 2 teaspoons at a time. Fold in well-beaten egg yolks; then gradually fold in flour, sifting about ¼ cup at a time over surface. Turn into ungreased 9-inch tube pan.

Oven, slow, 325°

Bake about 1 hour. Invert pan until cake is cold, about 1 hour.

ORANGE SPONGE: Follow recipe for Lemon Sponge Cake and substitute 1½ tablespoons orange juice for lemon juice; and 1 teaspoon grated orange rind for lemon rind. Cool and frost with Orange Blossom Frosting (page 202).

CHOCOLATE SPONGE: Make Orange Sponge but substitute 4 tablespoons cocoa for 4 tablespoons flour. Sift flour and cocoa together several times. Cool and frost with Cocoa Butter Cream Frosting (page 202).

HOT WATER SPONGE CAKE

Cake Flour, sifted, 1 cup
Baking Powder, 1½ teaspoons
Dash of Salt

Sift dry ingredients together.

Egg Yolks, 2
Sugar, 1 cup
Hot Water, 6 tablesps.
Vanilla, 1 teaspoon

Beat egg yolks until thick and lemon-colored. Gradually beat in sugar, hot water and vanilla. Beat in flour mixture. Beat batter until smooth.

Egg Whites, 2

Beat egg white until stiff but not dry. Fold into rest of batter; pour into 2 lightly buttered and floured 8-inch layer pans.

Oven, moderate, 350°

Bake about 20 to 25 minutes.

ROBERT E. LEE CAKE: Put Sponge Cake layers together with Lemon Filling. Cover top and sides with Seven Minute Frosting. (See Frostings, page 203.)

Sponge cake roll

Gingerbread served with a sweet sauce

PINEAPPLE PUDDING-CAKE

Crushed Pineapple, 1 large can **Coconut,** flaked, 1 can **Nuts,** chopped, ½ cup	In a 9″ × 13″ can pan, empty pineapple and spread evenly; spread coconut over pineapple, and sprinkle nuts over all. Spread cake mix just
Yellow Cake Mix, 1 package **Margarine,** 2 sticks	as it comes from the package and cover it with thin shavings of margarine.
Oven 325°	Bake 45 minutes.

When it comes from the oven it is soft like pudding, but when cold it can be cut and lifted out in portons. Serve cold, with a topping of ice cream if desired.

ANGEL FOOD CAKE

Cake Flour, sifted, 1 cup **Sugar,** ½ cup	Sift flour and sugar together 4 times.
Egg Whites, 12 (1½ cups) **Salt,** ¼ teaspoon **Cream of Tartar,** 1¼ teaspoons **Sugar,** 1 cup **Vanilla,** ½ teaspoon	Beat egg whites and salt with rotary egg beater. When foamy, add cream of tartar and continue beating until eggs are stiff enough to form peaks, but not dry. Add sugar, 2 tablespoons at a time, beating until just blended. Fold in vanilla. Then sift about ¼ cup of flour mixture over top of egg white mixture and fold in lightly. Repeat until all is used. Turn into ungreased 10-inch tube pan.
Oven, moderate, 375° **Shadow Frosting** (page 203)	Bake 30 to 35 minutes. Invert pan 1 hour or until cake is cold. Remove cake and frost.

CHOCOLATE ANGEL: Substitute 4 tablespoons cocoa for 4 tablespoons flour and sift together with flour several times.

YUM YUM CAKE
(no eggs!)

Sugar, 1 cup **Water,** 1 cup **Butter,** 3 tablespoons **Cinnamon,** ¾ teasp. **Salt,** ½ teaspoon **Raisins,** ½ cup	Boil sugar, water, butter, cinnamon, salt and raisins together for about 5 minutes. Cool.
All-Purpose Flour, sifted, 2 cups **Soda,** ½ teaspoon	Add sifted flour and soda to above mixture. Pour into 9″ × 5″ greased loaf pan.
Oven, slow, 325° **Chocolate Glaze** (page 202)	Bake about 50 minutes. Cool cake and frost.

APPLESAUCE CAKE

All-Purpose Flour, sifted, 1¾ cups **Soda,** 1 teaspoon **Salt,** ¼ teaspoon **Cinnamon,** 1 teaspoon **Cloves,** ½ teaspoon	Sift flour, soda, salt and spices together.
Butter, ¼ cup **Sugar,** 1 cup **Egg,** 1 **Applesauce,** 1 cup **Raisins,** ½ cup	In a large mixing bowl, cream room-temperature butter and sugar together until fluffy; add egg. Add flour mixture alternating with applesauce. Add raisins. Pour into greased 9″ × 5″ loaf pan.
Oven, moderate, 350°	Bake 30 to 40 minutes.

GINGERBREAD

All-Purpose Flour, sifted, 2 cups **Baking Soda,** 1 teaspoon **Salt,** ¼ teaspoon **Ginger,** ¾ teaspoon **Cinnamon,** 1 teaspoon **Nutmeg,** ¼ teaspoon	Sift dry ingredients together in a large mixing bowl.
Eggs, 2, beaten **Sugar,** ½ cup **Molasses,** ½ cup **Sour Milk** or **Buttermilk,** 1 cup **Butter,** ½ cup, melted	Combine eggs, sugar, molasses, milk and melted butter. Gradually add to flour mixture. beating thoroughly. Turn into greased 8-inch square pan.
Oven, moderate, 350°	Bake 35 to 45 minutes.

Serve with topping of applesauce or pineapple sauce (page 234), or with whipped cream.

FRUIT CAKE

Fruit Cake should be made several weeks in advance of Christmas, then wrapped in plastic wrap (not in foil) or in waxed paper and stored in a tightly lidded tin box. The easiest way to cut up the candied fruits is with scissors dipped frequenty in water.

DARK FRUIT CAKE

Raisins, seedless, ¾ cup
Currants, ½ cup
Candied Citron, ½ cup, chopped
Candied Orange Peel, ½ cup, chopped
Candied Cherries, ½ cup, chopped

Prepare and combine fruits and sprinkle with ¼ cup of the flour. Stir it well to separate the pieces of fruit.

All-Purpose Flour, 2 cups, sifted
Soda, ½ teaspoon
Cinnamon, 1 teaspoon
Clove, ¼ teaspoon
Allspice, ¼ teaspoon
Mace, ¼ teaspoon

Sift remaining flour and other dry ingredients together. Add prepared fruit.

Shortening, ½ cup
Sugar, 1 cup
Eggs, 4, unbeaten
Milk, ½ cup
Molasses, ½ cup

Cream shortening and beat until fluffy, gradually adding sugar. Add eggs, one at a time, beating after each until very light. Beat in molasses. Add flour mixture alternately with milk, in small quantities, mixing after each until blended. Divide batter between 2 greased 9″ × 5″ loaf pans.

Oven, slow, 300°

Bake 1½ hours, or until cake tester, or toothpick, comes out clean.

Wine or brandy may be substituted for ¼ cup of the milk if desired.

LIGHT FRUIT CAKE

Candied Orange Peel, ½ cup, chopped
Candied Citron, 1 cup, chopped
Candied Cherries, 1 cup, halved
Candied Pineapple, ½ cup, chopped
Almonds, 1 cup, blanched, sliced

Prepare fruits and nuts, and combine. Sprinkle with ¼ cup of flour; stir to separate individual pieces.

All-Purpose Flour, sifted, 2 cups
Baking Powder, 1 teasp.
Salt, ¼ teaspoon

Sift remaining flour with baking powder and salt. Add prepared fruit and nuts.

Shortening, 1 cup
Sugar, 1 cup
Eggs, 4, unbeaten
Lemon Juice, 2 tablesps.

Cream shortening until fluffy, adding sugar a little at a time. Add eggs, one at a time, beating after each one until light and fluffy; add lemon juice. Add flour mixture and blend until mixed. Turn into 2 9″ × 5″ greased loaf pans.

Oven, slow, 300°

Bake 1½ hours, or until cake tester, or toothpick, comes out clean.

Fruit cake with pecans and candied cherries

CHEESE CAKE

Unbaked Pie Crust, 9-inch	Start piecrust browning in 400° oven while you make the filling.
Sugar, 1 cup **Flour,** 2 tablespoons **Cottage Cheese,** 1 pound **Eggs,** 4, slightly beaten **Thin Cream,** 1 cup **Vanilla,** 1 teaspoon	Combine sugar and flour; add the cottage cheese and mix thoroughly. Combine eggs, cream and vanilla and add to cottage cheese mixture. Stir until creamy and well mixed. Pour into lightly browned crust.
Oven, moderate, 325°	Bake about 40 minutes.

CHERRY CHEESE CAKE

Follow recipe above for Cheese Cake, and pour into Graham Cracker Crust (page 182). Chill until cake is firm and top with Cherry Glaze.

Cherry Glaze

Red Sour Pitted Cherries, 19-ounce can	Drain cherries, reserving juice.
Sugar, 1 cup **Cornstarch,** ¼ cup **Salt,** ¼ teaspoon **Cherry Juice** **Water,** ½ cup	In saucepan mix ½ cup sugar, cornstarch and salt. Add cherry juice and water. Cook until very thick and clear, stirring constantly. Add ½ cup sugar and cherries. Stir until thoroughly mixed; cool. A little red food coloring may be added if desired. If mixture is too stiff, add 1 or 2 tablespoons water.

PINEAPPLE CHEESE CAKE

Follow recipe for Cherry Cheese Cake omitting Cherry Glaze. Instead, spread layer of drained, crushed pineapple on top of crumb layer and pour cheese mixture over it.

ITALIAN STYLE CHEESE CAKE

Sponge Layers	Line bottom and sides of a casserole with ½-inch thick slices of cake. Fill center with a filling made as follows:
Ricotta or **Creamy Cottage Cheese,** 1 lb. **Sugar,** 2 cups **Vanilla,** 1 teaspoon **Crème de Cacao,** 3 tablespoons **Semi-sweet Chocolate Pieces,** crushed, 2 tablespoons **Candied Cherries,** 2 tablespoons, finely chopped	Combine ricotta or cottage cheese with sugar, vanilla and crème de cacao in large bowl; beat until smooth and fluffy, using a mixer if you have one. Stir in chocolate and cherries. Pour into casserole, top with more cake; let stand in refrigerator overnight. Turn out on chilled serving dish. Sprinkle with confectioners' sugar.

To serve 4 to 6

CREAMY CHEESE CAKE
(no baking!)

Unflavored Gelatin, 1 envelope **Sugar,** ½ cup **Salt,** ⅛ teaspoon **Egg Yolk,** 1 **Milk,** ½ cup **Lemon Rind,** grated ½ teaspoon **Creamed Cottage Cheese,** 1½ cups, sieved **Lemon Juice,** ½ tablesp. **Vanilla,** ½ teaspoon	Mix gelatin, sugar, salt in top of double boiler. Beat egg yolk and milk together and add to gelatin mix. Cook over boiling water, stirring constantly until gelatin is fully dissolved, about 8 minutes. Remove from heat and add lemon rind. Stir in cottage cheese, lemon juice and vanilla. Chill, stirring occasionally until mixture mounds slightly when dropped from a spoon.
Egg White, 1, stiffly beaten **Heavy Cream,** ½ cup	When gelatin mix is thoroughly chilled fold in egg white and cream. Turn into 8-inch layer pan, top with crumb topping and chill until firm.

To serve 5 to 6

Crumb Topping

Butter, 2 tablespoons, melted **Sugar,** 1 tablespoon **Graham Cracker Crumbs,** ½ cup **Nutmeg,** ¼ teaspoon	Combine all ingredients and spread on top of cheese cake.

CRULLERS

All-Purpose Flour, sifted, 3½ cups **Baking Powder,** 4 teasps. **Salt,** 1 teaspoon **Cinnamon,** ½ teaspoon **Nutmeg,** ¼ teaspoon	Sift together flour, baking powder, salt and spices.
Butter, ¼ cup **Sugar,** 1 cup **Eggs,** 2, well-beaten **Milk,** 1 cup	Cream butter and sugar together; add eggs and beat until light and fluffy. Add flour mixture alternately with milk, combining lightly. Add a little more sifted flour if needed to make a soft dough. Turn dough on floured board; roll ¼-inch thick and cut with floured doughnut cutter.
Deep, hot fat, 360°–370°	Fry 2 to 3 minutes or until lightly browned, turning during cooking. Drain on paper towels.

Crullers may be dusted with confectioners' sugar or a mixture of sugar and cinnamon, or glazed (page 202).

CHOCOLATE CRULLERS: Omit spices, increase sugar to 1¼ cups, add 1½ squares melted unsweetened chocolate and ½ teaspoon vanilla to egg mix.

*Crullers
lightly dusted
with sugar*

JELLY ROLL

Cake Flour, sifted, ¾ cup **Baking Powder,** ½ teaspoon **Salt,** ¼ teaspoon	Sift flour, baking powder and salt together.
Eggs, 5, separated **Sugar,** ¾ cup **Vanilla,** ½ teaspoon	Beat egg yolks until thick and lemon-colored. Gradually add sugar, beating until light and fluffy. Stir in vanilla. Fold in egg whites beaten stiff but not dry. Gently fold in flour mixture. Pour evenly into 15″ x 10″ pan, greased, lined with waxed paper, and greased again.
Oven, moderate, 350° **Jam** or **Jelly** **Powdered sugar**	Bake 15 minutes. Turn out on clean towel dusted with powdered sugar. Carefully remove waxed paper and trim off crisp edges. Roll cake by gently lifting and pushing with the towel. Wrap towel around roll; cool on rack. Unroll cake, spread with jam or jelly, re-roll. Dust with powdered sugar, or garnish with whipped cream. Slice to serve.

To make about 8 slices.

ORANGE BLOSSOM ROLL: Spread roll with Orange Filling, page 204, and frost with Orange Blossom Frosting, page 203.

HOW TO DRESS UP A PLAIN CAKE MIX

Keep on hand a few packages of the excellent cake mixes now available for those times when you want a dressy dessert in a hurry. Make cake according to directions on package and use in one of the following ways:

JELLY CAKE: Spread layers with warm jelly and top with ready-whipped cream.

EASY BOSTON CREAM CAKE: Mix up a package of pudding mix, chill well and spread between layers. Top cake with powdered sugar or chocolate frosting (see page 203).

ITALIAN RUM: Use layers singly and spread with rum frosting (see page 203). Cut into portions and top each portion with a maraschino cherry.

STRAWBERRY "SHORTCAKE": Mash fresh sugared strawberries and spread between layers. Top with whipped cream and decorate with whole berries.

BANANA CREAM CAKE: Combine sliced bananas with whipped cream and spread between layers. Top with confectioners' sugar.

RUM BOSTON CREAM PIE

Yellow Cake Mix or **Store Sponge Cake**	Make cake according to directions on package in two layers, and let cool.
Soft Custard or **Instant Pudding Mix,** Vanilla **Rum,** 2 tablespoons **Chocolate Frosting** (page 203)	To make filling prepare a soft custard or package of pudding mix. Substitute 2 tablespoons of rum for 2 tablespoons of the milk. Chill. Split cake layers and spread filling between halves. Cover with chocolate frosting.

FROSTINGS

Frostings may be cooked or uncooked, depending on your taste. The uncooked variety is probably easier, and in fact, all the work can be done in the mixer. A cooked frosting must be of the right consistency to spread and hold its shape. Do not try to use one that is too thin. Test a little on the cake and if too thin, cook a little longer over hot water. If the frosting thickens too quickly, have boiling water at hand and add a teaspoon at a time until it is the right consistency.

SUGAR GLAZE

Confectioners' Sugar, sifted, 1 cup
Water, ¼ cup
Vanilla, ¼ teaspoon

Mix together until smooth. Tint with food coloring if desired. Makes thin frosting for Breakfast Cake, Cookies, etc. May be tinted any desired color with food coloring.

CHOCOLATE GLAZE

Butter, 2 tablespoons
Unsweetened Chocolate, 2 squares
Confectioners' Sugar, sifted, 1 cup
Boiling Water, 2 tablesps.

Melt butter and chocolate over boiling water. Remove from heat. Beat in sugar and water until smooth. A thin frosting for Doughnuts, Boston Cream Cake, etc.

CHOCOLATE VELVET FROSTING

Butter, ½ cup
Confectioners' Sugar, sifted, 3 cups
Unsweetened Chocolate, 2 squares, melted
Vanilla, ½ teaspoon
Milk, about 3 tablesps.

In a large mixing bowl, cream room-temperature butter and 1½ cups sugar until creamy. Add melted chocolate and beat until smooth. Add vanilla. Add remaining sugar alternately with milk, beating smooth after each addition.

Will frost one 8-inch layer cake

DREAMY CHOCOLATE FROSTING

Unsweetened Chocolate, 4 squares
Brown Sugar, ¾ cup
Butter, ¼ cup
Water, ⅓ cup
Salt, ¼ teaspoon

Combine chocolate, brown sugar, butter, water and salt in saucepan. Stir over medium heat until chocolate and butter are melted; then simmer 2 to 3 minutes longer until all are blended and slightly thick. Stir occasionally. Cool 5 minutes.

Confectioners' Sugar, sifted, 2 cups
Egg Yolks, 2, unbeaten
Vanilla, ¾ teaspoon

Add sugar gradually, beating well after each addition. Add egg yolks and vanilla; beat until smooth.

Will frost one 8-inch layer cake

CHOCOLATE MINT FROSTING

Add a few drops of peppermint extract to any one of the chocolate frosting recipes.

BUTTER CREAM FROSTING

Sugar, 1 cup
Cream of Tartar, ¼ teaspoon
Salt, ⅛ teaspoon
Milk, ⅓ cup

Combine in saucepan and cook to 240° on candy thermometer, or until a little of the mixture when dropped in cold water will form a soft ball that holds its shape.

Egg Whites, 3
Vanilla, 1 teaspoon

Beat egg whites until stiff but not dry. Add syrup very slowly to egg whites, beating constantly with beater. Add vanilla. Let get completely cold.

Butter, 1 cup

Cream butter well. Then add egg-white mixture 2 or 3 tablespoons at a time, beating well after each addition.

Will frost one 3-layer cake

Food colorings may be used to tint Butter Cream Frosting any desired shade.

COCOA BUTTER CREAM FROSTING: Reduce vanilla to ½ teaspoon and add 2 tablespoons cocoa along with sugar, salt and cream of tartar.

COFFEE BUTTER CREAM FROSTING: Substitute 2 teaspoons instant coffee for vanilla.

BOILED FROSTING

Sugar, 1½ cups
Water, ½ cup
Light Corn Syrup, 1 tablespoon
Egg Whites, 2, beaten
Cream of Tartar, ¼ teaspoon
Salt, dash
Vanilla, 1 teaspoon

Put sugar, water and corn syrup in saucepan and stir over low heat until sugar is dissolved; boil, covered, about 3 minutes, then boil uncovered without stirring until it reaches the soft ball stage (see page 236). Remove from heat and pour in fine stream over egg whites beaten stiff with cream of tartar, beating as you pour. Add salt and vanilla and continue beating until cool and of proper consistency to spread.

Will frost tops and sides of 2 layers, or 2 dozen cup cakes

WHITE MOUNTAIN FROSTING: Frost cake with Boiled Frosting, then lightly touch spatula to frosting and lift off. This pulls frosting up to form peaks.

BUTTER FROSTING

Butter, ½ cup
Confectioners' Sugar,
  sifted, 3 cups
Vanilla, 1 teaspoon
Cream, 3 tablespoons

In a large mixing bowl, cream room-temperature butter and 1 cup sugar until creamy. Add vanilla. Add remaining sugar alternately with cream, beating smooth after each addition.

Will frost one 8-inch layer cake or two dozen cup cakes

MOCHA FROSTING: Add 1 teaspoon instant coffee and 1½ tablespoons cocoa.

ORANGE BLOSSOM FROSTING: Flavor with ¼ teaspoon orange extract and 2 teaspoons grated orange rind.

Food colorings may be used to tint the base frosting any desired shade.

BUTTER-EGG FROSTING

Butter, ¼ cup
Egg Yolk, 1 large
Vanilla, 1½ teaspoons
Confectioners' Sugar,
  sifted, 3 cups
Cream, 3 tablespoons

Beat room-temperature butter and egg yolk together until blended. Add vanilla. Alternately stir in sugar and cream, beating until smooth after each addition.

Will frost one 8-inch layer cake

Food colorings may be used to tint the base frosting any desired shade.

The variations under Butter Frosting may also be used with Butter-Egg Frosting.

CREAM CHEESE FROSTING

Cream Cheese,
  8-ounce package
Confectioners' Sugar
  sifted, ¼ cup
Milk, ¼ cup
Vanilla, ½ teaspoon

Use cheese at room-temperature. Soften and blend with sugar. Add milk and vanilla. Beat until smooth.

Will frost one 8-inch layer cake

ORANGE FROSTING: Substitute ¼ cup orange juice for milk. Add 1 tablespoon grated orange rind.

RUM FROSTING: Omit vanilla and substitute 1 tablespoon rum for the milk.

CARAMEL FROSTING

Light Brown Sugar,
  2 cups
Light Cream, 1 cup
Salt, ⅛ teaspoon
Butter, ⅓ cup

Cook sugar, cream and salt, stirring until sugar is dissolved, to 234° (till mixture forms a very soft ball in cold water). Remove from heat, add butter and cool without stirring until bottom of saucepan feels lukewarm.

Vanilla, 1 teaspoon

Add vanilla and beat until frosting is creamy and barely holds it shape. Spread quickly on cake before frosting hardens.

Will frost one 8-inch layer cake

SEVEN MINUTE FROSTING

Egg Whites, 2
Sugar, 1½ cups
Dash of Salt
Water, ⅓ cup
Light Corn Syrup,
  1 tablespoon
Vanilla, 1 teaspoon

Beat together egg whites, sugar, salt, water and corn syrup in top part of double boiler; place over boiling water and continue beating with rotary beater about 7 minutes, or until frosting thickens and holds its shape when dropped from beater. Remove from boiling water, add vanilla and continue beating until stiff enough to spread.

Will frost one 8- or 9-inch layer cake or 24 cup cakes

MARSHMALLOW FROSTING: Beat ½ cup marshmallow whip into frosting before spreading on cake.

COCONUT FROSTING: Sprinkle Seven Minute Frosting with 1½ cups shredded coconut while frosting is soft.

ORANGE SEVEN MINUTE FROSTING: Substitute 3 tablespoons orange juice for 3 tablespoons water. Flavor with 1 teaspoon grated orange rind.

SEA FOAM FROSTING: Substitute 2 cups brown sugar for granulated sugar and omit corn syrup.

CHOCOLATE SEVEN MINUTE FROSTING: Melt 3 squares unsweetened chocolate and gently fold into frosting just before spreading on cake.

GINGER SEVEN MINUTE FROSTING: Add ¼ cup chopped candied ginger just before spreading on cake.

SHADOW FROSTING: Frost cake with Seven Minute Frosting. Melt 2 squares of unsweetened chocolate with 2 teaspoons butter. With spoon, drip chocolate mixture along top edges of cake to let it run down sides at intervals.

Food colorings may be used to tint Seven Minute Frosting any desired shade.

Applying marshmallow frosting

CAKE FILLINGS

Use these luscious fillings between the layers of your cakes with frosting on the outside, if you want to please the sweet-tooth members of the family.

CREAMY CHOCOLATE FILLING

Unsweetened Chocolate, 2 squares
Milk, 1¾ cups

Combine chocolate and milk and heat until chocolate is melted. Beat with rotary beater.

Sugar, 1 cup
Salt, ¼ teaspoon
Flour, ½ cup
Egg Yolks, 4
Vanilla, ½ teaspoon

Combine dry ingredients, add egg yolks slightly beaten. Add a little of the hot mixture and combine well, return to saucepan and cook. Stir constantly until thick. Add vanilla.

Ample quantity to spread between layers of large 3-layer cake

LORD BALTIMORE FILLING

Follow recipe for Seven Minute Frosting (page 203). Combine half of it with ¼ cup each of chopped blanched almonds, pecans, candied cherries and macaroon crumbs. Flavor with 2 teaspoons lemon juice and 1 tablespoon sherry. Use as filling between layers and frost cake with remaining frosting.

LADY BALTIMORE FILLING

Follow recipe for Seven Minute Frosting (page 203). Combine half of it with ½ cup each of finely chopped pecans and seeded raisins. Add 4 figs cut in strips and ½ teaspoon almond extract. Use as filling between layers and frost cake with remaining Seven Minute Frosting.

ORANGE FILLING

Sugar, ½ cup
Cornstarch, 2½ tablesps.
Dash of Salt
Egg Yolk, 1, slightly beaten
Orange Juice, ½ cup
Lemon Juice, 1 tablesp.
Water, ½ cup
Orange Rind, grated, 1 teaspoon
Butter, 1 tablespoon

Combine sugar and cornstarch; add salt and egg yolk. Add orange juice, lemon juice and water. Cook over direct heat until mixture starts to bubble, stirring constantly. Then cook over hot water 10 minutes longer, stirring occasionally. Add orange rind and butter. Cool.

To spread between layers of 2-layer cake

LEMON FILLING

Sugar, ¾ cup
Cornstarch, 2 tablesps.
Dash of Salt
Egg Yolk, 1, slightly beaten
Water, ¾ cup
Lemon Juice, 3 tablesps.
Grated Lemon Rind, 1 teaspoon
Butter, 1 tablespoon
Heavy Cream, ½ cup, whipped (optional)

Combine sugar, cornstarch and salt in top of double boiler; stir in egg yolk, water and lemon juice and cook over boiling water 5 minutes, stirring constantly; cook 10 minutes longer, or until mixture is thick, stirring occasionally. Remove from hot water and add grated lemon rind and butter; cool. If desired whipped cream may be folded in.

To spread between layers of 2-layer cake

LUSCIOUS LEMON-ORANGE FILLING

Cake Flour, sifted, ½ cup
Sugar, 1 cup
Salt, ¼ teaspoon
Orange Juice, 1½ cups
Lemon Juice, ¼ cup
Grated Orange and Lemon Rind, 3 tablesps.
Egg Yolks, 4

Combine dry ingredients in saucepan. Stir in orange juice, lemon juice, and grated rind. Cook, stirring, until mixture is clear and thickened. Beat egg yolks slightly, add a little of the hot mixture to them, stirring constantly and return all to the saucepan. Continue cooking until very thick. Cool.

Ample quantity to spread between layers of large 3-layer cake

Lady Baltimore cake

COOKIES

There are probably as many cooky recipes as there are cooks, so there is no need for monotony. Cookies are traditional treats at Christmas, in nearly every land, and many of these are included here.

Cooky doughs are often moist enough to drop from a spoon; stiffer doughs must be rolled to the desired thinness, or chilled and sliced. Chilling cuts down on the amount of flour otherwise needed: a tenderer cooky is the result.

Unbaked cookies may be frozen. Put drop or shaped cookies on baking sheet, freeze; then pack them in foil-lined box with foil between layers. Wrap the box. Bake when ready to use. Refrigerator cookies may be frozen efficiently in a roll.

TAKE CARE!

Do not make substitutions in ingredients. Do not use cake flour when all-purpose flour is called for. Do not use self-rising flour!

Always sift confectioners' sugar before using. Always pack brown sugar in the cup.

If your oven control is a little fast, the cookies will bake in a shorter time than indicated in the recipe, so keep your eye on them. Make sure they are not browning too much. If some brown before others, remove them from the pan to a cooling rack.

For best results, bake only one cooky sheet at a time in the the center of the oven.

COOKY-MAKING HELPS

COOKY SHEET: A large one, just a couple of inches smaller in size than your oven shelf. It's nice to have at least 2, so that one can be loaded while the other bakes.

WIRE COOLING RACKS: Place cookies individually on racks, not overlapping.

WIDE, THIN SPATULA: For lifting cookies from pan.

DECORATIONS: Look for the colored sugars and glitter sold in small bottles for decorating cookies.

STORING COOKIES

Don't store cookies, eat them up! They are better fresh. Soft cookies can be kept in the cooky jar as a rule. But in a very dry climate, moist or dry cookies will dry out and should be kept airtight. And in a moist climate, or in humid summer weather, crisp cookies won't stay crisp and should be kept in a tin with a tight-fitting lid. Keep all cookies in a cool place, and don't mix crisp ones with soft.

Remember in shipping cookies, that they will not last in good condition any longer than they would have at home. Do not try to mail perishable ones, or very delicate ones that will break from the jolting and vibration of travel.

DROP SUGAR COOKIES

Butter, ½ cup	Cream butter and add sugar
Sugar, 1 cup	gradually; beat until fluffy. Add
Egg, 1	remaining ingredients, beating
Cream, 1 tablespoon	well after each addition.
Vanilla, ½ teaspoon	
All-Purpose Flour, sifted, 1½ cups	Sift dry ingredients together and add to butter mixture. Mix well.
Salt, ¼ teaspoon	Arrange by teaspoonfuls on
Baking Powder, 1 teasp.	greased cooky sheet, 1-inch apart.
Oven, moderate, 375°	Bake about 8 minutes.

To make about 5 dozen

VANILLA DROPS

All-Purpose Flour, sifted, 2 cups	Sift dry ingredients together.
Baking Powder, 2 teasps.	
Salt, ½ teaspoon	
Butter, 1 cup	Cream butter, gradually adding
Sugar, 1 cup	sugar; beat until fluffy. Beat in
Vanilla, 1 teaspoon	vanilla and egg. Add flour
Egg, 1	mixture alternately with milk,
Milk, ½ cup	stirring well after each addition Drop from teaspoon on ungreased baking sheet.
Oven, moderate, 375°	Bake 8 to 10 minutes.

To make about 50 cookies

CHINESE ALMOND CAKES

To recipe for Drop Sugar Cookies add ½ cup ground unblanched almonds and 1 teaspoon almond extract. Omit egg. Drop in balls on ungreased cookie sheet and press out ⅛ inch thick. Place whole almond in center of each. Bake in 350° oven 12 to 15 minutes.

The blender may be used for grinding the nuts a few at a time.

Dropped cookies

Rolled cookies

Pressed cookies

Refrigerator cookies

BUTTERSCOTCH CRISPS

All-Purpose Flour,
sifted, ¾ cup
Baking Powder, 1 teasp.
Salt, ½ teaspoon

Sift dry ingredients together.

Butter, ½ cup
Brown Sugar, 1 cup,
packed
Vanilla, 1 teaspoon
Egg, 1
Nuts, ½ cup, finely
chopped

Cream butter and add sugar,
vanilla and egg. Beat until light.
Add sifted dry ingredients and
nuts. Drop by scant teaspoonfuls onto ungreased cooky
sheets.

Oven, hot, 400°

To make 8 dozen

Bake about 5 minutes. Remove
at once with spatula to cooling
rack.

OATMEAL COOKIES

Quick-cooking Oatmeal,
2¼ cups
Brown Sugar, 2¼ cups,
packed
Flour, 3 tablespoons
Salt, 1 teaspoon
Cinnamon, 1 teaspoon
Butter, 1 cup, melted
Egg, 1, slightly beaten
Vanilla, 1 teaspoon

Mix together oatmeal, sugar,
flour, salt and cinnamon. Stir in
melted butter and add egg and
vanilla. Stir until thoroughly
mixed. Drop by teaspoonfuls
2 inches apart on greased cooky
sheet.

Oven, moderate, 375°

To make about 5 dozen

Bake about 7 minutes.

RAISIN OATMEAL COOKIES: Sprinkle the 3 tablespoons of flour
over 1 cup seeded raisins and stir to separate raisins; then
add to oatmeal mixture.

PEANUT BUTTER GEMS

Peanut Butter, 1 cup
Lemon Juice, 1 teasp.
Salt, ¼ teaspoon
**Sweetened Condensed
Milk,** 1 can
Raisins, chopped, 1 cup

Mix peanut butter, lemon juice
and salt together. Gradually add
milk and raisins. Drop from
teaspoon onto greased cooky
sheet.

Oven, moderate, 375°

To make about 3 dozen cookies

Bake about 10 minutes.

BROWN-EDGED WAFERS

Soft Butter, 1 cup
Sugar, ⅔ cup
Vanilla, 1 teaspoon
Eggs, 2
Flour, sifted, 1½ cups
Salt, ¼ teaspoon

Cream butter and add sugar,
vanilla and eggs. Beat until
light and fluffy. Add flour and
salt; mix well. Drop by half-
teaspoonfuls onto greased
cooky sheet.

Oven, moderate, 350°

To make about 3 dozen

Bake about 10 minutes, or just
until the edges brown. Do not
overcook.

ROLLED SUGAR COOKIES

Follow recipe for Drop Sugar Cookies but add an additional
½ cup of flour; mix and chill 3 hours. Roll out ⅛ inch thick
on floured board and cut in desired shapes. These will bake
in less time than Drop Sugar Cookies.

DECORATED CHRISTMAS COOKIES

Make recipe for Rolled Sugar Cookies, cut out dough in
shapes of Christmas trees, stars, or as desired. Bake and cool.
Decorate with colored sugars or glazes (page 202).

CHOCOLATE COOKIES

Follow recipe for Drop or Rolled Sugar Cookies, but substitute ⅓ cup cocoa for ⅓ cup flour.

NUT COOKIES

Follow recipe for Drop or Rolled Sugar Cookies and add
½ cup chopped nuts.

SAND TARTS

Follow recipe for Rolled Sugar Cookies; cut out with round
cooky cutter. Brush with egg white and sprinkle with ¼ cup
sugar mixed with 2 teaspoons cinnamon.

SPICE COOKIES

Follow recipe for Rolled Sugar Cookies and add 1 teaspoon
cinnamon, ¼ teaspoon ginger and ¼ teaspoon cloves.

COCONUT COOKIES

Follow recipe for Rolled Sugar Cookies and add ½ cup
shredded coconut to mixture.

ORANGE THINS

Soft Butter, 1 cup
Sugar, 1¼ cups
Orange Rind, grated, 1
Egg, 1
All-Purpose Flour,
sifted, 4 cups
Salt, ¾ teaspoon
Almonds, ½ cup,
ground fine
Orange Juice, ¼ cup

Cream butter, add sugar, orange
rind and egg and beat until
light. Add remaining ingredients
and mix well. Roll very thin, and
cut with floured cooky cutters.
Place on ungreased cooky sheets.

Oven, hot, 425°

To make 10 dozen

Bake 6 to 8 minutes.

LEMON BUTTER COOKIES

Butter, 1 cup
Brown Sugar, 1 cup
Eggs, 2, well-beaten
Lemon Rind, grated, 1
Lemon Juice, ½ lemon
All-Purpose Flour,
sifted, 2 cups

Cream butter, gradually adding
sugar. Add eggs, lemon rind and
juice. Mix well. Add sifted flour
and blend well. Chill. Roll thin
and cut out. Place on ungreased
cooky sheet.

Oven, moderate, 350°

To make about 5 dozen

Bake about 10 minutes.

CHOCOLATE STARS

Butter, ⅔ cup
Sugar, 1 cup
Nuts, 1 cup, finely
   ground
Vanilla, 1 teaspoon
All-Purpose Flour,
   sifted, 1½ cups
Salt, ½ teaspoon
Semi-sweet Chocolate
   pieces, 2 6-ounce pkgs.

Cream butter and add sugar and beat until light. Add nuts, vanilla, flour and salt. (Mixture will be dry.) Roll to ⅛ inch thickness between two sheets of waxed paper. Cut with floured, star-shaped cooky cutter. Place on ungreased cooky sheets.

Oven, hot, 400°

To make about 5 dozen

Bake about 8 minutes. Cool. Melt chocolate over hot water, and spread on tops of cookies.

BRANDY WAFERS

Cake Flour, sifted,
   1¼ cups
Salt, ¼ teaspoon
Sugar, ⅔ cup
Ginger, 1 tablespoon

Sift dry ingredients together.

Molasses, ½ cup
Butter, ½ cup
Brandy, 3 tablespoons

Heat molasses to boiling and add butter. Remove from heat and add sifted dry ingredients, stirring constantly. Stir in brandy. Drop by half teaspoonfuls 3 inches apart on greased cooky sheet. Bake 6 cookies at a time.

Oven, slow, 300°

To make about 5 dozen

Bake for 8 to 10 minutes. Cool for 1 minute. Remove and roll at once around handle of wooden spoon. If removed too soon, wafers will break; if not soon enough, they will not roll.

MOLASSES COOKIES

All-Purpose Flour,
   sifted, 1⅛ cups
Soda, ⅛ teaspoon
Salt, ½ teaspoon

Sift dry ingredients together.

Molasses, ⅓ cup
Shortening, 3 tablesps.

Heat molasses to boiling point and pour over shortening. Add sifted dry ingredients. Mix dough until well blended and chill 1 hour or more. Turn out on floured board and roll ⅛ inch thick. Cut out and arrange on greased cooky sheet.

Oven, moderate, 350°
To make 50 cookies

Bake 8 or 10 minutes, or until crisp.

GINGERSNAPS: Follow recipe for Molasses Cookies and add 1 teaspoon ginger.

FILBERT BUTTER FINGERS

Soft Butter, ⅔ cup
Confectioners' Sugar,
   sifted, 6 tablespoons
Vanilla, 1 teaspoon
All-Purpose Flour,
   sifted, 2 cups
Salt, ¼ teaspoon
Almond Extract,
   ½ teaspoon
Filberts, 1 cup, chopped

Cream butter and add remaining ingredients; mix well. Press into 2 inch long finger-shaped pieces. Place on ungreased cooky sheet.

Oven, moderate, 325°

To make about 3½ dozen

Bake 15 to 20 minutes, or until lightly browned. While warm roll in fine granulated sugar.

Other chopped nuts may be used in place of filberts.

*Molasses cookies
in a variety of shapes*

Scotch shortbread

ALMOND BUTTER STRIPS

Butter, ¾ cup
Sugar, ¼ cup
Almond Extract,
   ½ teaspoon
All-Purpose Flour,
   sifted, 2 cups
Salt, ⅛ teaspoon

Cream butter and add sugar and flavoring; beat until light. Add flour and salt. Chill for several hours, until firm enough to roll. Roll to ⅛ inch thickness and cut in 1″ × 3″ strips. Put on ungreased cooky sheets.

Egg White, 1,
   slightly beaten
Sugar, 2 tablespoons
Cinnamon, ⅛ teaspoon
Blanched Almonds,
   ⅓ cup, finely chopped

Brush cookies with slightly beaten egg white. Combine sugar, cinnamon and almonds and sprinkle on tops of cookies.

Oven, moderate, 350°

Bake about 8 minutes.

To make about 6 dozen

PFEFFERNÜSSE

All-Purpose Flour,
   sifted, 3 cups
Brown Sugar, ⅔ cup
Pepper, ¼ teaspoon
Salt, ¾ teaspoon
Cloves, 1 teaspoon
Ginger, 1 teaspoon
Egg, 1
Soft Butter, ½ cup
Confectioners' Sugar

Combine ingredients, except confectioners' sugar, in large mixing bowl in order given and knead until dough no longer clings to hands. Pat dough out flat on lightly floured board and cut into small bars. Place on greased cooky sheets.

Oven, moderate, 325°

Bake about 15 minutes. Cool; roll in confectioners' sugar.

To make 5 to 6 dozen

SCOTCH SHORTBREADS

All-Purpose Flour,
   sifted, 2½ cups
Salt, ¼ teaspoon
Confectioners' Sugar,
   ½ cup
Butter, 1 cup

Sift dry ingredients together. Break butter in small pieces and work into dry ingredients until mixture is smooth and blended. Halve dough and roll each half to form a 6 inch round, ½ inch thick. Place on ungreased cooky sheet. With tines of fork, outline 6 wedges in each round. Prick wedges with fork.

Oven, slow, 275°

Bake about 45 minutes. Remove to wire rack and cool; break apart.

To make 1 dozen

FRIED TWISTS

Egg Yolks, 4
Heavy Cream, ¼ cup
Sugar, ⅓ cup
All-Purpose Flour,
   sifted, 1⅔ cups
Salt, ¼ teaspoon
Cinnamon, ¼ teaspoon
Confectioners' Sugar,
   sifted

Beat egg yolks until light. Add cream and sugar and beat well. Add flour, salt and cinnamon; mix well. Roll small amount of dough at a time to slightly less than ⅛ inch thick. Cut 1″ × 3″ strips with pastry wheel, cutting ends diagonally. Make a lengthwise slit in the center of each strip and pull one end through.

Deep Fat, 350°

Fry in deep fat 2 minutes or until lightly browned. Drain on paper towels and sprinkle when cold with confectioners' sugar.

To make about 4 dozen

SPRINGERLE

All-Purpose Flour, 2½ cups **Baking Powder,** ½ teasp. **Salt,** ½ teaspoon	Sift dry ingredients together.
Eggs, 2 **Sugar,** 1¼ cups **Lemon Rind,** grated, 1 **Anise Seed,** 1 teaspoon	Beat eggs until thick and lemon-colored. Add sugar gradually; beat with rotary or electric beater 20 minutes. Add flavorings and sifted dry ingredients. Mix well. Roll to ¼ inch thickness and let stand until dry on top. Emboss designs with springerle board by pressing very hard on dough. Cut around designs and let dry on board overnight. Remove to greased cooky sheets.
Oven, slow, 300° *To make about 3 dozen*	Bake for 25 to 30 minutes. Store in airtight container at least 1 week before using.

RASPBERRY BUTTER COOKIES

Butter, 1 cup **Sugar,** ½ cup **All-Purpose Flour,** sifted, 3 cups **Salt,** ¼ teaspoon **Raspberry Preserves** **Confectioners' Sugar,** sifted	Cream butter, gradually add sugar and beat until light. Add flour and salt. Roll to ⅛ inch thickness. Cut with floured 3-inch round cooky cutter. Cut out centers of half the cookies with floured 2-inch round cutter. Place cookies on ungreased cooky sheets.
Oven, hot, 400° *To make about 2 dozen*	Bake for 10 minutes or until lightly browned. Cool. Spread whole cookies with raspberry preserves, piled higher at center. Top with cooky rings and sprinkle with confectioners' sugar.

CHOCOLATE CHIP COOKIES

Butter, ½ cup **Brown Sugar,** ¾ cup **Egg,** 1, beaten **Salt,** ½ teaspoon **Soda,** ½ teaspoon **Hot Water,** 1 tablespoon **All-Purpose Flour,** sifted, 1⅛ cups **Vanilla,** 1 teaspoon **Nuts,** ½ cup, finely chopped **Semi-sweet Chocolate Pieces,** 6-oz. package	Cream butter until fluffy and add sugar gradually; beat until fluffy. Add other ingredients in order, dissolving the soda in the hot water. Mix well and drop by teaspoonfuls on greased cooky sheet.
Oven, moderate, 375° *To make about 3 dozen*	Bake about 8 minutes, or until delicately brown.

BUTTERSCOTCH NUT COOKIES

All-Purpose Flour, 2¾ cups **Salt,** ½ teaspoon **Soda,** ½ teaspoon	Sift dry ingredients together.
Butter, 1 cup **Sugar,** ½ cup **Brown Sugar,** ½ cup, packed **Vanilla,** 1 teaspoon **Eggs,** 2 **Nuts,** finely chopped, ½ cup	Cream butter and gradually add sugar, vanilla and eggs, beating well after each addition. Add dry ingredients and nuts. Chill about 2 hours. Shape into two loaves 2 inches square. Wrap in waxed paper, and chill overnight. Slice ⅛ inch thick and place on ungreased cooky sheets.
Oven, hot, 400° *To make about 6 dozen*	Bake 6 to 8 minutes.

SOUR CREAM COOKIES

All-Purpose Flour, sifted, 3 cups **Baking Powder,** 1 teasp. **Baking Soda,** ¼ teasp. **Salt,** 1 teaspoon	Sift dry ingredients together.
Butter, 1 cup **Sugar,** 1 cup **Brown Sugar,** ¼ cup **Eggs,** 2, well-beaten **Vanilla,** 1 teaspoon **Sour Cream,** ½ cup	Cream butter, gradually adding the sugars until mixture is fluffy. Add eggs and vanilla. Add flour alternately with sour cream; chill. Shape in rolls about 2 inches in diameter and wrap each in waxed paper. Chill thoroughly. Cut chilled dough in ⅛-inch slices, and place on ungreased cooky sheet.
Oven, hot, 400° *To make 9 dozen cookies*	Bake about 8 minutes.

HERMITS

Cake Flour, sifted, 2 cups **Baking Powder,** 1 teasp. **Salt,** ½ teaspoon **Cinnamon,** 1 teaspoon **Cloves,** ¼ teaspoon **Nutmeg,** ¼ teaspoon	Sift dry ingredients together.
Soft Butter, ½ cup **Brown Sugar,** 1 cup, packed **Eggs,** 2, beaten **Raisins,** seeded, chopped, 2 cups **Nuts,** chopped, ½ cup	Cream butter and gradually beat in sugar; add eggs. Beat until light and fluffy. Add sifted dry ingredients, raisins, and nuts; mix well. Drop by teaspoonfuls onto greased cooky sheet.
Oven, moderate, 350° *To make about 4 dozen*	Bake about 10 minutes.

PINWHEELS

All-Purpose Flour,
   sifted, 1¾ cups
Baking Powder, ¼ teasp.
Salt, ¼ teaspoon

Sift dry ingredients together.

Butter, ½ cup
Sugar, ¾ cup
Vanilla, 1 teaspoon
Egg, 1
Unsweetened Chocolate,
   1 square, melted

Cream butter; add sugar, vanilla and egg. Beat until light. Add sifted dry ingredients. Halve dough and add chocolate to one half. Chill for several hours, or until firm enough to roll. Roll white dough on floured board to a 9″ × 12″ rectangle. Roll chocolate dough to same size. Place on top of white dough and press gently with rolling pin. Roll up tightly; wrap in paper. Chill overnight. Slice ⅛ inch thick. Place on ungreased cooky sheets.

Oven, moderate, 350°

Bake about 10 minutes.

To make about 4½ dozen

BROWNIES

All-Purpose Flour,
   sifted, ¾ cup
Baking Powder, ½ teasp.
Salt, ½ teaspoon
Nuts, chopped, 1 cup

Sift dry ingredients together; add nuts.

Shortening, ⅓ cup
Sugar, 1 cup
Eggs, 2, well-beaten
Vanilla, ½ teaspoon
Unsweetened Chocolate,
   2 squares, melted

Cream sugar and shortening together; add eggs, vanilla and chocolate. Add flour-nut mixture and combine well. Turn into greased 8-inch square pan.

Oven, moderate, 350°

Bake 30 to 35 minutes. When cool, cut into squares.

FUDGE BROWNIES: Omit baking powder and bake in slower oven (325°) for about 30 minutes.

LECKERLI

Sugar, ½ cup
Honey, ½ cup
Candied Orange Peel,
   chopped, ½ cup
Candied Lemon Peel,
   chopped, ½ cup
Cloves, 1½ teaspoons
Nutmeg, 1½ teaspoons
Cinnamon, 1 tablespoon
Soda, 1 teaspoon
Cold Water, 2 tablesps.
Lemon Rind, grated,
   1 tablespoon
Unblanched Almonds,
   1 cup, sliced thin
Flour, sifted, 2¾ cups

Heat sugar and honey to boiling. Remove from heat; add peel, spices and soda dissolved in cold water. Mix well. Add lemon rind, almonds and flour. Knead until well-blended. Roll dough to ½ inch thickness. Put on greased waxed paper on cooky sheet.

Oven, moderate, 325°
Sugar Glaze (page 202)

Bake about 25 minutes. Turn out on wire rack and remove paper at once. Turn right side up. Frost with sugar glaze; cut into diamonds; store 1 week before using.

To make about 5 dozen

KISSES

See Meringues, page 229.

NO-BAKE BROWNIES

Unsweetened Chocolate,
   2 squares
Instant Coffee, 1 teasp.
Sweetened Condensed
   Milk, 1 cup
Graham Cracker
   Crumbs, 2 cups
Chopped Nuts, 1 cup

Melt chocolate in top of double boiler over boiling water. Add coffee and milk; cook, stirring until thickened. Remove from heat, add crumbs and ¾ cup of nuts, and mix well. Turn into buttered 9-inch square pan and press down. Sprinkle with remaining nuts. Chill. Cut in squares.

Brownies and macaroons

Date bars and assorted cookies are welcome gifts

DATE BARS

All-Purpose Flour,
  sifted, 1⅓ cups
Baking Powder, 1 teasp.
Salt, ¼ teaspoon

Sift dry ingredients together.

Honey, 1 cup
Eggs, 3, well-beaten
Vanilla, 1 teaspoon
Pitted Dates, 2 7¼-oz.
  packages, cut up
Nuts, chopped, 1 cup

Mix honey, eggs and vanilla. Beat well and add sifted dry ingredients; mixing well after each addition. Add dates and nuts. Spread in greased 13″ × 9″ × 2″ pan.

Oven, moderate, 350°

To make about 39 bars

Bake about 45 minutes. Cool in pan and cut 1″ × 3″ bars. Roll in fine granulated sugar if desired.

Chocolate nut squares

Christmas decorations add a festive touch

CHOCOLATE NUT SQUARES

Unsweetened Chocolate, 1 square
Butter, ¼ cup
Sugar, ½ cup
Egg, 1
All-Purpose Flour, sifted, ¼ cup
Salt, ⅛ teaspoon
Vanilla, ¼ teaspoon
Nuts, finely chopped, ⅓ cup

Melt chocolate and butter over hot water; remove from heat. Add remaining ingredients in order, except nuts. Spread in a greased 8-inch square pan. Sprinkle with nuts.

Oven, hot, 400°

Bake about 8 minutes or until just done. When cool, cut into squares.

FUDGE SQUARES

Butter, ½ cup
Unsweetened Chocolate, 3 ounces
Sugar, 2 cups
Eggs, 3
Vanilla, 1 teaspoon
All-Purpose Flour, sifted, 1½ cups
Salt, ⅛ teaspoon
Walnuts, chopped, 1 cup

Melt butter and chocolate together. Mix in sugar and eggs, one at a time, beating well after each addition. Add vanilla. Sift flour with salt and add to chocolate mixture; add nuts. Pour into greased 9″ × 9″ pan.

Oven, moderate, 350°

Bake about 30 minutes. When cool, cut into squares.

PECAN CHEWS

Eggs, 4
Light Brown Sugar, 1 lb.
Vanilla, 1 teaspoon
All-Purpose Flour, sifted, 2 cups
Baking Powder, 1 teasp.
Salt, ½ teaspoon
Pecans, chopped, 1½ cups

In top part of double boiler, beat 4 eggs slightly and stir in brown sugar. Put over boiling water and cook, stirring constantly, until thickened. Add vanilla and sifted dry ingredients. Stir in chopped nuts. Put into greased 13″ × 9″ pan.

Oven, moderate, 350°

Bake 25 to 30 minutes. When cool, dust with confectioners' sugar and cut into squares.

WALNUT BALLS

All-Purpose Flour, sifted, 2 cups
Sugar, ¼ cup
Salt, ½ teaspoon
Butter, 1 cup
Vanilla, 2 teaspoons
Walnuts, finely chopped, 3 cups

Sift flour, sugar and salt together. Work in room-temperature butter and vanilla. Add 2 cups nuts; mix well. Shape in 1 inch balls. Roll balls in remaining 1 cup nuts. Bake on ungreased cooky sheets.

Oven, moderate, 325°

Bake about 25 minutes, or until delicately browned.

To make about 4½ dozen

Pecans may be substituted for walnuts, in the above recipe. If desired, omit 1 cup of nuts and roll cookies while warm in fine granulated sugar.

RUM BALLS

Vanilla Wafers, 1 cup, crushed
Confectioners' Sugar, 1 cup
Pecans, 1½ cups, chopped fine
Cocoa, 2 tablespoons
Light Corn Syrup, 2 tablespoons
Rum, ¼ cup
Confectioners' Sugar

Mix crumbs, confectioners' sugar, 1 cup of nuts, and cocoa. Add corn syrup and rum and mix well. Shape in 1-inch balls. Roll half the balls in confectioners' sugar and the remainder in the ½ cup nuts.

To make about 3 dozen

BRANDY BALLS OR BOURBON BALLS: Substitute brandy or bourbon in the above recipe.

FROSTED FILBERT MACAROONS

Egg Whites, 4
Sugar, 1 cup
Vanilla, ¼ teaspoon
Filberts, ½ pound, grated

Beat egg whites until stiff, then gradually add sugar and continue beating for ½ hour; add vanilla and grated nuts. Refrigerate for several hours. Then drop by teaspoonfuls on unglazed paper-covered cookie sheets.

Oven, slow, 300°
Sugar Glaze, page 202

Bake about 1 hour, or until cookies can be lifted from paper. Frost while still warm with Sugar Glaze.

To make about 3 dozen

CHOCOLATE LACE

Butter, ½ cup
Syrup, light corn, ½ cup
Brown Sugar, ⅔ cup, firmly packed
Flour, sifted, 1 cup
Nuts, any kind, 1 cup finely chopped

Place butter, syrup and sugar in saucepan, bring to boil and remove from heat immediately. Blend in flour mixed with nuts. Drop by teaspoonfuls on greased baking sheet, 3 inches apart.

Oven, moderate, 325°
Semisweet Chocolate Pieces, 1 cup

Bake 8 to 10 minutes. Cool for a few minutes before removing from baking sheet. Stir chocolate over hot water until partially melted; then brush on cool cookies. Use chocolate as cool as possible to hasten drying.

To make about 6 dozen

COCONUT MACAROONS

Egg Whites, 2
Salt, ½ teaspoon
Almond Extract, ¼ teaspoon
Sugar, 1 cup
Shredded Coconut, 1 cup
Corn Flakes, 1 cup

Beat egg whites until stiff; add salt and almond extract. Gradually beat in sugar. Fold in coconut and cornflakes. Drop from teaspoon on greased baking sheet.

Oven, moderate, 350°

Bake about 20 minutes, or until golden. Remove from pan with spatula.

To make about 3 dozen

A variety of refrigerator cookies

DESSERTS

When we prepare meals in a hurry, dessert often arrives on the table without much advance planning, but actually it should be the dish that rounds out a balanced meal. It is an opportunity to provide the things that may have been missing from the rest of the meal, but that a good daily diet requires. Here is a chance to give the family its full fruit quota—if not by itself, then in combination with a custard sauce, or ice cream, or gelatin—all opportunities for additional protein, too.

Desserts need not be elaborate or time-consuming in preparation. Some of the simplest fruit desserts are the most delicious. Note the many easy ones in the fruit section.

Quick dessert improvisations with ingredients that you can keep on hand.

APPLE MALLOW

Combine 17-ounce can of applesauce with ½ cup miniature marshmallows. Chill several hours. Serve with a sprinkling of cinnamon.

QUICK HOLIDAY DESSERT

Miniature Marshmallows, 1 cup
Sour Cream, 1 cup
Fruit Cocktail, canned, 2 cups

Combine marshmallows, sour cream, and drained fruit; chill for several hours before serving.

To serve 4

Fresh fruit may be used in place of canned fruit cocktail, if desired.

BANANA ICE CREAM

Mix a package of lemon-flavored ice cream dessert according to directions. Add 2 mashed, ripe bananas; freeze with control set at coldest point and tray in quickest-freezing spot.

ITALIAN CREAM CHEESE CUSTARD

Ricotta, ½ pound
Cream, 2 tablespoons
Milk Chocolate, grated, ¼ cup
Walnuts, ¼ cup, finely chopped

Mix the ricotta with cream. Add chocolate and nuts and blend thoroughly. Serve in sherbet glasses.

To serve 4

HAWAIIAN LADYFINGERS

Dip both sides of unsplit ladyfingers lightly in pineapple juice, next in confectioners' sugar, then in flaked coconut. Serve at once.

EASY SHORTCAKE

Make individual biscuits according to directions on packaged biscuit mix; bake. Thaw frozen strawberries or peaches. Split biscuits, fill with fruit and top with whipped cream or ice cream.

Fresh fruit desserts that are simple yet elegant.

MELON COMPOTE

Make a compote of watermelon, honeydew and cantaloupe balls. Serve with lemon or lime wedges.

ORANGES WITH STRAWBERRIES

Peel oranges and cut crosswise into thin slices. Arrange slices on individual fruit plates and top each slice with a spoonful of strawberries (wild ones preferred, if you know where to pick them). Sugar lightly and serve at once.

STRAWBERRIES IN SOUR CREAM

Sugar a quart of berries to taste and let stand at room temperature until sugar dissolves. Then mix lightly with 1 pint of sour cream. Chill until ready to serve.

Try it with raspberries, too.

BLENDER APPLESAUCE

Combine ⅔ cup light syrup, ⅛ teaspoon salt, and 8 peeled and cored tart apples. Put into blender at medium speed until smooth. Add ¼ cup lemon juice. Chill.

To serve 4

APPLES AND CHEESE

Serve unpeeled quartered winesaps or a similar tart apple with a good sharp Cheddar cheese.

APRICOTS AND COTTAGE CHEESE

Arrange fresh fruit cut in quarters on individual plates around a serving of cottage cheese sprinkled with cinnamon.

Good with peaches, too.

BANANA ROYAL

Sugar sliced bananas and garnish with a spoonful of frozen lemonade.

BANANAS CORDIALE

Sprinkle banana slices with Cointreau.

BANANA-GRAPE CUP

Cut bananas into quarters lengthwise; then cut into chunks. Serve with halved and seeded red or black grapes.

Fruit and cheese for dessert

GRAPES SAUTERNE WITH SOUR CREAM

Seedless Grapes **Sauterne** **Sour Cream** **Brown Sugar**	Sprinkle chilled grapes with sauterne, top with sour cream and a sprinkling of brown sugar.

BRANDIED GRAPES

Remove stems from seedless grapes and place them in a bowl. Sprinkle with brandy and let marinate an hour in the re-refrigerator, stirring occasionally. Serve in chilled sherbet dishes topped with sweetened whipped cream.

WHITE PEACHES AND BLACKBERRIES IN KIRSCH

White Freestone Peaches, 4	Chill peaches for several hours.
Water, ½ cup **Sugar,** ½ cup **Vanilla,** ¼ teaspoon **Blackberries,** 2 cups, washed and drained **Kirsch,** 2 tablespoons	Boil water, sugar and vanilla to make syrup. Remove from heat, add berries. When cool add kirsch. Pour mixture over freshly peeled peach halves.

To serve 4

PEARS AND CHEESE

Halve dessert pears and serve with Roquefort or Bleu cheese.

MELON BOWL

Cut a piece from stem end of small round watermelon, scoop out pulp without piercing rind. Cut pulp in cubes and combine with several other fruits: pineapple, peaches, whole strawberries or raspberries. Sugar to taste and put fruit in melon. Pour over it 2 ounces of Kirsch or other liqueur or a dessert wine such as Muscatel. Put in refrigerator overnight.

AMBROSIA

Pineapple, 4 slices **Oranges,** 4, peeled **Coconut,** 1 cup, grated, fresh or packaged **Powdered Sugar** **Maraschino Cherries**	Cut fresh pineapples in cubes. Holding whole orange in left hand, cut orange along each side of membrane separating segments and lift out each segment. Remove seeds. Combine in bowl with coconut and sprinkle lightly with powdered sugar. Chill thoroughly. Garnish each serving with maraschino cherries.

To serve 4

Other fruits and fruit combinations may be used in the same way. Try fresh peaches, raspberries, or strawberries; or in combination and with bananas.

STRAWBERRY DIP

Arrange whole berries with the stems on, on small individual plates, surrounding a fluted paper muffin cup filled with confectioners' sugar for dipping.

STRAWBERRIES COINTREAU

Wash and hull strawberries, and cut in half. Add sugar and sprinkle with Cointreau. Let stand in refrigerator for 1 hour before serving. Serve with whipped cream.

RASPBERRY COOLER

Sugar raspberries and marinate in muscatel wine or rosé wine. Chill until ready to serve.

MIXED FROZEN FRUITS

Melon Balls, 1 package, frozen **Raspberries,** 1 package, frozen **Peaches,** 1 pkg., frozen	Defrost fruits to stage where they are still somewhat frosty, combine in a bowl and spike with a jigger of rum.

Glorified canned fruits for desserts in a jiffy.

APPLE SNOW

Applesauce, 2 cups
Lemon Juice, 1/4 cup
Cinnamon, 1/8 teaspoon
Salt, 1/8 teaspoon
Sugar, 2 tablespoons

Combine applesauce, lemon juice, cinnamon, salt and sugar and mix well.

Egg Whites, 2
Sugar, 1/4 cup
Red Sugar

To serve 4 to 6

Beat egg whites until foamy; add sugar gradually and beat until stiff. Fold in apple mixture and chill. Decorate with red sugar.

CHILLED APRICOTS WITH KIRSCH

Drain a 16-ounce can of apricots and pour 2 ounces of Kirsch over them. Chill thoroughly. Top with whipped cream.

Peaches may be substituted for the apricots. Good also with strawberries or raspberries.

FIGS IN WINE

Figs, 1 can
Port or **Claret,** 1/2 cup

Drain figs. Reserve 1/2 cup of syrup, combine with wine and pour over figs in bowl. Chill.

MANDARIN ORANGES IN RED WINE

Dry Red Wine, 1 cup
Sugar, 3/4 cup
Cinnamon Bark, 1 piece
Lemon, 2 slices
Mandarin Oranges,
  2 cans
To serve 4 or 5

Simmer wine, sugar, cinnamon, lemon and juice from oranges until syrupy. Remove cinnamon and lemon slices. Add orange segments to syrup; simmer few more minutes. Chill.

PEACH MELBA

Put large canned peach halves in sherbet dishes; put scoop of vanilla ice cream in hollow center of peach and top with following sauce:

Raspberries, frozen,
  12-ounce package
Red Currant Jelly, 1/2 cup
Cornstarch, 1 tablespoon
Cold Water, 1 tablespoon
Sherry, 2 tablespoons

To serve 4

Heat raspberries and jelly until jelly is melted; add cornstarch mixed with water. Cook, stirring until mixture is thickened. Add sherry. Chill.

ICY PEARS IN GINGER ALE

Cover drained, canned pears with ginger ale and chill thoroughly. Top with whipped cream.

A variety of apple snow, layered with clear apple sauce and topped with mint sprigs

PINEAPPLE JAMAICAN

Cubed Pineapple, 1 can
Rum, few tablespoons
Grated Coconut

Drain pineapple, marinate in rum. To serve, pile in individual sherbet dishes and sprinkle with coconut.

EASY PRUNE WHIP

Egg Whites, 2
Salt, 1/8 teaspoon
Sugar, 1/4 cup
Lemon Rind, 1, grated
Baby Food Prunes,
  8-ounce jar

To serve 4

Beat egg whites and salt until foamy. Gradually add sugar, beating until stiff. Sprinkle rind over it and add prunes; fold in and chill.

CANNED PRUNES IN PORT WINE

Prunes, 1 can
Cornstarch, 1 teaspoon
Port Wine, 1/3 cup
Whipped Cream

To serve 4 to 6

Cook juice from prunes until reduced to 1/2 cup. Mix cornstarch in wine; add to juice and simmer, stirring until sauce thickens and clears. Remove from heat; add prunes and chill several hours. Serve with whipped cream.

PARTY FRUIT COMPOTE

Combine drained canned pear and peach halves, apricots, dark sweet cherries, greengage plums and figs. Combine juices and to each pint add 1 tablespoon cornstarch; add 3 whole cloves, a stick of cinnamon and 1/2 cup grape jelly. Cook 10 minutes or until slightly thickened. Pour over fruits and chill. Serve with sour cream on the side.

Molded gelatin desserts are always sparkling and festive. They achieve importance with very little labor.

APRICOT-ORANGE NECTAR

Unflavored Gelatin, 1 envelope
Apricot Nectar, 12-ounce can
Orange Juice, ½ cup
Orange Rind, 1 tablespoon, grated
Whipped Cream

To serve 4 or 5

Sprinkle gelatin in ½ cup apricot nectar to soften. Heat until gelatin is dissolved. Add remaining nectar, orange juice and grated rind. Pour into square cake pan, chill. When set, cut in cubes, pile in sherbet dishes and serve with whipped cream.

SPANISH CREAM

Unflavored Gelatin, 1 envelope
Milk, 2 cups
Egg Yolks, 2
Sugar, 2 tablespoons
Salt, ¼ teaspoon

Soak gelatin in milk in top of double boiler 5 minutes. Place over boiling water and heat until gelatin is dissolved. Beat egg yolks slightly, add 2 tablespoons sugar and salt. Add a little of the hot milk, mix well, and return to double boiler. Cook, stirring constantly, until mixture coats a spoon. Cool, then chill until slightly thickened.

Egg Whites, 2
Sugar, 4 tablespoons
Almond Extract, ½ teaspoon

To serve 4

Beat egg whites until foamy; add sugar and continue beating until stiff. Fold in gelatin mixture, add almond extract. Pour into individual sherbet dishes or molds.

GRAPE PARFAIT

Grape-flavored Gelatin, 1 package
Ruby Port or **Dubonnet,** ½ cup
Heavy Cream, 1 cup

To make 4 servings

Dissolve gelatin in 1 cup of hot water. Add ½ cup port or other sweet red wine and cool. Whip cream and fold into gelatin mixture. Chill in freezing tray until somewhat thickened. Stir again; pile into parfait glasses. Keep in freezer until serving time.

MANDARIN ORANGE DESSERT

Orange Juice, 2 cups
Unflavored Gelatin, 1 envelope
Mandarin Oranges, 11-oz. can, drained

To serve 4

Soften gelatin in ¼ cup of orange juice; heat remaining juice and pour over gelatin; stir until dissolved. Chill until thickened but not firm. Add oranges and chill until firm.

LEMON SNOW WITH CHERRY SAUCE

Unflavored Gelatin, 1 envelope
Water, ¼ cup
Sugar, ½ cup
Salt, ⅛ teaspoon
Boiling Water, 1 cup
Lemon Juice, 3 tablesps.
Lemon Rind, grated, 1 tablespoon

Soak gelatin in cold water 5 minutes. Add sugar, salt and boiling water and stir until dissolved. Add lemon juice and rind. Chill until partially set.

Egg Whites, 3
Sugar, ¼ cup
Cherry Sauce (page 234)

To serve 4

Beat egg whites until foamy; add sugar gradually and beat until stiff. Add gelatin mixture slowly and beat with rotary beater. When blended stir until it holds its shape. Chill until set. Serve with Cherry Sauce.

CHOCOLATE BAVARIAN

Unsweetened Chocolate, 2 squares
Sugar, ½ cup
Milk, 2 cups
Egg Yolks, 2, slightly beaten

Melt chocolate in top part of double boiler over hot water; add sugar and combine. Add milk gradually, stirring constantly. Pour a little of the mixture over beaten egg yolks, mix and return to double boiler. Cook until mixture will coat a spoon. Remove from heat.

Unflavored Gelatin, 1 envelope
Milk, 2 tablespoons
Heavy Cream, ½ cup
Vanilla, ½ teaspoon

Dissolve gelatin in milk. Add to egg mixture. Cool and chill until partially set. Whip cream and vanilla and fold into mixture; pour into mold and chill until firm.

Sweetened Whipped Cream
Almonds
To serve 4

Unmold and decorate with whipped cream and blanched almonds.

RASPBERRY BAVARIAN

Unflavored Gelatin, 1 envelope
Cold Water, 2 tablesps.
Salt, ⅛ teaspoon
Boiling Water, ¼ cup

Soften gelatin in cold water and add salt. Add boiling water and stir until dissolved.

Raspberries, 2 cups
Lemon Juice, 1 tablesp.
Sugar, ¼ cup
Kirsch, 2 tablespoons

Crush raspberries and put through sieve. Add lemon juice and sugar. Stir in the dissolved gelatin. Chill until mixture partially sets. Stir in the kirsch.

Egg Whites, 2
Sugar, ¼ cup
Heavy Cream, 1 cup, whipped
Sweetened Whipped Cream
Whole Raspberries
To serve 6

Beat egg whites until stiff, adding sugar gradually. Fold meringue and whipped cream into gelatin mixture. Pour into a mold; chill until set. To serve, unmold and garnish with whipped cream and whole raspberries.

A charlotte decorated with raspberries

BLUEBERRY CHARLOTTE

Unflavored Gelatin,
  1 envelope
Cold Water, 1/4 cup
Boiling Water, 1/2 cup
Sugar, 1/3 cup
Blueberries, 1 cup,
  crushed
Lemon Juice, 1 tablesp.

Salt, 1/4 teaspoon
Egg Whites, 2
Heavy Cream, 1/2 cup,
  whipped

To serve 4

Sprinkle gelatin over cold water to soften. Dissolve in boiling water. Add sugar and dissolve. Add berries and lemon juice. Chill until partially set.

Add salt to egg whites and beat stiff; fold with whipped cream into berry mix. Turn into mold lined with sponge cake or lady-fingers, or into individual dessert dishes. Chill until set.

CRÈME DE LA CRÈME

Heavy Cream, 1 cup
Milk, 1/2 cup
Sugar, 1/2 cup
Salt, dash
Unflavored Gelatin, 1
  envelope, softened
  in cold water
Sour Cream, 1 cup
Kirsch, 2 tablespoons

Combine cream, milk, sugar and salt in saucepan and cook over low heat until sugar is dissolved. Remove from heat and stir gelatin into mixture. When dissolved, beat in sour cream with rotary beater until just blended and smooth. Blend in Kirsch. Pour into lightly oiled pint mold. Chill until firm. Unmold on dessert platter and serve surrounded by sweetened berries or any combination of fruit.

COCONUT ORANGE CREAM

Unflavored Gelatin,
  1 envelope
Cold Water, 1/4 cup
Orange Juice, 1 cup
Sugar, 1/3 cup
Salt, 1/8 teaspoon
Orange Rind, grated,
  1 tablespoon

Heavy Cream, 1 cup,
  whipped
Coconut,
  1/2 cup, shredded
Orange, 1/2 cup of pieces

To serve 4

Soften gelatin in cold water; heat 1/2 cup orange juice and add gelatin. Stir until dissolved. Add sugar and salt and dissolve. Add remaining juice and grated rind. Chill until partially set.

Whip gelatin mixture and fold in whipped cream. Add coconut and orange segments, trimmed of membrane and cut into small pieces. Chill until firm.

COFFEE-PECAN MOLDS WITH RUM CREAM

Strong Coffee, 4 cups
Cloves, 1/4 teaspoon
Cinnamon, 1/2 teaspoon

Unflavored Gelatin,
  2 envelopes
Water, 1/3 cup
Sugar, 3/4 cup
Pecans, 1/3 cup, chopped

Rum, 2 tablespoons
Sugar, 2 tablespoons
Heavy Cream, 1 cup,
  whipped

To make 4 to 6 servings

Simmer coffee and spices 5 minutes.

Soften gelatin in cold water, add coffee and sugar. Stir until gelatin is dissolved. Chill until mixture begins to set. Turn into bowl and whip. Fold in nuts. Pour into molds and chill.

Add sugar and rum to whipped cream. Unmold gelatin and serve with rum cream topping.

Delicious ways to use fresh fruit in cooked desserts. Many of these would make a satisfying light meal all by themselves.

CINNAMON BAKED APPLES

Wash and core firm, tart baking apples but do not cut all the way to bottom skin; place in baking dish. Fill each center with a mixture of sugar and cinnamon (1 teaspoon cinnamon to ½ cup sugar). Top with a small piece of butter. Cover bottom of pan with boiling water. Bake in moderate oven, 375°, 30 to 40 minutes, or until soft. Remove apples, pour over them any syrup in the pan. Serve warm or cold with cream.

MAPLE SUGAR APPLES: Fill centers with maple sugar or maple syrup.

ROSY SKILLET APPLES

Core and peel apples ⅓ down from top. In skillet make syrup of 1 cup sugar, 1½ cups water, 1 tablespoon lemon juice, few drops red food coloring. Put apples, tops down, in syrup and simmer 5 minutes. Turn over, cover skillet, and simmer 30 minutes, or until tender. Pour syrup over apples to serve, and fill centers with whipped cream, letting it pile up on top.

BAKED APPLE DUMPLINGS

Biscuit Dough (page 177) or **Pie Crust** (page 181)	Roll out dough ¼″ thick and cut in 6″ squares. Pare and core apples and place one in center of each square. Mix sugar, spices and raisins and fill center of each apple. Top with piece of butter. Fold dough together at top of apple and press edges together. Pierce dough in several places with fork.
Apples, 6 medium, tart	
Brown Sugar, ½ cup, firmly packed	
Cinnamon, 1 teaspoon	
Nutmeg, ¼ teaspoon	
Raisins, Seedless, ½ cup	
Butter, 2 tablespoons	
Oven, moderate, 350°	Bake 30 minutes. Serve with cream.

DUTCH APPLE CAKE

One-Egg Cake Batter (page 190)	Spread cake batter in 9″ x 13″ cake pan. Pare and core apples, and cut in eighths. Press pieces down into batter in neat rows. Mix cinnamon and sugar and spread with raisins over top of apples.
Tart Apples, 6 or 7	
Sugar, ½ cup	
Cinnamon, 1 teaspoon	
Seedless Raisins, ⅓ cup	
Oven, moderate, 350° **Hard Sauce** or **Lemon Sauce** (page 234)	Bake until apples are tender, about 25 minutes. Serve with Hard Sauce or Lemon Sauce.

This dessert may also be made with Biscuit Dough, page 177, and served with cream.

APPLE BROWN BETTY

Small Bread Cubes, 4 cups	Mix bread cubes, butter, cinnamon, salt and sugar. Arrange alternate layers of crumb mixture and apples in buttered 2-quart baking dish.
Butter, melted, ½ cup	
Cinnamon, 1 teaspoon	
Salt, ⅛ teaspoon	
Brown Sugar, packed, 1 cup	
Tart Apples, chopped, 4 cups	
Hard Sauce (page 234)	
Oven, moderate, 375°	Bake 1 hour or until apples are tender and top is golden brown. Serve with Hard Sauce or cream.
To serve 4	

SKILLET APPLE BROWN BETTY: Brown bread cubes in melted butter in skillet. Add remaining ingredients mixed together. Cover and cook 8 minutes, or until apples are tender.

PLUM BETTY: Substitute 4 cups sliced ripe plums for apples Substitute brandy for vanilla in Hard Sauce (page 234).

PEAR BETTY: Substitute 4 cups sliced, peeled pears for apples. Substitute Cointreau for vanilla in Hard Sauce (page 234).

APPLE CRISP

Apples, 6, tart	Peel and slice apples and arrange in bottom of shallow baking dish. Blend sugar, flour, cinnamon and butter with fingers to consistency of fine crumbs. Sprinkle over apples.
Brown Sugar, packed, ¾ cup	
All-Purpose Flour, sifted, ½ cup	
Cinnamon, ½ teaspoon	
Butter, ¼ cup	
Hard Sauce (page 234)	
Oven, moderate, 375°	Bake about 25 minutes. Serve warm with Hard Sauce.
To serve 4 to 6	

PEACH CRISP: Substitute 6 to 8 peaches for apples. Add ¼ teaspoon almond extract to hard sauce.

BLUEBERRY CRISP: Substitute 3 cups blueberries for apples and sprinkle over them the juice of half a lemon.

BLACKBERRY DUFF

Blackberries, 4 cups	In a deep kettle put blackberries, sugar, lemon juice and water. Bring to boil, cover with spoonfuls of dumpling batter. Cover tightly and cook 20 minutes over low heat without raising cover. Serve with light cream.
Sugar, ¾ cup	
Lemon Juice, 1 tablesp.	
Water, 2 cups	
Dumpling Batter (page)	
Light Cream	
To serve 4	

Apple dumplings

FRESH BLACKBERRY WHIP

Egg Whites, 2
Salt, dash
Sugar, ¼ cup

Lemon, 1, juice and
grated rind
Blackberries, 1 pint
Custard Sauce, page 226

To serve 4

Beat egg whites with salt until
stiff, then add sugar, beating it
in 1 tablespoon at a time.

Fold in lemon juice, grated rind
and washed blackberries; chill.
Serve with thin custard sauce
made with left-over egg yolks.

CURRANT-BLACKBERRY FLUMMERY

Currants, 1 cup
Blackberries, 2 cups
Water,
Sugar, 1 cup
Cornstarch, 6 tablesps.
Salt, ⅛ teaspoon
Lemon Juice, 2 tablesps.
Sour Cream or **Light
Cream**

To serve 4 to 6

Simmer currants and berries in
1 cup water about 5 minutes or
until soft. Put through sieve;
add water to make 3 cups.
Combine sugar, cornstarch and
salt and add to berries. Cook,
stirring constantly, over low
heat, until mixture thickens.
Add lemon juice. Cool and chill.
Serve with sour cream or light
cream.

3 cups of blackberries may be used if currants are not
available. Or 3 cups of blueberries may be substituted for
both.

SKILLET BLUEBERRY COBBLER

Blueberries, 3 cups **Sugar,** ½ cup **Water,** ¾ cup **Cornstarch,** 1 tablesp. **Water,** 2 tablespoons	Heat berries, sugar and water in skillet. Blend cornstarch with water; add to berries. Bring to boil, cook 1 minute stirring constantly.
Biscuit Mix, 1 cup **Sugar,** 1 tablespoon **Cream,** ⅓ cup *To serve 4 to 6*	Add sugar to biscuit mix, stir in cream. Drop dough by the spoonful over the berries. Cover and cook over low heat, 20 minutes. Serve hot with cream.

PEARS IN ORANGE SAUCE

Fresh Pears, 4	Core pears and peel one-third of the way down from the top. Put in 2-quart casserole.
Sugar, ¾ cup **Water,** 1 cup **Orange Juice,** ½ cup **Orange Rind,** grated, 2 teaspoons **Lemon Juice,** ½ lemon **Dash of Salt**	Combine sugar, water, orange juice, orange rind, lemon juice and salt in saucepan. Boil 5 minutes. Pour over pears. Cover, and bake.
Oven, hot, 400° *To serve 4*	Bake about 30 minutes. Remove pears; pour syrup into saucepan, and boil 10 minutes. Pour over pears. Chill.

STEWED PEACHES

Wash, peel and cut in half 3 pounds of firm, ripe peaches. Put them into a saucepan with the stones, skins, and about ½ cup of water. Cook them briskly, uncovered, turning each one over after it has boiled about 5 minutes. After 10 minutes lift out the stones and skins with a slotted spoon, letting the juice drain well into the pan. When peaches are just about tender (do not overcook) add ½ cup sugar, depending on sweetness of the fruit, and cook another minute or until sugar is dissolved, and juice boils up once more. Remove from heat and pour at once into a glass bowl. Cool and chill before serving.

STEWED PLUMS: Follow the above recipe for stewing red plums or blue prunes, leaving their skins on for flavor, and increasing the amount of sugar.

BROILED PEACH HALVES

Peaches, home-style, canned **Butter** **Brown Sugar** **Brandy** **Heavy Cream**	Place peaches, hollow up, in a flat baking dish. Fill each center with a little brown sugar, a dab of butter, and a teaspoonful of brandy. Add the peach juice to the dish around the peaches. Put under the broiler a few minutes, until the sugar melts. Serve with cream.

LEMONY PEARS

Fresh, ripe Bartlett Pears, 4 **Sugar,** ½ cup **Water,** ½ cup **Lemon,** 3 thin slices with peel *To serve 4*	Halve and core pears. In a large skillet dissolve sugar in water. Add lemon; heat gently for 2 or 3 minutes. Lay pear halves in skillet cut side down. Cook gently for 5 minutes; turn and cook 5 minutes longer, or until translucent. Chill and serve with heavy cream.

CHERRIES JUBILEE

Sugar, ½ cup **Salt,** dash **Cornstarch,** 1 tablesp. **Water,** ½ cup **Sweet Cherries,** 1 pound	In saucepan combine sugar, salt and cornstarch; add water and pitted cherries. Cook until thickened, stirring constantly. Cool.
Ice Cream, 1 pint **Brandy,** 4 tablespoons *To serve 4*	Place ice cream in individual serving dishes; cover with cherries. Add 1 tablespoon brandy to each, ignite with match and serve flaming.

GINGERED PEARS

Candied Ginger, ¼ cup, diced **Sugar,** ½ cup **Water,** ¾ cup	Make thin syrup with sugar, water and candied ginger.
Pears, fresh, 4 *To serve 4*	Peel pears, cut in quarters, simmer in syrup until tender, occasionally spooning the syrup over fruit.

Canned pears may be used, omitting sugar and using 1 cup of the syrup.

GINGERED PEACHES: Follow above recipe substituting peaches for pears.

STRAWBERRY SHORTCAKE

Make biscuit dough according to directions on page 177. Pat half of it into a 9″ layer pan; brush with soft butter. Roll out remaining dough and put on top. Bake in hot oven, 425°, 25 minutes or until golden brown.

Meanwhile wash and slice 1 quart of berries and sugar to taste. Split shortcake and fill with ½ the berries. Put remaining ones on top and serve with heavy pouring cream or whipped cream.

PEACH SHORTCAKE: Sliced sugared peaches, raspberries or other fresh fruit may be substituted for the strawberries.

Add nuts and raisins to dress up broiled peach halves

DRIED FRUITS

Dried fruits, such as prunes or apricots, must usually be soaked before cooking. Follow directions on package or soak until fruit plumps up. (Usually several hours.) Cook them slowly in the water in which they have been soaked.

SPICY BURGUNDY PRUNES

Soak prunes as usual, but substitute 1 cup of Burgundy or other red wine for 1 cup of the water. Add a small stick of cinnamon, several whole cloves, and a slice of lemon before cooking. Simmer until tender.

APRICOT FANCY

Prepare dried apricots according to directions on package, but substitute 1 cup of muscatel wine for 1 cup of the water.

PEACH ROLL

Prepare biscuit dough (page 177); roll ¼-inch thick. Pare and slice 6 peaches, place on dough and sprinkle with ½ cup sugar and 1½ tablespoons lemon juice. Roll as for jelly roll; place, seam down, on greased baking sheet. Brush with butter and bake in hot oven (400° F.) 25 to 30 minutes. Serve with Lemon Sauce (page 234). Approximate yield: 6 portions.

APRICOT ROLL: Substitute 1¼ cups sweetened, cooked dried apricots for peaches; omit sugar.

BLACKBERRY ROLL: Substitute 1 pint blackberries for peaches. Omit lemon juice and dust with cinnamon. Serve with whipped cream.

BLUEBERRY ROLL: Substitute 1 pint blueberries for peaches. Serve with Hard Sauce (page 234).

GOOSEBERRY ROLL: Substitute 1 pint gooseberries for peaches; sweeten with ¼ cup firmly packed brown sugar and omit lemon juice.

Cherries jubilee

Old English plum pudding

A hearty steamed pudding can be a satisfying conclusion to a light meal.

DATE AND NUT PUDDING

Butter, 2 tablespoons
Brown Sugar, $\frac{1}{2}$ cup, packed
Egg, 1
Vanilla, $\frac{1}{4}$ teaspoon
Flour, sifted, 1 cup
Milk, $\frac{1}{3}$ cup
Dates, chopped, $\frac{1}{2}$ cup
Nuts, chopped, $\frac{1}{2}$ cup
Whipped Cream

To serve 4

Cream butter and sugar until light. Beat in egg and vanilla. Add sifted flour alternately with milk, beating constantly. Fold in dates and nuts. Pour into greased 1-quart pudding mold. Cover tightly and steam 40 minutes. Serve with whipped cream.

OLD ENGLISH PLUM PUDDING

Baking Soda, 1 teasp.
Flour, 1 cup
Salt, $1\frac{1}{2}$ teaspoons
Cinnamon, $\frac{1}{2}$ teaspoon
Nutmeg, $\frac{1}{2}$ teaspoon
Clove, $\frac{1}{4}$ teaspoon
Ginger, $\frac{1}{4}$ teaspoon
Raisins, 1 cup, seeded
Currants, $\frac{1}{2}$ cup
Figs, $\frac{1}{2}$ cup, chopped
Citron, $\frac{1}{4}$ cup
Sugar, $\frac{1}{4}$ cup
Eggs, 4
Suet, $\frac{1}{2}$ pound, ground
Cider, 1 cup

To make about 12 servings

Sift together soda, flour, salt and spices; add fruits. Beat sugar into eggs until thick and lemon-colored. Add suet; mix with fruit mixture. Add cider and mix well. Turn into buttered 6-cup mold. Cover tightly and steam 3 hours.

Brandy may be substituted for part of the cider, if desired.

STEAMED BLUEBERRY PUDDING

Cake Flour, sifted, $1\frac{1}{4}$ cups
Baking Powder, 2 teasps.
Salt, $\frac{1}{8}$ teaspoon

Shortening, $\frac{1}{4}$ cup
Sugar, $\frac{1}{3}$ cup
Egg, 1
Milk, $\frac{1}{3}$ cup
Blueberries, 1 cup
Heavy Cream

To serve 4

Sift flour, baking powder and salt together.

Cream shortening and sugar until light. Beat in egg. Add sifted dry ingredients alternately with milk, beating constantly. Fold in blueberries. Pour into greased 1-quart pudding mold. Cover tightly and steam 40 minutes. Serve with heavy cream.

LEMON SNOWBALL PUDDING

All-Purpose Flour, sifted, 1 cup
Baking Powder, 1 teasp.
Salt, $\frac{1}{4}$ teaspoon

Egg Yolks, 3
Sugar, 1 cup
Water, 3 tablespoons
Lemon Juice, 2 tablesps.
Lemon Rind, grated, 1 tablespoon
Egg Whites, 3, stiffly beaten
Lemon Sauce (page 234)

To serve 4

Sift together flour, baking powder and salt.

Beat egg yolks, adding sugar gradually; beat until thick and fluffy. Add water, lemon juice and rind. Stir in flour mixture. Fold in stiffly beaten egg whites. Fill buttered custard cups $\frac{2}{3}$ full; cover tops with greased paper; place in wide kettle and steam 30 minutes. Turn from cups and serve with Lemon Sauce.

Custards and puddings are old-time favorites, and add nourishment to the meal.

CORNSTARCH CUSTARD

Egg, 1	In saucepan with rotary beater,
Milk, 2 cups	beat together egg and milk; beat
Sugar, 4 tablespoons	in sugar, salt and cornstarch.
Cornstarch, 2 tablesps.	Cook over moderate heat,
Salt, 1/8 teaspoon	stirring constantly, until mixture
Vanilla, 1 teaspoon	thickens. Add vanilla.

To serve 4

CUSTARD SAUCE: As a thinner custard to use on cake or fruit, use only 1 tablespoon of cornstarch.

CHOCOLATE PUDDING: Add 2 squares of unsweetened chocolate to melt as other ingredients heat, and increase sugar to 4 tablespoons.

BLANC MANGE

Cornstarch, 3 tablesps.	In top part of double boiler
Salt, 1/4 teaspoon	combine cornstarch, salt and
Sugar, 1/4 cup	sugar. Add milk and mix with
Milk, 2 cups	rotary beater. Cook over hot
Vanilla, 1/2 teaspoon	water 15 minutes, or until thick
	and smooth. Add vanilla. Turn
	into individual custard cups and
	chill until firm.
Dessert Sauce or **Fruit**	Unmold in dessert dishes and
	serve with chocolate or butter-
	scotch sauce, or with fresh or
To serve 4	canned fruit.

CREAMY TAPIOCA PUDDING

Egg Yolk, 1	In saucepan with rotary beater,
Milk, 2 cups	beat together egg yolk, milk,
Sugar, 2 tablespoons	sugar and salt; add tapioca.
Salt, 1/8 teaspoon	Cook over moderate heat,
Tapioca, quick-cooking,	stirring all the while, until
2 tablespoons	mixture comes to boil. Cook
Vanilla, 1 teaspoon	1 minute and remove from heat.
	Add vanilla.
Egg White, 1	Beat egg white stiff, adding
Sugar, 2 tablespoons	sugar gradually. Add to cooked
	mixture and fold in. Cool. Serve
	at room temperature, or chill, if
	desired. The pudding will
To serve 4	thicken as it chills.

TAPIOCA PUDDING SAUCE: To use as a dessert sauce on cake or fruit, use only 1 tablespoon of tapioca.

Baked custard, cup custard and blanc mange

BAKED CUSTARD

Eggs, 4	Break eggs into large bowl and
Sugar, 1/2 cup	beat with rotary beater or
Salt, 1/4 teaspoon	mixer; add sugar and salt, and
Milk, 4 cups	beat until thick and lemony in
Vanilla, 1 teaspoon	color. Add scalded milk and
	vanilla and beat until
	thoroughly mixed. Pour into
	baking dish.
Oven, moderate, 325°	Set baking dish in pan of hot
	water and bake 40 minutes or
	until silver knife inserted 1 inch
	from edge comes out clean.

To serve 4 to 6

RUM CUSTARD: Omit vanilla and add 1 tablespoon of rum.

CARAMEL CUSTARD: Melt 1/2 cup of sugar in heavy frying pan over low heat; when light brown in color remove from heat and add 1/4 cup of boiling water, slowly. Boil 10 minutes, or until caramel is dissolved. Add to milk in above recipe.

CUP CUSTARDS

To make custard in individual cups, follow recipe above. Set cups in pan of hot water, with water covering cup half way, and bake 20 to 25 minutes. A knife inserted in center will come out clean, when done.

SOFT CUSTARD

Eggs, 2, slightly beaten
Sugar, 4 tablespoons
Salt, ⅛ teaspoon
Milk, 2 cups, scalded
Vanilla, ½ teaspoon

Combine eggs, sugar and salt in top of double boiler. Gradually add hot milk and cook over boiling water, stirring constantly until mixture coats the spoon. Add vanilla and cool. Use as a dessert either plain or with a fruit or nut topping; or as a dessert sauce.

To serve 4

ALMOND CUSTARD: Substitute 1 teaspoon almond extract for vanilla and serve with a topping of chopped almonds.

FLOATING ISLAND

Egg Yolks, 4
Sugar, 3 tablespoons
Salt, ⅛ teaspoon
Milk, 2 cups, scalded
Vanilla, ½ teaspoon

Make custard following procedure for Soft Custard. Pour cooked custard into 4 to 6 dessert dishes.

Egg Whites, 4
Sugar, ¼ cup

Beat egg whites stiff, gradually adding sugar. In shallow baking pan put ½ inch boiling water. Drop stiff egg whites by heaping spoonfuls into water, and place pan in 350° oven for 10 minutes, or until needle inserted in the center comes out dry. Remove from water carefully with cake turner, draining off all water, and place on top of custard.

To serve 4

OLD-FASHIONED CREAMY RICE PUDDING

Rice, ¼ cup
Milk, 4 cups
Salt, ½ teaspoon
Sugar, ½ cup
Vanilla, 1 teaspoon

Oven, low, 275°

Combine ingredients in baking dish. Bake uncovered 3 hours at 275°. Stir up rice several times during first 2 hours, stirring under skin that forms on top of milk. Test grain of rice for doneness.

To serve 4 to 6

One-half cup of seedless raisins may be added if desired, and a dash of nutmeg sprinkled on top the last hour of cooking.

BREAD PUDDING

Eggs, 2, slightly beaten
Sugar, ½ cup
Salt, ½ teaspoon
Milk, 4 cups
Vanilla, 1 teaspoon
Bread

Oven, moderate, 325°

Beat eggs, sugar, salt, milk and vanilla in wide buttered baking dish. Cover top with several slices of buttered stale bread.

Bake 45 minutes, or until knife inserted 1 inch from edge comes out clean.

To serve 4

CHOCOLATE BREAD PUDDING: Blend 2 squares of melted unsweetened chocolate with the above ingredients by beating all together with roatary beater.

Blanc mange in a fluted mold

Zabaglione served with assorted cookies

ZABAGLIONE

Egg Yolks, 6
Sugar, ½ cup
Sherry, ⅓ cup (or Madeira)

Beat egg yolks and sugar together in top of double boiler until thick and lemon-colored, gradually adding sherry. Put top of double boiler over hot, not boiling water and not letting the bottom of the pan touch the water, beat with rotary beater until thickened.

Egg Whites, 6
Salt, ⅛ teaspoon

To serve 4

Beat egg whites and salt together until stiff. Fold into yolks; serve at once in sherbet glasses.

CHOCOLATE SOUFFLÉ

Unsweetened Chocolate, 2 squares
Milk, 2 cups
Sugar, ½ cup
All-Purpose Flour, ⅓ cup
Salt, ½ teaspoon
Butter, 2 tablespoons
Vanilla, 1 teaspoon
Egg Yolks, 4

Melt chocolate in milk in top of double boiler over boiling water. Mix sugar, flour and salt and add to chocolate, beating with rotary beater until well blended. Cook until thickened, stirring occasionally. Add butter and vanilla. Cool slightly. Beat egg yolks until thick and add to mixture. Mix well.

Egg Whites, 4
Whipped Cream

Beat egg whites stiff, fold yolk mixture into them. Pour into buttered 2-quart baking dish. Put in pan of hot water.

Oven, moderate, 350°

To serve 4

Bake 1¼ hours or until firm. Serve at once with whipped cream.

CHOCOLATE RUM SOUFFLÉ: Add 2 tablespoons rum to egg yolk mixture.

VANILLA SOUFFLÉ

Thick White Sauce, ¾ cup (page 90)
Sugar, ⅓ cup
Vanilla, 1 teaspoon
Almond Extract, ¼ teaspoon
Eggs, 3, separated

Prepare white sauce, add sugar and flavorings. Beat egg yolks until thick and lemon-colored and add to mixture. Beat egg whites until they form stiff peaks but are not dry, and fold them into mixture. Turn into straight-sided baking dish buttered on bottom only and place dish in pan of hot water.

Oven, moderate, 350°

Heavy Cream, ½ cup, whipped

To serve 4 to 6

Bake 50 or 60 minutes, or until firm. Serve at once from baking dish with sweetened whipped cream on the side, if desired.

RUM SOUFFLÉ: A tablespoonful of rum may take the place of vanilla and almond extract in the above recipe, if preferred.

PEACH SOUFFLÉ: Spread 2 cups of chopped canned peaches in bottom of baking dish and pour egg mixture over them. Bake as above.

TOP HAT SOUFFLÉ: See page 117.

Remember to keep these dessert mixes on the shelf for busy days:

Chocolate Fudge Pudding
Lemon Cake Pudding
Instant Pudding Mix
Ice Cream Mix
Flavored Gelatins
Cake and Cooky Mix

Petits pots de crème chocolat

PETITS POTS DE CRÈME CHOCOLAT

Sweet Chocolate, 1
  pound, grated
Instant Coffee, 1
  teaspoon
Milk, 1 pint
Egg Yolks, 8
Sweetened whipped
  cream

To make 8

Cook chocolate, coffee and milk in double boiler over boiling water until chocolate is melted, stirring constantly. Pour mixture over slightly beaten egg yolks and stir until smoothly blended. Strain through a fine strainer into custard cups. Refrigerate until cold. Serve with whipped cream.

FUDGE PUDDING CAKE

Butter, 2 tablespoons
Sugar, 1/2 cup
Vanilla, 1 teaspoon
All-Purpose Flour, 1 cup
Cocoa, 3 tablespoons
Baking Powder, 1 teasp.
Salt, 1/2 teaspoon
Milk, 1/2 cup

Sugar, 1/2 cup
Cocoa, 5 tablespoons
Salt, 1/4 teaspoon
Boiling Water, 1 2/3 cups

Oven, moderate, 350°

To serve 4 to 6

Combine butter, sugar and vanilla. Sift together flour, cocoa, baking powder and salt; add alternately with milk to first mixture.

Mix sugar, cocoa, salt and boiling water. Turn into 7″ × 9″ baking dish and drop first mixture by spoonfuls on top.

Bake 40 to 45 minutes. When finished there will be cake on top and sauce underneath. Serve warm or cold with plain or whipped cream. When cold, sauce becomes quite thick.

INDIAN PUDDING

Milk, 2 cups
Cornmeal, 2 tablespoons
Molasses, 1/4 cup
Sugar, 2 tablespoons
Ginger, 1/2 teaspoon
Salt, 1/4 teaspoon
Eggs, 2, slightly beaten
Vanilla Ice Cream

To serve 4

Scald milk in top of double boiler; add cornmeal a little at a time. Cook 20 minutes over boiling water. Add molasses, sugar, ginger and salt. Pour a little of the mixture over slightly beaten egg yolks, return to double boiler and cook few minutes longer. Serve slightly warm with ice cream.

CREAMY CHOCOLATE ROLL

Batter for Jelly Roll,
  page 201
Creamy Chocolate
  Filling, page 204

After baking, roll cake as described in Jelly Roll recipe. Cool, then unroll and spread with Creamy Chocolate Filling. Re-roll and place cake on its open end to hold it in position. If desired roll may be frosted with any chocolate frosting.

STRAWBERRY ROLL

Batter for Jelly Roll,
  page 201
Heavy Cream, 1 cup,
  whipped
Strawberries, sliced, 2
  cups

To make 8 slices

After baking, roll cake as described in Jelly Roll recipe. Cool, then unroll and spread with whipped cream and sliced berries. Re-roll and place cake on its open end to hold it in position. Chill until ready to serve.

MERINGUES

Meringues are pastry crusts or mounds made of white of egg and sugar. They are intended to hold rich fillings; or the meringue itself may be combined with a rich mixture of nuts or fruits.

Egg Whites, 4
Salt, ¼ teaspoon
Cream of Tartar,
  ¼ teaspoon
Sugar, 1 cup

Beat egg whites at room temperature until frothy, add salt and cream of tartar and beat, gradually adding sugar until mixture forms stiff peaks.

To make Meringue Crusts, spread over bottom and up sides of well-greased 9-inch pie pan. Bake in slow oven (275°) about 50 minutes or until dry and firm. Leave in oven to cool, but do not let brown.

MERINGUES GLACÉS: Shape mixture into large mounds with a depression in the center on brown paper. Bake as above. Remove from paper. Store in air-tight container. To serve, fill with fresh sugared fruit or chocolate filling (page 204), and top with whipped cream or ice cream.

KISSES: Small meringues shaped in mounds. Make them plain or add to the stiffly beaten whites, 1 cup of shredded coconut, or 1 cup finely chopped nuts, or 1 cup finely crushed nut brittle.

Meringues

*Strawberry
roll*

HEAVENLY CHOCOLATE PIE

Unsweetened Chocolate,
3 squares
Egg Yolks, 4
Sugar, ½ cup
Salt, ⅛ teaspoon
Water, 2 tablespoons

Melt chocolate in top part of double boiler over boiling water. Beat egg yolks and sugar, salt and water until light and fluffy. Stir into chocolate. Cook over boiling water, stirring constantly, until very thick. Remove from heat and cool.

Heavy Cream, 1 cup, whipped
Meringue Crust, 9-inch (see page 229)

Fold in whipped cream and pour into baked meringue crust. Chill 24 hours.

LEMON TORTE

Graham Cracker Crust (page 182)

Line the bottom and sides of a springform pan with graham cracker crust mixture. Make enough for larger pan and reserve some for topping.

Egg Yolks, 4
Sweetened Condensed Milk, 1 can
Lemon Juice, ⅓ cup
Lemon Rind, grated, 1 teaspoon
Nutmeg, ¼ teaspoon
Egg Whites, 4

Beat egg yolks until thick and gradually add milk, lemon juice, rind and nutmeg, beating constantly. Fold in stiffly beaten egg whites. Pour mixture into crust and top with reserved crumbs.

Oven, moderate, 325°

Bake 30 minutes, turn off oven and let cool in oven 1 hour.

PINEAPPLE UPSIDE DOWN CAKE

Butter, ¼ cup
Brown Sugar, packed, ½ cup
Pineapple, slices, 15-oz. can, drained

Melt butter in 8-inch square baking pan, add brown sugar and stir until mixed. Remove from heat and arrange pineapple in syrup.

Yellow Cake Mix, small size

Mix cake according to directions on package and pour over pineapple.

Oven, moderate, 350°
Whipped Cream

Bake 35 to 45 minutes. Loosen cake from sides and bottom of pan with spatula and turn over on cake plate, scraping out any syrup remaining in the pan. Serve with whipped cream topping.

The fruit may be garnished with walnuts or pecans if desired.

PEACH UPSIDE DOWN CAKE: Substitute canned peach halves for pineapple.

SHERRY TRIFLE

Ladyfingers or **Sponge Cake**
Jam
Sherry
Almonds, shredded
Lemon Peel, grated
Custard Sauce (page 226)
Whipped Cream

Line bottom of bowl with split ladyfingers or slices of sponge cake spread with jam. Sprinkle with sherry, shredded almonds and grated lemon peel. Pour over it a custard sauce, or prepared mix. Cover and let stand in refrigerator overnight. Serve garnished with whipped cream and a dab of the jam.

Refrigerator cake with chocolate frosting

Heavenly chocolate pie

CHOCOLATE REFRIGERATOR CAKE

Unsweetened Chocolate,
  2 squares
Hot Water, $\frac{1}{4}$ cup
Sugar, $\frac{1}{3}$ cup
Salt, $\frac{1}{8}$ teaspoon
Egg Yolks, 2
Vanilla, 1 teaspoon
Egg Whites, 2
Sugar, 2 tablespoons

Place chocolate and water in top of double boiler and melt over boiling water. Add sugar and salt; cook, stirring constantly, until slightly thickened. Add egg yolks, beat well and cook until slightly thickened. Remove from heat and add vanilla. Beat egg whites until foamy; add sugar gradually and beat until stiff. Fold in chocolate mixture and chill.

Heavy Cream, $\frac{1}{2}$ cup,
  whipped
Sponge Cake, 2-layer
  store cake
**Whipped Cream for
  garnish**

Fold in whipped cream. With a sharp knife split each layer of sponge cake horizontally. Cut and trim them to fit the bottom and sides of a 9″ × 5″ loaf pan. Add layers of chocolate mixture alternately with layers of sponge cake, ending with sponge cake. Chill 24 hours. Garnish with whipped cream.

To serve 8

APRICOT REFRIGERATOR CAKE

Dried Apricots,
  12-ounce package
Water, 2 cups

Cook apricots in water until tender and liquid is absorbed. Put through ricer or sieve and cool.

Butter, 1 cup
Confectioners' Sugar,
  sifted, 2 cups
Eggs, 4, separated
Lemon Juice and **Grated
  Rind,** 1 lemon
Sugar, $\frac{1}{3}$ cup

Cream butter; add confectioners' sugar, beat until light. Add egg yolks, one at a time, and beat well. Beat in apricot pulp, lemon rind and juice. Beat egg whites stiff; gradually adding granulated sugar until sugar is dissolved. Fold into apricot mixture.

Ladyfingers, 3 dozen
Heavy Cream, $\frac{3}{4}$ cup,
  whipped

Line deep 9-inch springform pan with split ladyfingers. Put in 3 alternate layers of mixture and remaining ladyfingers. Chill overnight. Remove sides of pan and garnish with whipped cream.

To serve 10 to 12

CHOCOLATE COOKY ROLL

Confectioners' Sugar,
  3 tablespoons
Heavy Cream,
  1 cup, whipped
Vanilla, $\frac{1}{4}$ teaspoon
Thin Chocolate Wafers,
  1 package
**Unsweetened Chocolate
  Shavings**
Candied Cherries

To serve 6 to 8

Fold sugar into cream and add vanilla. Spread between chocolate wafers. Frost tops and sides of filled wafers with cream. Decorate with chocolate shavings and cherries. Chill for at least 4 hours. To serve: cut diagonally across roll.

BAKED ALASKA

Cake, 1 layer of plain
  or sponge
Ice Cream, 1 quart, brick
Egg Whites, 3
Salt, $\frac{1}{8}$ teaspoon
Sugar, 6 tablespoons

Place cake on baking sheet. Put ice cream on top and trim cake with $\frac{1}{2}$ inch margin around ice cream on all sides. Beat egg whites stiff, adding sugar gradually. Spread thickly over ice cream and cake, making sure to cover ice cream completely.

Oven, hot, 450°

To serve 4 to 6

Bake 5 minutes, or until meringue is golden brown. Serve at once.

FROZEN DESSERTS

In making these frozen desserts set the refrigerator control for fast freezing before starting to work.

COFFEE ICE

Sugar, ¾ cup
Water, 4 cups
Instant Coffee, 4 teasps.
Heavy Cream,
 ½ cup, whipped

To serve 4

Heat sugar in water until mixture is hot and clear. Add coffee; pour into freezing tray, cool. Freeze to a mush, stirring once. Serve in sherbet glasses; top with whipped cream.

FRESH CURRANT ICE

Fresh currants, 4 cups
Water, 2¼ cups

Wash and stem currants. Cover with 2 cups of water, bring to boil, simmer 5 minutes or until soft. Force through fine sieve. Reheat.

Unflavored Gelatin,
 1 tablespoon
Sugar, 1 cup
Lemon, ½

To serve 4

Soften gelatin in ¼ cup water, add sugar and lemon juice, pour hot currant juice on gelatin and stir until dissolved. Cool and freeze in refrigerator tray until partly firm. Put in cold bowl and beat with rotary beater until fluffy. Return to tray and freeze firm.

LEMON SHERBET

Egg White, 1
Salt, few grains
Confectioners' Sugar,
 sifted, ¼ cup
Light Corn Syrup,
 ½ cup
Lemon Juice, 2 tablesps.
Milk, 2 cups

To serve 4

Beat egg white with salt until stiff. Beat in sugar, corn syrup and lemon juice. Stir in milk. Pour into refrigerator tray and freeze until almost firm. Turn into chilled bowl, and beat thoroughly. Return to refrigerator tray, and freeze until firm.

LEMON-APPLESAUCE SHERBET

Buttermilk, 2 cups
Applesauce, 16-oz. can
Sugar, 1 cup
Lemon Juice, 2 tablesps.
Grated Lemon Rind,
 1 teaspoon

To serve 6 to 8

Mix all ingredients and pour into 2 refrigerator trays; freeze until firm. Sprinkle each tray with grated rind.

WATERMELON SHERBET

Watermelon, ¼ large
Sugar, ½ cup
Salt, ⅛ teaspoon

Unflavored Gelatin,
 1 envelope
Lemon, 1

To make about 4 cups

Put watermelon pulp through food mill or sieve to get 3 cups of juice. Add sugar and salt.

Soften gelatin in ¼ cup of juice, dissolve over low heat. Add with lemon juice to watermelon juice. Freeze in ice cream freezer.

PEACH PARFAIT

Alternate peach and vanilla ice cream in parfait glasses. Top with frozen or canned sliced peaches, and whipped cream. Keep frozen until ready to serve.

CHOCOLATE RUM PARFAIT

Unsweetened Chocolate,
 2 squares
Hot Water, ½ cup
Butter, 1 tablespoon
Corn Syrup, ¾ cup
Vanilla, ½ teaspoon
Rum, ¼ cup

Combine chocolate, water, butter and corn syrup in saucepan and cook, stirring, until it boils. Remove from heat, stir in vanilla and rum.

Vanilla Ice Cream, 4 cups
Heavy Cream,
 ½ cup, whipped

To serve 6 to 8

Put alternate layers of ice cream and chocolate sauce in parfait glasses. Place in freezer until ready to serve. Top with whipped cream.

CHOCOLATE MOUSSE

Unflavored Gelatin,
 1 teaspoon
Milk, ½ cup
Unsweetened Chocolate,
 1½ squares
Confectioners' Sugar,
 ½ cup
Vanilla, ½ teaspoon

Soak gelatin in milk in top of double boiler for 5 minutes. Add chocolate and sugar and set top of double boiler over boiling water; heat until chocolate is melted and continue cooking, stirring constantly, until mixture is smooth. Add vanilla. Chill, stirring frequently.

Heavy Cream, 1 cup,
 whipped
**Whipped Cream for
 garnish**

To serve 4

Fold in whipped heavy cream, pour into freezing tray or mold, and freeze. If frozen too hard, remove from freezer ten minutes or so before serving. Top with whipped cream, with a sprinkling of instant coffee.

STRAWBERRY MOUSSE

Strawberries, 2 cups
Sugar, 4 tablespoons
Heavy Cream, 1 cup,
 whipped

Set refrigerator control
 for fast freezing

To serve 4

Wash and hull strawberries and crush with potato masher. Sprinkle sugar over them and stir until dissolved. Combine with whipped cream and pour into freezing tray. Freeze until partially hard, or if it freezes too hard, take it out to soften a while before serving.

PEACH MOUSSE: Substitute 2 cups crushed fresh peaches for the strawberries.

MAPLE MOUSSE

Maple Syrup, 1 cup
Egg Whites, 2
Evaporated Milk, 14-oz.
 can, chilled
Set refrigerator control
 for fast freezing

To serve 8

Cook maple syrup until it forms a soft ball in cold water. Beat egg whites until stiff; beat in syrup slowly, beating constantly until cool. Whip milk stiff; fold in maple syrup mixture and freeze in refrigerator.

ALMOND TORTONI

Egg White, 1
Sugar, 2 tablespoons

Beat egg white with rotary beater until almost stiff. Gradually add sugar.

Heavy Cream, 1 cup
Sugar, 4 tablespoons
Vanilla, 1 teaspoon
Almond, ¼ teaspoon
Almonds, blanched,
toasted, chopped,
¼ cup

Whip cream; fold in sugar and flavorings. Fold in meringue and nuts. Spoon into ¼-cup paper or foil cups and freeze at coldest setting in refrigerator freezing compartment until firm.

To make 8 servings

OLD-FASHIONED PHILADELPHIA ICE CREAM

A person who has eaten only the commercial ice cream on the market can have no idea of the delicious flavor and texture of the old-fashioned, hand-cranked product. If you have one of the old hand freezers, fill it with ice and rock salt, in the proportion of 8 parts of ice to 1 of salt; pour the ice cream mixture into the container, no more than ⅔ full, and then take turns cranking until that wonderful frozen substance makes cranking impossible. (Or a new electric freezer will take out all the work.) Remove dasher, cork up hole in lid, and pack it with additional ice and salt. Let it ripen, a few hours, or until ready to use.

Light Cream, 1 quart
Sugar, ¾ cup
Salt, ½ teaspoon
Vanilla, 2 teaspoons

Scald cream; add sugar and salt; cool. Add vanilla. Proceed as above.

To make 1½ quarts

BLACK AND WHITE BOMBE

Line a melon mold with a layer of Vanilla Ice Cream, 1 inch thick. Fill the center with Chocolate Mousse (page 232). Cover and fast freeze 3 hours.

If you do not have a mold, a loaf pan will do. Line bottom and sides with ice cream, fill center with mousse, and finish with ice cream on top. Use any combination of ice cream and mousse desired.

SPUMONE

Milk, 2 cups
Egg Yolks, 3, slightly
beaten
Salt, ⅛ teaspoon
Sugar, 1 cup
Vanilla, 1 teaspoon

In top of double boiler combine milk, egg yolks, salt and sugar. Cook over simmering water, stirring constantly, until mixture coats metal spoon. Cool; add vanilla. Pour into refrigerator tray and freeze at coldest setting.

Heavy Cream, 1 cup
Maraschino Cherries,
chopped, ¼ cup
Candied Orange Peel,
minced, 2 tablespoons
Almonds, 8, blanched,
chopped
Brandy, 2 tablespoons

Whip cream and fold in fruits, nuts and brandy. Line 2-quart melon mold with layer of frozen mixture, fill center with whipped cream mixture, cover and freeze in freezer or refrigerator freezing compartment until firm. Unmold by setting mold on cloth wrung out of hot water. Cut in wedges.

FRENCH VANILLA ICE CREAM

Egg Yolks, 4, slightly
beaten
Milk, 2 cups
Sugar, 1 cup
Salt, ⅛ teaspoon
Vanilla, 2 teaspoons
Heavy Cream, 2 cups

In top part of double boiler beat egg yolks and milk together. Add sugar and salt; cook over barely boiling water over low heat until mixture coats a metal spoon. Let cool. Add vanilla and cream. Freeze as directed under Philadelphia Ice Cream.

To make about 6 cups

BANANA ICE CREAM: Omit vanilla and add the sieved pulp of 2 large ripe bananas.

PINEAPPLE ICE CREAM: Omit vanilla and add 2 cups of sweetened chopped fresh pineapple, or canned crushed.

PEACH ICE CREAM: Omit vanilla and add 1 teaspoon almond extract. Add 2 cups sweetened crushed peaches.

STRAWBERRY ICE CREAM: Omit vanilla and add 2 cups sweetened crushed fresh strawberries.

Chocolate mousse served in sherbet glasses

DESSERT SAUCES

HARD SAUCE

Butter, ¼ cup
Confectioners' Sugar,
 sifted, 1½ cups
Vanilla, 2 teaspoons
Cream, 1 tablespoon

Cream butter until soft; add sugar and beat until smooth and fluffy. Add vanilla and cream and beat smooth.

Two tablespoons of rum or brandy may be substituted for vanilla and cream, if desired.

PEACH SAUCE

Frozen Sliced Peaches,
 2 packages
Water
Cornstarch, 2 tablesps.
Salt, few grains
White Corn Syrup,
 2 tablespoons
Brandy, 2 tablespoons

Defrost peaches according to directions on package. Drain juice, measure and add water if necessary to total 1¼ cups. Add remaining ingredients. Cook in a saucepan over low heat until slightly thickened. Cool and add peaches.

To make about 2½ cups

RASPBERRY SAUCE: Substitute frozen raspberries for peaches in the above recipe.

PINEAPPLE SAUCE

Crushed Pineapple,
 9-ounce can
Sugar, 2 tablespoons
Cornstarch, 2 tablesps.

Drain pineapple and to the juice add mixed sugar and cornstarch. Heat until thickened, stirring constantly. Cool, and stir in pineapple.

To make 1 cup

RED CHERRY SAUCE

Tart Red Pitted Cherries,
 1-pound can
 (water-packed)
Cornstarch, 2 tablesps.
Sugar, ¾ cup
Salt, dash
Red Food Color, few
 drops
Butter, 1 tablespoon

In saucepan combine cherries with cornstarch, sugar and salt. Cook over low heat, stirring constantly until thickened and clear. Remove from heat, add red coloring and butter.

Serve warm over squares of plain yellow or white cake.

BLUEBERRY SAUCE

Fresh or **Frozen Blue-**
 berries, ¾ cup
White Corn Syrup, ½ cup

Combine in saucepan and bring to boil. Serve hot over pancakes, ice cream or squares of cake.

To make 1½ cups

LEMON SAUCE

Sugar, ½ cup
Cornstarch, 1 tablesp.
Salt, ¼ teaspoon
Boiling Water, 1 cup
Lemon Rind, grated,
 1 teaspoon
Lemon Juice, 3 tablesps.
Butter, 2 tablespoons

Mix together all ingredients but lemon and lemon rind; bring to boil and cook about 5 minutes, stirring all the while until smooth, thickened and clear. Stir in lemon juice, rind and butter.

To make about 1¼ cups

Lemon sauce on blueberry turnovers

BUTTERSCOTCH SAUCE

Brown Sugar, 1 cup, packed
Heavy Cream, ¼ cup
Salt, ⅛ teaspoon
Light Corn Syrup, 2 tablespoons
Butter, 2 tablespoons

Combine ingredients in saucepan. Bring to boil and cook rapidly for 3 minutes (220° on a candy thermometer).

HOT FUDGE SUNDAE

Serve chocolate or butter pecan ice cream with Hot Fudge Sauce.

HOT FUDGE SAUCE

Unsweetened Chocolate, 8 squares
Sugar, 2 cups
Evaporated Milk, 14½-ounce can
Strong Coffee, 2 tablesps.
Salt, ⅛ teaspoon
Vanilla, 1 teaspoon

Melt chocolate in top of double boiler over boiling water, add sugar and stir. Cover and cook for ½ hour. Add milk, coffee, salt and vanilla. Beat until smooth and thick. Serve hot. Can be refrigerated and reheated over boiling water.

CHOCOLATE WALNUT SUNDAE

Serve vanilla ice cream with Chocolate Walnut Sauce.

CHOCOLATE WALNUT SAUCE

Butter, ½ cup
Walnuts, 2 cups, chopped
Semi-sweet Chocolate Bits

Melt butter in heavy skillet over low heat. Add walnuts and stir until lightly browned. Add chocolate bits and stir until melted and smooth.

FROSTY PINK MINT TOPPER

Heavy Cream, 1 cup
Confectioners' Sugar, sifted, ¼ cup
Mint Flavoring
Red Food Coloring

Beat cream stiff, adding sugar gradually. Add a few drops of mint to taste and a few drops of red food coloring to make it a delicate pink. Freeze in refrigerator tray until firm.

Serve on squares of chocolate cake or on ice cream.

ALMOND PRALINE BALLS

Vanilla Ice Cream, 1 quart
Almonds or **Pecans,** toasted slivered, 1 cup

Scoop 6 large balls of ice cream. Roll balls in toasted almonds and place in freezer to harden.

Light Cream, 2 cups
Butter, ¼ cup
Light Brown Sugar, 1½ cups
Corn Syrup, 2 tablespoons

Combine ingredients in heavy saucepan; cook over very low heat, stirring constantly, until mixture is smooth and has thickened slightly, about 5 to 10 minutes. Cool, stirring frequently. Serve with Almond Balls.

To serve 6

Almond praline balls

FOAMY YELLOW SAUCE

Butter, ⅓ cup
Confectioner's Sugar, 1 cup
Egg, 1, separated
Orange Juice, ¼ cup
Brandy, 1 tablespoon

Cream butter until soft. Gradually beat in sugar, then egg yolk, orange juice and brandy. Just before serving, fold in stiffly beaten egg white. Makes ¾ cup sauce.

Reminder for Instant Ice Cream Toppings:

    Fruit preserves
    Jellies, melted
    Liqueurs
    Chocolate syrup in cans
    Nuts in syrup
    Maple syrup
    Butterscotch syrup
    Frozen fruit

CANDY MAKING

Many home candies are easy to make and candy making can be a project to interest the whole family, or at least the younger members. One piece of equipment is practically essential to guarantee success and that is a candy thermometer: it is so much easier than testing in cold water, although that can be done in a pinch, and is described in the Candy Temperature Chart below.

Other equipment needed will be a large, heavy saucepan, a wooden spoon for stirring and beating, shallow pans for cooling, and, for some candies, a large platter or other smooth hard work surface.

COLD WATER TEST

To test candy syrup for doneness, put a few drops of the boiling syrup into a cup of cold water. Feel it with your fingers to judge the consistency described in the chart below. If it seems ready, remove pan from heat at once to prevent cooking. If it is not, cook a little longer and test again, using fresh water for each test.

BUTTERSCOTCH

Molasses, ¼ cup
Sugar, 1¾ cups
Water, 2 tablespoons
Vinegar, 1 tablespoon
Butter, ¼ pound

To make about 1 pound

Combine ingredients in skillet and stir over heat until thoroughly dissolved. Continue cooking, without stirring, to the light crack stage (272°). Pour into well-buttered shallow pans; as it hardens mark it off into squares. Or drop it from a spoon on waxed paper.

MOLASSES CANDY PULL

Butter, ½ cup
Sugar, 2 cups
Molasses, 1 cup
Water, ½ cup

To make about 2 pounds

Melt butter in heavy skillet, add sugar, molasses and water; cook to soft-ball stage (238°) and pour into greased pan. When cool enough to dent with the finger, gather it into a ball and knead with the fingertips until it is light in color and porous. Pull and roll into long strips and cut into pieces. Place on buttered plate.

CANDIED ORANGE AND LEMON PEEL

Use peel from
4 Oranges,
or 6 Lemons

Cover peel with cold water, bring to boil and cook until tender. Scrape white membrane from inside and cut peel into strips.

Sugar, 1½ cups
Water, ¾ cup

Combine sugar and water in saucepan, bring to boil and add peel. Cook until it has translucent appearance, about 15 minutes.

Sugar, 1 cup

Drain few pieces at a time from syrup, roll separately in sugar, and spread on wax paper to cool.

Food coloring, in red, green, or yellow, may be added to the syrup for a gay appearance.

CANDIED GRAPEFRUIT PEEL: Use the above recipe for the skins of 2 grapefruit; since grapefruit peel is more bitter, change the cooking water several times.

MOLASSES LOLLYPOPS

Molasses, 1 cup
Sugar, 1 cup
Vinegar, 2 teaspoons
Butter, ¼ cup

To make about 12

Stir molasses, sugar and vinegar over heat to dissolve; when boiling, add butter and continue cooking to light crack stage (270°). Drop by spoonfuls onto greased cooky sheet. Press wooden skewers into the warm candy to make lollypops.

CANDY TEMPERATURE CHART

Stage	Condition	Thermometer Reading
Soft Ball	Syrup dropped from a spoon into cold water can be gathered with the fingers into a ball.	236°–240°
Medium Ball	Somewhat firmer—will hold its shape.	242°–248°
Hard Ball	Firm, still plastic but not rigid.	250°–265°
Light Crack	When syrup forms threads that are hard but not brittle	270°–290°
Hard Crack	When threads form that are brittle and will shatter when tapped.	up to 310°

Dipping apples on a stick

APPLES-ON-A-STICK

Perfect Apples
Skewers

Put a skewer in each apple.

Sugar, 2 cups
Water, 1 cup
Light Corn Syrup, ⅔ cup
Red Food Coloring

Combine ingredients and stir over slow heat until sugar is dissolved. Continue cooking without stirring to the hard crack stage (290°). Remove pan from heat and plunge bottom in cold water to stop cooking: then put over pan of hot water to keep syrup from hardening. Add few drops of red coloring, if desired. Dip apples one at a time in syrup; place on greased cooky sheet to harden.

EASY PEANUT BRITTLE

Sugar, 2 cups
Roasted Peanuts,
  chopped, 1 cup
Salt, ½ teaspoon

In a skillet over low heat melt sugar to a thin syrup, stirring constantly. Add nuts and salt; mix thoroughly. Pour in thin sheet on large buttered pan. When completely hard and cool, remove from pan and strike with knife handle to shatter into bite-size pieces.

To make about 1¼ pounds

FUDGE

Unsweetened Chocolate,
  3 squares
Milk, 1 cup

Heat chocolate and milk slowly in saucepan until chocolate is melted; beat until mixture is smoothly blended.

Sugar, 3 cups

Add sugar, stir until mixture comes to a boil; then cook without stirring until it forms a soft ball when a little is dropped in cold water (238°).

Vanilla, 1 teaspoon
Butter, 3 tablespoons

Remove from heat, add vanilla and butter, do not stir. Let cool until lukewarm, then beat until thick and the mixture loses its gloss. Turn out quickly into greased 9-inch square pan.

To make about 1½ pounds

When firm, cut in squares.

MOCHA FUDGE

Instant Coffee, 2 tablesps.

Follow above recipe for Fudge, and add coffee with sugar.

PEANUT BUTTER FUDGE

Peanut Butter, 3 tablesps.

Follow Fudge recipe above, but add peanut butter in place of butter, before beating.

COCOA FUDGE

Cocoa, 1 cup

Follow Fudge recipe above; substitute cocoa for chocolate and mix it with sugar before adding to milk.

NUT FUDGE

Pecans, Walnuts or
  Almonds, 1 cup,
  chopped

Follow Fudge recipe above; add nuts just before turning into pan.

QUICK FUDGE

Sugar, 1½ cups
Evaporated Milk,
  14½-ounce can
Semi-sweet Chocolate
  Pieces, 12-oz. pkg.

Combine sugar and milk in saucepan and bring to boil; add chocolate pieces, remove from heat and stir until smooth. Cool slightly, beat by hand until creamy, and turn into buttered 8″ × 8″ × 2″ pan. When firm, cut into squares.

To make about 2 pounds

Assorted candies

Penuche

PENUCHE

Brown Sugar, 2 cups
Cream, ½ cup
Butter, 2 tablespoons
Vanilla, 1 teaspoon

Cook sugar and cream slowly, stirring to melt sugar, then continue until mixture reaches soft ball stage (238°). Remove from heat. Add butter and vanilla. When mixture has cooled a little, beat until thick and creamy. Pour into greased pan or drop by spoonfuls on waxed paper.

To make about 18 pieces

Whole pecan or walnut meats may be pressed into the top of each piece, if desired.

DIVINITY

Light Corn Syrup, ½ cup
Sugar, 2½ cups
Water, ½ cup

In saucepan heat syrup, sugar and water until sugar is dissolved, stirring constantly. Continue cooking without stirring to the firm ball stage (248°).

Egg Whites, 2

Meanwhile beat egg whites stiff, then pour syrup, a little at a time, over egg whites, beating constantly and returning syrup to heat between pourings.

Vanilla, 1 teaspoon
Walnuts, ½ cup, chopped fine

Continue beating until mixture is thick and begins to lose its gloss; add vanilla and nuts; drop by spoonfuls on wax paper or pour into buttered pan and cut into squares when cool.

To make about 24 pieces

REFRIGERATOR FUDGE

Cream Cheese, 3-oz. pkg.

Beat cream cheese until smooth.

Unsweetened Chocolate, 2 squares
Confectioners' Sugar, sifted, 2 cups
Vanilla, 1 teaspoon
Almonds or **Walnuts,** chopped, ½ cup

Melt chocolate over hot water, add to cheese with sugar, vanilla and nuts. Blend together thoroughly. Spread in greased baking pan; refrigerate until firm, then cut into squares.

To make about 1½ pounds

PRALINES

Sugar, 2 cups
Brown Sugar, 2 cups, packed
Cream, 1 cup
Salt, ¼ teaspoon

Combine ingredients and cook slowly to the boiling point, stirring all the while. Boil to the soft ball stage (236°).

Pecans, 2 cups, broken pieces

Stir nuts into syrup; remove from heat and place over hot water. Drop mixture by spoonfuls onto wax paper to make patties.

To make about 24

ALMOND DIVINITY

Almond Extract, ½ teasp.
Almonds, 1 cup, chopped

Follow recipe for Divinity above. Blanch almonds (see page 243) and chop them. Add extract and almonds to mixture just before turning it into pan, or dropping it by spoonfuls on paper.

Divinity fudge

CHERRY DIVINITY

Red Food Coloring
Candied Cherries

Tint Divinity a delicate pink while beating it. Drop by spoonfuls on waxed paper. Press a candied cherry lightly on the top of each piece.

TINTED DIVINITY

Pure food coloring can be used to tint Divinity any desired color. If you are making several batches, each can be tinted a different color.

ALMOND CRUNCH

Almonds, ½ pound

Blanch almonds, spread under broiler and toast lightly, then chop fine.

Butter, 1 cup
Sugar, 1 cup

Melt butter and sugar over low heat; add the nuts and cook to the very hard crack stage (310°). Pour into buttered 9″ × 9″ pan. Let cool.

Semi-sweet Chocolate, 4 ounces

Heat chocolate over boiling water until melted. Pour over nut mixture. When cool and hard remove from pan and crack into irregular pieces.

To make about 1¾ pounds

COCONUT CREAMS

Sugar, 2 cups
Cream, 1 cup
Coconut, moist, shredded, 1 cup
Vanilla, ½ teaspoon

Combine ingredients and cook over low heat, stirring constantly, until mixture forms soft ball (238°). Remove from heat and add vanilla. Cool to lukewarm, then beat until creamy. Drop by spoonfuls on buttered cooky sheet.

When cool and firm, candies may be chocolate coated if desired.

To make about 1¼ pounds

PINEAPPLE CREAMS

Candied Pineapple, 1 cup

Follow recipe for Coconut Creams above, omitting coconut. After beating, add candied pineapple chopped into small pieces.

Candied cherries may be substituted for pineapple.

CARAMELS

White Sugar, 1 cup
Brown Sugar, 1 cup
Light Corn Syrup, 1 cup
Light Cream, 2 cups
Butter, ⅓ cup

Combine sugar, syrup, butter and cream in large pan and cook slowly to the firm ball stage (248°), stirring all the while.

Vanilla, 1 teaspoon
Nuts, ½ cup, chopped

Remove from heat, add vanilla and nuts, stirring gently. Turn at once into 8″ × 8″ × 2″ buttered pan and let cool. Turn out of pan, cut in 1-inch squares, and wrap each in waxed paper.

To make about 2 pounds

CHOCOLATE CARAMELS: Add 3 squares unsweetened chocolate to the above recipe for Caramels.

Mints, chocolate logs and other candies

Serve assorted candies instead of a dessert

BUTTER TOFFEE

Sugar, 1 cup **Corn Syrup,** ¾ cup **Light Cream,** ¾ cup **Salt,** ¼ teaspoon	Stir sugar, syrup, cream and salt over heat until sugar is dissolved. Continue cooking until mixture forms firm ball in cold water (244°).
Butter, 2 tablespoons	Add butter and cook, stirring frequently until mixture forms hard ball (262°). Turn at once into buttered shallow pan. Mark into squares when cool, and when cold remove from pan and break apart with knife handle.
To make about 1¼ pounds	

RUM-BUTTER TOFFEE

Rum, 3 tablespoons, or
  Rum Flavoring,
  1 teaspoon
	Follow recipe for Butter Toffee above. Add rum or flavoring just before turning into buttered pan.

FONDANT

Combine 2 cups sugar, 1 cup water, and 2 tablespoons light corn syrup in saucepan. Stir over low heat until dissolved; boil, covered, about 3 minutes to dissolve crystals that collect on pan. Then boil uncovered to the soft ball stage. Pour out on platter or marble work surface that has been wiped with damp cloth. When cooled to lukewarm, work with wooden spoon or spatula until it becomes white and creamy; work in ½ teaspoon vanilla, then knead until smooth. Store overnight or several days in tightly covered jar before using. To make about 1 pound.

CHOCOLATE LOGS

Shape fondant into rolls 3″ × ½″ thick and roll in chocolate shot.

FRUIT DROPS

Shape balls of fondant candied cherries, squares of candied citron, or other candied or dried fruits. These may be served plain or with a chocolate coating, as above.

BONBONS

Fondant **Candied Fruits and** **Nuts for Centers**	Make fondant according to the above recipe. Reserve ⅓ of the batch and shape the remainder into balls with fruit or nut centers. Let stand on wax paper until firm.
Fondant Dip **Food Coloring** **Flavoring**	Melt reserved fondant over hot water but do not allow it to become hot. Add flavoring and food coloring as desired. Drop one center at a time into melted fondant, lift with fork and place on wax paper. Stir fondant frequently to prevent a crust from forming.
Decorations	Decorate bonbons with silver shot, colored sugar, or bits of nuts or fruit as desired.

MAPLE WALNUT FONDANT

Maple Extract, 1 teasp.
Walnuts, 1 cup, chopped

Add to above recipe for Fondant and knead in well. Press into buttered pan, mark off in squares, and let it set for a day before using.

If desired, the squares may be dipped in chocolate coating.

CREAM MINTS

Fondant, ¾ cup
Oil of Peppermint, 1 drop
Food Coloring

Make fondant by above recipe. Melt ¾ cup of fondant over hot water, flavor with oil of peppermint, color as desired. Drop from teaspoon on waxed paper, and let set until thoroughly dry.

Other flavorings may be substituted for peppermint—wintergreen, clove, or orange, for example.

The mints when dry can be chocolate coated if desired.

CHOCOLATE COATING

Use only special dipping chocolate: it should say "dipping" on package. The coating may be of bitter chocolate, sweet chocolate, or a combination of the two, depending on taste. Dry weather with a room temperature of 65° is best for coating.

Chocolate, 4 ounces
Butter, 2 tablespoons
Paraffin, 1 square inch
Vanilla, ¼ teaspoon

Combine ingredients in top of double boiler, over, but not touching, hot water. Stir until chocolate is melted, then cool to lukewarm, about 85°. Keep water in bottom of boiler at this temperature and place top part over it. Place candy centers one at a time in chocolate and lift out quickly with fork. Place on waxed paper to dry.

UNCOOKED FONDANT

Egg Whites, 2
Flavoring Extract,
    ¼ teaspoon
Confectioners' Sugar,
    sifted, 1 pound

To make about 1 pound

Beat egg whites slightly, then add sugar gradually, beating until stiff. Turn out on damp platter and knead until smooth and creamy. Flavor to taste with vanilla, almond, or a few drops of peppermint.

Fondant can be kept fresh for quite a while in an airtight jar or can, and used as desired. Combine it with candied fruits or chopped dates or figs, or chopped nuts, or preserved ginger. Use it to stuff prunes, dates, or figs.

ALMOND PASTE

Almonds, 1 lb., blanched

Grind almonds, using finest cutter. Regrind several times until very fine, or do a few at a time in the blender.

Sugar, 2¼ cups
Water, 1 cup
Orange Juice, ½ cup

To make about 2 pounds

Cook sugar and water to medium stage (240°). Add orange juice and chopped nuts. Remove from heat and stir until creamy; turn into pan dusted with confectioners' sugar and knead. When cool, pack in airtight containers. Store in cool place a week before using.

MARZIPAN

Almond Paste, 1 cup
Confectioners' Sugar,
    sifted, 1 cup
Rose Water, few drops
Vegetable Coloring

To make about ¾ pound

Mix all ingredients together. Knead 20 minutes on a cold platter dusted with confectioners' sugar.

Mold with fingers into any shape desired; traditionally miniature fruits and vegetables are used. Paint with vegetable coloring.

IRISH POTATOES

Roll round balls of marzipan in a mixture of cocoa and confectioners' sugar, equal proportions.

Marzipan in a variety of shapes

NUTS

Nuts are highly nutritious and can be used to add interesting flavor and texture to many dishes, particularly salads and desserts.

TO BLANCH NUTS: Pour boiling water over shelled nuts and let stand 5 minutes, or until skins are wrinkled. Drain; rub with fingers to remove skins. Dry thoroughly on absorbent paper or in warm (not hot) oven before using or storing.

TO TOAST NUTS: After blanching, drain and dry thoroughly, then spread out in a shallow pan and place in a moderate (350°) oven for 15 or 20 minutes, until thoroughly dry and lightly browned, stirring occasionally.

TO SALT NUTS: Place blanched nuts in a shallow pan, as above, and sprinkle evenly with salt, using about ½ teaspoon of salt to ¼ pound of nuts. The moisture will cause the salt to adhere to the nuts. Heat 15 or 20 minutes, or until thoroughly dry, stirring occasionally.

BUTTERED SALTED NUTS: Dry nuts after blanching, place in a bowl with melted butter, allowing about 2 teaspoons butter to 1 pound of nuts and stir around to coat nuts. Spread in shallow pan, sprinkle lightly with salt and brown in hot oven (400°) 10 to 15 minutes. Drain on paper towel.

SAUTÉED SALTED NUTS: Heat 2 tablespoons of butter in small frying pan. Add enough nuts to cover bottom of pan and heat slowly, stirring constantly, until delicately browned. Drain on paper towel and sprinkle with salt.

SUGARED NUTS: Blanch 2 cups of shelled nuts as described above; keep in warm place while preparing syrup. Combine 1 cup of sugar with ½ cup of water; stir over heat until sugar is dissolved, then boil, without stirring, until a small amount of syrup forms a soft ball in cold water (238°.) Hold pan of nuts several inches above heat and shake vigorously while slowly pouring syrup over nuts. Occasionally stir nuts, then add remaining syrup slowly until all is used. Nuts should be evenly coated. Store in closely covered tin box.

Assorted nuts with other appetizers

POPCORN BALLS

Molasses, 1 cup	Combine molasses, corn syrup, vinegar and butter. Boil rapidly to hard ball stage (250°). Place popped corn in large bowl. Pour syrup gradually into the center of the corn; stir with fork and gather corn, well coated with syrup, into balls. Butter hands and press balls between hands to pack hard.
Corn Syrup, 1 cup	
Vinegar, 1 tablespoon	
Butter, 3 tablespoons	
Popped Corn, 10 cups	
To make 8 to 10 balls	

Popcorn balls

APPETIZERS

The appetizer is a pleasant introduction to a meal, whether it is a simple fruit juice cocktail for a home dinner, or a more elaborate canapé or hors d'oeuvre for special company affairs. In any case it should spark the appetite, never dull it or satisfy it.

CLAM JUICE COCKTAIL

Make Clam Broth (page 104). Add a little lemon juice and horse-radish juice to taste. Chill.

Bottled clam juice may also be used.

TOMATO JUICE COCKTAIL

Serve tomato juice chilled as it comes from the can, or combine it with equal parts of sauerkraut juice or clam juice; or with an equal part of bouillon and serve hot in cups.

Or season it with a little lemon juice, grated cucumber, horse-radish, Worcestershire sauce, soy sauce, onion, curry powder, garlic salt, or Tabasco.

GRAPEFRUIT HALVES

Grapefruit, ½ per person	Wash and dry grapefruit; cut in half. With sharp knife cut around each section of fruit, close to membrane. Remove seeds.

BROILED GRAPEFRUIT

Grapefruit, ½ per person Brown Sugar, 1 table- spoon per half	Prepare as above. Sprinkle each half with brown sugar. Brown 10 minutes or until golden.
	May be flavored with rum or sherry before serving and garnished with cherries if desired.

MINTED FRESH FRUIT CUP

Combine a selection of fresh fruits in any combination desired. Flavor with chopped fresh mint and sugar to taste.

For variation, omit the mint and add a little of your favorite brandy, wine, or liqueur.

FRESH GREEN FIGS AND PROSCIUTTO HAM

Ripe Green Figs, 8 Prosciutto Ham, ¼ lb.	Serve 2 figs on small plate with prosciutto ham sliced thin and rolled.

To serve 4

WARMED COMPOTE OF FROZEN MELON BALLS

White Wine, ½ cup Ginger, ¼ teaspoon Frozen Melon Balls, 1 pkg.	Heat wine with ginger; remove from heat, add melon balls. Cover and allow to thaw. Serve warm.

To serve 4

MELON AND PROSCIUTTO HAM

Cantaloupe, 1 Prosciutto Ham, ¼ lb.	Cut melon into wedges and peel. Serve with prosciutto ham sliced thin and rolled.

Honeydew, Persian or Casaba melon may be used.

ANTIPASTO

On individual plates arrange thin slices of salami, little rolls of prosciutto ham, ripe, and green olives, pickled tiny red peppers, celery sticks, sliced hard-cooked eggs, and top each with an anchovy fillet. Serve with cruets of olive oil and vinegar.

SMOKED OR PICKLED FISH

Small portions of smoked or pickled fish make delicious appetizers: the variety includes whitefish, salmon (lox), sturgeon, herring, kippers. Serve accompanied with lemon wedges, sour cream, horse-radish, or a cruet of olive oil.

LOBSTER COCKTAIL

Chili Sauce, ¼ cup Mayonnaise, 2 tablesps. Horse-radish, 1 teaspoon Lemon Juice, 1 tablesp. Worcestershire, 1 teasp. Lobster, 2 cups, cooked, cut up	Combine all ingredients but lobster and put individual portions in small bowls in center of salad plates. Arrange cooked lobster in bite-size pieces on lettuce leaves surrounding the sauce. Serve well chilled.

To serve 4

SHRIMP COCKTAIL: Substitute jumbo-size shrimps in the above recipe. Chill thoroughly.

CRAB MEAT COCKTAIL: Substitute crab meat for lobster in the above recipe. Serve in chilled cocktail glasses and top with sauce.

TUNA COCKTAIL: Substitute a 7-ounce can of tuna fish for lobster in above recipe. Break tuna up into pieces with fork. Arrange in chilled cocktail glasses and top with sauce.

OYSTERS ON THE HALF SHELL

Have oysters opened at the fish market, or do it yourself (page 84). Serve each oyster on one half the shell, allowing at least 6 per person. Arrange on bed of crushed ice. Serve with a little dish of Cocktail Sauce (see Lobster Cocktail, above) and lemon wedges.

CLAMS ON THE HALF SHELL: Substitute clams for oysters in the above recipe.

Shrimps with remoulade sauce

CANAPÉS

Bread for canapés should be a day or two old; it is easier to handle. When making quantities you will save time by spreading a whole slice with soft butter, a soft cheese spread, or a little mayonnaise, then with whatever spread you are using, before cutting it up into squares or oblong strips. Round shapes are made with a cooky cutter and are more time consuming. The bread may be white, whole wheat or rye, toasted or plain, or crackers may be used instead.

Following are some suggested combinations for highly seasoned toppings to use in making these appetite teasers.

Cream cheese garnished with stuffed olive slice or radish, chopped chives

Mashed sardines topped with hard-cooked egg slices

Herring fillet chopped with pickles, onion, pimiento

Smoked salmon topped with thin strip of pimiento

Tuna mixed with mayonnaise into a paste, topped with sliced hard-cooked egg

Thin slice of ham garnished with pimiento rounds

Strips of anchovy decorated with thin slices of egg and pimiento

Cream cheese with chopped bacon and chives

Anchovy butter, garnished with sliced black olives

Rolled fillet of anchovy on creamed cheese

Roquefort cheese paste, garnished with sliced stuffed olive

Chopped egg spread, garnished with anchovy fillet

Cream cheese nest, filled with caviar and minced onion

Pimiento cheese, topped with cocktail onion

Deviled ham garnished with thinly-sliced gherkin

Camembert cheese topped with bits of bacon

Smoked salmon, spread with softened cream cheese mixed with a touch of horse-radish

CANAPÉ BUTTERS

To prepare any one of the following butters, beat the ingredients into ¼ cup butter, creamed; store in covered container in cold place until ready to use. If hard, leave in room temperature about 1 hour, or cream enough to soften before spreading on canapé base.

ANCHOVY BUTTER: Use 1 tablespoon anchovy paste, ½ teaspoon lemon juice and dash of paprika.

CAVIAR BUTTER: Use 1 2-oz. can caviar, mashed with soft butter.

CHEESE BUTTER: Use ¼ cup soft snappy cheese.

CHILI BUTTER: Use 2 tablespoons chili sauce.

CHIVES BUTTER: Use 1 tablespoon finely minced chives and 1 teaspoon lemon or lime juice, or a few drops of tarragon vinegar.

CHUTNEY BUTTER: Use 1 tablespoon chutney.

EGG BUTTER: Use 2 hard-cooked egg yolks, finely mashed, ½ teaspoon lemon juice and dash of Tabasco sauce; season with salt and cayenne.

GARLIC BUTTER: Allow one clove of garlic to stand 2 hours in ½ cup of butter; remove garlic before using as spread. Or mince fine and add to butter as spread.

GREEN SAVORY BUTTER: Mix together 3 tablespoons spinach purée, 1 tablespoon anchovy paste, 1 teaspoon capers, dash of paprika and salt to taste; force through sieve.

HERB BUTTER: Use ½ teaspoon dried tarragon and 1 tablespoon chopped chives or ½ teaspoon tarragon and ½ teaspoon dried rosemary. Rub together and let stand 20 minutes before using.

HONEY BUTTER: Use equal amounts of honey and butter. Stir until well blended. Use on hot biscuits, waffles and griddle cakes.

HORSERADISH BUTTER: Use 2 tablespoons horseradish.

KETCHUP BUTTER: Use 2 tablespoons ketchup.

LEMON BUTTER: Use a few gratings lemon rind and 2 teaspoons lemon juice. Lime or orange rind and juice may be substituted for lemon.

LOBSTER BUTTER: Use 1 tablespoon lobster paste, ½ teaspoon lemon juice and dash each of paprika and dry mustard.

MINT BUTTER: Use 2 tablespoons finely chopped mint leaves and 1 teaspoon lemon juice. Color a delicate green with vegetable coloring.

MUSTARD BUTTER: Use 1 tablespoon prepared mustard.

NUT BUTTER Use 2 tablespoons finely ground nuts; season with salt.

OLIVE BUTTER: Use 1 tablespoon olive paste and ¼ teaspoon lemon juice.

ONION BUTTER: Use 1 teaspoon onion juice.

PARMESAN BUTTER: Use 2 tablespoons Parmesan cheese.

PARSLEY BUTTER: Use 2 tablespoons finely cut parsley and 1 teaspoon lemon juice.

PEANUT BUTTER: Use ¼ cup peanut butter and 1 teaspoon honey; season with salt.

PIMIENTO BUTTER: Use 2 tablespoons mashed pimiento and 1 teaspoon finely chopped pickles.

ROQUEFORT BUTTER: Use 1 tablespoon Roquefort cheese.

SALMON BUTTER: Use 1 tablespoon salmon paste, 1 teaspoon lemon juice and dash of cayenne.

SARDINE BUTTER: Use 1 tablespoon sardine paste, ½ teaspoon each lemon and onion juice, and dash of paprika.

SHREDDED LOBSTER OR CRABMEAT BUTTER: Use 1 cup finely shredded lobster or crabmeat.

SHRIMP BUTTER: Use 1 cup shrimp. Rub through fine sieve. Add ½ teaspoon lemon juice and a dash of paprika or cayenne. Salt to taste.

WATER CRESS BUTTER: Use 2 tablespoons finely chopped water cress, 1 teaspoon lemon juice and a few drops Worcestershire sauce.

WORCESTERSHIRE BUTTER: Use ¼ teaspoon Worcestershire sauce.

SPREADS

Prepare a few attractive crocks of your favorite spreads, and keep them in the refrigerator to bring out at cocktail time. This is one of the jobs which the blender handles so well.

There are many ready-prepared spreads on the market which are useful for making canapés in a hurry. They may be used just as they come from the jar or combined with other ingredients to give them individuality. But let's please serve our "dips" on crackers or bread. It really is more sanitary, and there will be less damage to the furniture and carpets. Potato chips with a dip aboard are pretty fragile and may end up on the upholstery.

CHEESE SPREADS

CHEESE-CAVIAR SPREAD: Moisten cream cheese with cream; shape into tiny balls and roll in caviar. Serve on small crackers, buttered lightly.

CHEESE-ONION SPREAD: Mix ½ package (1½ oz.) cream cheese with 1 tablespoon minced onion and season with salt; add light cream to moisten. Serve on crackers or toast rounds. Sprinkle lightly with paprika or place sprig of parsley in center. Or spread on slices of dried beef, roll tightly and cut in 1-inch lengths.

CHILI-CHEESE SPREAD: Mix 1 3-oz. package cream cheese with enough chili sauce to moisten. Serve on crisp potato chips.

DILL CANAPÉS: Soften cream cheese with sour cream and season with finely chopped fresh dill, salt and pepper. Or mix chopped dill with the least possible amount of unsweetened butter or thick cream. Spread the mixture on long, thin slices of smoked salmon, roll them up and spear them with toothpicks. Serve chilled.

HAM BALLS: Combine 1 cup cottage cheese, ½ cup deviled ham, 1 tablespoon prepared horseradish, ¼ cup sour cream, ¼ teaspoon salt and dash of pepper. Form into balls and roll in ½ cup chopped water cress and 2 tablespoons chopped chives. Serve chilled.

HORSE-RADISH SPREAD: Combine 1 3-oz. package of cream cheese with 1½ teaspoons drained horse-radish, ½ teaspoon scraped onion and ⅛ teaspoon salt. Blend thoroughly and spread on toast rounds and top with bacon.

PISTACHIO CANAPÉ SPREAD: Combine 1 3-oz. package of Roquefort cheese and cream cheese with 1 tablespoon heavy cream, 1 teaspoon minced onion, 2 tablespoons chopped ripe olives, and ½ cup blanched pistachio nuts. Mix well and chill. Spread on rye wafers.

ROQUEFORT-CHIVES SPREAD: Mix Roquefort cheese with enough French dressing to moisten; season with chopped chives. Serve on crisp crackers, potato or corn chips.

BLUE CHEESE SPREAD: Blend ¼ pound blue cheese with enough cream or sour cream to spread. Add 1 teaspoon caraway seeds.

WINE-CHEDDAR SPREAD: Combine 1 cup soft Cheddar cheese with 2 tablespoons sherry wine and beat until well blended.

CHEDDAR-PEANUT SPREAD

Soft Cheddar Cheese, ½ cup	Combine cheese with finely chopped peanuts and add
Salted Peanuts, ¼ cup, chopped	enough cream to make it the right consistency for spreading.
Light Cream	

To make about 1 cup

FISH SPREADS

ANCHOVY-CHEESE SPREAD: Mix 1 part anchovy paste with 2 parts cream cheese. Spread on crackers. Garnish each with ½ anchovy or caper.

CAVIAR-EGG SPREAD: Mix 2 tablespoons caviar with 2 hard-cooked eggs, minced; moisten with mayonnaise. Serve on toast rounds.

A variety of canapés served on a cheese board

Appetizers can be as varied as they are tasty

Cheese served as it comes or in spreads

CAVIAR SPREAD: Mix 3 tablespoons caviar, 2 tablespoons finely chopped white onions and 1½ teaspoons lemon juice. Serve on toast points. Garnish with hard-cooked egg, daisy style.

DEVILED CRABMEAT SPREAD: Add 1 cup flaked crabmeat, 1 tablespoon each butter and onion juice, 1 teaspoon Worcestershire sauce and ¼ teaspoon mustard to ¼ cup Thick White Sauce (page 125), and heat thoroughly. Season with salt and pepper and serve hot on crackers.

KIPPERED HERRING SPREAD: Mix 1 cup mashed kippered herring, ½ cup minced cucumber and 2 drops onion juice. Serve on toast rounds.

SHRIMP SPREAD: Mix finely chopped shrimp with lemon juice and Tabasco sauce and season with salt and pepper. Spread on toast rounds and garnish each with section of pickled walnut.

TUNA FISH SPREAD: Mix ½ cup shredded tuna fish, 1 tablespoon lemon juice and 1 teaspoon grated onion with mayonnaise to moisten. Spread on toast squares and garnish with a half slice of lemon.

ANCHOVY SPREAD

Hard-Cooked Eggs, 2	Mince eggs and pimiento and
Pimiento, 1 tablespoon	blend with anchovy paste. Add
Anchovy Paste, tube	enough mayonnaise to make it
Mayonnaise	the proper consistency for
To make about 1 cup	spreading.

SARDINE SPREAD

Sardines in Oil,	Drain sardines, mash; combine
2 3¾-ounce cans	with lemon juice, onion and
Lemon Juice, 1 tablesp.	enough mayonnaise to make it
Onion, minced, 1 tablesp.	the right consistency for
Mayonnaise	spreading.
To make about 1 cup	

PINK SHRIMP SPREAD

Cream Cheese, 8-oz. pkg.	Blend cheese with seasonings.
Chili Sauce, ¼ cup	Mix in shrimp. Serve on
Lemon Juice, 2 teasps.	crackers, or carrot or celery
Onion Salt, ¼ teaspoon	slices. Mixture may be tinted a
Worcestershire Sauce,	deeper pink.
¼ teaspoon	
Shrimp, 5-ounce can,	
drained, finely	
chopped	
To make about 2 cups	

OTHER SPREADS

HAM-CHEESE SPREAD: Mix 1 cup finely chopped, cold boiled ham, ¼ cup grated American cheese, ½ teaspoon grated onion and 1 teaspoon catsup. Spread on crackers and place in center of each a bit of Horse-radish. Sprinkle with paprika.

PÂTÉ DE FOIE GRAS SPREAD: Mix 3 tablespoons pâté de foie gras with ¼ cup cream and season to taste. Rub through sieve and spread on toast fingers. Garnish with parsley.

LIVERWURST SPREAD: Remove skin from ½ pound liverwurst; mash well and add 1 teaspoon lemon juice, ½ teaspoon Worcestershire sauce and dash of paprika. Moisten with cream. Spread on toast rounds and garnish with Onion Butter (page 246).

AVOCADO SPREAD

Avocado, 1 medium	Peel and mash avocado. Com-
Mayonnaise, 2 tablesps.	bine with other ingredients. Put
Lemon Juice, 1 tablesp.	in bowl and spread top with a
Onion, minced, 1 tablesp.	little mayonnaise to prevent
Chili Powder, ⅛ teasp	discoloration. Just before
	serving, stir in mayonnaise.
To make about 1 cup	Serve on toast rounds or
	crackers.

DEVILED HAM SPREAD

Cream Cheese, 3-oz. pkg.	Blend cheese and deviled ham
Deviled Ham, 3-oz. can	with enough chili sauce to make
Chili Sauce	it the right consistency for
To make about ¾ cup	spreading.

MUSHROOM PÂTÉ

Mushrooms, sliced,
4-ounce can, drained
Potted Meat, 3-oz. can
Horse-radish, 1 tablesp.
Mayonnaise

To make about 1 cup

Combine mushrooms, potted meat and horse-radish with enough mayonnaise to make it the right consistency for spreading.

CHICKEN CURRY SPREAD

Boned Chicken, 6-oz. can
Parsley, 2 tablespoons
Onion, minced, 2 tablesps.
Curry Powder, 1 teasp.
Mayonnaise

To make about 1 cup

Chop chicken fine and add other ingredients with enough mayonnaise to make it the right consistency for spreading.

CHOPPED CHICKEN LIVERS

Onions, 2, sliced
Butter or **Chicken Fat,**
3 tablespoons
Chicken Livers, 1 pound
Egg Yolks, 3 hard-
cooked
Salt, 1 teaspoon
Pepper, ¼ teaspoon

To make about 2 cups

Sauté onions slowly in fat in skillet until golden; remove. Cook chicken livers slowly in skillet until tender. Grind or chop onions, liver and egg yolks fine and add seasonings. Serve on crackers, or on lettuce as a first course.

FRUIT SPREADS

AVOCADO-ONION SPREAD: Season mashed avocados with minced onion, salt and dash of Tabasco sauce. Serve on toasted bread rounds.

DATE SPREAD: Stuff dates with marshmallow cream which has been mixed sparingly with powdered coffee.

GUAVA-CHEESE SPREAD: Spread bread or crackers with cream cheese, then with guava jelly; sprinkle chopped nuts over top.

PINE AIGRETTES: Chop 6 slices of canned pineapple, or four of fresh pineapple, and set to drain. Add 2 tablespoons of grated American cheese, ⅛ teaspoon each of salt and pepper, 1 teaspoon of sugar, 2 teaspoons of toasted crumbs and the stiffly beaten white of an egg. Mix lightly, then heap on bread rounds and brown in the oven, but do not dry out or burn. Serve at once.

Appetizers for an outdoor party heated on a table grill

HOT HORS D'ŒUVRES

When you have lots of time to prepare for a party, you might want to serve a few hot hors d'oeuvres. These savory morsels make a big hit with guests; but don't have too many, or they become a meal rather than the appetizer.

HOT SHRIMP IN GARLIC BUTTER SAUCE

Fresh Shrimp, 1 pound,
cooked and deveined
Butter, ¼ pound
Garlic, 1 clove

Oven, moderate, 325°

Arrange shrimp in baking pan, melt butter with garlic clove cut in half; spoon over shrimp.

Heat five minutes in oven.

CRAB PUFFS

Crab Meat, flaked, 2 cups
Thick White Sauce,
½ cup (page 90)
Cucumber, 1, chopped
fine

Miniature Cream Puffs
(page 187)

To fill about 18 puffs

Use freshly cooked crab meat, or canned; pick it over for bits of shell and shred fine. Add to hot white sauce in top of double boiler. Add cucumber and mix well.

Fill miniature puffs and keep warm in oven until served.

TUNA PUFFS: Substitute tuna for crab meat and add 1 tablespoon lemon juice.

SALMAGUNDI PUFFS

Lean Beef, ground, ¼ lb.
Onion, 1 small, chopped
Green Pepper, 1, chopped
Tomato, 1, chopped
Butter, 2 tablespoons
Miniature Cream Puffs
(page 187)

To make about 24 puffs

In skillet fry beef, onion and green pepper until meat loses its red color. Add tomato and simmer 5 minutes. Season and fill puffs. Keep warm until served.

SAVORY PUFFS

Hard-cooked Eggs, 3
Parmesan Cheese,
 grated, $\frac{1}{3}$ cup
Parsley, chopped,
 1 tablespoon
Pimiento, minced,
 1 tablespoon
Salad Dressing
Miniature Cream Puffs
 (page 187)

Chop eggs fine and combine with other ingredients. Add enough salad dressing to moisten. Fill puffs and put under broiler until heated and lightly brown.

FILLED PASTRIES

Use recipe for Pie Crust (page 181); cut into 2 inch squares and mark each with diagonal line. Put a teaspoonful of one of the above fillings on half the pastry, fold over the other half, press edges firmly together, and bake in hot oven (400°) until golden brown.

BACON CHEESE PASTRIES

Bacon, 4 slices
Sharp Cheddar Cheese,
 $\frac{1}{4}$ pound
Pie Crust (page 181)

Fry bacon slowly until crisp; drain on paper towels and crumble. Chop cheese fine and mix with crumbled bacon. Fill pastry, press edges together tightly and bake in hot oven (400°) until lightly brown.

CAVIAR TRIANGLES

Fill each pastry with 1 teaspoon caviar. Press edges together firmly and fry in deep hot fat or bake in oven until golden brown.

TOMATO CANAPÉS

Slice small tomatoes thin and put each slice on a round of bread the same size. Spread with a little prepared mustard, then thickly with mayonnaise. Broil until mayonnaise becomes brown and puffy.

COLD TIDBITS

Spread a slice of boiled ham with prepared mustard and roll up around a finger of Cheddar cheese. Cut across in rolls, securing each with a toothpick.

Spread slices of rare roast beef with prepared mustard mixed with a little horse-radish. Roll up tight and cut into short lengths, securing each with a toothpick.

Stack boiled ham and cheese slices alternately with mustard between each slice. Chill and cut in cubes. Put a toothpick in each cube.

SANDWICHES

Everybody loves sandwiches—for many of us, in all their infinite variety, they are a standard part of our daily diet. If you pack sandwiches every day, it is easy to get in a rut and let the lunchbox become a monotonous affair. This section will serve as a checklist for lunch time menus at home, as well as provide varied fare to please the lunchbox carrier, whether small fry at school or adults at work.

THE LUNCHBOX

To make the job easier for you and to make the lunchbox convenient and attractive, provide all the suitable containers, utensils and accessories possible—waxed paper cups with lids, paper plates and napkins, salt and pepper, knife, fork and spoon. Disposable items are best—can be thrown away, to save dishwashing later. And, most important, a good vacuum bottle, for hot or cold coffee, tea, milk drinks, or soup.

As to Sandwiches

Vary the bread for sandwiches: white bread all the time becomes tiresome. So don't forget raisin, whole wheat, cracked wheat, rye, pumpernickel, Vienna, Italian, or whatever off-beat breads your market affords.

Vary the usual meat and cheese sandwiches with unexpected flavors. With lunch meats send along a tiny cup of chili sauce, catsup, mustard sauce, or pickle relish. Don't put it in the sandwich to become soggy.

With cheese, try spreading one slice of bread with chunky peanut butter. With cheese spreads, fry a slice of bacon crisp and crumble it, or add some chopped nuts. Liver pâté is good with cream cheese. With egg, combine chopped olives, or add an anchovy fillet or two.

And let's leave the lettuce out of the sandwiches. It makes them damp, and it becomes limp.

The Extras

For extras, include tiny cans of tuna fish or salmon, sardines in oil, or kipper snacks. Don't forget the can opener, and a few wedges of lemon. Add a well-seasoned deviled egg occasionally. A vacuum bottle of hot soup is a comfort in cold weather. (See the canned soup combinations on page 109.)

Slip in some greens, too—a celery heart, carrot strips, radishes, a few sprigs of water cress wrapped in wax paper or Saran wrap to keep fresh, the heart of lettuce with a small container of Russian dressing, or a sliced cucumber sprinkled with salt and freshly-ground black pepper. And don't forget relishes—pickles of all kinds, cranberry sauce, applesauce.

A container of salad can be a welcome change from sandwiches. Combine small cubes of left-over meat or poultry with chopped cheese, celery, and salad dressing. Or make it more filling with a little cooked macaroni or rice. Send muffins along.

Desserts

Cake, pie and cookies are standard items for dessert, but what about fresh fruits in season? Tuck in a container of blueberries, strawberries or raspberries, or sliced peaches with a little lemon juice squeezed over them to prevent darkening. And don't forget a small jar of sour cream on the side.

Canned fruits may also be used. Send them along in your own container, or use the little buffet-size cans (with can opener). And don't forget baked apples or puddings. Beware of custardy things in hot weather, though—they will spoil if left too long out of the refrigerator. For puddings or other cold dishes it is best to use a wide-mouthed vacuum jug: cold food is more appetizing served really cold.

KNIFE AND FORK SANDWICHES

You can build a whole meal around these. With salad and dessert they'll make a satisfying supper.

TURKEY DIVIDEND

On individual slices of toast arrange 2 tomato slices, 2 strips of bacon and a large slice of turkey. Make a cheese sauce (page 90) and spoon it over the turkey. Garnish with sliced stuffed olives.

WESTERN SANDWICH

Eggs, 4	Beat eggs with milk slightly,
Milk, ¼ cup	combine with other ingredients,
Ham, minced, ½ cup	pour into hot buttered skillet
Onion, minced, ½ cup	and cook until the mixture is
Green Pepper, minced,	firm. Serve between slices of
¼ cup	bread or toast.

To make 4 sandwiches

OPEN CHEESE AND TOMATO SANDWICH

Tomato Soup,	Heat soup in saucepan; add
10½-ounce can	cheese and butter, stirring over
American Cheese, ½ lb.	low heat until cheese is melted.
Butter, 2 tablespoons	Pour over toast.

To serve 4

SKILLET GRILLED SANDWICHES

Put slices of American cheese between slices of bread. Dip each into egg beaten with 2 tablespoons of milk. Fry in butter until golden-brown on each side. If desired, serve with tomato sauce, canned or homemade.

See suggestions for sandwiches on pages 254 - 255.

Sandwiches toasted in a special grill can be divided into bite-size portions

DOUBLE DECKER SANDWICHES

We'll settle for two decks: sandwiches taller than this look fabulous but are hard to bite into. Use three slices of bread or toast for each sandwich, combining white with whole wheat or rye. Use your own imagination in matching them up with fillers, or try the following suggestions:

TURKEY SPECIAL:

White bread, buttered
Large slice of turkey
Water cress
Whole wheat bread with Thousand Island Dressing (both sides)
Sliced ham
Cucumber slices
White bread, buttered

ITALIAN-STYLE:

Italian bread, buttered
Sliced salami
Onion slices
Italian bread with garlic butter (both sides)
Mozzarella Cheese
Anchovy Fillets
Italian bread, buttered

CORNED-BEEF CHALLENGE:

Rye bread, buttered
Corned-beef, mustard dressing
Sliced garlic dill pickle
Whole wheat bread, with mayonnaise (both sides)
American cheese
Sliced tomato
White bread, buttered

SEAFOOD BLUEPLATE:

White toast spread with salad dressing
Salmon
Chopped stuffed olives
Whole wheat toast, with salad dressing
Cream cheese
Sliced shrimp
White toast, with tartar sauce

CLUB SPECIAL

White toast spread with mayonnaise
Sliced white meat of chicken
Lettuce
White toast spread with mayonnaise (both sides)
Tomato slices
Crisp bacon
White toast spread with mayonnaise
Garnish with stuffed olives

MAMMOTH SANDWICHES

(The American favorite, called Hero, Submarine, Po' Boy)

Slice individual French or Italian loaves in half lengthwise. Arrange ham, cheese, salami on one side of loaf; cole slaw and tomatoes on other. Place halves together and cut diagonally into manageable portions.

CANOES

Scoop out centers from frankfurter rolls from end to end, leaving just a shell. Fill with chicken salad, or any salad made from cooked meat or poultry. Or combine cubes of cooked ham with creamy cole slaw.

FANCY SANDWICHES

ROLLED SANDWICHES: Remove crusts from thinly sliced bread. Lay bread between two damp towels and flatten out with rolling pin. Spread bread with cream cheese or other smooth filling and roll tightly. Keep in refrigerator covered with damp towel until ready to use.

PINWHEELS: Use uncut bread and slice it the length of the loaf. Follow directions in Rolled Sandwiches for dampening and rolling. Slice into ½-inch slices across the roll.

DECK OF CARDS: Cut assorted bread with cooky cutters into the shape of hearts, clubs, and spades. Shape diamonds with diagonal cuts.

BOX KITES: Put 2 kinds of filling between 3 slices of bread and cut into 1 inch squares.

*Mammoth
sandwiches*

A variety of sandwiches

FRUIT, CHEESE, NUT SANDWICH FILLINGS

Use for tea or fancy sandwiches, open or covered; crisp lettuce or water cress may be placed on bread if used soon after making.

APRICOT AND NUT FILLING: Mash 1 cup stewed apricots; add ½ cup chopped nuts and 2 tablespoons heavy cream.

DATE AND NUT FILLING: Chop dates and nuts and moisten with cream or mayonnaise.

ORANGE MARMALADE FILLING: Combine orange marmalade with cream cheese; chop oranges if pieces are large.

GLACÉ FRUIT SPREAD: Mix ½ cup minced glacé fruit, 1 tablespoon lemon juice, 1 cup cottage cheese and ½ teaspoon salt.

CHEESE AND PINEAPPLE SPREAD: Mix 1 3-oz. package cream cheese with 1 cup crushed pineapple, 2 tablespoons pineapple juice, 1 tablespoon grated carrot and ⅛ teaspoon salt.

ALMOND-CELERY FILLING: Mix ½ cup each chopped almonds and celery and moisten with mayonnaise.

PEANUT BUTTER AND HONEY SPREAD: Moisten peanut butter with honey to spreading consistency.

BLUE-CHEESE PIMIENTO SPREAD: Mash ½ cup crumbled blue cheese and combine with 2 tablespoons chopped pimiento and ¼ cup of salad dressing.

COTTAGE CHEESE SPREAD: Mix 1 cup cottage cheese with ½ teaspoon salt, 2 tablespoons sour cream and 1 tablespoon chopped pimiento.

CREAM CHEESE-GUAVA JELLY: Spread with cream cheese moistened with cream, then with guava jelly.

CREAM CHEESE AND CAVIAR SPREAD: Combine 1 8-ounce package cream cheese with ½ cup salad dressing, ½ teaspoon grated onion and 1 4-ounce jar caviar.

CREAM CHEESE AND GINGER: Mix cream cheese with minced preserved ginger and moisten with Cream Mayonnaise (page 163).

SPICY CHEESE SPREAD: Mix ¼ cup each softened butter and Parmesan cheese, dash of cayenne and a few drops of Worcestershire sauce.

SLICED CHEESE FILLING: Slice American, Old English, processed or Swiss cheese, spread lightly with prepared mustard, if desired, and place between slices of bread; toast until browned and cheese starts to melt.

CREAM CHEESE-HONEY: Spread with cream cheese moistened with milk, then with honey.

ORANGE PRUNE FILLING: Peel and remove pulp from 2 small oranges; chop and add ¾ cup pitted, chopped dried prunes and ¼ cup chopped walnuts. Mix with a little mayonnaise.

CARROT, NUT AND PINEAPPLE FILLING: Toss lightly together 1 cup grated raw carrot, ⅓ cup nut meats, finely cut, and 1 cup pineapple, drained and diced, and spread on whole wheat bread with mayonnaise.

APPLE, OLIVE AND NUT FILLING: Put 2 small quartered and cored apples through the food chopper. Then add ¼ pound chopped nut meats, 2 stalks of chopped celery and 3 chopped stuffed olives. Season with salt and paprika and moisten with mayonnaise.

MARASCHINO-CHEESE SPREAD: Mix finely chopped maraschino cherries with cream cheese and moisten with cherry liquor.

PEANUT BUTTER-BACON SPREAD: Moisten peanut butter with mayonnaise and mix with chopped crisp bacon.

BACON-HONEY SPREAD: Dice crisp bacon and add enough honey to form a spread.

Serve crackers with a choice of spreads

EGG SANDWICH FILLINGS

Use for luncheon or picnic sandwiches or for lunch box; garnish as desired. Chop hard-cooked eggs, season with salt and pepper and use one of the following combinations:

Eggs, minced onion and Mustard Salad Dressing (page 159)
Eggs, minced celery, pimiento and mayonnaise
Eggs, chopped pickles and mayonnaise
Eggs and Russian Dressing (page 163)
Eggs, chopped stuffed olives and Cooked Salad Dressing (page 165) or mayonnaise
Eggs, diced crisp bacon, or chopped boiled ham and salad dressing or well-seasoned mayonnaise
Eggs, canned salmon and chopped celery
Eggs, mashed shad roe
Eggs, chicken, tongue and Worcestershire sauce
Eggs, caviar and onion

TARTAR EGG SPREAD: Mash 6 hard-cooked eggs and combine with ¼ cup tartar sauce.

VEGETABLE SANDWICH FILLINGS

Use crisp vegetables with mayonnaise or other salad dressings for fillings for tea or fancy sandwiches, or for tasty sandwiches with a luncheon dish. Prepare just before serving. Some suggestions follow.

CARROTS: Grated and mixed with shredded cabbage or raisins.
CELERY: Chopped and mixed with chopped nuts and mayonnaise.

CUCUMBERS: Sliced thin or chopped and mixed with onion or nuts.
GREEN-ONION SPREAD: To ½ cup salad dressing add ¼ cup minced green-onion tops.
GREEN PEPPERS: Minced and sprinkled lightly over buttered bread.
OLIVE AND PECAN SPREAD: Combine 1 cup chopped pecans with 1 cup chopped stuffed olives and ¾ cup salad dressing.
RADISHES: Sliced thin. Use alone or with cucumber or green peppers.
SALAD GREENS: Lettuce, curly endive, water cress, tender spinach or young nasturtium leaves; use tender leaves, whole or shredded.
TOMATOES: Peeled and sliced thin, topped with finely sliced onion.
TUNA-FISH CELERY SPREAD: Combine a 6-ounce can of tuna with ¼ cup finely chopped celery, ½ cup salad dressing, 1 tablespoon lemon juice.
VEAL FORCEMEAT: Grind any leftover veal chopped nuts, pickle and stuffed olives. Add mayonnaise, season to taste. Mix lightly.
CORNED BEEF: Combine 1 cup ground or chopped corned beef with ¼ cup chopped water cress. Moisten with French dressing. Store in refrigerator. *Yield: filling for 4 sandwiches.*

SANDWICH SPREADS

See Canapé section (page 244) for butter, cheese, fish, meat and fruit spreads. There are fillings suitable for tea or fancy sandwiches and for more substantial ones.

BARBECUES AND PICNICS

The type of barbecue equipment you need will depend on whether you are a real devotee, do only an occasional cook-out in your small backyard, or limit yourself to the Fourth of July picnic. The elaborate portable rotisserie is for the cook who loves to move her kitchen to the terrace in the summer time; for the person who really feels that nothing equals the convenience of her kitchen stove, one of the small braziers for charcoal is adequate for occasional use. And for many, of course, the picnic basket and thermos jug fill the bill.

Actually there is a longer list of barbecuing equipment to choose from: the folding grill that fits across the camp fire, the hibachis, or small Japanese stoves that can easily be carried to beach or picnic ground, and the grill on a cart with shelf and storage space for food and dishes, easy to move wherever you want it. There are also permanent outdoor grills, built of stone, and simple camp stoves that burn kerosene, gasoline, bottled gas, or canned heat.

The rotisserie started out in life as an outdoor barbecue device, but soon became kitchen equipment for those who love to watch their meat broil on a revolving spit. Whether indoors or out, it must be motor-driven to be practical.

Cooking with Charcoal

Charcoal is the convenient fuel for all outdoor cooking. It eliminates the discomfort of trying to start a fire with damp wood; and a small brazier is more convenient than a campfire, and easy enough to take along with you.

Fill the bowl of the brazier with sand, gravel or cinders, level to the edge. This will protect the bowl and provide ventilation for the fire. Make a pile of the charcoal briquets, a dozen or so, and start them burning with paper or a chemical starter. As they burn they will look gray and ashy, and when they are entirely gray the fire is ready to use. Allow 20 to 40 minutes for this before you plan to start cooking.

When ready to cook spread the briquets over an area the size to be covered by the food you want to cook. Each briquet may be separated from its neighbor by an inch or two, and the heat will be ample for cooking. When ready to put food on the grill, knock the ash off the briquets. If the fire is too hot, the grill may be raised higher above it, or the briquets spread still farther apart.

In general, steaks and hamburgers may be cooked over a medium hot fire. Chicken requires a lower heat, for a longer period.

Experiment with simple foods first until you become familiar with this method of cooking.

What to Serve

Any piece of meat, poultry or fish that you would broil in your stove may be broiled over a charcoal grill. Consult the sections on steak and hamburgers, broiled chicken and broiled fish. Make a sauce in advance to baste the food with and to serve on the side.

Also see the section on game, if camp cooking is your problem.

Cooking on a Spit

Actually a spit for cooking a whole roast or bird may be rigged over any fire or grill, but as mentioned before, unless it is electrically operated turning the spit by hand every few minutes can be a nuisance.

In buying a motor- or battery-driven spit be sure its capacity will do the job you want done, so that in barbecuing a large cut of meat it will not cramp in the space, or strain the motor.

Prepare the charcoal fire in the same way as for cooking with a grill. Use a drip pan under the spit to catch the juices for basting, and ladle them over the meat when some have accumulated. It is advisable to use a meat thermometer when cooking a roast on a spit.

Small pieces of meat, chicken or fish may also be cooked on a spit by using a wire spit basket. Lay the piece flat in the basket; it will revolve and cook both sides of the meat without further attention.

PICNICS

To make a picnic really enjoyable the food should be as well prepared as though it were served at home. The food may be either hot or cold, but should be taken in thermos jugs so that it will be as advertised. Also take along all the equipment needed for everyone's comfort and convenience: gay tablecloths and table accessories that are disposable, yet will not disintegrate in use.

You might want to pack a complete individual lunch for each person, complete with sandwiches, salad, beverage, dessert, and so on in a gay package. Or not pack sandwiches at all, but just bring the makings and spread them out attractively on platters. See the suggestions in the section on Sandwiches, for help in making a picnic lunch interesting and delicious.

This is one time when your best homemade layer cake will be greatly appreciated. A big cake can usually be counted on to appease the last of the outdoor appetites. And take along plenty to drink in the way of coffee, lemonade, or iced tea, if you will be in a place where drinking water or cold soft drinks are not available. Don't forget plenty of fruit.

256

Portable rotisserie

Barbecued spareribs (page 45) cooked on an outdoor grill

Chicken barbecue

CORNISH ROCK HENS

Cook according to directions on page 70. When done, wrap at once individually in heavy foil and then in several layers of newspaper to keep hot. Serve within 4 hours, right in the foil.

SKEWERED LAMB
(In Russian it's Shaslik, in Armenian Shish Kebab)

Shoulder Lamb Chops,
  2 pounds
Onions, 8 small, peeled
Green Peppers, 2,
  cut in eighths
Tomatoes, 4, quartered
Mushrooms, 12 large caps

Salad Oil, ½ cup
Salt, 1 teaspoon
Pepper, ¼ teaspoon
Marjoram, ¼ teaspoon
Thyme, ½ teaspoon
Lemon Juice or **Vinegar,**
  2 tablespoons

To serve 4

Bone lamb and cut into cubes. Put with vegetables in bowl. Mix remaining ingredients and pour over lamb and vegetables. Store in refrigerator at least 1 hour.

Push pieces of meat alternately with vegetables on long metal skewers. Hold over hot coals or place under broiler, turning to brown all sides, 10 to 15 minutes.

SHRIMP KEBABS

Jumbo Shrimp, 1 pound
Garlic, 2 cloves, minced
Soy Sauce, ¼ cup
Lemon Juice, 2 lemons
Salad Oil, ¼ cup

To serve 4

Cut back of each shrimp to devein but do not remove shell. Wash thoroughly. Mix remaining ingredients and pour over shrimp. Let marinate in refrigerator several hours. To cook, divide shrimp into 4 portions and thread on skewers. Grill over hot coals 5 minutes, or until brown and done. Baste with marinade while cooking.

MIXED GRILL

Kidneys, 8 lamb
Mushrooms, 8 large
Rib Lamb Chops, 8 small
Brown and Serve
  Sausages, 4
Tomatoes, 4 medium
Salt and **Pepper**

Butter, ¼ cup

Split kidneys, remove fat and membrane, sprinkle with salt and pepper, wrap in foil package. Wipe mushrooms, place on foil, sprinkle with salt and pepper and a little melted butter. Fold foil and put both packages on grill over hot coals.

Broil chops, sausages, and tomatoes sliced in half crosswise and brushed with butter, to desired doneness.

FRANKFURTER KEBABS

Frankfurters, 4 large
White potatoes, 12 small,
  boiled
Onions, small, 12, peeled
Prepared Mustard, 1
  tablespoon
Salad Oil, ⅓ cup

To serve 4 skewers

Cut frankfurters in 3 or 4 pieces, place in bowl with potatoes and onions. Mix mustard with oil and pour over, coating frankfurters and vegetables thoroughly. Thread them alternately on long skewers. Grill over hot coals or under broiler, turning to brown all sides.

Other interesting kebab combinations can be made by combining cubes of lunch meat, such as chopped ham or salami, with little cherry tomatoes and peppers alternately on skewers.

Shrimps combined with onions, tomatoes, green peppers and mushrooms

A picnic might include cold meatloaf, pickles, macaroni salad, sandwiches, fresh fruit, ripe tomatoes and cookies

PICNIC BURGERS

Ground Beef, 1½ pounds
Salt, 1 teaspoon
Prepared Mustard
Steak Sauce
Ketchup

To serve 4

Make hamburger patties ahead of time. Mix beef and salt and shape into 4 patties. Wrap individually in foil, and freeze. To cook: put wrapped patties directly on coals and cook 4 to 10 minutes, depending on how well done you like them. Serve with condiments.

ONE-DISH PICNIC DINNER

To take along hot, or make on the site:

Spanish Rice Mix, 1 pkg.
Tomatoes, 16-ounce can
Frankfurters, 1 pound
Onions, 8-ounce can
Whole-Kernel Corn,
  16-ounce can
Green Lima Beans,
  16-ounce can

To serve 4

Make Spanish rice as directed on package. Add frankfurters cut in 1 inch pieces. Add remaining ingredients and simmer 5 minutes.

PICNIC SALAD

Baked Beans, 1 can
  (23-ounce)
Sharp Cheese, ½ lb.
Lunch Meat, 1 can
Scallions, 3
Celery, 1 cup, sliced
Eggs, 8, hard-cooked
Prepared Mustard,
  1 tablespoon
Tomatoes, 4 medium
French Dressing
  (page 159)
Salt and **Pepper,** to taste

To provide a complete picnic meal-in-a-dish for 8

Cut cheese and lunch meat into small cubes, chop onions, and quarter eggs and tomatoes. Mix all ingredients together with enough French Dressing to moisten; season to taste. Chill thoroughly, pack in vacuum container to take to picnic.

PICNIC BEAN LONG FELLOWS

Baked Beans, 2 16-ounce
  cans
Catsup, ¼ cup
Prepared Mustard,
  2 teaspoons
Worcestershire,
  1 tablespoon
Sweet Pickle Relish,
  2 tablespoons
French Loaves, 4 small

To serve 4

Combine all ingredients except bread in skillet and heat thoroughly. Split French loaves lengthwise and heat on grill. Serve bean mixture between bread halves.

GRILLED CORN-ON-THE-COB

Pull husks from corn, remove silk; replace husks and tie in place. Soak in cold salted water 10 minutes; drain. Roast on grill over hot fire or bury in hot coals, for about 10 minutes turning frequently. Remove husks and serve with butter, salt and pepper.

A hibachi can be carried easily and used anywhere

No utensils will be forgotten with a well-fitted picnic basket

Long-handled tools for the outdoor grill

PICNIC CLAMBAKE

Potatoes
Frying Chickens, cut up
Live Lobsters
Clams in the Shell
Corn in the Husk

Scrub potatoes and put them in the bottom of a very large kettle. Cover with pieces of chicken. Add as many live lobsters as clam-bakers, first rinsing them in clean water.

Add a layer of corn in the husk, then a layer of clams. Add 1 cup of water and cover tightly. Put over fire and steam for about 1 hour, or until clams open. Serve clams with melted butter for dipping and bowls to catch the broth, while the pot continues to cook. Serve corn next with butter and salt, and the remaining foods as they are done.

The quantities depend on how many people and how large the appetites. For each person you might provide ¼ chicken, 1 whole lobster, 6 or more clams, and 2 or 3 ears of corn

A clambake in the back yard

261

HOT AND COLD DRINKS

The world's peoples are united in one way, if no other, and that is by the universal love of tea and coffee. These are cheering, heartening drinks, that, hot or cold, wake us up in the morning, crown our daily meals and provide the basis for friendly get-togethers the world around. Milk drinks can provide an important part of our daily nutrition, and fruit drinks are indispensable in hot weather, and again are a gracious complement to many social gatherings.

GOOD COFFEE

Good quality fresh coffee, used in a generous amount, is the first essential. Next in importance is keeping the coffee fresh. Keep it in the refrigerator—an open can or jar at room temperature will soon lose its flavor because the volatile oils containing that wonderful flavor will simply dissipate. Of equal importance is using a clean coffee maker. A residue from old coffee can spoil the taste of the next batch you make, however fine and fresh the coffee. Wash the pot thoroughly with detergent after each using, and rinse with very hot water.

Coffeepot Coffee

In an old-fashioned coffee pot measure 2 level tablespoons of ground coffee for each 8-ounce cup of water. Add boiling water, place over heat and bring to boil. (Do not let it boil.) Stir well and remove from heat. Add dash of cold water to settle grounds. Let stand a few minutes over very low heat before serving. Unless used up at once, pour off through fine strainer into another container. Do not let it sit with the grounds in it.

Percolator Coffee

Measure 2 level tablespoons of percolator-grind coffee for each 8-ounce cup of water into coffee basket of percolator. Put cold water in bottom. Percolate 8 minutes after liquid in glass top has color, or until it looks strong enough. Remove coffee basket as soon as finished, and serve at once.

Drip Coffee

Measure 2 level tablespoons of fine-grind coffee into coffee section of drip pot for each 8-ounce cup. Pour boiling water into water section, put pot over low heat, and let water drip through. Do not let it boil. Remove water and coffee section from pot when finished and serve at once.

Vacuum-made Coffee

Measure water into lower bowl of vacuum pot; put upper bowl with filter snugly in place and put over heat. Measure 2 level tablespoons of extra-fine-grind coffee per cup into upper bowl. When water rises to upper bowl and boils, stir and remove from heat. Let all liquid go to bottom before taking off upper bowl.

Stronger Coffee

If you like your coffee very strong you may want to increase the amount of coffee used. The best way is to experiment until you find the right amount.

Every brand of coffee may require a different amount; some coffees are intended to give a light-bodied brew, while others are heavier-bodied. The correct grind for the coffee maker is also essential.

ICED COFFEE

Make coffee double the usual strength and pour it hot into ice-filled tall glasses.

For one glass, use instant coffee in the way described on the label.

Left-over coffee may be poured while still fresh into ice trays to freeze, and the cubes used to chill iced coffee.

GOOD TEA

A clean pot for tea is just as important as for coffee (see above) and it should be rinsed thoroughly to make sure no suds are left in it. Before making tea fill the pot with scalding water to heat it, then pour off when ready to use the pot.

The water for tea should be drawn from the cold water tap, and reheated water should not be used, as it will taste flat.

The water must fully boil, not just be hot.

Into the hot pot measure 1 teaspoon of tea (or 1 tea bag) per cup. Pour boiling water over it, and let brew 3 to 5 minutes depending on how strong you like it. Brewing too long makes it bitter; *never* boil it.

If you like weak tea, make it just as described above, then dilute the individual cup with a little hot water.

Serve plain or with milk (not cream) or a touch of lemon. Sugar is optional.

ICED TEA

Make the tea as described above, but use twice the amount of tea per cup and brew 4 minutes. Pour hot into ice-filled tall glasses. Serve with lemon and sugar. Mint sprigs, wedges of orange, lime or lemon, or pineapple spears may be added for looks and for flavor as well. A little cinnamon may be added for a spicy flavor. If iced tea becomes cloudy, add a little boiling water and stir.

HOT COCOA

Cocoa, 2 tablespoons
Sugar, 2 tablespoons
Milk, 3 cups
Water, ¼ cup

To serve 4

Mix cocoa and sugar together in saucepan; add water and boil gently over low heat, stirring. Add milk, heat thoroughly, but do not boil. Beat with rotary beater to blend smoothly.

HOT CHOCOLATE

Unsweetened Chocolate, 2 squares **Sugar,** ⅓ cup **Water,** ½ cup **Milk,** 3 cups **Whipped Cream**	Cut up chocolate, mix with sugar and water in top of double boiler and melt over boiling water. Stir in milk and serve with a dollop of whipped cream on each cup.

To serve 4

ICED CHOCOLATE

Use the above recipe for Hot Chocolate, doubling the amount of chocolate, or use canned chocolate syrup, 2 tablespoons to 1 cup of milk. Beat with a rotary beater until frothy and pour over cracked ice in tall glasses. Top with a dollop of whipped cream.

MOCHA CHOCOLATE FROSTY

Make Iced Chocolate, as above, and add a scoop of coffee ice cream; stir and serve at once.

ICE CREAM MILK SHAKES

Milk Shakes may be made in a cocktail shaker, a blender, or beaten with a rotary beater. Add any desired flavoring along with the ice cream. You might try powdered coffee, chocolate syrup, or crushed fresh fruit.

Milk Shakes may also be made by substituting an egg, in place of the ice cream, for each cup of milk, and sweetened to taste.

DEMITASSE

Prepare strong coffee, using 2 to 3 tablespoons coffee for 1 cup boiling water. Serve hot in small cups. After-dinner coffee is usually served black.

VIENNA COFFEE

Prepare demitasse coffee, as above. Top each cup with whipped cream.

CAFÉ AU LAIT

Prepare strong, hot coffee and an equal quantity of scalded milk. Pour both coffee and milk into the cup simultaneously— a pot in each hand, so that the combination is half of each.

MINTED BRACER

Pour 1 quart boiling water over 8 teaspoons of tea and several sprigs of fresh mint, chopped; let steep 5 minutes; strain into large ice-filled pitcher. Add ⅓ cup sugar dissolved in a little of the hot tea or plain boiling water, and 1 large lemon sliced paper thin. Mix well.

The blender will make fruit or milk drinks in seconds

LEMONADE

Add the juice of one lemon and ¼ cup of sugar syrup (see below) to ½ cup of water for each glass of lemonade. Pour it over a tall glass of cracked ice and garnish with mint leaves, slices of orange or pineapple.

LIMEADE: Substitute juice of 1 lime for each lemon.

ORANGEADE: Substitute juice of 1 orange and ¼ lemon for all lemon juice.

SUGAR SYRUP

Boil equal quantities of sugar and water for three minutes. Pour into a sterilized jar, cover, and keep chilled. Use for sweetening all cold drinks.

FRUIT PUNCH

Canned, frozen or fresh fruit juices may be used in any pleasing combination. You might combine orange, lemon, pineapple and add crushed strawberries or raspberries for color. Or grape juice may be added. Sweeten to taste and pour over tall glasses of cracked ice or serve in style in a punch bowl, if preferred, with punch cups.

MULLED CIDER

Add a few pieces of stick cinnamon, ¼ teaspoon of allspice and ¼ teaspoon of cloves to a quart of sweet cider. Simmer 10 minutes and strain into mugs. Serve steaming hot. To make about 4 portions.

LEMON PICK-ME-UP

Make ice cubes from a 6-ounce can of frozen lemonade concentrate, diluted according to directions on can. Fill tall glasses with cubes. Pour double-strength tea, strained, over lemonade ice cubes. Garnish with slices of lemon.

FROSTED COFFEE

Half fill 6 tall glasses with chopped ice; pour hot strong coffee over ice until glasses are three-fourths full, and top each with a heaping tablespoon of vanilla ice cream.

BLACK COW

Put a large scoop of vanilla in a tall glass. Fill with chilled root beer and stir until ice cream is partly melted.

CHOCOLATE ICE-CREAM SODA

Put 2 to 3 tablespoons of chocolate syrup into tall glass. Add ¼ cup of cold milk and a large scoop of chocolate ice cream. Fill glass with chilled sparkling water and stir.

MINTED FROSTY

In a thoroughly chilled glass put the juice of 1 lime, 2 teaspoons of sugar and 2 or 3 fresh mint leaves. Thoroughly crush the leaves with a long-handled spoon. Fill glass with crushed ice, cover and shake until heavily coated with frost. Garnish the top with a fresh mint leaf and serve with a straw.

The best iced tea

Fruit punch served in a hollowed-out watermelon

RASPBERRY SODA

Put 2 tablespoons of partially defrosted, frozen raspberries in tall glass. Fill three-quarters full with chilled carbonated water. Add scoop of vanilla ice cream and garnish top with raspberries.

FROSTED PEACH NECTAR

For each serving fill a tall glass three-quarters full with chilled peach nectar; add a scoop of vanilla ice cream. Stir until ice cream is partially dissolved.

CRANBERRY-ORANGEADE COCKTAIL

Mix 1 pint of cranberry-juice cocktail and 1 6-ounce can of frozen orange juice with 2 cups of water. Pour over ice cubes.

GRAPE FIZZ

Combine equal amounts of grape juice and ginger ale, and serve in tall glasses filled with ice cubes.

GINGER PUNCH

To 1 quart of cider add ½ cup of crushed pineapple, 1 orange in paper thin slices, 3 sprigs of mint, crushed, and chill thoroughly in refrigerator. When ready to serve pour into punch bowl and add 1 quart of ginger ale, serve in punch cups.

ORANGE FREEZE

For each serving put 2 tablespoons of frozen orange-juice in tall glass with 3 or 4 ice cubes. Fill glass three-quarters full with ginger ale and add a scoop of orange sherbet on top.

OLD-FASHION COOLER

For each serving, put 3 or 4 ice cubes in a tall glass. Add 1 strip of pineapple, 1 slice each of orange and lemon, 1 maraschino cherry. Fill glass with ginger ale.

ABOUT WINES

Wine with meals is a pleasant European custom that Americans have been slow to follow, but are coming more and more to appreciate. Since there are such fine domestic wines produced mainly in California and New York State, as well as a plentiful supply imported from the great wine-producing countries of the world, it is hoped that more people will learn to know and enjoy these perfect accompaniments to fine food.

The final arbiter of the wines you serve and what you serve them with should be your taste and preference. However, certain traditions have been established about the compatibility of specific wines with certain foods, so following is a brief guide to the most familiar types and how they are generally used. It is not necessary to buy special glasses for each type of wine, although they are available for those who want them. If you want just one all-purpose glass, a champagne glass is a good choice for table wines and is useful for many cocktails, too.

GUIDE TO SERVING WINES

Type of Wine	Examples	To serve with	How to serve
Appetizer Wines	Sherry—dry to semi-sweet Vermouth—dry French, sweet Italian Madeira—dry	Before meals; with hors d'oeuvre; with soups	Serve at room temperature or slightly cooled, in 2½ to 3-ounce sherry glasses
Red Table Wines	Burgundy—dry Claret—dry (Cabernet, Zinfandel) Chianti—dry	Hearty dishes; red meats, game, spaghetti, cheese dishes	Serve at room temperature in 5 to 8-ounce wine glasses
	Rosé	Good with all foods	Serve chilled
White Table Wines	Rhine Wine—very dry and tart to medium (Riesling, Traminer, Sylvaner) Chablis—dry, less tart Sauterne—dry to medium	Fish, shellfish; chicken or other light meats; omelets	Serve chilled in 5 to 8-ounce wine glasses
Dessert Wines	Port—sweet (red, white or tawny) Tokay—less sweet Muscatel—sweet Sherry—sweet Madeira—sweet Sauterne—sweet	Fruit, nuts, cookies, fruit cake, cheese	Serve at room temperature in 2½ to 3-ounce glasses
Sparkling Wines	Champagne—brut is very dry, sec is medium dry, doux is sweet Sparkling Burgundy—semi-sweet	Dry with appetizers or main courses; sweet with desserts	Serve chilled in 5-ounce champagne glasses

Types of glasses used for a variety of drinks

WINE IN COOKING

The quality that makes a wine harmonize with a certain food on the table, also makes it the perfect ingredient to enhance that particular dish in its cooking; therefore we can be guided by the serving chart opposite when choosing wines for cooking. In general, use red wines in game or red meat dishes, white wines in cooking chicken, seafood, or light meats. Sherry is used in soups, sauces or desserts, and in many other special dishes. Wine should provide a background to other flavors, never be the dominating flavor in any dish. The alcoholic content is lost in the cooking. Wine that has soured may be used in salad dressings.

WHERE SOME WELL-KNOWN WINES COME FROM

French and German Wines

Bordeaux Wines come from the Bordeaux area of France. This area is divided into districts, each of which gives its name to the wine produced there: Médoc, Graves, Sauternes, Saint Emilion, Pomeral, Barsac, etc. "Claret" is an English term applied to all red Bordeaux wines.

Burgundy Wines come from 3 separate districts in France: the Côte d'Or, the Maconnais and Beaujolais, and Chablis. From the Côte d'Or come the full-bodied red Burgundies and the great white Burgundies; from Chablis comes the wine we know by that name.

Rhine Wines from the French side of the Rhine are the white table wines familiarly known as Riesling, Traminer, Sylvaner. From the German Rhine come Piesporter, Zeltinger and Bernkasteler, and many other important wines. Moselle is a German wine from the Moselle river valley.

Champagne comes from the Department of the Marne in France.

Some wines from Bordeaux

Typical bottle shapes: left to right, Italian sparkling wine, Spanish muscat wine, port, Rhine or Austrian wine, sherry

Italian Wines

Italy produces many wines—red and white table wines and sweet dessert wines. Probably the best known red wine is the familiar Chianti which is exported in the straw-covered flasks from the district of Tuscany. Other familiar ones are Orvieto, from Umbria, Barola and Barbera, from the Piedmont area. Arbanello, Malvasia and Marsala are sweet wines from Sicily. Italian Vermouth is a white wine flavored with herbs and spices and is sweeter than the Vermouth made in France.

Spanish Wines

Sherry is, of course, the wine we think of first when we think of Spanish wines. Sherry is actually a blend of wines and it may range in taste from very dry to sweet. Fino Sherry is very dry; Amontillado, dry to medium; and Olorosa or Amoroso, sweet.

Portuguese Wines

Port is the wine of Portugal and the only true port in the world. It is an after-dinner wine. Madeira is another familiar Portuguese wine which ranges in taste from dry to sweet.

Some well-known California and New York wines

South American Wines

Wine is produced in Argentina, Peru and Chile, most of it from European vines and bearing European names. The wines of Chile are mostly of the Rhine type and of superb quality.

North American Wines

California produces the great percentage of North American wines. Due to its great variety of climate, most European grapes can be grown there, and the wine names are taken from the great wines of Europe. There is great variation in the quality of Californian wines and it pays to try as many kinds as you can to find the best. Many fine ones come from small vintners who can produce only limited quantities.

New York State wines come from the Finger Lakes district of New York. They include red and white table wines, and sparkling wines, made from native grapes, and they rival many of the imported wines in flavor.

VINTAGE WINES

French and German wines are dated with the year of the vintage and this is sometimes very important in making a choice. In a year when the rainfall and growing season is just right, the grapes are at their best, and this is known as a great, or very great, year. Likewise frost or drought can affect the crop and produce a poor vintage. Many wine importers provide charts listing the quality of each year's vintage. American wines are not designated in this way.

COCKTAILS

Cocktails are very regional drinks, varying greatly in the method of making from one section of the country to another. In addition, they are a very personal ritual with many people, so we can only attempt to give very general recipes for making them.

A one-ounce jigger used in making the following recipes, will produce one cocktail. Multiply the quantities by the number you wish to make. Cocktails may be stirred in a pitcher or tall drinking glass, shaken, where indicated, in a shaker, or made in the blender.

Alexander—1 jigger Cognac, 1 jigger Crème de Cacao, 1 jigger cream. Shake well with ice and strain

A small cabinet arranged for wine storage

A shallow closet makes an efficient wine cellar

into cocktail glass. Gin may be used in place of Cognac if desired.

Bacardi—2 jiggers Bacardi rum, 1 jigger grenadine, juice ½ lemon. Shake with ice and strain into cocktail glass.

Daiquiri—2 jiggers rum, juice ½ lime, 1 teaspoon sugar. Shake well with ice, strain into cocktail glass.

Gibson—2 jiggers gin, ½ jigger dry Vermouth. Stir well with cracked ice; strain into cocktail glass. Add pearl onion.

Manhattan (dry)—2 jiggers rye whiskey, 1 jigger French Vermouth. Stir with cracked ice, strain into cocktail glass. Add twist of lemon peel.

Manhattan (sweet)—Substitute Italian Vermouth for French in the above recipe; substitute maraschino cherry for lemon peel.

Martini—2 jiggers gin, ½ jigger dry Vermouth; pour over cracked ice, stir well and strain into cocktail glass. Garnish with olive, if desired, or with twist of lemon peel.

Old-Fashioned—Crush lump of sugar in 1 teaspoon water with dash of bitters, in old-fashioned glass. Add ice cubes. Pour over ice, 1 jigger of rye, Scotch, or bourbon, as desired. Stir well and garnish with slice of orange, slice of pineapple, and maraschino cherry.

Pink Lady—2 jiggers gin, 1 jigger applejack, juice ½ lemon, 1 teaspoon white of egg, 2 dashes grenadine. Shake well with ice, strain into cocktail glass.

Whiskey Sour—1 jigger rye, juice ½ lemon, 1 teaspoon powdered sugar. Shake well with ice, or put into blender. A drop of egg white will make a nice froth on top.

TALL DRINKS

Claret Lemonade—Juice of 1 lemon, 1 teaspoon sugar, 4 ounces claret. Serve with ice cubes in 10-ounce collins glass. Stir well.

Cuba Libre—Put juice of ½ lime, 1 jigger rum into collins glass with ice cubes. Fill with cola drink, stir.

Milk Punch—1 cup milk, 1 jigger brandy or rum, 1 teaspoon sugar. Shake with ice, strain into collins glass, sprinkle with nutmeg.

Planter's Punch—Mix juice of 1 lime, 1 teaspoon sugar, 1 jigger rum, 2 dashes Curaçao. Pour over shaved ice in collins glass. Garnish with fruit and serve with straws.

Rye Highball—Pour jigger of rye into 8-ounce highball glass containing ice cubes. Add water or soda and stir. Highballs may also be made of Scotch or rum.

Tom Collins—Mix juice of 1 lemon, 1 teaspoon sugar, 1 jigger gin. Pour over ice in collins glass. Fill with soda.

Gin and Tonic—Pour jigger of gin over ice in highball glass. Fill glass with bottled quinine water. Garnish with twist of lemon or lime peel.

Mint Julep—Use 12 ounce glass or pewter mug. Dissolve 1 teaspoon granulated sugar in just enough water to cover it. Crush a sprig of mint with the sugar and water and leave it in the glass. Fill with finely cracked ice. Pour in Bourbon whiskey to within ½ inch of top. Stir until glass is thoroughly frosted. Decorate with mint sprigs.

Bloody Mary—For one portion combine a jigger of Vodka, 2 jiggers of tomato juice, juice of ½ lemon, and Worcestershire Sauce, salt and pepper to taste. Shake well with ice, strain and serve. This can be a good choice if you need to serve an alcoholic drink before an early Sunday dinner or Sunday lunch, and for a crowd the desired amount can be made up in a pitcher beforehand and served over ice cubes or crushed ice.

Tom and Jerry— Mix 1 egg yolk with 1 teaspoon powdered sugar. Pour on ½ jigger brandy and ½ jigger Jamaica rum. Stir thoroughly. Add the white of 1 egg, beaten, and while stirring pour in hot milk or boiling water, to fill the cup. Sprinkle nutmeg on top.

Hot Buttered Rum—Put 1½ ounces Jamaica rum, 1 lump sugar, 1 small slice butter in old-fashioned glass or mug. Fill with boiling water. Stir and sprinkle nutmeg on top.

EGGNOG

6 eggs, separated	Beat egg yolks until thick and
Sugar, ¾ cup	light-colored, add sugar and
Cognac or Rum, 2 cups	beat until well blended; slowly
Milk, 4 cups	add brandy, then the milk and
Heavy Cream, 4 cups	cream. Beat egg whites until
Dash Nutmeg	stiff and fold into milk mixture.
	Add a sprinkling of freshly
	grated nutmeg to each serving.
To make about 20 portions	Serve in punch cups.

FROSTED COFFEE ROYALE

Fresh, strong coffee, 3 cups	Combine cold coffee and brandy and sweeten to taste.
Brandy, ½ cup	Pour over crushed ice in small
Sugar, 3 teaspoons, if desired	highball or on-the-rocks glass.

CHAMPAGNE PUNCH

Brandy, ¼ cup	Pour Brandy and Triple Sec
Triple Sec or **Cointreau,** ¼ cup	over fruit rinds and sugar in quart jar. Put lid on tight and
Rind of ½ **Orange**	let marinate for several hours.
Rind of ½ **Lemon**	
Sugar, ¼ cup	
Sauterne, 1 quart	Add sauterne and chill. Strain
Champagne, 1 quart	mixture into punch bowl over
Orange and **Lemon** slices	block of ice, and add chilled Champagne. Garnish with several slices of orange and lemon, or with some large strawberries. Serve in punch cups.

This amount will make about 12 servings; multiply recipe for a larger crowd.

FROZEN FOODS

Women no longer have to be sold on the convenience of frozen foods as the number of home freezers throughout the country will testify. It is possible, however, that all of these freezers are not being used as effectively as they might be. One of their major uses should be the storage of cooked foods, so that one meal's preparation time actually produces two or three meals. In other words, the quantity cooked may be doubled or tripled and the surplus frozen and stored for future use. With a freezer full of this sort of treasure a woman with many outside interests, or the working wife, is never at a loss to produce a home-cooked meal, and she can do her big cooking jobs when convenient.

In this section we give a brief summary of the methods for freezing foods. For complete and detailed description of the freezing of individual items, consult the pamphlets on the subject that are distributed by the United States Department of Agriculture* and your own state college of agriculture. The latter will deal with products grown in your own locality, and are usually distributed free of charge.

WHAT THE FREEZER CANNOT DO

The freezer will not *improve* food. What comes out of the freezer will be only as good as what went in. So don't skimp on quality, in the mistaken notion that it does not matter. Don't, for example, buy lower grade meat than you would normally use on your table. Don't waste freezer space on vegetables that are past their prime. And don't save on packaging materials. Frozen foods will not retain their flavor and quality unless well wrapped. They might even take on any stale or "off" odor in the freezer.

Freeze only foods in good condition—cold does not kill bacteria or mold; it simply arrests their life cycle, which will continue when the food is thawed. For this reason, it is safer to thaw frozen foods in the refrigerator, rather than at room temperature.

FAST FREEZING

Fast freezing, on which the quality of frozen food depends, is done at temperatures of 10 or 15 degrees below zero. So if you plan to freeze produce at home, get a freezer that will go below zero, or which has a fast-freeze compartment separate from the regular storage space and with lower temperatures possible. Otherwise you would do better to have fresh food fast-frozen at a locker plant and use your freezer for storage only.

You can store frozen food satisfactorily at zero, which is the lowest temperature of most freezers. But fresh meats, fruits and vegetables frozen at zero will be of inferior quality. The reason is that slow freezing causes huge ice crystals to form in the cells, which breaks them down much faster than the small crystals formed by fast freezing. How freezing affects tissue cells is best demonstrated by the limp condition of raspberries, after they are completely thawed. There is no cell structure left to support the shape of the original food. This does not apply to cooked foods, however—prepared dishes, or the leftover turkey or roast—foods already in liquid form, like fruit juices. These can be frozen satisfactorily at zero, as can baked goods.

A popular misconception is that you can properly freeze fresh foods in the across-the-top frozen food compartment of your refrigerator. If you do you'll find the results most disappointing. Use this compartment only to store frozen foods, ice cream, or to make frozen desserts. Or you can use it for freezing properly packed cooked foods for a few weeks.

When you freeze be sure to use properly treated wrappings or containers. Ordinary waxed paper or thin foil is not good enough—you need a wrapping that will not tear and that is moisture-proof and vapor-proof.

Date each package and label it. Keep a check list near your freezer to help you turn over your inventory within a reasonable length of time. Make sure you do not lose track of things, and keep food longer than its freezer life, for the quality will become impaired thereafter.

---

* U.S. Department of Agriculture Bulletins: "Home Freezing of Fruits and Vegetables," 15 cents. "Home Freezers—Their Selection and Use," 10 cents.

Wrapping food in foil for freezing

FREEZING COOKED MAIN DISHES

Do not overcook foods that you are planning to freeze. They will be heated up later, so a little undercooking is preferable.

Cool foods quickly after they are cooked. This stops the cooking at once, thereby retaining flavor and texture. To cool, plunge uncovered pan of food into iced water or set pan on ice. Keep water cold until food cools.

Put food into moisture-proof containers as soon as cool, packing it tightly to eliminate air; but semi-liquid foods should have head room at the top for expansion. Use containers that hold only enough for one meal. For semi-liquid dishes the container should be rigid. (Casserole dishes may be frozen in the dish in which they were made, if desired.) Containers should then have lids adjusted, and be sealed with freezer tape. If bags are used, they may be sealed, then put into waxed cardboard boxes, or wrapped in freezer paper.

When freezing dishes with gravy or meat stock, cool, then skim off all fat before freezing.

Freezing a mixed dish when only partially completed is also possible. For example, in making a stew, the cooked meat could be frozen by itself, and the fresh vegetables added when you are ready to serve it. This would insure that the vegetables would not be overcooked and too soft. Seasonings could be added at the same time.

THINGS TO GUARD AGAINST
IN FREEZING COOKED MIXTURES

In general all prepared food may be frozen if you keep the following pointers in mind:

· hard-cooked egg white becomes tough

· fried foods lose their crispness, may become soggy

· mayonnaise tends to separate

· strong flavors such as pepper, onions, clove, and synthetic vanilla may become bitter; and should be added to a dish later if possible

· salt loses its savor and will need an additional amount added when serving

· sauces tend to separate; beating them at high speed in the blender just before freezing may prevent this; rice flour will make a smoother sauce for freezing

THAWING

Cooked food may be thawed in the oven, if it is in an oven-proof container. Or it may be thawed slightly at room temperature, then turned into the top part of a double boiler for heating. Or it may be heated in a saucepan, providing it can stand a lot of stirring, to prevent sticking, without damaging the texture.

FREEZING BAKED GOODS

Yeast Rolls and Bread are more dependable if frozen after baking; dough frozen before baking sometimes fails due to chemical changes that take place in the dough during storage. Cool baked bread or rolls, package, and freeze immediately.

Bought breads, coffee cakes and rolls may be frozen in their original wrappers for two weeks, or up to three months if put into freezer wrapping.

To serve, heat frozen rolls in a tight bag in the oven; toast slices of frozen bread; thaw bread, wrapped, at room temperature.

Quick breads may be frozen before or after baking, but the quality is apt to be better if frozen after baking. The storage life of unbaked muffins or biscuits is limited to 2 to 3 weeks.

Cakes frozen after baking are less likely to fail, but will lose crispness of crust during storage and thawing. This may be an important factor in frosting a cake. Cakes frozen, then baked may have a smaller volume, but the flavor may be better. Moreover frozen batter takes up less storage space than a baked cake. Angel food and sponge cakes *must* be baked and then frozen.

Freeze a frosted cake before you wrap it, so as not to damage the frosting. Frosting will crack after a few weeks of freezing; however, a butter frosting will last better than a boiled one.

Thaw frosted cakes in their wrappings in the refrigerator. Use them up as soon as possible, as they get stale quickly.

Pies may be frozen before or after baking; however, those frozen unbaked are apt to have a fresher flavor. Pies frozen after baking should be thawed and warmed in the oven to avoid a day-old pie flavor.

Freeze pies before wrapping to avoid spilling. Use metal rimmed paper, or aluminum pie plates.

Fruit pies need the same treatment to prevent discoloration as frozen fruit does. (See below.)

FREEZING VEGETABLES

Prepare vegetables as described on page 131. Then put them into a strainer, collander, or wire basket and plunge them into boiling water for the length of time specified in the list below. Lift them out of the boiling water and immediately plunge them into ice water for the same length of time. Drain well and pack in a convenient package or rigid container.

The reason for this process is to stop the enzyme action which causes the vegetable to mature. It also softens the vegetable, making it easier to pack. Use one gallon of boiling water for one pound of non-leafy vegetables; two gallons for one pound of leafy vegetables.

FREEZING FRUITS

Freeze fruits at 15 or 20 degrees below zero. If your freezer will not go that low, it is better to have them frozen at a locker plant, then store in your own freezer.

Fruits are better flavored and textured if packed with sugar or a sugar syrup. However, for dietetic purposes they may be frozen without sweetening.

SYRUP PACK: Prepare syrup ahead of time and chill until ready to use. In general a 40% syrup is used for most fruits. Dissolve 3 cups of sugar in 4 cups of water to make 5½ cups of syrup. Use ½ cup of syrup for each 2-cup container of fruit.

To pack sliced fruit, put syrup into containers. Peel and slice fruit right into syrup. Leave ½-inch head room at top of container. Put crumpled parchment paper on top to push fruit under syrup. Wipe edges clean, cover with lid and seal. Label with name and date. Put whole fruit into containers and pour syrup over. Finish in the same way.

SUGAR PACK: Spread fruit in shallow dishes. Sprinkle with sugar and mix gently with pancake turner until sugar is dissolved. Put fruit and juice into containers. Press fruit down with crumpled paper. Close and seal.

UNSWEETENED PACK: Pack prepared fruit in containers without added liquid or sweetening; or cover with water containing ascorbic acid, if needed (see below). Press fruit down with crumpled paper. Close and seal containers.

TO KEEP FRUIT FROM DARKENING: Fruits that have a tendency to darken should have ascorbic acid (vitamin C) added to them. This is obtainable in crystal form and can be dis-

BOILING WATER BATH	*One Minute*	*Two Minute*	*Three Minute*	*Four Minute*
Peas	Lima Beans	Asparagus	Brussels Sprouts	
Turnip Greens	Green Beans	Broccoli	Celery	
	Beet Greens	Carrots		
	Kale	Cauliflower		
	Spinach	Mushrooms		
	Swiss Chard	Summer Squash		

Corn on the cob (young ears), 7 minutes.
Cut Corn (use older ears), 7–10 minutes depending on size; cut grains from cob after chilling.

solved in a little cold water. Add it to the liquid used (½ teaspoon to 4 cups of liquid); or, in sugar packs, sprinkle it over the fruit before adding sugar. Lemon juice may be substituted but is not as effective in preserving the color of the fruit.

For specific instructions on each fruit see "Home Freezing of Fruits and Vegetables," the U.S. Department of Agriculture bulletin.

FREEZING MEATS

Meat should be frozen at 15 or 20 degrees below zero. (See the section, Fast Freezing, page 272.) If your freezer will not go that low, it would be best to have your meat frozen at a locker plant and store it in your own freezer.

To prepare meat for freezing, trim off excess fat. Fat is the hardest thing to keep, it has a tendency to turn rancid. So if your freezer should develop an "off" odor, look first for the offending fat. It will have a waxy dark look.

Wrap meat tightly in freezer wrapping, making a tight double fold with the edges of the paper, and seal securely. Label clearly, showing the kind, date and number of servings. Put into stockinette bags for protection from tearing.

Frozen meat may be cooked thawed, or unthawed, but recent tests have proved that meat retains its flavor and nutrients better if cooked in the frozen state. So increase the cooking time for frozen meat and use a meat thermometer to tell when a roast is cooked through.

Roasts can go right into the oven frozen, allowing more time per pound for cooking. Use a meat thermometer to make sure it reaches the right degree of doneness. Steaks and chops require about twice the usual cooking time, if cooked frozen.

To freeze roast meats, separate the sliced and small bits from the large chunks and freeze separately for different purposes. Wrap the large pieces well in freezer wrap, and put the others in containers with stock or gravy to protect the flavor.

FREEZING POULTRY

Freeze only young poultry uncooked. Older birds are better made up into special dishes, then frozen.

To freeze, prepare poultry as for cooking, leaving it whole for roasting, or cut up for frying and broiling. Package it securely in freezer wrapping, separating the pieces with two sheets of foil or paper so that they will separate easily for speedy thawing. Stockinette may be used over the wrapping to protect the package from tearing. Label clearly for specific uses.

FREEZING SEAFOOD

Freeze only very fresh fish, right out of the water. Clean it and freeze whole, or in halves, fillets, or steaks. Wrap securely and label.

To use, thaw in its container and use promptly.

Poultry, corn, chopped meat and pie, ready for the freezer

WHAT TO DO
WHEN THE FREEZER STOPS

It is well to face the fact that the day may come when the current goes off. This may be due to some mechanical failure in the freezer itself, or to some general catastrophe like a hurricane, that tears up power lines throughout a whole area. When the contingency arises you will be glad if you have selected a freezer with good insulation. A short current failure is nothing to worry about, because the food will stay frozen for about two days if the box is well filled. With half a load, it will stay frozen one day. *Just don't open the freezer*—keep that cold sealed in as long as possible, and the better the insulation the longer it will stay cold.

If, however, you know that you are going to be without current for several days you must take steps to preserve the food. You might wrap it in blankets and take it to your local freezer-locker plant—provided of course it isn't affected by the emergency.

If locker space is not available, try to obtain dry ice from a local dairy or cold-storage warehouse. Fifty pounds will keep food frozen for about 36 hours. Put heavy cardboard over the packages of food, and the dry ice on the cardboard. Putting a blanket or quilt over the cabinet will help, but be sure not to cover up the air-vent openings, in case the power should go on unexpectedly. Be careful when using dry ice—it will "burn" you if you touch it with your bare hands.

In general, thawed food should never be refrozen; the quality will not be improved by the second freezing. It is better to use what you can at once, cook as much of the balance as possible, then freeze it; or canning may be the only solution.

Fruit can be used up for making pies, jams, jellies and preserves. Be careful of thawed vegetables, shellfish and cooked foods. Bacteria multiply very rapidly in these foods, and the odor doesn't always tell you whether or not they are spoiled. Make sure meat and poultry has not started to spoil. If the odor is questionable, get rid of it.

CANNING AND PRESERVING

The home canning of fruits and vegetables has largely been replaced by freezing, because the latter is quicker and preserves food more nearly in its natural state. For those who are still interested in canning, the United States Department of Agriculture Bulletins, "Home Canning of Fruits and Vegetables" and "Home Canning of Meat" are very complete and can be obtained from the Government Printing Office, Washington, D.C. We give only a brief summary of the subject in this chapter.

CANNING

Because there is a danger of spoilage, with serious results to the user, in improperly canned vegetables, only the boiling water bath or the pressure cooker methods are acceptable. The boiling water bath is sufficient for fruits and tomatoes because of their natural acid content. The oven or open kettle methods should be avoided.

EQUIPMENT

You will need a large covered kettle or a large pressure cooker, depending on the process used. Use only canning-type jars, with new covers for each canning. The covers may be glass-lined zinc, used with rubber rings, or glass or metal tops with screw bands. Use new rubber rings each time. When buying new jars, get wide-mouthed ones for ease in filling. Do not use any jar with a crack or a nicked edge. Wash and rinse jars and covers, and sterilize by boiling covered in water 10 minutes. Keep in sterilizing water until ready to fill. Handle with tongs.

CANNING FRUITS AND VEGETABLES

For finest flavor, can vegetables that are young and tender, and fruit that is fully ripe but sound, and can them as soon as possible after picking, within an hour if possible. Prepare vegetables as you would for cooking. (See page 131.)

BLANCHING

Blanch all vegetables before packing in jars. It drives the air out of the vegetable for better preservation, softens it for packing, preserves color, and the vegetable is close to boiling point before processing starts.

To blanch vegetables, put enough produce for just one jar at a time into a wire basket and dip it, for the length of time specified on the canning chart, into a large kettle of boiling water.

Blanching also makes skin removal easier, as with tomatoes and peaches. Scald the fruit first, then plunge into cold water and remove skin.

Tomatoes and fruits may be packed cold in the jars, or precooked for a tighter pack. To precook fruits prepare the syrup recommended, add fruit and simmer according to directions. Then pack in jars, allowing $\frac{1}{2}$-inch head-room; add a few grains of salt to each one, place tops in position and screw firmly but do not force. After processing, do not touch vacuum lids; put on rubber ring jars, complete final turn.

Process in your pressure cooker, following the manufacturer's directions if you have them, or the Canning Chart below; or place the hot jars in boiling water to cover and time the boiling according to the chart.

CANNING CHART FOR VEGETABLES

Vegetable	Blanching Time	Boiling Water Bath	Pressure Cooked at 10 Pounds Pressure
Asparagus	4 minutes	2 hours	30 minutes
Beans, green or wax	3 minutes	3 hours	30 minutes
Lima Beans	5 minutes	3 hours	50 minutes
Broccoli	3 minutes	2 hours	30 minutes
Carrots	3 minutes	2 hours	30 minutes
Corn	3 minutes, cut off kernels	3 hours	60 minutes
Greens (Spinach, Chard, etc.)	cook until wilted	3 hours	60 min. at 15 lbs. pressure
Peas	3 minutes	3 hours	45 minutes
Tomatoes (see Canning Chart for Fruits and Tomatoes)			

SUGAR SYRUPS

FOR FRUITS

Type of Syrup	Sugar	Water	Approx. Sugar Content
Light	1 cup	3 cups	25%
Medium	1 cup	2 cups	33%
Heavy	1 cup	1 cup	50%

CANNING CHART FOR FRUITS AND TOMATOES

Fruit	Preparation and Pre-cooking Time in Syrup	Type of Syrup, or Sugar	Boiling Water Bath
Apples	Pared, cored, sliced. Boil 5 minutes.	Light	15 minutes
Applesauce	Prepare as usual, pack boiling hot	—	15 minutes
Apricots	Blanch and peel; or leave whole unpeeled. Heat to boiling in syrup	Light to Medium	20 minutes
Berries (except strawberries and currants)	Fill jar with raw fruit, shake down for full pack. Cover with boiling syrup made with juice.	Light to Medium	20 minutes
Cherries	Bring to boil in syrup	Medium	10 minutes
Peaches	Blanch, slip off skins. Halve and pit, or slice. Drop fruit into boiling hot syrup and pack at once	Light to Medium	15 minutes
Pears	Peel, halve and core. Drop into boiling hot syrup and pack at once	Medium	15 minutes
Pineapple	Peel, core, remove "eyes"; slice or cut in pieces. Add ½ cup sugar, cover and heat slowly 10 to 15 minutes. Pack hot, cover with juice	Sugar	25 minutes
Plums and Prunes	Prick skin or cut in halves. Heat to boiling in syrup	Light to Medium	15 minutes
Rhubarb	Cut in ½-inch lengths; add ½ cup sugar to each quart and let stand until juicy. Bring to a boil and pack hot	Sugar	10 minutes
Strawberries	Stem; add ½ cup sugar to each quart. Bring slowly to boil. Let stand overnight to plump berries. Bring quickly to boil to pack	Sugar	10 minutes
Tomatoes	Scald, skin, and remove stem ends of perfect ripe tomatoes. Leave whole or quarter and bring to boil, stirring constantly. Add 1 teaspoon salt to each quart	—	10 minutes
Tomato Juice	Remove stem ends, cut in pieces and simmer until softened. Put through fine sieve or food mill. Add 1 teaspoon salt to each quart. Re-heat to boiling. Leave ½-inch head space in jars	—	15 minutes

MAKING JELLY

Two pounds of prepared fruit will yield about a pint of juice, or about 4 jelly glasses of jelly, when sugar has been added. To increase the yield from fruit it is advisable to add pectin. Also, many fruits are low in pectin, and really require its addition to make them jell. When you buy one of the commercial brands of liquid or powdered pectin on the market, a complete book of instructions will come with it which should be followed faithfully.

Another way to extend the precious juice that you extract from berries or cherries is to cook apples and combine the apple juice with the other. Thus you may make your jelly a combination of strawberry and apple, cherry and apple, blueberry and apple, and so on.

Preparing the Fruit

Wash the fruit thoroughly to remove any insecticides that may have been sprayed on it, but do not remove the skin for it is rich in pectin which makes the jelly jell. It also adds to the color. Cook the fruit with only enough water to keep it from burning, crushing the fruit in the kettle with a potato masher. Berries require only 2 or 3 minutes cooking, hard apples may take 15. As soon as fruit is soft and full of juice, pour it into a jelly bag, supported above a large bowl. Do not squeeze the bag, but let it drip slowly, perhaps overnight, if you want a really clear jelly. If you do not mind a cloudy jelly, you may squeeze the bag, or even make a second extraction.

To make a second extraction, do not squeeze the pulp but return it to a saucepan, cover with cold water, stir to mix and bring slowly to boil. Boil 10 minutes, then drain through jelly bag. Use separately or add to first extraction.

Fruit Juice

The juice you obtain may be canned, if desired, to use as cold drinks or to make into desserts and dessert sauces. To can it, add 3 tablespoons of sugar to each quart, bring it to the boiling point, and fill hot sterilized jars to overflowing. Put the jars into a simmering water bath for 5 minutes. This juice may be made into jelly at a more convenient time.

Making the Jelly

Add sugar to fruit juice and heat, stirring until sugar dissolves. Boil rapidly until a jelly thermometer registers 220°, or test with a spoon as follows: take up a spoonful of juice, cool slightly, then pour back into the kettle from the side of the spoon. When cooked sufficiently, the jelly will come together at the edge of the spoon and "sheet" off all together. If it comes off in drops, it is not quite ready.

When ready, skim jelly, pour into hot sterilized glasses. Cover with thin layer of paraffin that is just melted, but not smoking, over low heat. Let first layer of paraffin harden, then repeat, tilting glass so that paraffin will cover entire surface. The two layers together should be about ⅛-inch thick. Label and date glasses. Store in cool, dark place.

SUGAR CHART FOR JELLY	*Add ⅔ cup of sugar to 1 cup of juice of—*	*Use 1 cup of sugar to 1 cup of juice of—*	
	apple	currants	blackberries
	crab apple	grapes	damson plums
	quince	beach plums	guavas
	half apple and half cherry, blueberry, raspberry, pineapple, or peach		

For jelly made with commercial pectin, consult directions that come with it.

MAKING JAM

Jam may also be made with commercial pectin for quick jelling and to increase the yield. If you prefer to do it that way follow the instructions that come with the pectin.

STRAWBERRY JAM

Make jam in small amounts so that it cooks quickly, to preserve color and flavor. Wash berries and crush in large kettle. Heat slowly until juice flows freely, then boil rapidly until fruit is very soft. Measure fruit and add ⅔ cup of sugar for each cup of fruit. Boil rapidly until it sheets from a spoon (220°) stirring occasionally to prevent sticking. Pour into sterilized glasses and cover at once with paraffin or seal in hot sterilized jars.

RASPBERRY, BLACKBERRY, and BLUEBERRY JAM may be made the same way. If the fruit is very seedy, it may be put through a sieve before the sugar is added.

CONCORD GRAPE JAM

Separate skins from pulp and cook pulp. Put pulp through sieve to remove seeds. Add skins to pulp and measure. Add ½ cup sugar to each cup fruit. Boil rapidly until it sheets from a spoon (220°) stirring occasionally to prevent sticking. Pour into sterilized glasses and cover at once with paraffin, or seal in hot sterilized jars. 4 pounds of grapes make about 8 glasses of jam.

SPICED ELDERBERRY-GRAPE JAM

Elderberries, 2 quarts
Grapes, Wild or Concord, 2 quarts
Water, ¼ cup
Sugar, 1 pound
Vinegar, 1 cup
Allspice, ½ teaspoon
Cloves, ½ teaspoon

To make about 9 cups

Wash elderberries and put through sieve to remove seeds. Add water to grapes and cook until soft; put through sieve. Combine berries and grapes and add sugar, vinegar and spices. Boil rapidly until jam is clear and sheets from spoon, stirring constantly to prevent burning. Pour into hot glasses and cover with paraffin.

ORANGE MARMALADE

Cut oranges up in small pieces and measure. Add 3 cups of water for each cup of fruit; let stand overnight. Boil slowly until tender, and add 1 cup sugar to each cup of fruit. Continue cooking until syrup sheets from a spoon. Pour into sterilized glasses and cover at once with paraffin. Six oranges will make about 8 glasses of marmalade.

FREEZER PEACH JAM

Peaches, 4 cups, cut up
Lemon Juice, ¼ cup
Powdered Pectin, 1 pkg.
Light Corn Syrup, 1 cup
Sugar, 5½ cups

Sprinkle peaches with lemon juice as you cut them up, to prevent darkening. Crush peaches with potato masher in a kettle. Sprinkle with pectin and let stand 20 minutes, stirring occasionally to blend pectin with fruit. Add sugar and syrup and place over low heat until just warm. Do not cook. Pour jam into sterilized jars, leaving ½ inch head space and cover with lids. Let stand until jelled and then store in freezer.

PRESERVES AND CONSERVES

Preserves are usually whole fruits or pieces in heavy sugar syrup. When two or more fruits are combined, it is called a conserve. Preserves are best when made in small batches.

Hard fruits, such as winter pears, pineapples, or quinces, should first be boiled in water until tender. Drain them and use the water to make syrup.

In general, use ⅔ pound of sugar for each pound of fruit; strawberries require 1 pound for each pound of fruit. Boil fruit in syrup, stirring frequently, until fruit is clear and tender and syrup is thick. Turn into hot sterilized jars and seal at once.

QUINCE PRESERVES

Quinces, 1 pound	Pare, quarter and core quinces. Cook in 4 cups of water for 1 hour, or until nearly tender.
Sugar, 1½ cups Lemon, 1	Cut lemon in thin slices and remove seeds. Add sugar and lemon to fruit and continue cooking until fruit is tender and clear. Put fruit in sterilized jars, cook syrup until it is heavy and fill jars. Seal at once.

About 2 pint jars

GREEN TOMATO PRESERVES

Green Tomatoes, 1 pound Lemon, 1 Brown Sugar, ¾ cup, firmly packed Ginger, 2 teaspoons, tied in cloth bag	Slice tomatoes and lemon in thin slices; cook together with brown sugar and ginger until thick. Remove ginger before pouring into sterilized jars. Seal at once.

To make about 2 half-pints

PINEAPPLE PRESERVES

Slice and pare 1 pineapple and remove hard centers; cook in boiling water to barely cover until tender. Drain, reserving liquid. Weigh fruit and add ¾ pound of sugar for each pound of fruit; dissolve sugar in 1 cup of fruit liquid. When syrup boils, add pineapple. Cook until clear, fill sterilized jars and seal.

SPICED CRAB APPLES

Leave stems on crab apples, cut out blossom ends, and boil until they are tender in a syrup made as follows: for each pound of crab apples, 1 cup of brown sugar, ¾ cup of cider vinegar, ½ inch of stick cinnamon, and ½ teaspoon cloves. Place cooked fruit in sterilized jars, with a piece of cinnamon and some cloves in each, fill jars with syrup, and seal.

SPICED SECKEL PEARS: The above recipe may also be used for seckel pears.

BRANDIED PEACHES

Select ripe, flawless peaches. Dip each one quickly in hot water and dry with a towel to remove the fuzz. Weigh the peaches and for each pound of fruit use 1 cup of sugar and 1 cup of water for the syrup. Put the peaches into the boiling syrup and boil 5 minutes, then place peaches carefully in sterilized jars. Cook syrup until thick, then add it to the peaches with an equal quantity of brandy. An easy way to do this is to add syrup and brandy alternately with a small cup or dipper until the jar is full. Seal jars. These improve when set aside a few months before using.

Fresh Orange Conserve (see page 282)

GOOSEBERRY AND PINEAPPLE CONSERVE

Gooseberries, 1½ quarts
Water, ½ cup
Pineapple, shredded, 2 cups
Seeded Raisins, 2 cups
Sugar, 4 cups

Boil gooseberries in water until skins burst; add pineapple and cook 10 minutes. Add raisins and sugar; cook until thick and clear, and seal in sterilized jars.

To make about 4 half-pints

GINGERED PEACH CONSERVE

Dried Peaches, 1 pound
Water, 4 cups
Oranges, 2
Seedless Raisins, 1 cup
Crystallized Ginger, chopped, ¼ cup
Lemon, 1
Sugar, 2 cups

Soak peaches in 4 cups of water until soft. Add 1 orange, thinly sliced; add raisins, ginger, juice of 1 orange and lemon, and sugar. Cook until thick and clear, and seal in sterilized jars.

To make about 4 half-pints

CURRANT-BERRY CONSERVE

Currants, stemmed, 4 cups
Gooseberries, stemmed, 5 cups
Blackberries, 2½ cups
Sugar, 7 cups

Cook all ingredients together until thick and clear. Seal in sterilized jars.

To make about 7 half-pints

GINGERED TOMATO CONSERVE

Tomatoes, 4 pounds
Preserved Ginger, chopped, ½ cup
Lemon, 1
Sugar, 8 cups

Peel, slice and drain tomatoes. Cook with ginger, juice and grated rind of lemon, and sugar. When clear and thick seal in sterilized jars.

To make about 6 half-pints

FRESH ORANGE CONSERVE

Oranges, 12 small, thinly sliced
Lemons, 2, thinly sliced
Sugar, 6 cups
Vanilla Extract, 1 tablespoon

Measure thinly sliced oranges (there should be 9 cups). Add sliced lemon. Place in a large preserving kettle with 4 cups of water. Cover and soak overnight. Cook, uncovered 1½ hours or until tender. Measure the mixture (there should be 6 cups). Add 6 cups of sugar or use equal parts of sugar and cooked orange and lemon mixture. Cook until thickened, about 1½ hours, stirring occasionally. Remove from heat and stir in pure vanilla extract. Ladle into hot sterilized jars. Seal at once.

6 jars, ½ pint each

PICKLES AND RELISHES

BREAD AND BUTTER PICKLES

Cucumbers, 6 large
Onions, 3 large
Salt, 1 teaspoon
Vinegar, 1 cup
Sugar, 1 cup
Celery Seed, 1 teaspoon
Mustard Seed, 1 teasp.
Turmeric, ¾ teaspoon
Pepper, ¼ teaspoon

To make 2½ pints

Wash and peel cucumbers; peel and slice onions. Combine remaining ingredients and bring to boil; add cucumbers and onions, and cook 2 minutes, over low heat. Turn into sterilized jars, seal.

GARLIC DILL PICKLES

5-Gallon Crock
Dill Plant, 1 pound
Cucumbers, 40 or 50 small
Pickling Spice, handful
Salt, coarse cooking or Kosher, 1 pound
Cider Vinegar, 1 quart
Water, 2½ gallons

Place a layer of dill in the bottom of crock; cover with several layers of cucumbers, a layer of dill, pickling spice and a few pieces of garlic. Repeat layers until crock is almost full, topping with a layer of dill. Cover with brine of salt, vinegar and water, and place a weighted plate on top to keep the cucumbers under the brine. Cover the top with clean cloth or paper and let stand 3 to 5 weeks in cool place. Inspect occasionally; remove scum and add new brine when necessary to keep cucumbers covered.

MUSHROOM CHUTNEY

Mushrooms, ¼ pound

Apples, chopped, 2 cups
Onions, ½ cup, chopped
Green Pepper, ½ cup, chopped
Crystallized Ginger, ½ cup, chopped
Seedless Raisins, 1 cup
Brown Sugar, 1 cup
Nutmeg, ¼ teaspoon
Cinnamon, ¼ teaspoon
Allspice, ¼ teaspoon
Vinegar, ¼ cup
Salt, 1 teaspoon

To make about 2 pints

Drop mushrooms in boiling water, drain at once, chop into pieces.

Combine mushrooms with other ingredients in large saucepan. Bring to boil and simmer, covered, over low heat 45 minutes. Pack in sterilized jars.

WATERMELON PICKLE

Trim off the outer green skin of watermelon rind and any remaining pink flesh, using only the white part. Cut into small cubes and measure. To crisp it, soak 1 hour in lime water to cover, made by adding 1 tablespoon lime (Calcium oxide) to 4 cups water. Drain and cover with fresh water to cover. Bring to boil, simmer 30 minutes. Drain, cover with salted water and simmer again for 30 minutes; drain and reserve water.

Sugar, 9 cups
Vinegar, 6 cups
Cooking Water, 2 cups
Whole Cloves, 2 tablesps.
Stick Cinnamon, 2 tablespoons
Gingerroot, small piece
Prepared Rind, 12 cups

To make about 5 to 6 pints

Boil sugar in vinegar and water to make a syrup; add spices in cheesecloth bag. Add prepared watermelon rind (see above) and cook slowly about 1 hour, or until rind is clear and syrup thick. Remove spice bag, pour into sterilized jars and seal.

SPICED PEACHES

Sugar Syrup, 2 cups
Cider Vinegar, 1 cup
Whole Cloves, 1 tablesp.
Stick Cinnamon, 1 stick broken in pieces

Follow procedure for canned peaches (page 278), but add the listed ingredients to the sugar syrup with spice in spice bag. Drop peaches into the syrup as you remove the skins and boil 10 minutes. Remove from heat and let peaches sit overnight. Remove spice bag, put peaches in jars, reboil syrup and fill jars. Process.

SPICED PEARS: Use the above recipe for pears.

Commercially canned peaches and pears may be spiced by boiling the juice with the spices and pouring it hot over the fruit.

CHILI SAUCE

Tomatoes, 24 large
Onions, 8
Sweet Red Peppers, 3
Sweet Green Peppers, 3
Sugar, 1 cup
Salt, 2 tablespoons
Vinegar, 4 cups
Cloves, 1 teaspoon
Cinnamon, 2 teaspoons
Allspice, 1 teaspoon

To make about 8 pints

Wash and chop vegetables; combine with other ingredients. Cook slowly for about 1 hour, or until thick. Pour into hot sterilized jars, filling to overflowing, and seal at once.

TOMATO CATSUP

Tomatoes, blanched and
  chopped, 16 cups
Sweet Red Peppers,
  chopped, 1 cup
Onions, chopped, 1 cup
Salt, 1 tablespoon
Sugar, 1 cup
Celery Seed, 1 teaspoon
Mustard, 1 teaspoon
Stick Cinnamon, 1 stick
Whole Cloves, 1 tablesp.
Vinegar, 2 cups

Cook tomatoes, peppers and
onions together until soft. Put
mixture through food mill or
sieve. To pulp add salt and
sugar; tie celery and mustard
seed, stick cinnamon and cloves
in cheesecloth bag and add.
Cook briskly 1 hour. Remove
spice bag. Seal in hot, sterilized
jars.

To make about 8 pints

CHOWCHOW

Green Tomatoes,
  20 medium
Cucumbers, 10 small
Green and Red Sweet
  Peppers, 4
Cauliflower, 1 medium
  head
Onions, 6 medium
String Beans, 2 pounds
Salt, 3 tablespoons
Vinegar, 8 cups
Mustard Seed, 2 tablesps.
Turmeric, 4 tablesps.
Pepper, 2 teaspoons

Wash vegetables and chop into
small pieces. Mix with vinegar,
seasonings and spices and bring
to boiling point. Simmer 1 hour,
stirring occasionally. Pour into
sterilized jars and seal tightly.

To make about 10 pints

CORN RELISH

Sweet Corn, 12 ears
Onions, 2 chopped
Sweet Green Peppers,
  2 chopped
Sweet Red Pepper, 1
  chopped
Cabbage, Chopped 1
  cup
Salt, 2 tablespoons
Pepper, ¼ teaspoon
Dry Mustard, 1½
  tablespoons
Sugar, 1 cup
Vinegar, 2 cups

Cut corn from cob, but do
not scrape the ear; mix with
onions, peppers and cabbage
and add remaining ingre-
dients. Cook slowly 1 hour,
stirring occasionally. Turn
into hot sterilized jars, filling
to overflowing, and seal at
once.
Canned kernel corn may be
substituted for ear corn; use
6 cups, drained, and proceed
as for fresh corn.

To make about 2 pints

PICCALILLI

Green Tomatoes,
  chopped, 8 cups
Green Pepper, chopped,
  1 cup
Onion, chopped, 1 cup
Vinegar, 2 cups
Salt, 1 tablespoon
Celery Seed, ½ tablesp.
Mustard Seed, 1 tablesp.
Stick Cinnamon, several
  pieces, broken
Sugar, 2 cups

Combine ingredients, bring to
boiling point, simmer 1 hour,
stirring from time to time. Pour
into sterilized jars, putting a
piece of the cinnamon in each.
Seal tightly.

To make about 4 pints

PEPPER RELISH

Red Peppers, 12
  chopped
Green Peppers, 12
  chopped
Onions, 12 chopped
Vinegar, 2 cups
Brown Sugar, 1 cup
  firmly packed
Salt, 2 tablespoons
Celery Seed, 2
  tablespoons

Drain peppers and onions,
cover with boiling water and
simmer 15 minutes. Drain
again and add vinegar, sugar,
salt and celery seed. Boil 15
minutes and pour into hot
sterilized jars and seal at
once.

To make about 2 pints

SPICED ORANGE PEEL

Orange Peel, 1 quart
  cubed
Vinegar, 1½ cups
Sugar, 1½ cups
Cinnamon, 4 sticks
Cloves, 12

Scrape all flesh from orange
peel and soak overnight in
cold water. Cover with fresh
water and bring to a boil.
Repeat twice and cook peel
until tender. Combine vinegar, sugar, cinnamon and
cloves, bring to a boil, add
peel and simmer 3 minutes.
Pack into hot sterilized jars
and seal completely.

To make about 5 pints

SPICED BLACKBERRIES

Brown Sugar, Packed
  4 cups
Vinegar 2 cups
Blackberries, 5 pounds
Whole Cloves, 1
  tablespoon
Cinnamon, 2 sticks
Allspice, 8 whole

Dissolve sugar in vinegar;
add blackberries and spices
tied in a cloth bag. Boil
rapidly until thick. Remove
spices, pour into hot sterilized jars, filling to overflowing, and seal at once.

To make about 5 pints

FOOD FOR A CROWD

When you start to plan a meal for guests, one of the chief considerations will be the quantity of food to prepare. The recipes in this book, as you have probably noted, are usually planned to feed four people, so the arithmetic is simple when you are going to feed multiples of four. Doubling or tripling a recipe is applicable to most meats, vegetables, prepared main dishes and simple desserts, but never with cake recipes or complicated desserts. Instead bake each cake recipe separately, and mix the dessert in separate batches. Pie crust, too, is better made in individual recipes—it requires less handling, therefore has less chance to become overworked and tough.

For groups of eight or twelve, you will find that a roast or a ham is a real economy, and also will stretch to feed unexpected guests. Since it can be prepared in advance it will be less trouble for the cook than having to do short-order broiled or fried dishes after guests have arrived. Another reliable solution to the company dinner is a casserole dish that can stay warm in the oven without harm until serving time. You should have several of these in your cooking repertoire. For suggestions, refer to "Casseroles" in the index.

You may occasionally be called upon to plan food for still larger groups—a church supper or a club gathering in your own home. Let this be fun for yourself as well as others, by having menus that are easy to handle and a well-organized committee to help with food preparation and serving. Again there will be less last minute work and confusion if the food is all of the kind that can be prepared well in advance and kept warm in the oven until needed, for these affairs can sometimes stretch out for several hours until everyone is fed.

Following is a marketing list to guide you in buying food for as many as fifty people:

PURCHASING FOOD FOR FIFTY

Food	Approximate Size of Serving	Amount to Purchase for 50 Servings
Meat		
Beef: roast		
Rib, rolled, boned	2½ to 3 ounces cooked	17 to 20 pounds
Rib, standing	3 to 3½ ounces cooked	20 to 25 pounds
Chuck, pot roast	3 to 3½ ounces cooked	20 to 25 pounds
Beef: round steak	4 to 4½ ounces clear meat uncooked	17 to 20 pounds
Beef: stew		
Chuck and plate clear meat	5 ounces stew	10 to 17 pounds
Lamb: roast		
Leg	2½ to 3 ounces cooked	20 to 35 pounds
Shoulder, boneless	2½ to 3 ounces cooked	15 to 20 pounds
Lamb: stew		
Shoulder and brisket—clear meat	5 ounces stew	17 to 20 pounds
Pork: roast		
Loin, trimmed	2½ to 3 ounces cooked	20 to 25 pounds
Ham:		
Fresh	3 to 3½ ounces cooked	20 to 25 pounds
Smoked, tenderized	3 to 3½ ounces cooked	17 to 20 pounds
Veal: roast		
Leg	3 to 3½ ounces cooked	20 to 35 pounds
Shoulder, boneless	3 to 3½ ounces cooked	17 to 20 pounds
Veal cutlet	4 to 5 ounces uncooked	12 to 17 pounds

Food	Approximate Size of Serving	Amount to Purchase for 50 Servings
Meat (continued)		
Hamburger	4 to 5 ounces uncooked 1 or 2 cakes	17 to 20 pounds
Meat loaf or extended meat patties	4 to 4½ ounces cooked meat loaf	12 to 15 pounds
Bacon: medium	3 strips	5 to 6 pounds
Sliced, wide	2 strips	5 to 7 pounds
Canadian, sliced	2 or 3 slices	7 to 10 pounds
Sausage:		
Links	3 links	17 to 20 pounds
Cakes	6 to 8 ounces raw meat 2 cakes	20 to 25 pounds
Frankfurters	2 wieners	12½ to 14 pounds
Fish		
Fresh or frozen fish fillets	4 to 5 ounces	14 to 17 pounds
Oysters:		
For frying, large	4 to 6 oysters	7 to 8 quarts
For scalloping, small		4 to 5 quarts
For stew, small	4 to 6 oysters	3 quarts
Poultry		
Chicken: Fryers	¼ fryer	35 to 40 pounds, dressed 25 to 30 pounds, eviscerated
Fowl: Fricassee	4 to 6 ounces including bone	35 to 50 pounds, dressed 25 to 35 pounds, eviscerated
Fowl: For dishes containing cut-up cooked meat	1 to 2 ounces of clear meat	17 to 20 pounds, dressed 13 to 17 pounds, eviscerated
Turkey	2 to 2½ ounces of clear meat	35 to 50 pounds, dressed 25 to 35 pounds, eviscerated
Vegetables		
Asparagus	3 ounces or 4 or 5 stalks	12 to 16 pounds
Beans: Green or Wax	2½ to 3 ounces or ½ cup	10 to 12 pounds
Beets	2½ to 3 ounces or ½ cup	12 to 14 pounds
Broccoli	2½ to 3 ounces	17 to 20 pounds
Brussels sprouts	2½ to 3 ounces	10 quart baskets or 12 lbs.
Cabbage:		
Raw	1 to 2 ounces	8 to 10 pounds
Cooked	2½ to 3 ounces or ½ cup	12 to 15 pounds
Carrots:		
Cooked	2½ to 3 ounces or ½ cup	14 to 16 pounds
Raw, strips	2- to 3-inch strips	2 to 2½ pounds
Cauliflower	3 ounces or ½ cup	28 to 32 pounds
Celery:		
Raw		3 to 4 bunches
Cooked	2½ to 3 ounces or ½ cup	7 to 10 bunches
Lettuce	⅙ or ⅛ head	4 to 5 heads for garnish 6 to 8 heads for salad
Onions	3 to 3½ ounces or ½ cup	14 to 16 pounds

Food	Approximate Size of Serving	Amount to Purchase for 50 Servings
Vegetables (*continued*)		
Potatoes:		
White	4 to 4½ ounces or ½ cup mashed or creamed	15 to 20 pounds
Sweet	3½ to 4 ounces	17 to 20 pounds
Spinach	3 to 3½ ounces or ½ cup	17 to 20 pounds
Squash:		
Summer	2½ to 3 ounces or ½ cup	13 to 16 pounds
Winter, mashed	3 ounces or ½ cup	25 to 30 pounds
Tomatoes		10 pounds fresh for slicing
Turnips (white)	3 ounces or ½ cup	15 to 20 pounds
Frozen Vegetables		
Asparagus tips	2½ ounces	10 pounds (4 40-oz. pkg.)
Beans, cut green	2¼ ounces	7½ pounds (3 40-oz. pkg.)
Beans, baby Lima	2¼ ounces	7½ pounds (3 40-oz. pkg.)
Beans, Fordhook	2¼ ounces	7½ pounds (3 40-oz. pkg.)
Broccoli	2½ ounces	10 pounds (4 40-oz. pkg.)
Cauliflower	2½ ounces	10 pounds (4 40-oz. pkg.)
Corn, whole kernel	2¼ ounces	7½ pounds (3 40-oz. pkg.)
Peas	2¼ ounces	7½ pounds (3 40-oz. pkg.)
Spinach	2½ ounces	10 pounds (4 40-oz. pkg.)
Fruits		
Apples	½ cup sauce	15 to 20 pounds for sauce or pie
Bananas	1 small	15 pounds
Cranberries	¼ cup sauce	4 pounds for sauce
Fruit cup	⅓ to ½ cup	4 to 6 quarts
Fruit juice	½ cup or 4 ounces	2 cans, No. 10 or 6½ quarts
Lemons		25 to 30 lemons (1¼ quarts juice) for lemonade for 50 glasses
Oranges		4 to 6 doz. medium oranges (6 quarts juice) for 50 4-oz. glasses
Peaches	3 ounces or ½ cup	10 to 12 pounds for slicing
Pineapple	½ cup cubed	5 medium
Rhubarb	½ cup sauce	10 pounds
Strawberries	½ cup	10 to 13 quarts
	⅓ cup for shortcake	8 to 10 quarts
Miscellaneous Foods		
Bread		Usually allow 1½ slices per person to accompany meal
Butter		2 pounds
Cheese:		
Brick		3¼ pounds sliced for sandwiches
Cottage		6 pounds
Coffee	1 cup	1 pound and 2½ gallons water for 50 cups

Food	Approximate Size of Serving	Amount to Purchase for 50 Servings
Miscellaneous Foods (*continued*)		
Cream:		
Heavy (40 per cent)	1 rounded tablespoon whipped	1 pint
Light (20 per cent) or top milk	1½ tablespoons	1¼ quarts
Honey	2 tablespoons	5 pounds
Ice cream:		
Brick		7 to 9 bricks
Bulk		2 gallons
Potato chips	¾ to 1 ounce	2 pounds
Puddings	½ cup	6 quarts
Rolls	1–2	6 to 7 dozen
Salad mixtures	½ cup	7 to 8 quarts
Salad dressing:		
Mayonnaise	1 tablespoon garnish for each salad	3 to 4 cups
French	1 to 1½ quarts for mixed salads	¾ to 1 quart
Soups	scant 1 cup	3 gallons
Tea	1 cup	50 individual tea bags
		3 ounces bulk tea to 2½ gallons water and chipped ice
Canned foods (in general)		2 No. 10 cans
Pickles: sweet		1½ quarts
Three-inch	½ pickle	25 pickles
Macaroni		5 to 6 pounds
Spaghetti, Italian style		6 to 8 pounds
Jam		3 pints

APPENDIX

THE KITCHEN STOVE

Some cooks swear by gas and others by electricity —some claim that electricity is cleaner than gas, is easier on the bottoms of your pans; some feel it is safer because it eliminates an open flame on which you might, in a careless moment, ignite a sleeve. Gas has always been considered faster than electricity and more flexible because the heat is instant, while the electric burner takes time first to heat up and then cool off when you no longer need it. However, the more recent electric stoves are overcoming the slow-heating objection with faster coils, and the slow-cooling factor can be used to advantage because you can turn off the current when food is almost finished and it will continue to cook for a few more minutes while the burner holds its heat. If a recipe calls for switching quickly from high to low heat, and you are using an electric stove, have a second burner going at low heat to make the change.

High heat is not needed for cooking most foods. In most recipes it is specified only as a means of bringing water or a mixture to a boil, then usually the heat is reduced for the remainder of the cooking

An
electric stove

A gas stove

period. Low oven heat and longer cooking period is used these days for roasting meats—it causes less shrinkage, improves the flavor and keeps your oven free of spattering fat. Too high heat should not be used in pan frying with any sort of fat or oil because it will cause the fat to break down and smoke.

In top-of-the-stove cooking you can judge the amount of heat you are using by its effect on the food being cooked. Moderate heat should produce a steady bubbling of the contents of a saucepan that has been first brought to a boil. Low heat will produce a gentle simmering or agitation.

When you are preparing a dish to be cooked in the oven, first be sure to check the oven temperature shown at the bottom of the list of ingredients and turn on your oven to preheat 10 or 15 minutes while you are preparing the recipe. Your experience with your own stove will teach you exactly how much time is required for preheating.

POTS, PANS, TOOLS, ETC.

Following is a list of cooking and food preparation equipment which is divided into two groups—a minimum list, the bare essentials if you are just starting out, or if you have a tiny kitchen, and a supplemental list from which you can select things as you find you need them.

	Begin With These	*Add These*
Cooking Utensils	coffee maker large skillet with cover small skillet with cover double boiler, also serves as mixing bowl or 2 saucepans 1-qt. saucepan 3-qt. saucepan 6-qt. kettle with lid rectangular roasting pan casserole	griddle teakettle teapot pie pans cake pans cooky sheets bread pans muffin pan cooling rack canning equipment roasting racks
Tools	rotary beater can opener (wall type) corkscrew, bottle and jar opener long-handled fork long-handled spoon long-handled perforated spoon pancake turner spatula potato masher paring knife vegetable scraper vegetable brush slicing knife rubber scraper	butcher knife French cook knife grapefruit knife scissors ladle rolling pin cutting board wooden fork and spoon pastry blender pastry brush chopping bowl knife sharpener candy, deep fat, and oven thermometers sugar and flour scoops nut cracker graters and shredder funnel tongs timer
Equipment for Food	set of mixing bowls measuring cups	additional measuring equipment—pint, quart, fractions of cup
Preparation and Storage	measuring spoons reamer colander wax paper and aluminum foil	flour sifter flour shaker pepper mill strainers, medium and fine mesh custard cups refrigerator dishes food chopper fruit juicer bread box canisters molds food mill

When you are starting in to outfit a new kitchen, it is much better to begin with just a limited number of good quality, general purpose pans and tools and add the more specific things when you find out in just which direction your particular cooking flare is taking you. If steak-broiling and salad-making are your favorite branches of the culinary art you'll want different equipment than the cook who does lots of baking and fancy dessert making. Choose each piece with care so there will be no useless duplication to clutter up the cupboards and drawers in your kitchen.

HOW TO SEASON A NEW PLANK

Hardwood planks are sold at housewares stores, or you can obtain the lumber and sandpaper it down to make your own. Soak the plank in cold water for several hours, dry the surface and rub thoroughly with salad oil, as much as it will take up. Pay particular attention to the edges. To clean after using, scrape and rinse off, let it dry slowly, not near heat. Re-oil before using.

SMALL ELECTRICAL APPLIANCES

The advantage of many electrical appliances is that they can free you from the kitchen stove and permit you to do your cooking on the spot in the dining room, or outdoors, when you want to. In selecting ones that will be most useful to you, consider that many are quite versatile, and one will often do the job of several. For instance, you can make a stew in the electric deep-fat fryer, bean pot, corn popper, skillet, roaster, or sandwich grill with its insert pan in place; and you can fry chicken in any one of them; or make pancakes on a table grill, range griddle, skillet, grill in the roaster-oven, or the grill top of the rotisserie.

Keep on file, so that you can frequently refer to them, the manufacturer's directions that come with every new piece of equipment. These will teach you all its uses, how to operate it efficiently, and how to prolong its life with proper care.

Frequently used utensils conveniently hung on peg board

294

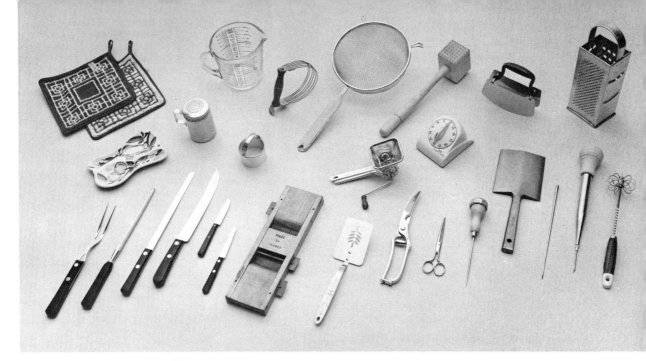

The most important utensils and others that may be added

The Electric Food Mixer

Keep the mixer and its attachments conveniently at hand for immediate use. Use it to mix batters and doughs, squeeze oranges, make milk drinks, mash potatoes, whip cream, grate and shred vegetables; and, with some kinds, chop ice, grind meat, sift flour, grind coffee, and whatever other odd jobs the manufacturer suggests.

When you select a mixer, look for the following points: adequate speed controls—more than 3 are necessary for all the jobs a mixer performs; automatically revolving bowl to leave hands free for adding ingredients; beaters that go in and out of their sockets easily; a detachable power head so that it can be held for mixing things at the stove; a juicer conveniently positioned so that it will not splash.

If you don't do a great deal of heavy batter beating, and if space is at a premium, a hand-held mixer is useful: it can be kept in a drawer or hung on the wall.

An electric food mixer

The Blender

The blender takes the manual labor out of food preparation jobs that require pounding, crushing, grating, grinding, sieving and liquefying. Use it to simplify the work in making puréed soups, salad dressings, gravies and sauces, fruit drinks, and strained baby foods; also to pulverize nuts, crush fruits, chop parsley, or grate cheese.

Caution: A blender is not for heavy duty mixing—most cake batters require a regular mixer. It can be used for cake mixes if you do one in small batches, then combine it by hand. It is possible to grind coffee beans, but not easy to get a uniform grind. Some blenders claim to crush ice. However, don't try to crush a whole ice cube—break it up first with a hammer, then crush it in the blender.

The Electric Roaster

An electric roaster can be used for any type of baking or roasting. It is claimed that whole meals can be cooked in it at one time, but actually this puts an undue strain on the roaster and you may find that extra time is required for food to be done properly. Some roasters also have broiling units and grids so that you can use them for such things as steak and pancakes.

An electric roaster is useful for getting the cooking out of the kitchen in hot weather. Use it on a porch or terrace by providing a long heavy extension cord.

To get the most efficient performance from your roaster follow the manufacturer's directions regarding time and temperature. The following general statements apply to most types:

Always preheat—depending on the temperature setting this may take from 15 to 30 minutes. Removing the lid while the food is cooking causes heat loss and retards browning. Leave the inset pan in the bottom of the roaster when cooking. Use a rack for baked foods, to permit circulation of air. Place a roast on a trivet in the inset pan, and use the pan itself to make soups and stews.

An electric blender

The Rotisserie

A rotisserie is a rotating spit with vertical heat, either gas or electric, behind it. The juices from the meat or fowl on the spit drop into a pan, where they can be recovered for basting. Though originally a method for cooking outdoors, rotisseries have now come into the kitchen. Use a rotisserie for cooking such things as a rolled roast of beef or leg of lamb, or whole chicken, on the spit; or in the broiling basket, cook hamburgers, lamb chops, cut-up chicken or other small portions of meat.

The dimensions of the heating element differ in various makes. In selecting one, make sure the actual broiling area is adequate for the amount of food you must cook at one time.

The Deep Fat Fryer

This appliance should encourage the cook to try those deep-fat fried foods that she may have thought were beyond her skill. Use it for fritters, croquettes,

Electric skillet

proper temperature will not absorb or transmit food flavors.

The Electric Skillet

Another appliance that permits you to cook away from the kitchen, to cook your eggs right at the breakfast table, if you like. Use it as you would any skillet, for fast frying or for braised or stewed dishes that require long, slow cooking. Use it, also, for making pancakes.

The Electric Toaster

Select a toaster that has a thermostatic control, with a dial which can be adjusted for light or dark toast. Use your toaster for split English muffins, corn cakes and the like, as well as for bread. Toast frozen bread slices as they come from the freezer.

and doughnuts, and for chicken, small fish or fillets, shell fish, vegetables such as eggplant, cauliflower and onions, and, of course, potatoes.

The deep fat fryer may be used for other things too—to make a stew or soup, or a small pot roast, or to cook vegetables. Use it to warm rolls or muffins.

Follow carefully the directions that come with your deep fat fryer. Use the amount of fat specified— if you use too much it will bubble over or spatter; if you use too little, the food will not be properly submerged and the cooking will be unsatisfactory. Some kinds of fat have a higher smoke point than others. Experience will teach you which are best for this. In general, the oils and some lards have a higher smoke point. To get the best results, always follow the suggested temperature for the food you are cooking, and time the cooking period carefully. Fat that is overheated breaks down and will affect the quality of the food that is next cooked in it. With proper care and temperatures, the fat may be saved and used a number of times. Fat that is used at a

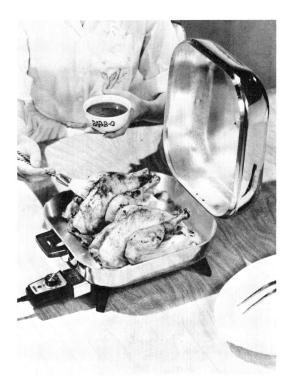

Multicooker
large enough to roast a ham or
two chickens

Two sizes of double boilers

Electric can-opener

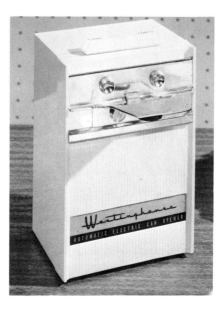

LEFT TO RIGHT: *Dutch oven, frypan, saucepan, griddle and smaller frypan*

Electric Coffee Makers

The important feature about an electric coffee maker is that it keeps the coffee always piping hot. In choosing one, find out how long it requires to brew the coffee—some will do a potful in as little as 7 or 8 minutes. See the section on coffee, for the several methods of making, and how to always have good coffee.

The Electric Waffle Baker

Some waffle bakers come preseasoned from the factory, while others need to be treated before they are used. Read the instructions to see if seasoning is required.

Heat the waffle baker to correct temperature before you pour in the batter. Waffles will stick if the grids are not hot enough. Or if the baker is not automatic, test it by sprinkling the grid with drops of water. When moderately hot the water will form balls and roll around on grids; on too-cool grids, water will bubble slowly and boil away.

If griddle is properly seasoned, and the temperature correct, but the waffles stick, perhaps your recipe contains too little melted shortening. Try adding a little more.

Table Grills

As with all appliances, read the directions carefully. If the grill has interchangeable waffle grids, they will require the same treatment as waffle bakers.

Use the grill for pancakes, for hamburgers, and for grilling sandwiches; or for whatever other uses the manufacturer recommends.

The Pressure Cooker

Pressure cookers are particularly useful to save time with foods that require long cooking—the cheaper cuts of meat, stewing chickens, and the like. Women who go to work often find them invaluable. Pressure-cooked food cannot be expected, however, to taste like oven cooking—steam is moist heat, and its effect upon food quite different from dry, oven heat.

Some modern pressure cookers are electrical,

Electric coffee maker

thermostatically controlled, and can be used for all-purpose cooking as well as pressure cooking. Choose the size that is most useful for your purpose. A 4-quart one is good for stews and pot-roasts.

Don't be careless with the pressure cooker and don't leave it unattended. For both safety and good cooking results, study the directions carefully and follow them exactly. Each type varies in the details of its operation. And don't forget that *timing* is the most important factor to prevent food from being overcooked. This is particularly important when cooking vegetables, to preserve their texture.

THE MICROWAVE OVEN

Microwave ovens have been in existence for about twenty years, but at this writing they still are not the general use in spite of their many advantages to the homemaker. The reason is largely due to the problem of making them absolutely safe, because the rays can be very damaging to human tissue. Every safeguard must be used in their manufacture, which in turn makes them very costly. Especially must precautions be taken against the possibility of having the rays leak out around joints or doors that are not perfectly fitted. It seems that each time a break-through in technology brings a newly designed oven to the market, criticism and safety warnings are not long in following. So this is a field to keep your eye on—when ovens are made to fully comply with the highest standards set by the United States Department of Health, Education and Welfare, and have had sufficient use and testing, they will be something well worth having.

The microwave oven cooks with rays, not heat, and so they cook *cool* and you can use any sort of utensil. You can cook, defrost and reheat, in paper plates, glass or ceramic utensils. And you can cook everything in just a matter of minutes, even to the baking of potatoes in about ten minutes. But before you acquire one of these marvels, just be sure it is safe.

STORING FOOD

Following are some tips on the ideal temperatures and conditions under which various foods should be stored, and the length of time they are at their best, *under ideal conditions*. Since the homemaker usually must store staple foods at ordinary kitchen temperatures rather than at the low temperatures that are most favorable, the period of time in which they remain in top condition will be shorter.

Perishable Foods	*Are at their best*
Meats—*fresh*	Refrigerate at 40° or below, wrapped loosely.
	Beef—keep large cuts up to one week—ground *beef* no longer than 2 days.
	Pork, lamb or *veal*, keep no longer than 5 days.
cooked	Will keep covered tightly, 4 to 6 days.
frozen	Keep at 0° or less, *beef*—up to 1 year; *lamb*—up to 9 months; *pork and veal*—up to 6 months; *sausage* up to 3 months.
Poultry—*fresh*	Refrigerate under 38°, 2 or 3 days. Cut-up parts spoil more quickly.
cooked	Wrap tightly in moisture-proof wrap for 2 or 3 days.
frozen	Keep up to 8 months.
Fish and Sea Food—*fresh*	Refrigerate at 35° to 40°. Spoils quickly—use the first day.
cooked	Use quickly.
frozen	Keeps at 0° or less 6 to 12 months.
Dairy Products	*Butter* keeps 1–2 weeks at 45° or less. Don't store in special "keeping" compartment longer than few hours.
	Milk and Cream—keep tightly covered at 40° to 50°. Don't use pasteurized milk longer than 5 days after purchase—it may spoil without souring.
	Cottage Cheese—keep at 40° to 50° 2 or 3 days.
	Cheese—store at 45° to 50° in tight container or cloth moistened with vinegar, to retard drying.
Margarine	Keep 1 to 2 weeks in tight containers at 40° to 45°. Don't store in special "keeping" compartment longer than few hours.
Eggs	Keep best in moist atmosphere. Don't store with strong-flavor foods. Refrigerate with large ends up at 40° to 50°, 2 to 3 weeks. Do not wash eggs, as washing destroys natural seal.
Lard, Cooking Fats and Other Shortenings	Refrigerate and protect from light, air and moisture.
Salad Oils	Keep at room temperature for short periods, or refrigerate.
Bakery Foods	*Bread, rolls and doughnuts* will keep in tightly wrapped vapor-proof wrapper at under 75° for 5 days.
	Layer cakes, tightly wrapped, keep 1 week. *Cream-filled cakes* and *custard pies* keep in refrigerator no more than 2 days. Have definite bacterial hazard.
	Cookies will keep crisp in dry, tight container for 3 to 4 weeks.
	Baked foods can be tightly wrapped in freezing paper and stored in freezer for several months.

Perishable Foods	*Are at their best*
Fruit	Fresh *apples*, *pears* and *peaches* will keep in a cool, dry, dark place with temperature from 40° to 55° for 2 to 3 weeks. Otherwise refrigerate in covered container. Keep *melons* in cool ventilated place to store, 3 to 6 days; refrigerate to serve.
	Keep *bananas* and *avocados* out of refrigerator until really ripe. Bananas bought green may last as long as 2 weeks. *Berries* are the most perishable fruit, will keep in 40° to 50° only 2 or 3 days at most. Sort out soft ones before storing. *Citrus* fruits keep 3 to 6 weeks at 40° to 50°, but lose in flavor and texture unless in moist atmosphere. Keep *juice* in tightly closed container in refrigerator —loses flavor and vitamins after 1 day.
Vegetables	Keep *spinach* and *salad greens* in moisture-proof containers in refrigerator to preserve crispness, 2 to 5 days. Wilting hastens vitamin loss. *Cabbage* keeps best in moist, but well ventilated, temperature 32° to 36°.
	Potatoes can be stored at room temperature for 1 to 2 weeks, for longer periods at temperature 36° to 40° with ample air circulation and protection from light.
	Keep *carrots*, *beets* and *turnips* under 60° in dry, dark place for 2 to 4 weeks.
	Onions will keep at room temperature a short time, but keep best dry at 32°. Keep *sweet potatoes* dry and well-ventilated at 45° or above, up to 2 weeks.

Staple Foods	*Are at their best*
Canned Fruits, Vegetables, Meat and Milk	Keep best under 60° in dry atmosphere so that cans can't rust. Will keep unopened 1½ to 2 years; flavor deteriorates somewhat after 1 year.
Coffee	Air and age cause aromatic oils to become rancid. Keep tightly closed in refrigerator 1 to 2 weeks.
Crackers	Retain their crispness and flavor in dry, tight container up to 1 month. One of the new dehydrated crisping cans will keep opened crackers crisp.
Ready-to-eat Cereals	Lose flavor and crispness—keep only 1 to 3 months.
Spices, Flavorings and Dried Herbs	If kept tightly covered and dry under 60°, *herbs* and *spices* will keep their flavor for a year, *flavorings* 1 to 2 years.
Sugar	Keep *granulated* and *powdered* sugar in airtight containers to prevent absorption of moisture.
	Keep *brown* the same way to *retain* moisture and prevent lumping.
Syrups, Jams and Preserves	Will keep sealed 1 year at 45° to 50°. Surface mold is harmless and can be removed. Deeper mold affects flavor. Keep opened jams and jellies in refrigerator.
Tea	Loses flavor with age and exposure to air. Keep for 1 to 2 months tightly closed.
Flour	Stored in dry and air-tight rust-resistant container at temperatures under 65°, *white flour* will keep 1–2 years. *Whole-grained flour* and *cereals to cook* only 2 to 4 months. All flours are subject to rancidity and weevils at high temperatures.
Rice, Uncooked Cereals, Prepared Pancake, Biscuit and Cake Mixes, Macaroni Pastes, Pudding Mixes	Keep dry and tightly covered up to 1 year. All flour products become rancid and weevily if improperly stored.

ABOUT CANS

You will notice upon opening that some cans have gold-colored enamel linings. These are used to preserve the color of red fruits, or to prevent the sulphur in some foods from staining the interior of the can. Contrary to all superstition about opened cans, it is perfectly safe to keep food in the can it comes in, if the can is kept *covered tightly* in the refrigerator.* Uncovered food in cans will get a tinny taste that makes it unpalatable but not harmful.

* The Bureau of Human Nutrition and Home Economics of the Dept. of Agriculture.

Name of Can	*Quantity*
Buffet	Holds 8 ounces—or 1 cup of baby foods, fruits, etc.
Picnic	Holds 10½ ounces—or 1¼ cups soup
Vacuum	Holds 12 ounces—or 1½ cups vacuum packed corn
No. 300	Holds 14 to 16 ounces—or 1¾ cups pork and beans
No. 303	Holds 16 to 17 ounces—or 2 cups fruits, vegetables, ready-to-serve soups
No. 2	Holds 1 lb., 4 ounces (or 1 pt. 2 fl. oz.)—or 2½ cups fruits, juices, vegetables
No. 2½	Holds 1 lb., 13 ounces—or 3½ cups fruits, pumpkin, sauerkraut, tomatoes
46 ounce	Holds 3 lbs., 3 ounces (or 1 qt. 14 fl. oz.)—or 5¾ cups fruit, juices, vegetables, whole chicken
No. 10	Holds 6½ to 6¾ lbs.—or 12 to 13 c. fruits, vegetables, for restaurants, institutions

COMMON SIZES OF CANS

BUFFET	PICNIC	VACUUM	NO. 300	NO. 303
Holds 8 ounces— or 1 cup of baby foods, fruits, etc.	Holds 10½ ounces— or 1¼ cups soup	Holds 12 ounces— or 1½ cups vacuum packed corn	Holds 14 to 16 ounces— or 1¾ cups pork and beans	Holds 16 to 17 ounces— or 2 cups fruits, vegetables, ready-to-serve soups

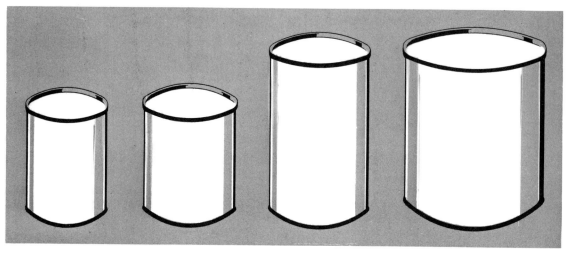

NO. 2	NO. 2½	46 OUNCE	NO. 10
Holds 1 lb., 4 ounces (or 1 pt. 2 fl. oz.)— or 2½ cups fruits, juices, vegetables	Holds 1 lb., 13 ounces— or 3½ cups fruits, pumpkin, sauerkraut, tomatoes	Holds 3 lbs., 3 ounces (or 1 qt. 14 fl. oz.)— or 5¾ cups fruit, juices, vegetables, whole chicken	Holds 6½ to 6¾ lbs.— or 12 to 13 c. fruits, vegetables, for restaurants, institutions

TABLE SETTINGS

HOW TO SET
A DINNER TABLE CORRECTLY

1. Cloth or mat. 2. Napkin (on or to left of plate). 3. Place plate. 4. Salad plate (serve after seating). 5. Bread-and-butter plate. 6. Cup and saucer (omit 5 and 6 for formal dinner). 7. Water glass (wine glass to right of this, if used). 8. Dinner fork. 9. Salad fork. 10. Butter spreader (parallel to either table edge). 11. Dinner knife (sharp edge toward plate). 12. Dessert spoon. 13. Teaspoon (omit 12 and 13 for formal dinner; substitute soup spoon if necessary and bring in dessert silver with dessert). 14. Salt and pepper.

A BUFFET TABLE SET FOR A COCKTAIL-SUPPER PARTY

ABOVE: *Snacks to accompany the drinks, with hot dishes at each end*

BELOW: *Follow the same pattern for the supper dishes to make the change quickly and without confusion*

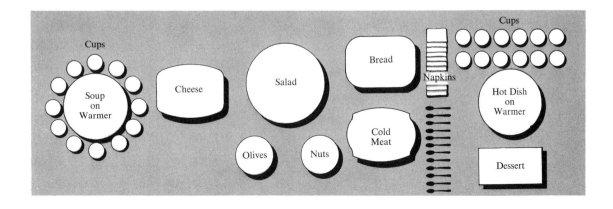

Place setting for breakfast

A table set for a lunch or an informal dinner

Lunch or supper for two

*Place setting
for dinner*

A table set for a formal lunch or an informal dinner

The end of the meal: the table is cleared except for fruit plates and finger bowls

Informal dinner for two

*A convenient counter set
for lunch or supper*

*An informal meal
out-of-doors*

HERBS

AND OTHER

SEASONINGS

Herbs are used in many recipes throughout the book. Believing that the majority of women do not have access to fresh herbs from the garden, the recipes call for dried thyme, marjoram, basil and the like. If you are fortunate to have fresh ones, increase the quantity, substituting about a tablespoon of the fresh leaves for a teaspoon of the crumbled dry product. Parsley we use fresh, for it can be bought fresh in most places, but if this is unavailable, substitute the packaged dry leaves. Fresh chives can often be bought in produce stores, or you might grow a small pot of them, along with a pot of parsley, on your kitchen window sill.

HOW TO COOK WITH HERBS

Use herbs sparingly since their aromatic oils are very strong. Do not use them in several dishes at the same meal—use them for variety and accent only. Blend judiciously for different purposes; have a leading flavor and combine two, three or four less pronounced flavors with it. Never emphasize more than one of the very strong herbs in a blend, except perhaps for sausage. Blends should be so subtle that only the expert can tell which herbs are used. Chop savory leaves very fine. For some purposes, grind them in a mortar. The more the cut surface is exposed, the more completely the aromatic oil can be absorbed. Blending or heating with butter or other fats is the best way to draw out and extend the flavor of the aromatic oils. It's well to remember when using herbs in recipes that one tablespoon of freshly chopped herbs is equal to 1 teaspoon of dried or ½ teaspoon of powdered herbs. Soaking dried herbs in a few drops of water or lemon juice for 15 minutes before using helps to point up the flavor. For soups and gravies, add sprigs of fresh herbs tied in tiny bunches or use ground herbs in cheesecloth bags. Remove them after they have served their purpose. Herbs left too long in soups or gravies will impart unpleasantly strong flavors. They are best added a short time before the cooking is finished.

Herbs may be grouped as very strong, fairly strong and delicate in flavor. The very strong herbs are: Rosemary, sage and winter savory. The fairly strong herbs are: Basil (sweet), balm (lemon), mint, marjoram (sweet and pot), thyme, dill, fennel and tarragon. The delicate herbs are: Summer savory, chervil, parsley, chives. The delicate herbs are excellent for general use.

HERB BOUQUETS

To season soups, stews and sauces make bouquets of dried herbs (bouquet garni). Prepare a quantity of them at one time and store until ready to use. Making them is simple. Cut small cheesecloth bags about 1½ to 2 inches square and fill these with mixtures of dried, crushed herbs. Store the bouquets in tightly covered and labeled containers. The bags are added to the soup, sauce or stew toward the end of the cooking period. They should remain long enough for the soup (or sauce) to achieve a fine herbal aroma and should then be removed. Do not let them stand indefinitely in the soup or it will become bitter and over-seasoned. Use only once, then discard.

The cooking term *fines herbes* is applied to a selection of fresh herbs chopped fine and either sprinkled over the food as it cooks or combined with the sauce or gravy.

Fines herbes may be made by chopping finely a combination of the following: ½ onion, 2 scallions, 2 sprigs parsley or chervil, ½ leek and 1 tablespoon fresh marjoram. You may prefer another combination of your own.

HERB BUTTER

To prepare herb butter minced tender leaves of fresh chives, fennel, chervil, tarragon and marjoram and a few crumbs of dry bread are ground with a pestle in a mortar with a drop or two of brandy, or an aromatic liqueur. This is then blended with butter and forced through a fine sieve. (The crumbs and liqueur help distribute and hold the flavor of the herbs in the butter.) The mixture is chilled and rolled into balls with wooden butter paddles. A ball of herb butter is placed on piping hot steak or broiled fish and

Herbs in pots: chives, parsley, oregano, sage (at back), rosemary, burnet

allowed to melt into it, or the mixture is used as a savory cracker or sandwich spread.

MIXED HERB VINEGAR

Take leaves of balm, mint, marjoram, savory and tarragon, stalks of chives and chervil, add a few shallots and a little basil. Fill jar one-third full, cover with a fine quality vinegar. Cover tightly and let stand for 2 weeks. Strain, bottle, label and store in a cool place. Use these herb vinegars for flavoring salad dressings, soups, fish sauces, pickles, etc.

HOW TO USE HERBS AND SPICES IN COOKING

APPETIZERS

TOMATO JUICE: A dash of mace or marjoram, basil or tarragon or finely chopped parsley

CRANBERRY JUICE: A tiny dash of ground cloves

AVOCADO: Freshly ground pepper, onion juice, onion salt, chili powder season the mashed avocado pulp, wedges or halves

STUFFED CELERY: Paprika for appearance and flavor

SMOKED SALMON: Paprika, black pepper

CREAM CHEESE SPREAD: Onion juice, onion salt, celery seed

HAM SPREAD: Onion juice, onion salt, celery seed

SOUPS

In general the following herbs may be used: Basil, bay leaf, caraway seeds, chervil, chives, cloves, coriander seeds, marjoram, mint, parsley, peppercorns, rosemary, savory, tarragon (especially with tomato), thyme (particularly with onion).

CREAMED CHICKEN OR TOMATO: Mace, paprika
CREAMED TOMATO OR PEA: Cloves, paprika (a dash of nutmeg in split pea soup), tarragon
VEGETABLE: Thyme, savory, garlic
CHOWDER: Poultry seasoning, thyme, bay leaf
CONSOMMÉ: Ground allspice, thyme, or sage
VICHYSSOISE: Chervil
MULLIGATAWNY: Curry powder, mace, cloves
CHICKEN: Nutmeg
LAMB BROTH: Mace, curry powder
OYSTER STEW: Light touch of mace, nutmeg, cayenne and dash of paprika
BEAN SOUP: Cloves, thyme, mustard
BEEF: Cloves, allspice, garlic, bay leaf, dash of nutmeg
MOCK TURTLE: Basil, bouquet

MEATS

Fines herbes may be used with most broiled, baked or braised meat: anise, basil, bay, chervil, chives, horse-radish, lemon balm, mace, marjoram, mint (with lamb), parsley, peppercorns, rosemary, sage, savory and thyme.

ROAST BEEF: Onion or garlic rubbed into meat before cooking; rosemary; thyme sparingly

POT ROAST: Cloves, allspice, bay leaf, garlic, ground ginger (sometimes rubbed on meat before cooking), marjoram, savory

BOILED BEEF: Cloves, bay leaf

HAMBURGER: Onion, allspice, poultry seasoning, savory, marjoram, basil, rosemary, occasionally pickling spice, thyme sparingly

BEEF STEW: Celery seed, bay leaf, pepper, nutmeg, thyme sparingly, occasionally pickling spice, basil, rosemary

HAM: Whole cloves

CHICKEN: Rosemary, onion, mace or nutmeg, curry, poultry seasoning, basil, chervil, sage, tarragon, thyme

LAMB: Garlic, freshly ground pepper, marjoram

MEAT LOAF: Celery, onion, cloves, allspice, parsley, ground pepper, garlic, poultry seasoning, marjoram, sage, savory, thyme

CROQUETTES: Poultry seasoning, sage, celery seed

SWEETBREADS: Onion juice, mace, white pepper, paprika

COOKED MEAT: Curry

SPARERIBS: Garlic, chili powder, bay leaf, paprika, marjoram, savory, thyme

FISH

In general basil, bay leaf, chervil, chives, dill, fennel, lemon balm, marjoram, mint, parsley, peppercorns and tarragon are used; whole allspice, mustard, Worcestershire sauce, onion, celery, curry and pickling spice (steamed fish).

Season to taste with herbs and spices

STUFFINGS

Poultry seasoning is generally used in combination with onion, parsley, and celery, but if there is none available, use the following combination: onion, sage, thyme, pepper and mustard.

EGGS

In general good herb combinations are basil, chervil, chives, marjoram, parsley, rosemary and tarragon.

OMELETS

Basil, chervil, marjoram, tarragon and occasionally rosemary.

VEGETABLES

Besides the specific herb musts below, basil is particularly good with tomatoes, potatoes and peas; bay leaf with tomatoes; marjoram and mint with peas, carrots and green vegetables; rosemary and sage with vegetable-cheese dishes; tarragon is usually used with vinaigrette vegetables and thyme is particularly good with scalloped dishes.

BEETS: Cloves, bay leaf

KIDNEY BEANS: Chili powder, bay leaf

STRING BEANS: Sage, savory, basil, bay leaf, whole cloves

CABBAGE: Onion, celery seed, curry

RICE: Curry

CAULIFLOWER: Poppy seeds, celery seed

SWISS CHARD: Onion, salt, marjoram

WHITE POTATO: Paprika, parsley, basil, dill

SQUASH: Cinnamon, marjoram

ONIONS: Celery seed, cloves

TOMATOES: Allspice, celery, basil, marjoram, sage, tarragon, bay leaf

SWEET POTATOES: Nutmeg, cloves

BAKED BEANS: Pepper, mustard, allspice

CORN: Paprika, pepper, chili powder

EGGPLANT: Allspice, bay leaf, sage

KALE: Nutmeg

RED CABBAGE: Allspice (especially with apples)

SUCCOTASH: Nutmeg

SPINACH: Nutmeg, marjoram, mint

LIMA BEANS: Cayenne, celery, onion, savory, basil, chives

CARROTS: Thyme, marjoram, mint

PEAS: Thyme, rosemary, tarragon, basil, marjoram, mint

SAUCES

Bay leaf, chervil, chives, curry powder, horse-radish, mace, parsley, saffron (particularly to impart a yellow color), tarragon (in vinegar or white sauce and in French dressing) may be used.

CREAM SAUCE: Onion juice, celery, mace or nutmeg (with chicken and veal), cayenne, mustard, paprika and parsley

BROWN SAUCE FOR MEATS: Onion juice, garlic, allspice, pepper

FISH SAUCE—BÉARNAISE, TARTAR SAUCE, *etc.:* Tarragon, chives

TOMATO SAUCE: Onion, garlic, celery, celery seed, cloves, black pepper and basil

MUSHROOM SAUCE: Onion, nutmeg, pepper

SALADS AND SALAD DRESSINGS

Among the many herbs, both fresh and dried, that can be used in salads are: Anise (leaves), basil, borage, burnet, chervil, chives, fennel, lemon balm, mint, parsley, rue, sorrel and tarragon.

COLESLAW: Generous amounts of celery seed, pepper, paprika, caraway seeds

TOMATO ASPIC: Bay leaf, celery salt, onion juice, cloves, cayenne, basil and tarragon

COTTAGE CHEESE: Onion, marjoram, sage, thyme, chives

PEAR SALAD: Add ginger to the dressing

COOKED SALAD DRESSING: Pepper, mastard, paprika

SPICED VINEGAR: Savory, cloves, mace, allspice, pepper, chives, celery seed and bay leaf

FRUIT SALAD DRESSING: Ground mustard, nutmeg

FRENCH DRESSING: Curry, freshly ground pepper, chervil, savory, basil, marjoram, tarragon

CALORIE CHART*

	Name of Food	Quantity	Approx. Calories
MILK AND MILK PRODUCTS	Milk, fresh, whole	1 cup	165
	Milk, fresh, skim	1 cup	85
	Milk, evaporated	1 cup	345
	Milk, condensed	1 cup	980
	Milk, dry, nonfat solids	1 tablespoon	30
	Cheese—Cheddar	1 inch cube	115
	Cheese—Processed	1 inch cube	105
	Cottage Cheese	1 ounce	25
	Cream Cheese	1 inch cube	105
	Cream, light	1 tablespoon	30
	Cream, heavy	1 tablespoon	50
	Ice Cream	½ pint	288
SEAFOOD	Clams, raw	4 ounces	90
	Crab Meat, cooked	3 ounces	90
	Flounder	4 ounces	80
	Haddock	1 average fillet	160
	Halibut steak	1 average	230
	Oysters, raw	1 cup (13 to 19 med. size)	200
	Scallops, raw	4 ounces	90
	Shad	4 ounces	190
SEAFOOD, CANNED	Mackerel	3 ounces	155
	Salmon, pink	3 ounces	120
	Sardines, in oil	3 ounces	180
	Shrimp	3 ounces	110
	Tuna fish	3 ounces	170
MEAT AND POULTRY, COOKED	Bacon	2 slices	95
	Beef, hamburger	3 ounces	315
	Beef, Sirloin, boneless	3 ounces	255
	Beef, Chuck, boneless	3 ounces	265
	Chicken, boneless	3 ounces	170
	Lamb, leg roast	3 ounces	230
	Liver, Beef, fried	2 ounces	120
	Pork, loin or chops, boneless	3 ounces	285
	Pork, cured Ham, boneless	3 ounces	340
	Pork lunch meat, canned	2 ounces	165

* Excerpted from "Food Values in Common Portions" by the Bureau of Human Nutrition and Home Economics, USDA, Washington, D.C. (Obtain from Superintendent of Documents, Washington 25, D.C. Price 5 cents per copy.)

	Name of Food	Quantity	Approx. Calories
MEAT AND POULTRY, COOKED (*continued*)	Sausage—pork	4 ounces	340
	Sausage—frankfurter	1	125
	Sausage—bologna	average slice	465
	Veal cutlet	3 ounces	185
FATS AND OILS	Butter	1 tablespoon	100
	Vegetable Fats	1 tablespoon	110
	Oils, Salad or Cooking	1 tablespoon	125
	Lard	1 tablespoon	125
	Salad Dressing—French	1 tablespoon	60
	Salad Dressing—home-cooked	1 tablespoon	30
	Mayonnaise	1 tablespoon	90
EGGS	Raw Egg, whole	1 medium	75
	Egg White	1 medium	15
	Egg Yolk	1 medium	60
VEGETABLES	Asparagus, cut spears, cooked	1 cup	35
	Asparagus, canned	6 spears	20
	Beans, green limas, cooked	1 cup	150
	Beans, green, snap, cooked	1 cup	25
	Beets, cooked, diced	1 cup	70
	Broccoli, cooked	1 cup	45
	Brussels Sprouts, cooked	1 cup	60
	Cabbage, raw, shredded	1 cup	25
	Cabbage, cooked	1 cup	40
	Carrots, raw or cooked	1 cup	45
	Cauliflower, cooked	1 cup	30
	Celery, raw or cooked	1 cup	25
	Collard, cooked	1 cup	75
	Corn, cooked	1 med. ear	85
	Corn, canned	1 cup	170
	Cucumbers, raw	6 slices	5
	Lettuce, raw	2 large leaves	5
	Mushrooms, canned	1 cup	30
	Onions, young, green	6	25
	Parsnips, cooked	1 cup	95
	Peas, cooked	1 cup	110
	Peppers, green, raw	1 medium	15
	Potatoes, baked	1 medium	95
	Potatoes, boiled in skin	1 medium	120
	Potatoes, French fried	8 pieces	155
	Potato Chips	10	110
	Pumpkin, canned	1 cup	75
	Radishes, raw	4 small	5
	Sauerkraut, canned	1 cup	30

	Name of Food	Quantity	Approx. Calories
VEGETABLES (*continued*)	Spinach, cooked	1 cup	45
	Squash—summer, cooked	1 cup	35
	Squash—winter, cooked	1 cup	95
	Sweet potatoes, baked	1 medium	185
	Sweet potatoes, boiled	1 medium	250
	Tomatoes, raw	1 medium	30
	Tomatoes, canned	1 cup	45
	Tomato Juice	1 cup	50
	Turnips, cooked	1 cup	50
DRIED BEANS, PEAS; NUTS	Almonds, shelled, unblanched	1 cup	850
	Beans—Red Kidney, canned	1 cup	230
	Beans—Navy with Pork and Tomato Sauce	1 cup	295
	Beans—Navy with Pork and Molasses	1 cup	325
	Beans—Lima, dry	1 cup	610
	Brazil Nuts, shelled	1 cup	905
	Coconut, dried, shredded, sweetened	1 cup	345
	Peanuts, roasted, shelled	1 cup	805
	Peanut Butter	1 tablespoon	90
	Peas, split, dry	1 cup	690
	Pecans, halves	1 cup	750
	Soybeans, dry	1 cup	695
	Walnuts, English, halves	1 cup	655
FRUITS	Apples, raw	1 medium	75
	Apple Juice	1 cup	125
	Applesauce, sweetened	1 cup	185
	Apricots, raw	3	55
	Apricots, canned in syrup	4 halves	95
	Apricots, dried, cooked, unsweetened	1 cup	240
	Avocados, raw	½	280
	Bananas, raw	1 medium	90
	Blackberries, raw	1 cup	80
	Blueberries, raw	1 cup	85
	Cantaloups, raw	½	35
	Cherries, raw	1 cup, pitted	65
	Cherries, canned, sour	1 cup, pitted	120
	Cranberry sauce, sweetened	1 cup	550
	Dates, dried, cut up	1 cup	505
	Figs, raw	3 small	90
	Figs, dried	1 large	55
	Fruit Cocktail, canned	1 cup	180
	Grapefruit, raw	1 cup sections	75
	Grapefruit Juice, unsweetened, canned	1 cup	90
	Grapefruit Juice, frozen concentrate	6-ounce can	295
	Grapes, slip-skin	1 cup	85
	Grapes, adherent skin	1 cup	100
	Grape Juice	1 cup	170

	Name of Food	Quantity	Approx. Calories
	Lemon Juice	¼ cup	15
	Oranges	1 medium	70
	Orange Juice	1 cup	110
	Orange Juice, frozen concentrate	6-ounce can	300
	Papayas, raw	1 cup	70
	Peaches, raw	1 medium	45
	Peaches, canned in syrup	1 cup	175
	Peaches, dried, cooked, unsweetened	1 cup	225
	Pears, raw	1 medium	95
	Pears, canned in syrup	2 med. halves	80
FRUITS (*continued*)	Pineapple, raw, diced	1 cup	75
	Pineapple, canned in syrup	1 large slice	95
	Pineapple Juice, canned	1 cup	120
	Plums, raw	1	30
	Prunes, cooked, unsweetened	1 cup	310
	Prune Juice	1 cup	170
	Raisins, dried	1 cup	430
	Raspberries, raw	1 cup	70
	Rhubarb, cooked with sugar	1 cup	385
	Strawberries, raw	1 cup	55
	Strawberries, frozen	3 ounces	90
	Tangerines	1 medium	35
	Watermelons	½ slice (10″ × ¾″)	45
	Candy—Caramels	1 ounce	120
	Candy—Chocolate, sweetened, milk	1 ounce	145
	Candy—Fudge, plain	1 ounce	115
	Candy—Hard	1 ounce	110
	Candy—Marshmallows	1 ounce	90
SUGARS, SYRUPS AND	Chocolate, unsweetened	1 ounce	140
CANDIES	Chocolate Syrup	1 tablespoon	40
	Honey	1 tablespoon	60
	Jams, Marmalades, Preserves	1 tablespoon	55
	Molasses	1 tablespoon	50
	Sugar, granulated or brown	1 tablespoon	50
	Table Syrup, blended	1 tablespoon	55
	Blancmange	1 cup	275
	Custard, baked	1 cup	285
	Ice Cream, plain	½ pint	288
	Apple Betty	1 cup	345
	Gelatin Dessert, plain	1 cup	155
DESSERTS	Sherbet	½ cup	120
	Cakes—Angel Food	¹⁄₁₂ of 8″	110
	Cakes—Plain or Cupcakes	1 cupcake	130
	Cakes—Layer, with Icing	¹⁄₁₆ of 10″	410
	Cakes—Sponge	¹⁄₁₂ of 8″	115
	Doughnuts, cake type	1	135
	Fruit Cake, dark	1 slice, 2″ × 2″ × ½″	105

	Name of Food	Quantity	Approx. Calories
DESSERTS (*continued*)	Gingerbread	1 piece, 2″ × 2″ × 2″	180
	Cookies, plain	1 3″	110
	Pies—Apple	4″ sector	330
	Pies—Custard	4″ sector	265
	Pies—Lemon Meringue	4″ sector	300
	Pies—Mince	4″ sector	340
	Pies—Pumpkin	4″ sector	265
GRAIN PRODUCTS	Biscuits, baking powder	1	130
	Bran Flakes	1 cup	115
	Bread—Boston brown	1 slice	105
	Bread—Rye	1 slice	55
	Bread—White	1 slice	65
	Bread—Whole Wheat	1 slice	55
	Corn Flakes	1 cup	95
	Corn Grits	1 cup	120
	Crackers, graham	2 medium	55
	Crackers, soda	2	45
	Farina, cooked	1 cup	105
	Macaroni, cooked	1 cup	210
	Muffins	1	135
	Noodles	1 cup	105
	Oatmeal	1 cup	150
	Pancakes, wheat	1 cake	60
	Pretzels	5 sticks	20
	Rice, cooked	1 cup	205
	Rice, puffed	1 cup	55
	Rolls, plain	1 (12 per pound)	120
	Spaghetti, cooked	1 cup	220
	Waffles	1	215
	Wheat Flours, Whole or All-purpose	1 cup	400
	Wheat Germ	1 cup	245
	Wheat, shredded	1-ounce biscuit	100
ALCOHOLIC DRINKS	Ale	8 ounces	144
	Beer, light	8 ounces	120
	Beer, bock	8 ounces	136
	Brandy, cognac	1 ounce	88
	Champagne, dry	4 ½ ounces	112
	Champagne, sweet	4 ½ ounces	161
	Gin	2 ounces	136
	Liqueurs	¾ ounce (cordial glass)	80
	Manhattan Cocktail	2 ½ ounces	200
	Martini, dry	2 ½ ounces	160
	Rum	1 ounce	88
	Stout	8 ounces	152
	Whiskey, American	1 ounce	88
	Wine, dry	4 ounces	85
	Wine, sweet	1 ounce	42

	Name of Food	Quantity	Approx. Calories
	Carbonated Beverages, cola type	1 cup	105
	Bouillon Cubes	1	2
	Olives, "mammoth" size, green	10	70
	Olives, "mammoth" size, ripe	10	105
MISCELLANEOUS	Pickles, dill	1 large	15
	Pickles, sweet or mixed	1 pickle	20
	Vinegar	1 tablespoon	2
	White Sauce, medium	1 cup	430
	Yeast, dried	1 tablespoon	20

VOCABULARY OF COOKING TERMS

Appetizer: The first course of a meal consisting of a small portion of food or drink to whet the appetite.

Aspic: A savory jelly used to garnish meat or fish or to make a mold of meat, fish or vegetables; served cold.

Bake: To prepare food by cooking in a dry heat, as in an oven, or under coals.

Barbecue: To roast or grill meat, fowl, etc. before an open fire, on a griddle or revolving spit, basting with a highly seasoned sauce.

Baste: To moisten roasting meat with melted butter, pan drippings, or other liquid, to prevent burning and to add flavor.

Batter: A mixture for cake or biscuits consisting of flour and liquid, and thin enough to drop from a spoon.

Beat: To make a mixture smooth and incorporate air.

Bisque: A rich cream soup thickened with purée; or an ice cream containing powdered nuts or macaroons.

Blanch: To remove the skin of, by scalding or to prepare fruits and vegetables for freezing or canning.

Blanquette: A fricassee with a white sauce.

Blend: To thoroughly combine two or more ingredients.

Boil: To cook food by immersing it in a boiling liquid.

Boiling Point: The point at which a liquid is hot enough that it just begins to bubble.

Bombe: A mold, usually melon-shaped, lined with one kind of ice cream and filled with another.

Bouillon: A clarified and seasoned stock served as a soup, usually made from beef.

Bouquet Garni: Same as herb bouquet.

Braise: To cook meat by first browning in a small amount of fat, and then simmering in a covered pan with a little added liquid.

Bread: To cover with bread crumbs before cooking, as breaded veal cutlet.

Bread Crumbs: Crumbs made from dry bread, crushed fine and sifted and designated as dry bread crumbs; or from fresh bread crumbled, called soft bread crumbs.

Brochette: A small spit or skewer.

Broil: To cook by direct exposure to radiant heat, as on a grid over live coals, or beneath a gas flame or electric wires.

Broth: A simple soup made from meat, flavored with vegetables and sometimes containing rice or barley.

Brown: To cook food on both sides in a small amount of fat until lightly brown.

Brush: To spread with butter or other substance using a small paper or pastry brush.

Calorie: The amount of heat required to raise 1 kilogram of water 1 degree centigrade.

Canapé: An appetizer consisting of a round of bread or toast, or cracker, covered with a highly seasoned spread.

Candy: A confection; to cook a fruit or vegetable in a heavy syrup until transparent; to glaze.

Caramelize: To heat sugar until melted and brown.

Casserole: A food baked and served in an earthenware or other heatproof dish; also the dish itself.

Caviar: The prepared and salted roe of certain large fish.

Chantilly: A dish made with whipped cream.

Charlotte: A dessert usually of gelatin made in a mold lined with sponge cake or ladyfingers.

Chiffonade: A mixture of finely cut or shredded vegetables used in soup or salad dressing.

Chill: To put under refrigeration until cold.

Chop: A particular cut of meat; to cut repeatedly.

Chowder: A soup, usually made with milk, containing salt pork, clams, fish, and sometimes vegetables.

Clabber: Curdled milk in which the curd has not separated from the whey.

Coat: To cover food with another substance, such as flour, egg, etc.

Coddle: To cook slowly and gently in water just below the boiling point, such as eggs.

Compote: A dish of fruits cooked in syrup in such a way that they keep their form.

Condiment: Something used to give relish to food; a seasoning.

Consommé: A light colored clear soup.

Cook: To prepare food for eating.

Court Bouillon: A seasoned broth for poaching fish.

Cream: To prepare with cream or cream-like sauce; to beat butter until it is of a light, creamy consistency.

Crêpe: A French pancake, usually very thin.

Crisp: In a state of being brittle; easily shattered.

Croissant: A crescent-shaped roll of rich dough.

Croquette: A ball made of minced meat, fowl, rice, etc., coated with egg and bread crumbs and fried in deep fat.

Croustade: A kind of crisp patty shell.

Croutons: Small pieces of bread toasted or fried crisp.

Cube: To cut into small pieces whose sides are equal in size.

Curry: An Indian seasoning; a dish cooked with curry powder.

Custard: A sweetened mixture of milk and eggs, baked or boiled.

Cut In: To cut through shortening and flour with two knives or pastry cutter until pieces of shortening are small and well coated.

Cutlet: A small thin piece of meat, usually from the leg, for broiling or frying.

Deep Fry: (See fry).

Demitasse: A small after-dinner cup of strong coffee.

Deviled: Highly seasoned food.

Dice: To cut into small cubes.

Dissolve: To liquefy a solid; to melt.

Dot: To cover with tiny bits, in no particular pattern.

Dough: A soft mass of moistened flour, thick enough to knead or roll.

Dredge: To coat lightly with flour.

Drippings: Residue of juice and fat after meat or poultry has been cooked.

Dry Ingredients: Ingredients having no liquid or fat base.

Dust: To sprinkle lightly with sugar or flour.

Entrée: Originally a dish served between the main courses; now usually the main course.

Fat: Shortening, such as butter, lard, vegetable oils, or margarine.

Filet or *Fillet:* The tenderloin of meat; or fish without bones.

Flake: To break into small flat pieces.

Fold In: To combine two mixtures with a spoon using a motion that carries some of the top layer to the bottom, then reverses to bring some of the bottom layer to the top.

Fondue: A baked dish similar to a cheese soufflé but containing bread crumbs; a Swiss chafing dish cheese sauce.

Forcemeat: Meat or fish chopped fine.

Fork-tender: Tender enough so fork will pierce easily.

Frappé: A mixture chilled to mushy consistency.

French Fry: (See fry).

Fricassee: A dish cooked by braising.

Fritters: Small quantity of batter fried in deep fat or sautéed.

Frosting: A mixture of sugar, flavoring, and other ingredients used on baked goods.

Fry: To cook in a small amount of fat, called sautéeing or panfrying; or, to cook in deep fat, called deep-fat or French frying.

Fry Out: To render the fat from, as salt pork.

Galantine: Poultry, fish or meat, freed of bones, stuffed with forcemeat, cooked, pressed, covered with aspic and served cold.

Garnish: To decorate or ornament.

Gelatin: A substance high in protein used in desserts, etc.

Glacé: The effect of being frozen, iced, candied or covered with thin icing.

Glaze: To cover with thin, glossy covering.

Goulash: A ragout of beef or veal flavored with paprika and vegetables.

Grate: To rub on grater to produce particles in varying textures.

Grease: To coat lightly with fat, oil, butter or shortening.

Grill: To broil.

Grind: To reduce to small particles.

Gumbo: A mixture using okra.

Herb Bouquet: A combination of herbs that blend well together.

Hors d'œuvre: An appetizer served at the beginning of a meal.

Ice: Any frozen dessert not containing cream or milk.

Icing: Another term for frosting.

Julienne: Cut into thin strips.

Junket: Sweetened, flavored milk set firm with rennet.

Knead: To work by repeated motions into a smooth, well-mixed mass.

Lard: To place strips of fat on top of meat, or to insert fat in gashes in meat, or to thread fat into lean meat by means of a larding needle.

Legume: Any edible bean.

Lyonnaise: Cooked with chopped onions.

Macedoine: A fruit or vegetable mixture.

Marinade: A flavored mixture in which food is placed to soak in order to improve taste or tenderness.

Marinate: To season food by soaking it in a flavored mixture.

Mask: To completely cover, as with mayonnaise or a sauce.

Melt: To liquefy by heat.

Meringue: A quickly browned mixture of beaten egg white and sugar.

Mince: To cut or chop in very small pieces.

Mix: To blend into one mass or mixture.

Mocha: A variety of coffee; having coffee flavoring.

Mousse: A frozen dessert of sweetened or flavored whipped or thin cream and gelatin, frozen, without stirring; a similar unsweetened produce made of cheese, vegetables, fish, meat or poultry.

Nesselrode: A dessert containing nuts and chopped fruits; often served in a chilled or frozen state.

Pan-Broil: To cook in a very hot pan with little or no fat.

Pan-Fry: (See fry).

Parboil: To boil until partially cooked.

Parch: To dry to extremity; to shrivel with heat.

Pare: To cut away the outside skin.

Parfait: A frozen dessert of whipped cream, eggs, and flavoring, frozen without stirring.

Paste: A smooth food mixture made by mixing or grinding.

Pasteurize: To sterilize milk by heating it to a temperature of 145° F. for 30 minutes, followed by a rapid cooling to below 50°F.

Pâté de Foie Gras: A paste of goose liver and truffles.

Patty: A flat cake, as of meat.

Patty Shell: A puff paste case made to hold filling.

Peel: To strip off the outside skin.

Petit Fours: Small, iced cakes.

Pièce de Résistance: The most substantial or main dish of a meal.

Pilaf or *Pilau:* An oriental dish made of rice boiled with meat, fowl, fish, spices, etc.

Pit: To remove pit or seeds.

Plank: To broil or bake on a plank, as fish or meat.

Poach: To cook gently in hot liquid kept below the boiling point.

Pot Roast: A roast cooked on top of the stove by braising; usual method for tougher cuts of meat.

Poultry: Any domesticated birds which serve as a source of food.

Precook: To cook food partially.

Preheat: Turning on heat 10–20 minutes before actual oven use is started.

Purée: To put food through a blender or sieve; also a soup made with such a mixture.

Rabbit or *Rarebit:* Melted cheese mixed with beer or ale, served on toast or crackers.

Ragout: Highly seasoned stew.

Ramekins: Individual baking dishes.

Ravioli: Little shells of thin noodle dough containing a savory forcemeat.

Reduce: To lessen quantity by boiling away; to lower.

Relish: Pickle or other tart dish served with food for added flavor.

Render: To separate fat from its connective tissue by heating.

Rennet: Enzyme used to curdle milk.

Rice: To separate into small particles by putting through a sieve or ricer.

Rissole: A ball or roll of minced meat, fish, or potato, covered with pastry and fried in deep fat.

Roast: To cook by dry heat in an oven; bake.

Roll: To press or level with a roller.

Roux: Cooked mixture of flour and butter used to thicken soup and sauces.

Sauce: A dressing for meats, poultry, fish, vegetables, or desserts.

Sauté: (See fry).

Scald: To bring a liquid to just below the boiling point.

Scallop: To bake a food in a casserole, usually with a sauce covered by crumbs.

Score: To criss-cross a surface with lines running in two directions.

Scramble: To stir while cooking.

Sear: To brown surface of meat quickly with high heat.

Season: To render palatable by adding salt and pepper, and sometimes spice.

Set: To settle into a firm state.

Sherbet: A sweetened, flavored frozen mixture containing milk, egg white or gelatin.

Shirr: To bake eggs in a dish.

Shortening: Any fat used in cooking.

Shred: To cut or tear into narrow, long pieces.

Sift: To put dry ingredients through a fine sieve.

Simmer: To cook in liquid just below the boiling point.

Singe: To remove the hairs on poultry with a lighted match or taper.

Skewer: To fasten meat or poultry together with a metal or wooden pin.

Sliver: Sharp, slender slices or fragments.

Snip: To cut with scissors in a series of short quick strokes.

Soak: To let become saturated or softened in liquid.

Soufflé: A hot, spongy dish into which stiffly beaten egg whites are folded just before baking.

Spice: An aromatic seasoning.

Sponge: Dough after it has been raised or converted by yeast or other leavening; a porous pudding of gelatin, sugar, fruit juice and beaten egg whites.

Steam: To expose to the action of steam for cooking or softening.

Steep: To extract the essence of by soaking.

Sterilize: To completely destroy all germs.

Stew: To cook in a little liquid over gentle heat without boiling.

Stir: To mix food with the repeated circular motion of a spoon.

Stock: Liquid resulting from the cooking of meat, fish or vegetables.

Syrup: A solution of sugar with liquid.

Thicken: To make less liquid by adding flour, egg or cornstarch.

Timbale: A seasoned mixture cooked in a mold.

Toast: To brown by exposure to fire, gas flame, or electric radiation.

Torte: Rich cake containing nuts, fruits.

Toss: To throw lightly with quick motions.

Truss: To fasten, by skewer, or needle and thread, fowl's wings to body before roasting.

Try Out: Same as fry out.

Whip: To beat rapidly to incorporate air and increase volume.

20 RULES FOR SAFETY IN THE KITCHEN

Every year about 4,000,000 people are seriously injured in their own homes and many of these accidents occur in the kitchen. Check the following points to see whether you are perhaps carelessly courting an accident.

1. Wipe up spilled food or grease on the kitchen floor; don't risk slipping on it.
2. Don't over-wax the floor to make it slippery.
3. Replace worn floor covering before you catch your heel in it and trip.
4. Never stand on a rickety chair to reach a high shelf; invest in a sturdy step stool.
5. Have plenty of light at all work surfaces so that you can see what you are doing at all times.
6. Keep doors and drawers of kitchen cabinets closed to prevent painful bumps.
7. When adding electrical appliances to your kitchen, make sure you are not overloading the circuits. Do not use sub-standard equipment, or worn electric cords.
8. Never touch an electric cord or switch with wet hands or while one hand is in water. Remember that water conducts electricity.
9. Never light the gas oven with the oven door closed. Open it first so that if any gas fumes have collected, they will escape. Don't look into the oven while you light it: stand to the side. Apply the match quickly after the gas is turned on.
10. Make sure gas burners are turned off all the way when not in use. Always be sure to check them after something boils over, to see that the flame has not gone out.
11. Keep kitchen knives in a knife holder, not loose in a drawer. Slice away from you, not toward your hand.
12. Do not put sharp knives in the dish water with other utensils. Do not leave sharp knives where children can reach them.
13. Sweep up broken glass carefully and put in closed container. Use damp tissue to pick up small slivers. If glass breaks in the dishpan, empty it at once and remove broken glass.
14. Use can opener that leaves a smooth edge. Handle the open lid with care—it is sharp.
15. Do not put pans of hot liquids on the edge of stove where they can be accidentally upset. Turn the handles inside, out of reach of children. Keep tea-kettle spout away from you and lift pot lids on the side away from you so that the steam will not rise in your face.
16. Keep small children out of the kitchen when you are handling hot liquids.
17. Use a deep kettle for deep fat frying and don't fill it more than $\frac{2}{3}$ full. Don't let water fall into fat, and place foods in it carefully with tongs.
18. Use generous size pot holders for hot dishes and pans, not a towel that can brush against the burner and catch fire.
19. Use your pressure cooker safely. Study carefully the directions that come with it and observe the safety precautions.
20. Keep a fire extinguisher in the kitchen: there is hardly a cook alive who has not had one fat fire. If it happens in the oven it is easily controlled: turn off the heat and keep the door shut until it goes out. Or throw a handful of salt or baking soda on it. A fat fire on top of the stove may spread before you realize what has happened, so use the fire extinguisher at once. Never try to put out a fat fire with water, you will simply spread the flames.

The best types of extinguishers for fat fires are liquid carbon dioxide under pressure, or aluminum sulphate and bicarbonate of soda (foam type).

HIGH ALTITUDE COOKING

If you live in a very high altitude your cooking methods and the sea-level cooking times given for recipes in this book will need adjusting. This is particularly true in baking cakes, and you should consult your state agricultural college extension service for information in regard to your locality.

In general, these rules apply:

Water boils at 1° less than 212° for every 500 feet above sea level—this means longer cooking times for vegetables, stews, sugar syrups and deep fat frying.

Yeast bread dough rises more rapidly at high altitudes and should be carefully watched.

Baking powder breads may have the baking powder decreased slightly, though they are not as affected as much.

Pressure cooking times and pressures need adjusting—consult the directions that came with your cooker.

INDEX

INDEX

PICTURE SOURCES

ABERCROMBIE & FITCH: 260 (3 pictures)

AMERICAN LAMB COUNCIL: Title-page Spread

AMERICAN MEAT INSTITUTE: 26, 36, 42, 47, 48, 51, 167

AMERICAN SPICE TRADE ASSOCIATION: 97 (2 pictures), 100 *bottom*, 105, 119 *bottom*, 123, 166, 193, 195, 225, 253, 255, 257 *bottom*, 312

THE APPLE PANTRY OF THE WASHINGTON STATE APPLE COMMISSION: 217

BEST FOODS-CORN PRODUCTS COMPANY: 57, 150, 154, 160, 161, 162, 177, 182, 183, 187 (2 pictures), 203, 206 (4 pictures), 209, 212 (2 pictures) 213, 214, 221, 226, 237, 238 (2 pictures), 239, 240, 241, 242, 243 *bottom*, 258

BLACK, STARR & GORHAM, INC.: 308 (upper 2), Table designs

BORDEAUX WINE INFORMATION BUREAU: 267 *bottom*

THE BORDEN COMPANY: 77 top, 80 *bottom*, 169, 223, *top*, 228, 231

BUITONI FOODS: 128

CAMPBELL SOUP COMPANY: 102

CHERRY GROWERS AND INDUSTRIES FOUNDATION: 223 *bottom*

COLONIAL WILLIAMSBURG: 176, 199, 307 (2 pictures)

COMMITTEE OF STAINLESS STEEL PRODUCERS: 306 *bottom*, 308 *bottom*

CORNING GLASS WORKS, *Corning, New York*: 94, 96

DENMARK CHEESE ASSOCIATION: 216, 247 top, 248

FINGER LAKES WINE GROWERS ASSOCIATION: 268 *bottom right*

FORMICA CORPORATION: 309 *top*

FRENCH-ITALIAN WINE AND SPIRIT CORPORATION: 268 *top*

FRIGIDAIRE DIVISION-GENERAL MOTORS CORPORATION: 291

GAS APPLIANCE MANUFACTURERS ASSOCIATION: 292

GENERAL ELECTRIC COMPANY: 296, 297 *top*, 300

GENERAL FOODS KITCHENS-DREAM WHIP DESSERT TOPPING MIX: 229 *top* (Hugh J. Stern Photograph), 299 *top*

GRANDMA'S UNSULPHURED MOLASSES: 198, 208, 212

R. S. GRIER, *courtesy Mrs. L. H. Brague*: 10, 13

HAMILTON BEACH: 263

HAMMACHER SCHLEMMER: 259 *top*, 267 *top*, 294, 295 *top*

INTERNATIONAL SILVER COMPANY: 306 *top*

KITCHEN AID: 295 *bottom*

LOUISIANA YAM COMMISSION: 155

PICTURE SOURCES

NATIONAL DAIRY COUNCIL: 126 *bottom*, 235

NATIONAL FISHERIES INSTITUTE: 77 *bottom*, 80 *top*, 81, 83, 86 (2 pictures), 87

NATIONAL LIVE STOCK AND MEAT BOARD: 24 (*upper* 2), 25, 27, 37 *top*, 38, 41, 42 *bottom*, 43, 46, 49

NATIONAL PEANUT COUNCIL: 243 *top*

NESTLE COMPANY: 233

PEPPERIDGE FARM, INC.: 188

BEATRICE AND JULES PINSLEY AND THE HERALD TRIBUNE-*Today's Living:* 109

POULTRY AND EGG NATIONAL BOARD: 59 (*upper* 2), 65, 68, 69, 112, 114 (3 pictures), 115 (3 pictures), 118 *top*

REVERE WARE: 298 *top*

REYNOLDS WRAP: 211, 223, 224, 229 *bottom*, 230, 249, 254, 257 (upper 2), 259, 261, 273, 275

ROQUEFORT ASSOCIATION, INC.: 118 *bottom*

SHRIMP ASSOCIATION OF THE AMERICAS: 245

SUGAR INFORMATION, INC.: 191, 194, 197, 201, 234, 280

SUNBEAM CORPORATION: 252, 297 *bottom*, 299

SWANS DOWN CAKE FLOUR: 173 *bottom*, 189, 190

SWIFT AND COMPANY: 180–181 (7 pictures)

SWITZERLAND CHEESE ASSOCIATION, INC.: 118 *top*

THE TAYLOR WINE COMPANY, INC.: 39, 93 *top*, 100 *top*, 107, 227, 247 *bottom*, 265

TEA COUNCIL OF THE U. S. A.: 173 *top*

THE TOOL SHED HERB NURSERY, *Salem Center, N. Y.*: 311

UNCLE BEN'S, INC.: 63, 82, 122 (2 pictures)

UNITED FRESH FRUIT AND VEGETABLE ASSOCIATION: 103, 133, 135 (2 pictures), 137, 138, 139, 142, 143, 147 (2 pictures), 156, 157, 164, 184, 186, 204, 217, 219, 264, 281

WEAR-EVER ALUMINUM, INC.: 126 *top*, 127

THE WEST BEND COMPANY: 14, 30, 132

WESTINGHOUSE: 298 (*lower* 2)

WHEAT FLOUR INSTITUTE: 174 (4 pictures)

WINE INSTITUTE: 29, 37 *middle*, 219, 268 *bottom left*, 269, 270

COLOR
ILLUSTRATIONS

Brunch: CAMPBELL SOUP COMPANY, *facing page* 24

Roast chicken: DUDLEY-ANDERSON-YUTZY, *facing page* 26

Shrimp: SHRIMP ASSOCIATION OF THE AMERICAS, *facing page* 88

Hamburgers: CARNATION EVAPORATED MILK, *facing page* 152

Pies, Puddings: DUDLEY-ANDERSON-YUTZY, *facing page* 184

Sherbet: EVAPORATED MILK ASSOCIATION, *facing page* 232

EQUIVALENT AMOUNTS

Food	Weight	Approximate Measure
Apples	1 lb.	3 medium (3 cups sliced)
Bananas	1 lb.	3 medium (2½ cups sliced)
Berries	1 qt.	3½ cups
Bread crumbs, fresh	1-lb. 1-oz. loaf	11 cups fresh bread crumbs (with crusts)
Butter or margarine	¼-lb. bar	½ cup (8 tablespoons)
	1 lb.	2 cups
Cheese, American	½ lb.	2 cups grated
Cheese, cream	3-oz. pkg.	6 tablespoons
Cheese, cottage	½ lb.	1 cup
Chocolate	1 square (1 oz.)	5 tablespoons grated
Coffee, ground	1 lb.	80 tablespoons

Makes about 50 serving cups beverage (2 tablespoons ground coffee per cup)
or makes about 36 serving cups beverage (3 tablespoons ground coffee per cup)

Food	Weight	Approximate Measure
Cream, heavy	½ pt.	2 cups whipped
Dates, pitted	7¼-oz. pkg.	1¼ cups cut up
Egg whites, fresh	about 8–11 whites	1 cup
Egg yolks, fresh	about 12–14 yolks	1 cup
Flour: All-purpose	1 lb.	4 cups sifted
Cake	1 lb.	4¾ to 5 cups sifted
Whole-wheat	1 lb.	about 3½ cups unsifted
Lemon juice	1 medium lemon	3 tablespoons lemon juice
Lemon rind	1 medium lemon	1 tablespoon grated rind
Macaroni	1 cup	2 cups cooked
Milk: Evaporated	14½-oz. can	1⅔ cups
	6-oz. can	¾ cup
Sweetened condensed	14-oz. can	1¼ cups
	15½-oz. can	1⅓ cups
Nuts in shell: Almonds	1¼ lb.	1 to 1¾ cups nut meats
Brazil nuts	1 lb.	1½ cups nut meats
Peanuts	1 lb.	2 cups nut meats
Pecans	1 lb.	2¼ cups nut meats
Walnuts	1 lb.	1⅔ cups chopped
Nuts, shelled: Almonds	1 lb. 2 oz.	4 cups
Pecan meats	1 lb.	4 cups
Walnut meats	1 lb.	4 cups
Brazil nut meats	1 lb.	3 cups
Orange juice	1 medium orange	⅓ cup juice
Orange rind	1 medium orange	2 tablespoons grated rind
Potatoes: White	1 lb.	3 medium (2⅓ cups sliced)
Sweet	1 lb.	3 medium (3 cups sliced)
Raisins	15-oz. pkg.	3 cups (not packed)
Rice (uncooked)	1 lb.	2 cups uncooked
	1 cup	3 to 4 cups cooked
Saccharin	¼ grain	1 teaspoon sugar
Succaryl	1 tablet	1 teaspoon sugar
Sugar: Brown	1 lb.	2⅓ to 3 cups (firmly packed)
Confectioners'	1 lb.	4 cups sifted
	1 lb.	3⅓ cups unsifted
Granulated	1 lb.	2⅓ cups
Tomatoes	1 lb.	3 medium